BANGKOK
TO BALI

BANGKOK
TO BALI

FRANK KUSY

Robertson McCarta

To President Daisaku Ikeda,
Soka Gakkai International.
In gratitude.

Note: every guide goes out of date sooner or later. Prices change, tourist offices move, new hotels open, old ones close, etc. If you spot any errors or inaccuracies, or have any tips or suggestions to pass on to us (and therefore to other travellers) we'd love to hear from you.

Every care has been taken to ensure that all the information in this book is accurate. The publishers cannot accept any responsibility for any errors that may appear or their consequences.

Designed by Colin Lewis
Production by Bob Towell
Cover design by Prue Bucknall
Phototypeset by Bookworm Typesetting, Manchester, England
Printing, binding and manufacture in Spain by Graficas Estella, S.A.

First published in 1990 by
Robertson McCarta Limited
122 Kings Cross Road
London WC1X 9DS

© Frank Kusy
© Photographs, Steve Merchant, Rowan McOnegal

British Library Cataloguing in Publication Data

Kusy, Frank
    Bangkok to Bali
    1 South-East Asia. Visitors' Guides
    I. Title
    915.90453

ISBN 1 85365 215 6

Contents

List of Maps

Acknowledgements

Special thanks go to Henderson, Ken and Folly (Robertson McCarta); to Mike Gooley, Gail Randall and Genevieve West (Trailfinders); to Steve Merchant and Rowan McOnegal (for photographs); to Jonathan Clayton, Jonathan Beeley, John Patient, Richard Plaistowe, Lindsay Wiseman, Caroline Trowsdale, Lucy Tod, Aislinn O'Dwyer, Ide Salim Felicio and Jackie Sloggett (for sharing a great Trailfinders tour); to Steve Pettitt and Nigel Berry of Pettitt's India (for flights); to Tony Richards, Brenda Baldwin, Lee Geok Suan and the Singapore Tourist Promotion Board (for showing what a tourist board can do when it really pulls out all the stops); to Jennifer Smith, Anton Partono and Putu Suwandi of Aerowisata Hotels (for showing me how the rich live in Bali); to I Gede Budasi and I Nyoman Ginaka of Menyali village (for the memory of a lifetime – a full Balinese-style wedding); to Nicola Wingrove (for everything else).

Literally hundreds of travellers, tourist officers and local people have contributed to this guide. Thanks to you all, and especially to: Rohita Apui, Andrea Bailey, Endang Beratan, Dave Burton, Roy Collins, Karen Grey, Roger Martin, Stephen Muenzer, Jeannie Scott, Erich Steiner, Karl Watkin (Bali), Roggie Cale, Rusty Muchfree and Marjo van Rijn (Bandung), Oranud Kuptabathin and TAT, Dave Ware, Sukhum and Mongkon (Bangkok), Abu, Sjafrudin Bastami, Klaus Billair, Lucy Dowling, Steve van Paassen (Bogor), Pip Darvall, D.P. and Uschi Digdoyo (Bromo), Sutan Armyangah and Martin Rinaldo, Terry and Louise Gregory, Richard Guiness, Charles Parkin, Linda van Gelder, James Welsh, David Wolstenholme (Bukittingi), James McGrath (Bukit Lawang), Sally Herdon and Nasir (Cherating), Wisoot Buachoom and TAT, Stewart Davidson, Suriyan Khamsitha, Anan Manthong, Nat, Madame Nok (Chiang-Mai), Viyada Biriya Sombat and TAT (Hat Yai), Mark Davies and Headrock Cafe, Tipawan Tampusana and TAT (Hua Hin), Willem Kwakman, Nathaniel Lawalata, Brian Mullally, Tuta Soedjono, Henk van Dan, Ingrid van der Linde (Jakarta), Dr Eko Budi, Mr Soekokgo (Kalibaru), Somboon Pinyen and TAT, Sunya and Sunya Rux restaurant (Kanchanaburi), Franco Ce (Koh Pee-Pee), Jerome Brownsteen, Elizabeth Engle, Porn and Poh (Koh Samui), Noor Azlan, Anuar, Leang, Badriah and Town Guest House, Mr Lee and Town Garden House, Kirke Mahy, Darren McAvoy (Kota Bahru), Mrs Lee and Rong (Krabi), Mohd Jeffri and Tina Travel, Ramchand and MSL Travel (Kuala Lumpur), Mr Effendy, M. Yamin and TDC, Ibrahim Mohammed (Kuala Terranganu), James Chaney, David Holme, Deborah Seitler, Mark Stanton (Lake Toba), Nanang Hermansyah, Sarah Marshall, Eugene O'Docherty, Rusma Wadi, Wim Min and Saviatri Travel (Lombok), Joseph Chong and Jonkers restaurant, David Lee, Gary Nicholson, Roy Rodrigues, Kate and Phillipa Rumble, Pauline Schwartz, Sue Whitehouse (Malacca), Ken and Christina Waldeck (Malang), Kamal Ruzaman Suleiman (Marang), A.B. Sianipar and Jacky (Medan), Ali, Paul Jamal, Dr Hasanuddin and TIC, Harry van Pelsen, Sip van der Werff (Padang), Diyanto, Willy Franssen, Mette Hansen (Pangandaran), Rosehana and TDC, Ruby K.C. Lim and PTA (Penang), Chia Boon Hee, Ellen Rozena (Singapore), Cukkert Asa, Robert Barr, Celia Fraser, Pete and Joy Merrett, Fiona Seth-Smith, Harry, Mawardi Moeslich (Solo), Peter Cheng, Catherine Hartley, Rachel Simmonds (Tioman), Marsha, Heru Purnomo, Hadi Wusono and TIC, W.S. Soedalhar, Jane and Kim Timson (Yogyakarta).

Introduction

Bangkok to Bali (and vice versa) has long been part of the overland route for Europeans heading for Australia and Antipodeans coming to Europe. The route is ideal as a holiday in its own right, a stopover on a longer round-the-world itinerary, or as a trans-Asian journey to Australasia.

There are several reasons for the sudden popularity of South-East Asia as a holiday destination. A major one is the large number of Europeans now going out to Australia for working holidays – many return back home via Bali-Bangkok, on the overland trail. Second, it is still so cheap. Living not on the baseline but staying at reasonable accommodation (a room of your own, with a shower) and travelling by bus and train, you can stay in Indonesia, for example, for about £40 a week, and that includes one decent meal a day, a lot of fruit and a selection of street food.

Third, there is so much variety. Here you have tropical beaches, active volcanoes, Amazonian rain forests, cool hill stations, magnificent temples, colourful festivals and fabulous handicrafts. One day you could be snorkelling for coral off a remote palm-fringed island, the next chatting to a monk at a busy Bangkok traffic intersection! Fourth, the route is an easygoing one, safe, much less hassle than, say, India or Nepal, and the locals are invariably friendly. If there is one good reason for travelling from Bangkok to Bali, it must be the friendliness of the people – the Indonesians and Thais especially. I would not quite put the Malaysians into the same category – they are a little more Westernised and, as Muslims, rather more formal. Indonesia is also Muslim, but here interpretation of the faith is far less strict than in many other Islamic countries. The Indonesians are some of the friendliest people around. Even more helpful and hospitable, however, are the Singaporeans – rather surprising for such a Westernised city.

The overexposure of Thailand to foreigners has left it far less the 'land of smiles' than it once was, especially in the tourist centres, although if you take the trouble to smile first, you will always get one back. The only country whose people I have heard complaints about is Sumatra – and that is only because it is still so far off the beaten track and is unused to foreign visitors.

Jakarta, Yogyakarta and Bali are the main hassle-centres – very pushy – and in all three places you will need both humour and patience. You will not want to stay long. In certain other places, like Bangkok, Bandung, Malang and Medan, because of the traffic pollution (one sniff of the air in Medan, and your eyes start to run!). Out of these more urbanised areas however, as soon as you hit the islands, the beaches and the out-of-the-way villages with their beautiful scenery, laidback atmosphere and smiling families, you will want to stay *too* long! It's the old, old story – as soon as you go somewhere (like backwoods Java) where there have not been many Westerners yet, you will find local people at their best, and that is the most important requirement for a successful trip.

South-East Asia is very busy at the moment. It is still a place for adventurers, but there are a lot more people (and much better facilities) than, say, two years ago, especially in Thailand where tourism has recently taken off. Up until now, the weak infrastructure of the region (poor transport, accommodation, etc.) dissuaded all but rough-living backpackers from taking a holiday here. The breakthrough was Thailand's phenomenally successful 'Year of Tourism' in 1987, which encouraged several neighbouring countries to follow suit. There is a 'Visit Malaysia' year in 1990, 'Visit Indonesia' year in 1991, and in 1992 Singapore will be reopening (after revamping) a whole host of major sights and attractions. Bali is already a haven for Australian package-tourists, and other paradise islands like Tioman, Lombok and Sumatra are poised on the brink of development. The next five years – from 1990 to 1995 – will see the whole area opening up, and there is no better time to go than the present!

Planning your trip is important. Bangkok to Bali is a vast area – four countries and 3,700 km add up to a lot of travel – so you will have to be selective if you are to make the best use of your time. The first thing to do is to read up on the area. Scour your local libraries, browse around the big travel bookshops, and order a heap of brochures from various tour operators. I did not do this, and so was astonished to find, as I drifted down from Bangkok to Penang, to Kuala Lumpur and Singapore, and finally to Jakarta, how 'Western' these cities had become. The big illusion about South-East Asia is that it is still backward and Third World. Nothing could be further from the truth. It is, in fact, very progressive. What a lot of Westerners do not understand is that South-East Asia is actually passing them by. Only recently, the *Straits Times* in Singapore carried an article about London being the dirtiest city in Europe! Singapore is far cleaner than London any day. So are Bangkok and Kuala Lumpur. If there is a city which is dirty, it is Penang, which has both rubbish and rats. Jakarta has a modern aspect, certainly, but look down the sidestreets, along the edge of the canal and the railway line, and you will see an Eastern slum development

Java is Asia, but it is not all dirty and it is not all backward. There is obviously a lack of money, and there are a lot of people living on a small piece of land, but there is no outright poverty. Yes, there are slums, but you also find these in any Western city like London or Liverpool. If you can accept this reality; if you can accept that East and West share the same fundamental problems, then you have probably got the right attitude for travelling. The mistake that many Europeans make, which spoils their trip, is to wander round South-East Asia like a colonial overlord, treating the locals as second-class citizens. This kind of attitude will not win you any friends. Unless you are polite and respectful and ask for things nicely, you will run up against Asian forgetfulness and awkwardness in their severest forms!

How long should a trip from Bangkok to Bali take? I think that is up to you. Going flat out, you could cover the ground by train, bus and a flight (Singapore to Jakarta) in six days. So, even with just a month to spare, flying into Bangkok and flying out of Denpasar in Bali, either to travel onwards to Australia or to return to Europe, you could take in quite a lot on the way. Personally, I think six to eight weeks would be a pleasant length of time. I wouldn't want to do it in much less. Bear in mind that you will have a two-month visa for Indonesia. So, if you decide (as many do) to have a holiday in Bali – shopping, touring and lazing around on beaches – you should allow an extra two or three weeks. If you want to take in the Thai beaches, that will use another two weeks, so, in all, ten weeks would be about right. Living on the cheap (though comfortably so), you could do the whole thing for £500 (about £50 a week) but allow an extra £100 for shopping/ emergencies, and then take into account any time spent in Singapore or Bangkok (expensive).

This guide is obviously selective. It covers some 50 points of major interest, along with a number of 'off-the-beaten-track' options for the adventurous traveller. If you wanted to go right through the book, visiting every place mentioned, you could probably do it in 100 days and for as little as £1500. For a quick but comprehensive overview of the territory, and to get you from Bangkok to Bali in just 20 days, I would suggest the (very well-priced) Trailfinders Rover. After that, you could rest up in Bali for a week, and then use this island as a base for side-trips to Lombok and east Java (three to four days apiece). From Bali, you can start working your way back to Bangkok. If you have come with Trailfinders, you can skip north Java, Singapore and west-coast (from June-September, east coast) Malaysia. You will however need two weeks to travel through central Java (Malang-Solo-Yogya-Pangandaran) to west Java (Bandung and Bogor) to Jakarta. From here, the time-saving option is the short flight to Padang, followed by an eight- to ten-day tour of Sumatra (Bukittingi-Toba-Brastagi, etc.), flying out of Indonesia from Medan to Kuala Lumpur. Personally, I would not spend too long in Malaysia – you can zip round the highspots (Kuala Lumpur to Medan, then up the east coast via Tioman, Cherating and Marang, to Kota Bahru) pleasantly in two weeks.

The last month you could devote exclusively to Thailand – from the beaches of the south (Krabi, Samui, Hua Hin) up to Bangkok; then two side-trips to Kanchanaburi and Koh Samet; finally, the long haul north to Chiang Mai (for trekking and last-minute shopping) and the slow drift back south, via the ruins of Sukhothai and Ayutthaya, to Don Muang airport for the flight home. If you cannot manage all this in one trip, don't worry – there is always a next time!

Bangkok-Bali is a year-round destination. There are only two seasons – the wet and the hot – and it makes little difference when you go. Whenever you turn up, there is going to be a wet season at one or other of the countries en route. Even in Thailand it is wet in the north when it is dry in the south, and vice versa. In Malaysia all the tour companies switch between the east and west coasts, depending on the individual rainy seasons. Trailfinders, for instance, offer a west coast itinerary (Penang, Cameron Highlands, Kuala Lumpur) between November and March, and switch to the east coast from June to September. Meanwhile, Java comes into its wet season from November to January, and it gets very wet. Sometimes there is a gap (just possibly) at the end of October through to early November, when you could do the whole tour with no rain involved. You could slip out of Bangkok on a couple of dry days, find Penang warm and clement, nip down west-coast Malaysia to Singapore (which has always a chance of rain), and clear Java and Bali just before the rains arrive – if, that is, there is a late monsoon!

The chart opposite gives you a general idea of the weather to expect. The climate at all times of the year is very warm and humid. It can (and does) rain at any time, but even the worst rains are often accompanied by periods of brilliant sunshine.

Many Australians cannot afford the long flights into Bali or Java. Instead they fly to one of the southernmost islands of the Indonesian archipelago, and then island-hop their way overland to Bali. This is much cheaper.

GETTING THERE

FROM THE UK
Official return fares from London to Bangkok start at £598 with Thai International (tel: 01-491 7953); unofficial rates booked through Trailfinders (tel: 01-938 3366) cost from £250 one-way, £451 return. The cheap season for tickets is October/November and mid-January to mid-June. It's worth shopping around; many cheap bargains are advertised in magazines like *Time Out, LAM, TNT* and *Australasian Express,* and there are several discount travel agencies round Earls Court, London.

Garuda fly from London to Jakarta, where you can catch a connecting flight to Bali on Monday, Wednesday and Thursday. In the quiet season (1 February to 15 June, 1 October to 30 November), Trailfinders offer London to Jakarta for £325, and London-Bali return for £616. Bangkok-Bali is £185 throughout the year.

You can now travel from London to Singapore nonstop in less than 13 hours on a scheduled daily flight. Trailfinders have flights from £253 one-way, from £506 return. Jakarta to Denpasar (Bali) is only £60, and if you are heading for Australia, Denpasar to Sydney or Melbourne is £175.

FROM AUSTRALIA
It is now about A$1000 return to Bali from Sydney on Qantas (A$50 more on Garuda) without shopping around. That includes two weeks' free accommodation in reasonable mid-bracket comfort in Bali! If you do not want accommodation, the flight is around A$700 from Sydney and only A$400 from Perth. Cheap flight specialists in Sydney include STA at la Lee St, Railway Square (tel 2126744) and Sydney Flight Centre in Martin Place (tel: 2212666). STA also have offices in Perth, Melbourne and Darwin.

GETTING BACK

Do not forget to reconfirm airline tickets for coming home. Singapore is a good place to do this as it is quick and efficient. All too often people are knocked off the flight list because they did not contact their airline early enough to reconfirm their tickets. During the high season months especially (approximately November to March), all international flights should be confirmed at least two weeks ahead. A common stumbling block is Bali – Australians have their holiday period around Christmas and the New Year, and towards the end of January there is often a heavy backlog of people fighting for a seat on the few planes back to Australia.

If you are planning a long tour of South-East Asia, it may be worth flying out on a one-way ticket (Trailfinders offer London-Bangkok from £250, London-Bali from £308). You can find really cheap return flights by shopping around in Bangkok, Singapore or Penang.

ORGANISED GROUP TRIPS

In the UK, four main companies run trips from Bangkok to Bali – Trailfinders, Asian Overland (booked through Exodus), Top Deck, and Dragoman. They all use public transport (i.e. local trains and buses), and the travel cost covers all journeys plus hotel-to-station transfers, etc. Local transport for sightseeing is left to the individual, to allow more freedom. Some optional excursions may cost extra, but rarely more than £10 in total. Those with visions of flag-waving tour leaders, shepherding flocks of people, need not worry. The tours are designed with maximum flexibility in mind. There is very little in the way of 'organised' sightseeing, and apart from

		J	F	M	A	M	J	J	A	S	O	N	D
BANGKOK	Av. Fahrenheit	79	82	84	86	85	84	83	83	82	81	80	78
	Av. no. dry days/mth	30	27	28	27	22	20	18	18	15	17	25	30
SINGAPORE	Av. Fahrenheit	80	81	82	82	82	82	82	82	82	81	81	81
	Av. no. dry days/mth	14	17	17	15	16	17	18	17	16	15	12	12
JAKARTA	Av. Fahrenheit	79	79	80	81	81	80	80	80	81	80	81	79
	Av. no. dry days/mth	13	11	16	19	22	23	26	27	25	23	18	17
BALI	Av.Fahrenheit	82	82	82	82	82	79	80	81	81	81	81	81
	Av. no. dry days/mth	15	6	12	15	22	29	26	27	21	13	6	10

sticking to the departure timetable, nothing is obligatory. Although no age limit is enforced, the group's average age is under 30, and the maximum group number is 20. The tour leader saves you time and hassles, and supplies you with as much useful information as possible. The prices quoted below include an air ticket to cover flights from Singapore to Jakarta.

Trailfinders, 42-48 Earls Court Road, London W8 (tel: 01-938 3366). This company provides a complete travel service – insurance, inoculations, information, visas and cut-price air tickets. Also a 20-day 'Bangkok to Bali Rover', covering (from November to March) Bangkok, Hua Hin, Cameron Highlands, Penang, Singapore, Cirebon, Bandungan, Yogyakarta, Mt Bromo and Bali. From April to October, the itinerary switches from Hua Hin/Cameron Highlands to Kuala Lumpur, Taman Negara and Kuantan. The cost of the tour, exclusive of food and accommodation, is £365. Accommodation is reserved by the tour leader, but there is no obligation to take it and you are entirely free to go off and arrange this for yourself.

Full information and xeroxed tact sheets are supplied at each stop along the route, and on arrival in Bali the tour leader gives a full rundown on the island. Departures are every month, or more frequently as the tours fill up. Book as far in advance as possible as this trip is proving very popular, probably because it is the best value around. As an independent traveller, arranging your own transport, hotels and sightseeing, you would be hard pressed to cover the same area in 30 days, never mind 20, and you certainly would not save much (if any) money. You would also lose the convenience of having forward-booked transport (hotels too), the cheaper hotel rates offered to groups, and reserved seats on the trains – almost impossible to get in, say, Indonesia!

Trailfinders also offer a ten-day 'North Thai Rover', visiting Bangkok, Tha Ton, Chiang Mai, Chiang Rai, Ayutthaya and Khao Yai National Park. This costs £275 and includes chartered transport, an experienced tour-leader and a variety of accommodation from simple hilltribe huts to comfortable air-conditioned hotels. It is real value for money and worth considering!

'Dragoman', 10 Riverside, Framlingham, Suffolk IP13 9AG (tel: 0728 724184). Prices are far higher than Trailfinders, but so is the standard of accommodation provided. The 22-day 'S. E. Asian Explorer' tour starts at £495 and takes in Bangkok, Penang, Cameron Highlands, Kuala Lumpur, Malacca, Singapore, Jakarta, Jogyakarta, Mt Bromo and Bali.

PRE-DEPARTURE

DOCUMENTS
Passports should be valid for at least six months longer than the duration of your trip. Visas are not required for Malaysia and Singapore, or (provided you hold an onward air ticket out of the country, and your passport is still good for six months) for Indonesia. Visas are only required for Thailand if you stay over 15 days. An international driving licence, available from any AA office, is essential if you wish to drive vehicles abroad. Student cards like ISIC (International Student Identity Card) and the International Youth Hostel Card can save you a lot of money, especially on airline tickets and Asian hostel accommodation.

JABS AND TABS
Although not compulsory, vaccinations against cholera, typhoid, tetanus, polio and infectious hepatitis are all highly advisable. Contact your doctor at least six weeks prior to departure to arrange injections. If you are short on time, use the (quick) vaccination services offered by Thomas Cook, 45 Berkeley St, London Wl (tel: 01-499 4000), the Hospital of Tropical Diseases, 41 Pancras Way NWl (tel: 01-387 4411), or Trailfinders. Also check with your doctor about malaria tablets. Start them a week before departure, and keep on taking them for four weeks after your return. If you want to avoid the unpleasant side-effects of many brands of malaria tablets, why not try the homoeopathic variety. While you are with the doctor, pick up some drugs to relieve diarrhoea. Those most widely prescribed are Imodium and Lomotil.

INSURANCE
Travel insurance is strongly recommended. If your bank or travel company cannot recommend a good policy – one which covers lost luggage, money and valuables, personal liability and travel delay – go to Trailfinders or Topdeck Travel in Earls Court Road. Both companies offer a comprehensive scheme with a 24-hour telephone number to contact in medical emergencies. So does Jardine's at 25 Collingwood St, Newcastle-upon-Tyne (tel: 091 261 8002) and STA Student Travel at Priory House, 6 Wrights Lane, London W8 6TA.

MONEY
You do not have to change any foreign currency in Britain. Exchange facilities are readily available on a 24-hour basis at international airports like Bangkok, Bali, Jakarta and Singapore. Rates are often better locally than those quoted in the UK. For safety, buy travellers' cheques (American Express are best) in small denominations, and (to assist claims)

keep a record of the numbers in a separate place. If you are bringing cash, bring big bills as you get a much better exchange rate on 50 and 100 dollar bills than on 10s or 20s. Credit cards are useful for unexpected purchases, and for acquiring a fresh injection of cash when you spend too much in the shops. Major cards like Visa, American Express and Master Charge are widely accepted in South-East Asia.

COSTS

It is hard to set a budget for any South-East Asian country. What you spend depends on a lot of factors – if you can speak a little of the local language, everything becomes cheaper; if you drink beer, it will double the cost of your meal; if you stay put in one place, rather than travelling around, you will save on transport and (where long-stay discounts are given) on accommodation too.

I always tell people to allow £15 a day, without their shopping. Included in that amount is a beer or two in the evening, two decent meals a day, a reasonably comfortable room, and day-to-day transport costs. Malaysia and Thailand are pretty similar pricewise, but you should allow £5 extra per day to cover living expenses in Singapore.

Bali is cheap, Java cheaper and Sumatra cheapest of all. You can get by in Sumatra on less than £10 a day, and that is really living it up! If you are on a tight budget, you can cover most places (except Singapore) on as little as £5 a day, provided you do not move around a lot and are prepared to live on rice and noodles. 'We lived quite well at budget level on US$150 a week in Bali and for only US$100 in Java', reported one couple, 'but we don't smoke and we don't drink!' Two people can travel far cheaper than one – most hotels and guest houses charge more or less the same for a single room as for a double, so it makes sense to find a travelling companion and to share costs. Trailfinders, a tour company used to catering for independent travellers, suggests a budget of £6 a night for accommodation (if there are two of you), £6-10 a day for food, and a maximum of £10 a day to cover all optional excursions. In practice, having taken one of their tours myself, it was much cheaper!

WHAT TO TAKE

Travel as light as possible – take only essentials. You can buy everything else you need (clothes, luggage, toiletries, etc.) in Bangkok, where they are often much cheaper than at home. Remember, heavy baggage is very tiring to carry in the heat! Try to pack everything in one large soft bag or a frameless rucksack with a top carrying handle, strong zips, and lots of pockets. All small items (camera, Walkman, books, maps, etc.) can go in a shoulder bag or day-sack, which will come in handy later on for sightseeing or day outings.

Clothing

Cool cotton clothes are best. You are heading into hot, humid tropical climes. Clothes dry quickly in these conditions, so bring only a few and wash them often. Your packing list should include the following:

T-shirts/cotton shirts (3)	thongs/sandals/ flip flops
shorts (1)	light waterproof
trousers/jeans (2)	lightweight jacket
skirts/dresses (2)	swimwear
socks/underwear (2)	towel
	sun hat

You'll also need a warm sweater and a pair of comfortable flat shoes for jungle walks in cool hill stations (e.g. Cameron Highlands) and for climbing high-altitude volcanoes like Mt Bromo.

Equipment

mosquito net (buy Blacks)	combination padlock
sheet sleeping bag (or duvet cover)	toilet paper (flat pack)
money belt (I prefer an armband wallet)	water bottle water-purification tablets (Puritabs are best)
torch (try a Magnalight – small, strong, ideal for travelling)	personal toiletries/ mirror/sewing kit
alarm clock (with illuminated time)	personal medical kit/mosquito repellent
inflatable pillow	playing cards/
Walkman/tapes	reading matter/
camera/film	writing matter
snorkel/mask	sunglasses/sun
washing line/soap powder	cream/ Chapstick
penknife with openers	spare spectacles/ contact lenses

MAPS AND INFORMATION

Maps and information are available from tourist offices throughout South-East Asia, or from the following addresses in the UK:
Thailand, 49 Albemarle St, London W1 (tel: 01-499 7679)
Malaysia, 57 Trafalgar Sq., London WC2 (tel: 01-930 7932)
Singapore, 1st floor, Carrington House, 126-130 Regent St, London W1 (tel: 01-437 0033).

Detailed country maps (ask for APA or Nelles) are sold by map specialists like

Robertson McCarta Ltd, 122 Kings Cross Rd WCl (tel 01-278 8276) or The London Map Centre, 22-24 Caxton St, London SW1 (tel: 01-222 2466). Trailfinders has an excellent travel library at 194 Kensington High St, London W8 (tel: 01-938 3999), ideal for advance reading and research. Three good bookshops with a large travel section are Stanfords, 12-14 Long Acre, London WC2 (tel: 01-836 1321), Compendium, 234 Camden High St, London NW1 (tel: 01-485 8944) and the Travellers' Bookshop, 25 Cecil Court WC2 (tel: 01-836 9132).

TRAVEL INFORMATION

GETTING AROUND

Travel is very easy, especially in Malaysia and Singapore, where people do go out of their way to help you. It is most difficult in Sumatra, where if they tell you a bus is coming, or a boat has just gone, it either isn't or hasn't.

BUSES

Throughout the region, buses are the quickest and cheapest way of getting from place to place. Bus travel is most interesting (and most hazardous) in Indonesia. Indonesian bus-drivers all have different philosophies on the best way to make money: there are those who will drive very quickly all the time and just cover their route as fast as they can; then there are those who kerb-crawl. They go *really* slowly over the entire route, stopping at any organic creature to ask if it wants a ride, and then they will drive as *fast* as they can until somebody gets off. As soon as there is a spare space they go back to a standstill again until it is filled. Public buses throughout Indonesia – particularly in Jakarta (where they know the power of money) – can be classified this easily.

Regarding where to sit, always try for a back seat on buses. It gives you the ability to stuff your backpack behind your head, and leaves your long legs free to dangle! This is the only solution for those lengthy, hot, overcrowded bus journeys through Java and Sumatra. The back seats get the worst of the bumps, but you get a lot of breeze (by the door) and if there is an accident you will be one of a handful of people to escape injury.

TRAINS

It is easy to reserve train seats/berths in Thailand and Malaysia. Everything is computerised, and you can buy your ticket at the same time. In Java, however, you cannot buy a ticket for another country until you arrive. The only way you can get a booking in, say, Jakarta (Gambir station) is to go along and buy a ticket – ideally the moment you arrive. The only problem is that there is probably a two- or three-day wait until there is a seat, and meanwhile you are stuck in Jakarta!

SIGHTSEEING

This can be hot, tiring work. Get up early (around 6 or 7 a.m.), do your sightseeing while it is cool, and collapse back into the haven of your fan-cooled/air-conditioned room by noon. Have lunch and a short siesta, then start off again around 4 p.m., when the heat has dropped. Another way to be kind to your body is to travel by night buses or trains – it is so much cooler. You may lose some sleep, but just think of the money you are saving on that night's accommodation!

DRESS

In South-East Asia, as in any distinctly poor Third World area, you will be expected to dress well. Hippie wear is not smiled on. From their point of view, you are a Westerner, who has had every opportunity to to do well. You have been born in a rich country, have had an education, and you should, simply by virtue of the fact that you have been able to afford to come out here, have some money. So if you do not dress like you have some money, you are obviously an idiot. You have evidently done nothing with all those opportunities; you have absolutely wasted them. If you wander round in frayed shirts, dirty shorts and cheap thongs, they will wonder what you are doing? Who are you kidding? You must be able to afford some smart, clean clothes, so why are you trying to look poorer than us?' Although hippies are not in vogue any more, there is certainly still a travelling band of people trying to go back in time. You will get a far better reaction from the locals, especially from hippie-hating officials, if you dress up for formal occasions like applying for visas at embassies, extending visas at immigration offices, arriving at border posts and entering airports.

WOMEN TRAVELLERS

Most women travellers have the time of their lives in South-East Asia, especially in Thailand, where the Thai men treat them with the highest respect. If there is a problem, it is in strongly Muslim countries like Malaysia and Java, where Western women travelling on their own are regarded with some suspicion. 'Take special care in Malaysia!', warned one girl, 'There's no such thing as a casual date out here, and wearing skimpy clothing labels you a (very) available lady. Whatever you do, don't rashly accept any invitations for strolls down the beach or into people's homes at night.' Women rarely travel on their own in Malaysia – they soon team up with a man (which makes them non-existent to Malaysian flashers and hasslers) or with another girl.

Matters are not much better in Bali, especially on Kuta beach and in Ubud. 'I spent a night in Ubud', was one report, 'and the *losmen* cook took a fancy to me. I locked my door at night, and when I opened it in the morning I found him asleep on the porch. That's what I call dedication!' But the worst reports come from Java, where 'the men hassled us all the time, even when we were wearing wedding rings. The women, by contrast, blanked us out – I think they thought we were prostitutes. We met a Javanese guy on a train, and he wanted us (three girls) to go to his sister's wedding. He asked us "Are you married?", and we said "No", and he said "Oh, you're still *virgins* then!" That's the way they think out there.'

A few more tips for women travelling in Java: 'It's a good idea to wear a bra – wearing anything too exposing really provokes the Javanese men. If any of them touches you, even an arm or an elbow, bear in mind that they're not allowed to touch their own women. You're quite within your rights to give them a stern look and to say "Hands off!" It may shock them if you act outraged, but they'll back down immediately. Also, when talking to them, lower your eyes at intervals – prolonged eye-contact is a real come-on!' Throughout the region, modest dress cuts down the hassle-ratio by about half. Despite equatorial temperatures, cover arms and legs, and button up to the neck. It won't make you invisible, but it will help. Last, bring a good supply of tampons or sanitary towels. They're hard to get out here.

DRUGS

Thailand, Malaysia and Singapore operate the death penalty for possession of illegal substances, so the simple message with drugs is *don't*. Lots of foreigners go to jail for lengthy terms because they have ignored this warning, and South-East Asian jails are not pleasant.

PHOTOGRAPHY

Keep your photographic gear to a minimum. Even for the serious photographer, a 35 mm camera with two zoom lenses (one from about 28 mm to 90 mm, the other from 70 mm to 200 mm) will cover most pictorial needs. As for film, I would recommend a medium fast colour film for best results: Kodachrome 64, Ektachrome 100, or Fujichrome 100 for slides; Ektacolor 100/200 or Fujicolor 100/200 for prints. Apart from Singapore, film is more expensive abroad, so bring a good supply from home. If you need a new camera, or your existing one needs repair, Singapore is the place to

go. If you have an electronic camera, be sure to carry extra batteries. If you do not want your photos washed out by bright tropical sunlight, avoid taking snaps in the middle of the day. When taking photographs of people, ask permission first. It's a nice touch to have some of the photos you take of local people developed overnight (easy to do, most South-East Asian towns have a quick Fuji or Kodak service) and to hand them out next day. They just love it – so many travellers take their photos, and so few show them the result.

LANGUAGE

This is not really a problem. You can get by with English in most places, especially in Malaysia and Singapore. It is worth learning the numbers in Thai and Indonesian as you will then get a much better deal when bargaining.

BARGAINING

You will quickly learn to bargain for everything: taxis, food, souvenirs or accommodation. On Kuta beach in Bali, I have even bargained over the price of a newspaper! Contrary to popular belief, there is no 'formula' for securing a good deal. You cannot say: 'I'll cut his price by a half or a quarter'. It doesn't work. Neither does haggling. Haggling is for tourists! The best way to get a good price is not to say anything. The seller will ask 'Well, what's your price?', but don't give him one. If you do, you will probably offer too much and then he will bargain you up from there. Keep your mouth shut and let him do the talking. Allow yourself the occasional laugh (to indicate amusement at his inflated prices) and keep shaking your head. If you can keep this up, he will lower his prices a dozen times without you uttering another word!

Shopping around is the best way to get a bargain. Actually, it's the only way. Even if you think the price is fair, check somewhere else. If one shop has got this item, rest assured that another will have it too. And just watch the price come tumbling down as you walk out of the shop!

There are two more points worth remembering: you get what you paid for, and it's not a bargain if you don't want it. Asians believe that once you have started negotiating for something, you have almost committed yourself to purchasing. I have lost count of the number of people who have bought things they didn't want simply because they began bargaining!

An important tip, which is likely to save you a lot of trouble, is not to get too 'serious' about money. Sure, bargaining is the rule, and you don't want to pay high prices just because you are a tourist, but accept that you are going into a poor part of the world. In Java, for example, where the average wage is a pitiful £25 a month, you will often see travellers having desperate arguments with their *becak* driver over 200rps (8 pence). 'He's ripping me off!' is the familiar complaint, but how can you be 'ripped off' for 8p? He might be making a little bit extra, but who can blame him? He has probably been cycling 76 kg of plump European flesh around for four hours and feels entitled to a small tip.

HEALTH

With the exception of Singapore, you have to watch what you eat and drink. Do not drink tap water. Stick to (cheap) bottled mineral water, and be wary of ice in drinks (although it is nearly impossible to avoid it altogether). Go easy on street food, but don't pass it by just because it *is* a street stall. Some of the best food in South-East Asia is out there on tiny trays and barrows, and it is simply too good to miss. Just check that it has been freshly cooked, and look to see where the food is stored before it is cooked. Are the sticks of *satay* (meat on skewers) kept out in the open, where flies or dust from passing trucks can get at them? Are the dishes you are going to eat off being washed in clean, soapy water or in a bucket of stagnant slime? Basically, if you keep an eye on the food, you can avoid a lot of problems. The sudden change in diet can sometimes cause stomach upsets (local versions: Bangkok Boogie, Java Jive, Bali Belly), so it is wise to steer clear of spicy food and raw vegetables/salads for the first few days. If you do get a tummy bug, drink plenty of fluids (to prevent dehydration) and restrict your diet to small amounts of bland food (boiled rice, bananas) and warm tea. Also, go easy on alcohol and hot sun. The two most common causes of ill-health in Thailand, are drinking too much Mekong whisky or Singha beer and sitting too long in the sun. People do not take sunburn seriously, but it is a problem. If you have a parting in the centre of your hair (or no hair at all), wear a hat. If you have spent all year in an office wearing shoes and socks, you will have to protect your feet. One man I met was so crippled by sunburn on the tops of his feet that he could not walk for three days!

If you have anti-malaria tablets, remember to take them, and *do* bring a sufficient supply. I ran out halfway through one trip, and had to beg more from a succession of other travellers – most embarrassing. Malaria is not a nice thing to catch, and it can recur for years. The choloroquine-based tablets currently on the market are not very effective, but they are better than nothing. A mosquito net is the best antidote to malarial mosquitoes, which are rife throughout South-East Asia and which come out after dark. You can also keep these little bloodsuckers at bay by burning mosquito coils and by covering bare skin at night. A good anti-histamine cream like Anthisan works wonders with mosquito bites – it really takes the sting out of them!

Bilharzia is present, most often in warm stagnant waters off Bali and other tropical islands. The best prevention is to wear shoes and clothing if wading or bathing in infected areas. When snorkelling for coral, wear a pair of light canvas shoes to avoid coral cuts. The two things *not* to step on are sea-urchins and fire-coral (brown with white tips and hairy). It is generally a bad idea to go swimming in South-East Asian seas with open wounds. If you get coral-dust in them, you could end up with tropical ulcers. In damp, humid climes like these, even simple cuts and scratches can become infected. Make sure that they are kept dry and clean, and apply a good antiseptic powder like Cicatrin, which is an excellent curative for burns, open sores and wounds. After clearing the infection, follow up with a waterproof healing cream like Conotrane.

Ear infections are rife, especially amongst people who do a lot of swimming. This 'tropical ear' is a fungal infection, caused mainly by not drying the ears after a swim or shower. If you do not deal with it straightaway (a local chemist will always know what eardrops to prescribe), it flares up and can be very painful.

Throughout South-East Asia, you do not need a prescription to buy a broad-spectrum antibiotic. One of the best ones to use out here is double-strength Bactrim, which is available over the counter from most Indonesian *apotiks* or chemists if you cannot find it anywhere else.

SECURITY

Penang used to have a reputation for bag-snatching, and Jakarta still does, but the rest of South-East Asia is generally very safe. Personal security depends a lot on sticking to your normal routines. If you are used to carrying your valuables in a shoulder bag, keep right on doing it. Ignore the prophets of doom with their warnings of bag-snatchers and slash-thieves – there have been too many cases of people changing routine, and stashing their cash in hotel safes (or even under their pillow!) and then not remembering where they have put it until aboard a 22-hour bus to somewhere else. But do use hotel safes when you can. If the hotel does not have one, lock up your valuables (including any money not needed for that day's expenses) in a bag in your room. A good strong combination lock is usually enough to dissuade any light-fingered room cleaner.

It is generally a bad idea to carry all your travellers' cheques, airline tickets, passport, etc. around on the streets, unless, that is, you keep them all in a money belt or (much better, in my opinion) an armband wallet. The main targets of street-thieves are small pieces of hand-luggage which they assume (often correctly) contain cameras, wallets and personal valuables. They do not often go for rucksacks and big bags, which are simply too bulky or heavy to run off with. Pickpockets tend to work public buses and trains, and anywhere where there are crowds, so keep an eye out for them as they will be watching you! A big 'don't' throughout South-East Asia is to leave bags or valuables unattended. In Thailand, for instance, what you would call 'theft', they would call 'loss'. If you put your bag on a restaurant table, wander off to get your coat, and come back to find it gone, you have just 'lost' it. The fact that somebody picked it up is purely a result of it being left unattended. It looked like it needed a new owner, and now it's got one. In a case like this, the police are not going to be very helpful. All they are likely to do is give you a form to send to your insurance company.

On the whole, the individual traveller is more prone to theft than people travelling in couples or in groups. If there are two of you, one can always mind the bags while the other joins a queue for bus tickets, has a swim or goes to the toilet. If you are on your own, and you have loads of luggage, it is going to be difficult even to get into a toilet in Asia! The lone traveller is particularly at risk on long overnight bus journeys in Thailand. If he drops off to sleep (or is helped to do so by 'kindly' strangers offering drugged food or drinks) he will lose everything but his shirt.

ACCOMMODATION

In general, accommodation in South-East Asia is not as cheap as you might expect (especially if you are coming from India) and prices are increasing fast. Here are a few tips: (1) don't arrive at big cities at weekends, school holidays or Chinese New Year – room rates go sky-high, and you will be lucky to find anywhere decent to stay; (2) always aim to arrive in a town or city by noon at the latest. That gives you time to look around for a good hotel/guest house suited to your budget; (3) always check rooms for vermin/bugs, especially under beds, in dark corners, waste bins and toilets; (4) always check mosquito netting on windows; (5) establish whether the room rate includes (a) breakfast, (b) tax,

(c) service charge. Nearly everywhere in Bali gives breakfast inclusive with the cost of your room. The quality of accommodation in Java is lower than in Bali and more expensive. In Singapore and Malaysia, the best budget lodges are often Chinese-run. They often have single rooms with large double beds (quite adequate for couples) and are good value for money.

Note: hotel rates quoted throughout this guide are subject to increase without notice – expect a 5-10 per cent rise for the 1990 season.

FOOD

South-East Asia has everything from street food stalls and night hawker markets to burger joints and international restaurants. In most places you can pick and choose from a variety of different cuisines, and it is all very cheap. The region can be a bit tough on vegetarians, however, especially in Muslim countries like Malaysia and Indonesia. Muslims cannot really relate to the concept of vegetarianism, and if you order a vegetarian meal, don't be at all surprised if it turns up garnished with pieces of chicken or prawn!

The milk situation is bad throughout South-East Asia. Very few places have anything but sickly-sweet condensed milk for tea and coffee. It is always worth asking in restaurants for Nescafé with UHT milk or Coffee-Mate powder. The alternative is to drink it black.

The mineral water in Java is called Ades. If you ask for water (*aqua*) they sometimes don't understand, but if you ask for Ades, they know exactly what you mean! Wherever you go, there is a bewildering variety of fresh fruit, from snakeskin *salaks* and lychees to mangoes, pineapples, watermelons, papaya, pomegranates, strawberries, and over 20 varieties of banana in Thailand alone. The king of the fruits has to be the 'durian'. Weighing several kilos, with a skin of armour-piercing spikes, it smells of sewage. It is an acquired taste which few travellers ever acquire!

COMMUNICATIONS

Postal services in this part of the world are good. Mail can be sent to poste restantes (most post offices have them) or to hotels. When getting friends/family to write to you, ask them to (a) print your name clearly; (b) underline the surname; (c) put the surname *before* the Christian name (e.g. **SMITH** John). This will save your mail being 'misfiled' and lost.

If you are on a long hike and you need to call home, the cheapest place to make

IDD phone calls is Singapore – only £1.20 per minute to the UK! You can dial direct from the comfort of your hotel bedroom, but a 20/30 per cent surcharge will then be added.

CONSERVATION

The rapid growth of tourism in this part of the world has had serious repercussions on the environment. All those beach bungalows, traditional-style wooden guest houses, and wood/bamboo rafts for river-rafting have led to a serious depletion of the forests. The severe flooding of southern Thailand in late 1988 forced this country to become environmentally aware – the widespread deforestation of the higher land of the north meant that there was nothing to stop the rains flooding down into the lowland south. Trees retain 70 per cent of the water that falls on them, and they gradually release this over period of months into the land. With all the logging that has been going on (over half of Indonesia's 120 million hectares of tropical forest is now producing logs for industrial purposes), the treeline over much of South-East Asia has simply disappeared. The Thais and the Javanese are now rapidly replanting trees, but as yet the Malaysians have not.

Meanwhile, the rain forests of Sumatra are fast disappearing. Following the recent drop in oil prices, the government has decided to raise more cash crops (palm oil, rubber, cocoa) by clearing vast expanses of rain forest and turning them into big plantations. This wholesale destruction of forested areas (the levelled trees are just left to rot; they are not even towed away for timber) has threatened the wildlife of the area, particularly large animals like elephants who rely on the forest for survival. There are not that many elephants in Sumatra to begin with, only four or five thousand. As a tourist travelling through these areas, you can do your bit for conservation by refusing to endorse products which further endanger the wildlife. *Don't* buy stuffed turtles or turtle-shells (or eat turtle *satay* and turtle soup) in Bali or Yogya, and *don't* order crocodile or elephant curry (or buy crocodile, snake or elephant shoes/handbags) in Thailand. Many of these products are banned for export anyway, as you will find if you check with your embassy. Finally, *don't* tread on live coral when snorkelling – it kills it.

WILDLIFE

There is much wildlife (spiders, snakes, scorpions, cockroaches and mosquitoes) knocking around basic bamboo huts on islands such as Koh Phangan and Koh Samui. They are particularly fond of damp bathrooms. Mosquitoes are fairly low-profile in Malaysia and Thailand. They are worse in Indonesia, but in general they are not a big problem, mainly because most hotels have good netting on windows, mosquito coils, sprays for rooms and mosquito nets. If you are in a high-risk area (e.g. Koh Samet) keep your door shut, especially after dark and in the early morning. If there are any such vampires in your room, try leaving the door open with the light off and leave the room yourself. Javanese mosquitoes are particularly cunning. They don't just hide under toilet seats. They lurk under the rim!

Snakes are not much in evidence. Apart from obvious spots like Penang's Snake Farm (full of pit vipers, which do not bite and are draped over visitors) and the odd one or two in Taman Negara or on trek in northern Thailand, you will be lucky to see one. Spiders tend to hang out in cheap bungalows with leaky bamboo roofs. I only came across large spiders in Koh Samui and Pai (Thailand), Baloran Game Park (Java) and Kota Bahru (Malaysia). The tarantula I found under a telephone receiver in Bangkok was something else!

Wherever you stay, gekko lizards are a common sight – over your window, climbing round your room, hanging around by the lights, etc. They are harmless enough, and they eat mosquitoes! Cockroaches are found in all but the best hotels. If you are on a low budget, and want to avoid them, ask for a room without a bathroom. Jellyfish rash is common when swimming off places like Hua Hin, Kuantan and (if you are brave enough to swim here) west-coast Malaysia. If stung, apply an anti-histamine cream like Anthisan.

Leeches, which you will come across in rainy areas like the Cameron Highlands, bring out the worst passions in people. Leeches have amazing heat-detection senses. They sit on the edge of a damp path, waiting for a warm leg to come along. If it is your leg that they find, you can just flick them off. Funnily enough, travellers are far more horrified by leeches (which just draw a bit of blood and leave no infection) than they are by something really dangerous like mosquitoes which carry malaria, phalaria, dengue fever, etc. – all potential killers.

Note: if you don't like crawlies, your only guarantee of a good night's sleep is a mosquito net. I never travel without one!

Thailand

Thailand has something for everyone, which is just as well since everyone wants to go there. It is a rare combination of beautiful beaches, magical islands, tropical jungles, mountain valleys, ancient ruins and bargain shopping. It is also the only country in South-East Asia which has never been colonised, which probably explains the wealth of indigenous culture and the extraordinary friendliness of the people. The 'Land of Smiles' is famous for its warmth, generosity and hospitality to foreigners. Everybody gives you a smile and a cheery 'sawadee!', no matter how busy they are.

This is a Buddhist country and the religion is very much alive. Even in the modern, cosmopolitan capital of Bangkok, saffron-robed monks still walk the pavements at dawn collecting alms. Blessed with a rich art and culture and a wealth of sights to see, Thailand is one of the safest and most pleasant countries in the world to travel around. Nearly everybody speaks English and even those who do not (mainly persistent students) are eager to learn!

THE LAND

Thailand, the fabled land of Siam, takes up a large part of the Indo-China peninsula. About the size of France, it occupies an area of about 518,000 sq km and is bordered by Burma on the west, Kampuchea on the east, Laos on the north and Malaysia on the south. There are four distinct geographic regions: the mountains of the north, the vast plateau of the north east, the long, narrow isthmus of the south and the flat, damp central plains, ideal for rice-growing.

The Thai economy is still based on rice, tin and rubber (the main three exports) although tourism has recently become the top foreign earner. Sex and sin are still very saleable 'commodities' – over 70 per cent of the three million or so tourists who visit the country each year are single men! One of the dichotomies of the Thai brand of Buddhism is that it condones (or fails to acknowledge) the existence in Bangkok of one million prostitutes. All roads in Thailand lead to the modern metropolis of Bangkok, next to which the second city, Chiang Mai, is practically a village. Most of the land outside the capital is countryside and some 80 per cent of the population are still agrarian.

Thailand offers a lot more than shopping in Bangkok, trekking in Chiang Mai and beachcombing in Koh Samui. These three centres are all that most people allow time for, but there are some excellent alternatives for the adventurous traveller, like the Buddhist ruins of Sukhothai, the beach resorts of Koh Samet and Hua Hin, the offshore islands of Krabi, or the beautiful countryside (and river-rafting) around Kanchanaburi. Make time for at least a couple of these less tourist-visited attractions before pushing on to Malaysia. Do not be in too much of a hurry to cover Thailand. Of all the countries in South-East Asia, this is the one with the most to offer!

CLIMATE

The climate of Thailand is tropical but there are three seasons: hot and humid from March to June, hot and rainy from July to October and cool from November to February. The 'cool' season is only called cool because it is less hot and humid at night. Temperatures range from 61-95°F (16-35°C) in Bangkok and from 68-82°F (20-28°C) in Chiang Mai.

HISTORY

Often referred to as 'Muang Thai' or Land of the Free, Thailand has fought off successive waves of invaders to keep its unique culture, customs and traditions intact. Until quite recently, it was generally thought that the Thai people originated some 4,500 years ago in Mongolia. A constant series of migrations took them to southern China, where they founded the Nan Chao kingdom and then further south into the Asian peninsula. This theory was upturned during the 1960s, however, when a string of prehistoric sites was discovered – at Kanchanaburi, Mae Hong Son and Ban Chiang, which suggests that Thailand was probably the home of the world's oldest Bronze Age civilisation, dating back over 5,000 years.

In the twelfth century, some Thais (known then as 'Syams' or dark people) made a living as mercenaries in the armies of the Khmer, a powerful empire which had driven westward into Thailand from present-day Kampuchea. In 1238 Thai princes seized the Khmer-ruled town of Sukhothai, which became the first Siamese capital. Not long after, other Thai kingdoms began to appear, first under King Mengrai in Chiang Rai in north Thailand, then under the Prince of Utong in Ayutthaya, 64 km up the Chao Phya river from modern Bangkok. Founded in 1350, Ayutthaya quickly replaced Sukhothai as the capital of Siam and it enjoyed two centuries of unsurpassed power before being totally destroyed by the Burmese in 1767. The Siamese, under General Taksin, quickly re-

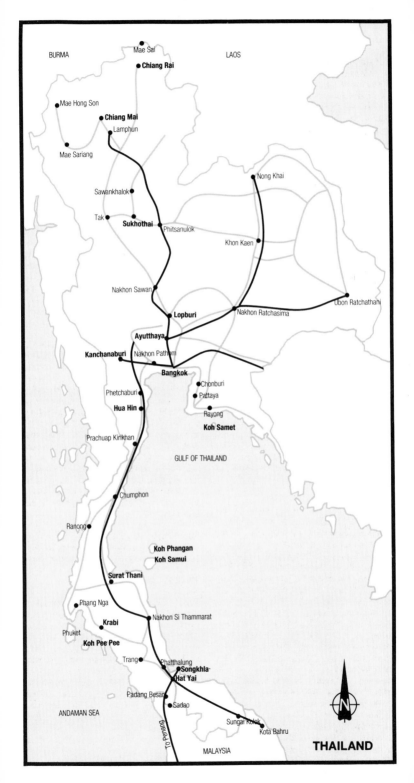

grouped and ousted the Burmese, but Ayutthaya was never again occupied.

A new capital was founded at Thonburi, which in 1782 moved across the river to its present site of Bangkok. Taksin was executed (after going mad) and General Chakri became Rama I, the first king of the continuing Chakri dynasty. In the nineteenth century, while the rest of South-East Asia fell under colonial rule, Siam managed to retain its independence. A clever series of trade treaties between Rama III (of 'The King and I' fame) and Britain, France and the United States, saw to that. On 24 June 1932, a peaceful coup transformed the country from an absolute into a constitutional monarchy and in 1939 Siam was renamed Thailand.

After the Second World War, political power passed to a series of dictatorial military premiers. Only in 1973, following a student revolt, was there a brief interlude of democracy. The military seized the reins again in 1976 and since then, under the progressive Prime Minister Prem Tinsulanonda, Thailand has returned to some sort of stability. Not that it has ever been particularly unstable, however. As far as the Thais are concerned, it matters little who governs the country, just so long as the king is safe on the throne. The stability of the crown as a counter-balance to each new politicial coup has meant that nothing much changes from one government to the next, since each new government since 1932 has sought the king's approval. The present ruler, King Bhumibol (Rama IX), may be only a constitutional monarch but he remains the spiritual and temporal head of the nation, the lynchpin of Thai unity.

PEOPLE AND RELIGION

The other national rallying point is Theravada Buddhism, which is the professed religion of over 90 per cent of all Thais. There is a small minority of Muslims in the south and a few Christians to the north, but all over the country Buddhist monks can be seen at dawn collecting their first meal of the day. Every Thai male spends at least a few months in a monastery, preparing himself for adulthood and every Thai family who gives food to a monk (or helps a foreign tourist across the road) is acquiring merit for their next life. The politeness, modesty and friendliness of the Thai people stem directly from their belief in Buddhism, which extends its influence to every aspect of daily life.

The people of Thailand, of whom there are approximately 60 million, are a mixture of several different racial and ethnic groups – mainly Thai, Chinese, Mon, Khmer, Lao, Malay, Indian and Persian. Small, dark-haired and fine-boned, they are generally considered (especially the women) the most attractive people in South-East Asia. This has as much to do with their temperament as with their physical attributes. The Thais are the nicest, smiliest people around and they are great fun to be with. Be warned, however, those smiles can sometimes conceal a sudden, unpredictable temper!

A basic etiquette should be observed to avoid giving offence in Thai society. Insulting the royal family, for example, doesn't go down at all well. Neither does climbing sacred monuments for photos, displaying physical affection in public places, or going skinny-dipping on beaches. Touching anyone *older* than you on the head is a big 'don't', as is pointing your feet at people or at images of Buddha. In Thailand, the head is the most sacred part of the body (since it houses the spirit) and the feet the most defiled (since they are in direct contact with the earth). Smart dress is essential when entering Thai houses, Buddhist temples or Islamic mosques, and do not forget to remove your shoes!

VISAS

No visa is required for a stay of up to 15 days, but this cannot be extended once in the country, nor can the 30-day transit visa which costs £5. If you are going to spend any time in the country, it is worth paying out for a 60-day tourist visa (£8) which can be extended, at minimal cost and with little fuss, at immigration offices in Hat Yai, Chiang Mai and Bangkok. In the UK, visas are issued by the Thai embassy (tel: 01-589 2857) at 30 Queensgate, London SW7, open 9.30 a.m. to 12.30 p.m., weekdays. For convenience, if you book your flight with Trailfinders, their visa service can obtain a visa for you. The charge for this service is an additional £11.50.

Note: Bangkok is a good place for getting visas for other countries, notably Burma, India, China, Nepal and Bangladesh.

DOMESTIC TRANSPORT

Air

Thai Airways fly to all major centres in Thailand and fares are very cheap. A few popular routes, like Bangkok-Chiang Mai (1275B) and Bangkok-Hat Yai (1760B), are discounted by 20 per cent if you take the night flight. To Malaysia, there are regular flights from Bangkok/ Hat Yai to Penang/Kuala Lumpur. In Bangkok, Thai Airways have a head office at 6 Larn Luang Rd (tel: 2800090) and a desk at Don Muang airport (tel: 5238271).

Rail

There are four rail lines, running north, north-east, east and south. Timetables/

reservations are available from Bangkok's Hualamphong station (tel: 2233790), which is open for bookings from 8.30 a.m. to 6 p.m. weekdays, until 12 noon at weekends. Popular trains, like the Bangkok-Butterworth International Express and the Bangkok-Chiang Mai Express, should be booked well in advance. In addition to regular passenger fares, there are surcharges of 20B for rapid trains and 30B for express trains. Berth charges on express trains are 170 to 200B second class, or 250 to 350B first class.

Trains are quick and comfortable and they usually run on time. They are particularly recommended for long-distance travel. Overnight trains serve meals and drinks and they make several stops where you can pick up fruit, snacks and magazines. Use express trains wherever possible; they reach their destinations far quicker than rapid trains (which are not rapid at all) or slow ordinary trains.

Note: Don Muang Airport is on the north-south rail link between Bangkok and Chiang Mai. If you are at the end of your journey and do not wish to go back into the capital, make your last ports of call Chiang Mai, Sukhothai and Ayutthaya, in that order. The airport is only 40 minutes down the line from Ayutthaya.

Road

Public state-run buses travel throughout the country, but though cheap, they are uncomfortable and subject to accidents. Private 'tour' buses run between major tourist centres like Bangkok, Hua Hin, Koh Samet, Koh Samui, Chiang Mai, Hat Yai and even Butterworth in Malaysia. They cost a bit more, but provide comforts like pillows, blankets, meals, videos and sometimes reclining seats. In general, I would recommend public buses for short trips of four hours or less and private buses (if available) for longer hauls. All-night buses are prone to theft. Don't travel alone on them, and if you must, do not go to sleep and do not accept (possibly drugged) food, drinks or sweets from strangers. Any refreshments you need, you can get without moving from your seat. A cheerful procession of youths will board your bus at every stop it makes (there will be several) selling fizzy drinks, barbecued chicken on sticks, vegetarian snacks, diced pineapples, cigarettes and chewing gum. Like the Indonesians, the Thais like to spend long, boring bus journeys either eating, drinking or smoking.

Notes: most overland travellers cross into Malaysia from Hat Yai, either by shared taxi to Penang (west coast), or by bus/train to Sungai Kolok for Kota Bahru (east coast).

LOCAL TRANSPORT

Taxis and motorised *tuk tuks* (noisy three-wheelers known locally as *samlors*) are found in Bangkok and several regional centres. There are also small pickup trucks called *songthaews*, with two rows of seats and a more or less fixed route. *Songthaews* have a standard charge (usually 4/5B), but taxi and *tuk-tuk* fares should always be negotiated before setting off. Taxis have meters (but rarely use them) and because they are air-conditioned they ask around 10/15B more than *tuk-tuks*. If you are not sure of the correct fare, ask a local person. Local buses operate in many larger cities like Bangkok or Chiang Mai. They are cheap but slow, and because their destinations are posted in Thai, you will need a good town map to work them out. Also cheap and slow are the bicycle *samlors* (cycle rickshaws) found in all of the smaller towns of Thailand. Hired cars are available in Bangkok and Chiang Mai and you can rent bicycles, motorcycles and jeeps in centres like Koh Samui, Krabi, Hua Hin and Kanchanaburi. An international driving licence is required to drive any vehicle in Thailand.

SHOPPING

Thailand provides one of the big shopping trips of the east, with a multitude of quality products at bargain prices. Good buys include teakwood carvings, bronze-ware, silver jewellery, ceramics, niello-ware, silk and gems. Bangkok has a superlative choice of handicraft outlets: try Silom Rd for silk and gemstones, Sukhumvit Rd for leatherware and River City, next to the Royal Orchid, for rarer, older antiques, woodcarvings, bronze and silverware. Chiang Mai is famous for its hilltribe handicrafts, especially hand-woven costumes in richly embroidered and colourful cottons. Elsewhere, shop for blue sapphires (from the local mines) at Kanchanaburi, beautiful cotton fabrics at Hua Hin and Koh Yaw (near Song-khla) and cheap hi-fi equipment (mostly smuggled in from Singapore) at Hat Yai. Fashion clothes, copied designer goods and pirated music cassettes are best bought in Bangkok where quality is guaranteed. Wherever you shop, bargaining is expected. The Thais love to bargain. As soon as you have given them a good battle, they will give you a sensible price! You will soon learn to enjoy this feature of Thai shopping.

ENTERTAINMENT

Few Thai attractions pull in more tourists than the music and dance of old Siam. Of the five main forms of classical dance drama which thrive today (all of them influenced by India and Sri Lanka) the *khon chak* is performed the most often and is most effectively produced by the College of Dramatic Art in Bangkok, where most students learn their trade. At hotels like the Indra Regent, you can see a truncated version of the original dance drama which lasts anything from 45 minutes to two hours – a far cry from past days, when it used to go on all night. Instant culture shows like this are pretty touristy, but the costumes are superb, the dancers beautiful and the music (played on gongs, xylophones and flutes) is the genuine article. Up in Chiang Mai, you can see a whole procession of northern hilltribe dances included in the cost of a traditional *khantoke* dinner.

ACCOMMODATION

Thailand is quickly pricing itself out of the backpacker market. In the short space of 18 months, from late 1987 to early 1989, several Bangkok hotels, particularly in the mid-range, doubled their prices. This means a (very) short stay in the capital for many shoestringers – a couple of nights in a noisy, airless cell in Banglampoo and they are off to Chiang Mai or Koh Samui, where living is cheap.

Bangkok has the full range of accommodation, from £40 a night luxury hotels (with pools, bars, restaurants and air-conditioning) to £20 second class hotels (fewer facilities, often no pool) down to £1/2 guest houses, with little more than a bed, a chair or two, a ceiling fan and a common shower/toilet.

Out of Bangkok, prices slip around 20 per cent, but so do standards, at least at the top end of the market. Chiang Mai probably gives the best all-round value for money. It has clean, comfortable hotels and guest houses at sensible prices and generous low-season discounts. Anywhere else, you can expect to pay as much as £25 a couple for an old-colonial hotel in Hua Hin, or as little as £2 for two in a simple beach bungalow on a remote island like Koh Phangan. It is generally a good idea to travel with a friend as most places charge more or less the same for a single room (with a big double bed) as for a double. Between May and September (low season) many high-class and mid-bracket hotels offer discounts of between 20 and 40 per cent, sometimes more, if you book through a hotel travel agency. From November to February (high season) you will be lucky to get a room at all, let alone a reduced tariff, so book well ahead!

FOOD

The Thais love their food, but they very rarely sit down to a full set meal. They prefer to pick at things – a bit of this, a bowl of that – all day long. There is no shortage of food in Thailand, it is on offer right round the clock. The only problem is the chillies, which are exceedingly hot! If you do not like your food fiery, ask for something *mae pet* (not hot) or order less spicy Chinese food instead. If you stay at Western-style hotels at resorts, the Thai dishes are invariably bland and tasteless. 'We chose half-board at an otherwise good hotel in Samui,' reported one couple, 'and even our specific complaint to the cook that the hot and sour soup [*tom yam*] was neither, produced no remedy, only an apology. It was only when we later had a little chat with him and asked for "proper", not "Europeanised" Thai food that we got superb results, as good as the Rim Naam Terrace restaurant at Bangkok's Oriental Hotel, our benchmark so far.'

Real *tom yam* is found on the street, along with a galaxy of other 10B dishes like *kai yang* (spicy barbecued chicken), *hor mok* (fish in a chilli, onion and garlic sauce), *kang kiew wan kai/nua* (chicken/beef curry), *pat thai* (fried noodles with onions, peanuts, vegetables and egg) and *tom yam kung* (the standard Thai soup, with shrimp, lemon grass and mushrooms). The backpackers' staple diet is *kao pat* (fried rice with onions, vegetables and sometimes an egg) or *kao pat kai/muu/kung* (chicken/pork/shrimp fried rice). Don't be afraid to experiment – Thailand has some of the best street food in the world. As long as it has been freshly cooked, it is perfectly safe.

Western cuisine is widely available if you want it. All the major beach resorts and tourist centres now cater for foreign appetites, which means you can get pizzas, steaks and banana pancakes all the way down from Chiang Mai to Hat Yai! Most of the high-class restaurants are in Bangkok, where you can choose from around a dozen international cuisines.

MONEY

The currency of Thailand is the *baht* (B), which is divided into 100 *satang*. There are notes of 10, 20, 50, 100 and 500 *baht*, and coins of 1, 2 and 5 *baht*; 25 and 50 *satang*. No more than 2,000 *baht* per person may be brought into Thailand and only 500 *baht* per person may be taken out without special permission. At the time of writing, there are approximately 40 *baht* to the £ and 25 *baht* to the US$.

TIME

Thai time is seven hours ahead of GMT. Thus, when it is 12 noon in Bangkok, it will be 5 a.m. in London, 1 a.m. in New York and 3 p.m. in Sydney.

ELECTRICITY

Electrical current in Thailand is 220 volts and 50 cycles, but most hotels have

110-volt outlets for shavers and similar electrical appliances.

LANGUAGE

Even in Bangkok and the other major tourist centres, where English is generally understood, it makes sense to learn a few Thai words – shopping, bargaining and getting around town suddenly becomes much easier! Despite the complexities of the Thai language, acquiring a basic vocabulary is child's play. Verbs have no tenses and there are a lot of useful one-syllable words which can be strung together to form simple sentences. Saying everything in a neutral monotone is best. This avoids the potential minefield of tonal variations, whereby every word, depending on how it is pronounced, can have up to five different meanings! Polite speech requires the addition of *kup* (for men) and *ka* (for women) to the end of each sentence. This shows respect for the listener and denotes agreement or understanding. The all-purpose word for 'you' is *khun*, while 'I/me' is *pom* for men and *dee-chan* for women. Because the Thais have difficulty pronouncing the letter 'r' (which often becomes 'l') you'll often be better understood if you say you come from 'Anglit' rather than from 'Angrit'. The following vocabulary should suffice for most occasions, but if you need a proper phrasebook the one published by Lonely Planet (Joe Cummings, 1984) makes a useful travelling companion.

Civilities

hello/goodbye	*sawadee-kup (ka)*
how are you?	*sabai-dee-kup? (ka)*
I am fine/happy	*sabai-sabai!*
thank you	*khop-khun-kup (ka)*
you are welcome/ no problem	*mai pen rai*
excuse me/sorry	*kaw-thot*
pleased to meet you	*yindee tee-ruja khun*
what is your name?	*khun cheu arai?*
my name is Frank	*pom cheu Frank*
my name is Mary	*dee-chan cheu Mary*
how old are you?	*khun ayuu tao rai?*
I am 20 years old	*pom (dee-chan) ayuu yee-sip pi*
I'm from England/ USA	*pom (dee-chan) khon Angrit/ Saharat Amerikaa*
do you speak English?	*put Angrit?'*
I don't understand	*chan mai kao chai*

Simple Words

yes (statement)	*chai*
yes (agreement)	*kup (ka)*
good	*dee*
very good	*dee maak*
no good (bad)	*mai dee*
big	*yai*
small	*lek*
hot (temp)	*rawn*
hot (food)	*pet*
cold	*yen*
beautiful	*soWAY* (*say the 'way' with a rising tone emphasis, or you could be wishing someone bad luck!)

Money

how much?	*tao rai?*
how many *baht*?	*ki baht?*
too much	*phaeng bai*
no way, forget it	*ma dai!*
please discount	*lot noi*
I do not want it	*may ao kup (ka)*
I do not have it (e.g. enough money)	*mai mee kup (ka)*

Food

rice	*kao*
fried rice with ...	*kao-pat ...*
chicken/pork/crab/ shrimp	*kai/muu/puu/ kung*
noodles	*kuaytiaw*
barbecued chicken	*kai yang*
spicy papaya salad	*som-tam*
curry	*kaeng*
fish	*pla*
eggs	*khai*
fruit	*phon-la-mai*
water	*nam*
ice	*nam-khaeng*
coffee, without sugar	*kaafay, mai sai nam-taan*
tea, with milk	*nam-cha, sai nom*
delicious	*aroi*
enough	*por lao*
what's your special dish?	*mee arai phe-set?*
I'm vegetarian	*pom (dee-chan) kin jeh*

Numbers

0	*soon*
1	*nung*
2	*song*
3	*saam*
4	*see*
5	*ha*
6	*hok*
7	*jet*
8	*paet*
9	*kao*
10	*sip*
11	*sip-et*
12	*sip-song*
13	*sip-saam*

Vegetable market

20	*yee-sip*
21	*yee-sip-et*
30	*saam-sip*
42	*see-sip-song*
100	*roi*
1000	*nung pan*
10,000	*nung muen*
1 million	*laan*

Time

minute	*na-thee*
hour	*chua-mohng*
year	*pee*
today	*wan-nee*
tommorrow	*pung-nee*
yesterday	*meau wan-nee*
how many hours?	*kee chua-mohng?*

Travel

where is the ...	*yuu thee nai...*
bus station	*sathanee rot meh*
railway station	*sathanee rot fai*
police station	*sathanee tam-ruat*
boat	*reua*
bank	*thanaakhaan*
where are you going?	*bai nai?*
I'm going to Bangkok	*cha bai Bangkok*
do you have a room ...	*mee hong mai ...*
for two people	*song khun?*
do you have a toilet?	*mee hong-nam mai?*

BANGKOK

Thailand's capital is one of the great cities of Asia, with a population approaching six million. Set on a broad plain formed by the meandering Chao Phya River, Bangkok, like most Asian cities, combines the old and the new, the tranquil and the chaotic, the exotic and the mundane. Despite the traffic congestion and the modern façades of hundreds of new Western buildings, numerous sections of Bangkok retain the charm of the past and provide visitors with fascinating insights into the traditional life of Thailand. A city of palaces and temples as well as markets and shops, Bangkok is the seat of government, the commercial and business centre, the country's leading port and a crossroads for travel and communication in South-East Asia.

When Rama I moved his capital here from Thonburi in 1782, he was looking to recreate, as closely as possible, the old capital of Ayutthaya destroyed by the Burmese in 1767. By the late nineteenth century, his dream had come to fruition, Bangkok was no longer a tiny mosquito-infested fishing village but a vital, bustling international port, complete with numerous *klongs* (canals) and hundreds of glittering, eye-catching temples. In the mid-1960s, the city gained a new lease of life when it was selected as an R&R base for American troops from Vietnam. There followed a boom in hotels, cine-

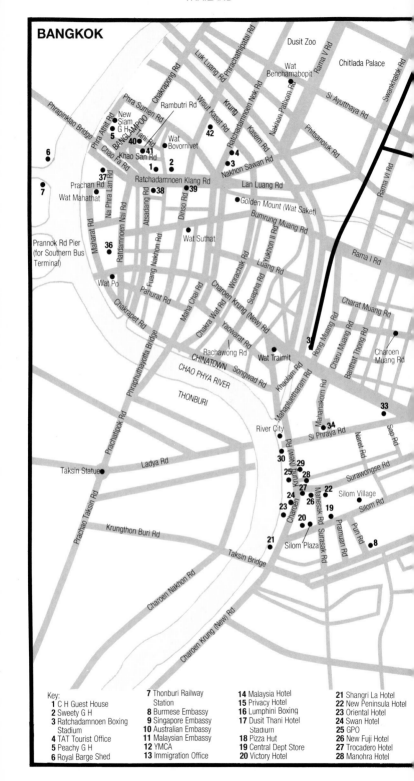

BANGKOK

Dusit Zoo

Chitlada Palace

Wat Benchamabopit

Phrapinklao Bridge

Phra Sumen Rd

Rambutri Rd

New Siam G H

BANGLAMPOO

Thani Rd

Phra Athit Rd

Chao Fa Rd

Khao San Rd

Wat Bovornivet

Luk Luang Rd

Phrachathipatai Rd

Wisut Kasat Rd

Krung

Ratchadamnoen Nok Rd

Kasem Rd

Nakhon Sawan Rd

Lan Luang Rd

Golden Mount (Wat Saket)

Bumrung Muang Rd

Ratchadamnoen Klang Rd

Prachan Rd

Wat Mahathat

Na Phra Lan Rd

Maharat Rd

Ratdamnoen Nai Rd

Atsadang Rd

Dinso Rd

Fuang Nakhon Rd

Wat Suthat

Prannok Rd Pier (for Southern Bus Terminal)

Wat Po

Pahurat Rd

Maha Chai Rd

Chakrapet Rd

Chakra Wat Rd

Charoen Krung (New) Rd

Worachak Rd

Luang Rd

Supha Rd

Nukhon II Rd

Rama I Rd

Rama IV Rd

Charat Muang Rd

Phrapinklao Bridge

Phrapinklao Bridge

Prachatipok Rd

Phraphutthayotfa Bridge

Rachawong Rd

CHINATOWN

Yaowarat Rd

Wat Traimit

Songwad Rd

CHAO PHYA RIVER

THONBURI

River City

Khaolam Rd

Mahapruetharam Rd

Mahanakhon Rd

Charoen Muang Rd

Banthat Thong Rd

Rong Muang Rd

Charu Muang Rd

Si Phraya Rd

Narat Rd

Sap Rd

Surawongse Rd

Silom Village

Silom Rd

Pramuan Rd

Pun Rd

Taksin Statue

Ladya Rd

Prachao Taksin Rd

Krungthon Buri Rd

Silom Plaza

Taksin Bridge

Charoen Naknon Rd

Charoen Krung (New) Rd

Si Ayutthaya Rd

Swankhalok Rd

Rama V Rd

Phitsanuloke Rd

Nakhon Pathom Rd

Rama VI Rd

Maneak Rd

Surasak Rd

Key:

1 C H Guest House
2 Sweety G H
3 Ratchadamnoen Boxing Stadium
4 TAT Tourist Office
5 Peachy G H
6 Royal Barge Shed

7 Thonburi Railway Station
8 Burmese Embassy
9 Singapore Embassy
10 Australian Embassy
11 Malaysian Embassy
12 YMCA
13 Immigration Office

14 Malaysia Hotel
15 Privacy Hotel
16 Lumphini Boxing
17 Dusit Thani Hotel Stadium
18 Pizza Hut
19 Central Dept Store
20 Victory Hotel

21 Shangri La Hotel
22 New Peninsula Hotel
23 Oriental Hotel
24 Swan Hotel
25 GPO
26 New Fuji Hotel
27 Trocadero Hotel
28 Manohra Hotel

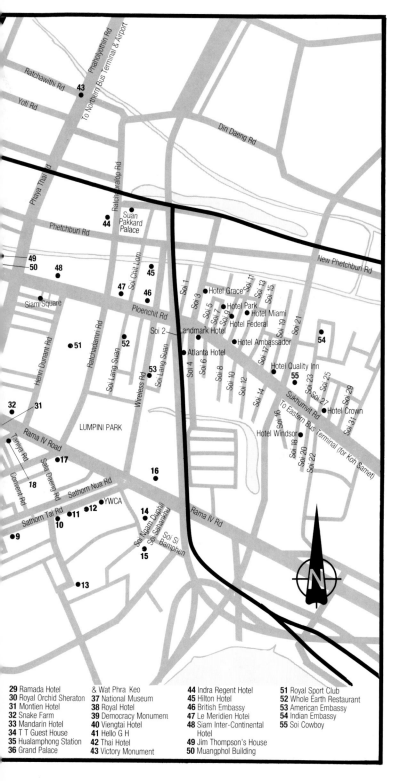

29 Ramada Hotel
30 Royal Orchid Sheraton
31 Montien Hotel
32 Snake Farm
33 Mandarin Hotel
34 T T Guest House
35 Hualamphong Station
36 Grand Palace

& Wat Phra Keo
37 National Museum
38 Royal Hotel
39 Democracy Monument
40 Viengtai Hotel
41 Hello G H
42 Thai Hotel
43 Victory Monument

44 Indra Regent Hotel
45 Hilton Hotel
46 British Embassy
47 Le Meridien Hotel
48 Siam Inter-Continental Hotel
49 Jim Thompson's House
50 Muangphol Building

51 Royal Sport Club
52 Whole Earth Restaurant
53 American Embassy
54 Indian Embassy
55 Soi Cowboy

mas, bars, restaurants and massage parlours, and Bangkok's reputation as the leisure (and sex) capital of the world was born. Nowadays, while many people certainly do come for the entertainments and the shopping, it is the sheer variety of Bangkok that attracts and which brings visitors back again and again. This is not one city, but many, a jigsaw of self-contained villages loosely strung together to form a metropolis of innumerable facets with no nucleus. Chinatown, Silom, Sukhumvit, Siam Square, Banglampoo – each of these areas can claim to be Bangkok's 'centre', but the truth is that the city has no centre at all. The heart of Bangkok is where you are at any moment – sipping a cocktail at the Oriental Hotel, crossing the road with a chatty saffron-robed monk, watching a 'sexotic' show in steamy Patpong, gazing awestruck at the glittering spires of the Grand Palace, or simply watching a video in a Ko Sahn Rd bar. Beyond the initial impressions of noise, pollution and traffic, Bangkok has a charm and charisma all of its own – a few days here and you'll be hooked!

Bangkok is one of the safest cities in the East, but you should still take sensible precautions. Beware of pickpockets (especially on buses and in crowds), check surplus cash into a hotel safe-deposit (never carry lots of money or valuables on the street), and avoid so-called 'English students' offering trips to expensive restaurants, shops or nightclubs. Don't lose your smile, but temper friendliness with caution!

ARRIVAL/DEPARTURE

Bangkok's Don Muang International Airport, 25 km north of the city, is served by some 30 international airlines and is a major stopover for around-the-world flights between East Asia, the Near and Middle East and Europe. The international terminal has desks for tourist information, hotel-booking and money-exchange. There is also a cheap baggage deposit (20B per piece per day) and a good restaurant up on the observation floor. If you need somewhere to stay while waiting for a flight, the luxury Airport Hotel (tel: 5661020) is attached to the airport, with rooms from 1900B. Or try the Bamboo Guest House, right across from the terminal, opposite Don Muang Police Station, with air-conditioned rooms at US$15/20 and dormitory beds at US$5. If you give them a ring from the airport (tel: 5313506), they will pick you up.

You can go from airport to city by 250B air-conditioned limousine, 121B Ambassador car, or 50B coach, all bookable from the Thai Limousine counter in the international lounge. Taxis can be hired at the airport exit – only 150B per

load if you bargain hard. From the main road outside the terminal, air-conditioned buses 4 and 29 go to Silom/Hualamphong, via Rama I and Rama IV roads, for 15B; or take ordinary bus 59 to Banglampoo/Khao San Rd for just 3B. Don Muang rail station, a short walk from the terminal (via the Airport Hotel pedestrian bridge) has regular trains into Hualamphong station for only 5B.

When leaving Bangkok, allow good time (one and a half hours) for the return journey to the airport. Also have your airport tax handy: 200B for international flights, 20B for domestic flights.

Rail

Most destinations out of Bangkok are served by Hualamphong railway station on Rama IV Rd. Trains to Kanchana-buri, however, leave from Bangkok Noi station, across the river in Thonburi. Hualamphong station has an advance-booking desk (open 8.30 a.m. to 6 p.m. weekdays, and until 12 noon weekends) and a tourist information counter. Book well ahead for the daily express trains to Chiang Mai (dep. 7.40 p.m., 12 hours) and to Penang (dep. 3.15 p.m., 21 hours). The Butterworth train is only 618B (US$25) for a second-class lower berth sleeper and the 100B extra for air-conditioning is worth it. From Bangkok to Singapore is a tiring 40-hour journey, but you can sleep most of the way in a comfortable US$50 berth.

Road

Travel agents in Ko-Sahn Rd, Soi Si Bamphen and Silom (TT Guest House) sell tickets for quick, super-comfy VIP buses to Chiang Mai (350B), Koh Samui (400B) and Hat Yai/Krabi (450B); there are also ordinary air-conditioned buses to Chiang Mai (200-220B), Samui (250B), Hat Yai (350B), Krabi (330B), Hua Hin (150B), Koh Samet (140B), Penang (550B), Kuala Lumpur (570B) and Singapore (650B).

If you want to arrange things yourself, there are regular buses daily to Chiang Mai, Chiang Rai, Ayutthaya and Sukhothai from the Northern Terminal on Phaholyothin Rd (tel: 2794484), buses to Kanchanaburi, Hua Hin, Samui and Hat Yai from the Southern Terminal (tel: 4114978) across the river in Thonburi and buses to Ancient City and Koh Samet from the Ekamai bus station (tel: 3913301) beyond Sukhumvit Soi 40. All three terminals have left-luggage facilities.

TOURIST SERVICES

The main TAT (Tourism Authority of Thailand) office at 4 Ratchadamnoen Rd (tel: 2821143) is open 8.30 a.m. to 4.30 p.m. daily. A visit here, to plan your tour of the country, will save you a lot of

View over the Royal Palace at Wat Arun

questions later. Pick up an armload of free printed information, a free copy of *Bangkok This Week* (full of up-to-date information) and a 40B *Nancy Chandler's Map of Bangkok*. A 35B bus-map of the city (sold at TAT, bookshops and stationers) is also a good investment; ask for the one by K. S. Thaveepholcharoean. Malaysia TDC office (handy if you are heading that way) is right opposite McDonald's in Patpong (Silom Rd).

The central GPO on New Rd (Charoen Krung) has a very efficient poste restante counter and is open 8 a.m. to 8 p.m. weekdays, 8 a.m. to 1 p.m. weekends and holidays. It also has a cheap parcel-packing service – open 8 a.m. to 4.30 p.m. weekends, 8 a.m. to 12 noon Saturdays, which is ideal for sending excess clothing and gifts home or onwards. Overseas calls at the telephone office behind the GPO (down a side alley, open 24 hours) are 240B for the first three minutes and 60B per minute thereafter. Connections are normally quick and good.

Banks are open 8.30 a.m. to 3.30 p.m. weekdays, but closed at weekends and on public holidays. Money changing is possible throughout the day, however, as most banks have kiosks which open early and close late. Recommended bookshops include Asia Books at 221 Sukhumvit Rd, Bookseller at 81 Patpong Rd, Silom, Bangkok Books at Siam Square, Soi 4 and Chalermnit at 2 Erawan Arcade, Erawan Hotel, Ploenchit Rd.

Travel agents in the Banglampoo and Soi Ngam Duphli areas offer a wide range of services: sightseeing tours, hotel reservations, bus/car hire, visas for Burma, Nepal, India and China, travel insurance, student cards and cheap round-the-world flights. Some typical one-way air fares out of Bangkok include London (8800B), New York (15,000B), Bombay (5000B), Kathmandu (4500B), Singapore (2000B), Sydney (10,000B) and Bali (7700B). You may well buy cheaper flights by shopping around, but in the main it is best to stick to reliable, well-established agents like Thai Student Travel at Thai Hotel, 78 Prachatipatai Rd, Banglampoo (tel: 2815314-5) or Sunny's Tropical Tour (tel: 2868897) at 2-3 Soi Si Bamphen.

Bangkok embassies include Australia, 37 Sathorn Tai Rd (tel: 2873680), Burma, 132 Sathorn Nua Rd (tel: 2332237); France, 35 Custom House Lane, New Rd (tel: 2340950); India, 46 Soi Prasarnmitr, Sukhumvit Rd (tel: 2580300); Indonesia, 600-2 Petchburi Rd (tel: 2523135); Malaysia, 35 Sathorn Tai Rd (tel: 2861390); Nepal, 189 Soi Puengsuk, Sukhumvit 71 (tel: 3917240); Singapore, 129 Sathorn Tai Rd (tel: 28621ll); UK, 1031 Ploenchit Rd (tel: 2530191); USA,

95 Wireless Rd (tel: 2525040). Most embassies receive visa applications between 8 a.m. and 12 noon and require your passport overnight.

Major airlines with offices in Bangkok include Air France (tel: 2339477), British Airways (tel: 2368655), Cathay Pacific (tel: 2336105), JAT Yugoslav Airlines (tel: 2350500) and Qantas (tel: 2360102), all at Charn Issara Tower, 942/51 Rama IV Rd; Biman Bangladesh Airlines (tel: 2340300) and Philippine Airlines (tel: 2332350) at Chongkolnee Bldg, 56 Surawong Rd, Bangkok Airways at 144 Sukhumvit 46 (tel: 2534114), China Airlines at Peninsula Plaza, 153 Rajadamri Rd (tel: 2534438), Gulf Air at Panunee Bldg, Ploenchit Rd (tel: 2547931), KLM Royal Dutch Airlines at 2 Patpong Rd (tel: 2355155), Korean Air at 3rd floor, Dusit Thani Bldg, Silom Rd (tel: 2349283), LOT Polish Airlines at 12 Silom Rd (tel: 2352223), Pakistan International Airlines at 52 Surawongse Rd (tel: 2342961), Singapore Airlines at 12th floor, Silom Centre Bldg, Silom Rd (tel: 2360440) and Thai Airways at 89 Vibhavadi-Rangsit Rd (tel: 2800070 domestic, 2333810 international).

GETTING AROUND

Apart from a stroll to the local shops, few people tackle Bangkok on foot. It is a hot, humid and noisy city, not at all conducive to walking. Local transport is cheap and plentiful, but if you are new to Bangkok and have not appreciated the traffic yet, beware of the evening rush-hour period (4-7 p.m.) – severe congestion, with the occasional motionless waits of up to ten minutes at a time. Don't be caught out, especially if you have a plane or train to catch!

Taxis and *Samlor*

Taxis are the easiest way to get around the city, especially if you are short on time. No taxis use meters, so you must negotiate a fare *before* setting off. As a rough guide, they charge 30-40B for short hops and 50-80B for trips across town. Avoid the taxis hanging around outside hotels – they cater for rich tourists and charge accordingly. *Samlors*, the noisy three-wheelers known as '*tuk-tuks*', are a little cheaper than taxis but you still have to haggle over the fare in advance.

Buses

Travel by public bus (once you have worked out how to use the bus-map) is dirt cheap. For just 2B, you can go all the way on, say, bus No. 17 from Banglampoo in the north down to Silom in the south. By *tuk-tuk*, this long haul would cost you 60B minimum. Crossing Bangkok by bus can, however, be a very wearisome business – hot, slow and time-consuming. Air-conditioned buses (5B for the first 10 km) are more comfortable, less crowded and less frequented by pickpockets than standard buses. Route signs are in Thai only, so ask your hotel about route numbers and stops.

Boat

The Chao Phya Express – a long river-taxi with a red board and a man at the back urgently blowing a whistle – travels up and down the Chao Phya River all day, avoiding the traffic jams and making a number of very useful stops (Oriental Hotel, GPO, Grand Palace, National Museum, Banglampoo, etc.). One comes along every 20 minutes or so and fares range from 3B to 9B, depending on the distance travelled. Slower cross-river ferries operate from several jetties and just go back and forth across the river. Fast long-tail taxis zip to and from the Grand Palace and the Oriental pier. They cost 100B one-way and are best chartered by a group. Boats offering guided tours cost a little more and can be negotiated for at the Oriental Pier. Share-fare longtail boats leave every half-hour or so from Tha Tien pier (behind Wat Po) for the picturesque side-klong trip down Klong Mon (highly recommended).

SIGHTS

To see Bangkok's major attractions in three or four days (which is all most people allow) requires dedication. You need to be up early in the morning (to avoid the heat), you need to be smartly dressed for the temples (no sleeveless T-shirts or shorts) and you need a good city map. If you are particularly short on time, consider an organised tour from a hotel or guest house. Otherwise, try the following suggested itineraries:

Day One

If you are an early riser, start at the small **Flower Market** between the Oriental Hotel and the Shangri-La Hotel. This is very pretty, especially around dawn. From here, you can walk down to the Oriental Pier for an express boat to **Wat Arun**, located on the Thonburi side of the river. This impressive Temple of the Dawn is built primarily in the Cambodian style, though with strong Thai and Chinese features. The royal statue of King Taksin is here, in the sanctuary in front of the pagoda, along with artistic statues of demons and angels.

There are 99 stupas in the compound and four large *prangs* surround the central spire which soars to a height of 79 m. You can climb halfway up this high pagoda for excellent views of the river and the city. Each of the five major *prangs* has a stucco exterior studded with pieces of glazed Chinese pottery, some whole, some in fragments. Admission to Wat Arun is 5B and it is open 8.30 a.m. to 5.30 p.m. daily. If you want to avoid the crush of tourist boats, do not turn up between 10 a.m. and noon. If you are on a scheduled tour, you may not have much choice – but you can sometimes persuade your boatman to visit the Royal Barges first and to return to Wat Arun later on.

The **Royal Barges** are located up a small side-klong, just past Wat Arun. In former times, these richly decorated boats were used for royal and military ceremonies. Nowadays they stand idle in large air-hanger sheds where, because they are out of the sunlight, you cannot get the true colours. Occasionally, you may see them out on the river, practising for some important occasion and then they are truly spectacular, all gold and decoration glinting in the sun. The official King's Barge, *Sri Supannahong* is here, with a large bagged jewel hanging from its nose. It is around 44 m long, requires a crew of 61, and its figurehead represents Brahma's vehicle, the sacred swan. Several others of these teakwood barges have figureheads taken from the Hindu tradition – look out for Hanuman, the famous white ape of the Ramayana epic, the red *garuda* bird (vehicle for the Lord Vishnu) and the seven-headed *naga* or serpent. Admission to the barges is 10B and they are open to view from 8.30 a.m. to 4.30 p.m. daily unless they are being used at the time.

Wat Pho, the Temple of the Reclining Buddha, is a couple of riverboat stops back down the Chao Phya, on the Bangkok side. Built by Rama I nearly 200 years ago, this is one of the oldest and largest temples in the city. It has just been restored (at an estimated cost of £1 million) to all its former glory. The showpiece 46-m-long reclining Buddha looks brand new and is covered in shiny gold leaf from head to toe. The soles of its massive mother-of-pearl feet are inscribed with the 108 extraordinary signs by which the true Buddha is recognised. Wat Pho is open 8 a.m. to 5 p.m. daily, admission is 10B and you can hire guides at the entrance.

The **Grand Palace**, a short stroll up from Wat Pho, is nearly a square kilometre of dazzlingly beautiful temples and palaces. Surrounded by high white walls, it was constructed by the early Chakri kings as a city within a city, able to be defended in times of strife. Today, it features a royal coins and medals pavilion (wonderfully air-conditioned), two stunning halls of audience (closed at weekends), the ornate Chakri Palace (built 1876 in the Italian Renaissance style) and, in the main chapel, **Wat Phra Kaeo** or the Temple of the Emerald

Buddha. The tiny 'emerald' (actually jasper) figure within is the most revered Buddha image in Thailand. Believed to be over 1,000 years old and to have originated from Ceylon or northern India, it first came to light in Thailand when it was discovered inside a stucco Buddha in Chiang Mai (1486). It later migrated to Vientiane when captured by the Laotians, but was recaptured by the Thais in 1778. The palace complex is open every day from 8.30 a.m. to 11.30 a.m. and from 1 p.m. to 3.30 p.m. The 100B entrance fee includes admission to **Vivanmek Palace**, a 20B *tuk-tuk* ride away near Dusit Zoo. This beautiful three-storey teakwood palace, built as the home of Rama V, is one of Bangkok's finest sights, full of priceless art objects and royal memorabilia. Guided tours in English are run every hour (on the hour) from 9 a.m. to 3 p.m. and they are excellent.

Day Two
The **National Museum**, formerly the palace of the deputy king (*upraja*), is one of the largest and best presented museums in Asia, built in 1782 with over 1,000 exhibits. To get there, take the express riverboat to the Grand Palace pier, then make a short walk across the Pramane Ground. Turn up at 9.30 a.m. for free guided tours in English on Tuesdays (Thai Art and Culture), Wednesdays (Buddhism) and Thursdays (Pre-Thai Art). The museum is open 9 a.m. to 4 p.m. – closed Mondays and Fridays, and admission is 20B.

Wat Mahathat, the Temple of the Great Relic, is a few minutes' stroll south of the museum, on Na Prathat Rd. This is a famous meditation wat, with an impressive *bot* containing a sacred relic of the Buddha. I spent a whole afternoon at the university here, being chatted up by students, teaching a little English, and being shown around classrooms. The market round the back is a weekend one, with a wonderful layout and opportunities for good photography.

Wat Bemchamabopit (Marble Temple) is a 40B *tuk-tuk* ride north, on Si Ayutthaya Rd. Built in 1899 during the reign of Rama V, this temple is made of white marble imported from Carrera in Italy and is regarded as one of the finest examples of modern Thai architecture. In the courtyard behind the *bot*, there is an interesting gallery of 51 Buddhas (most of them copies) from many styles and periods. Admission to the temple is 10B and the best time to visit is early morning (around 7 a.m.) when Buddhist monks are chanting in the chapel. If you are staying nearby, you might fit it in before the National Museum!

Dusit Zoo offers a good escape from the city noise. The entrance is in Rama V Rd (near Chitlada Palace), a ten-minute walk from the Marble Temple. Established in 1938 by Rama VII, the zoo today plays an important part in preserving many of South-East Asia's rare animals and birds from extinction. Within its well-landscaped 17 hectares can be found Sumatran rhinos, American bison, rare Thai mouse deer and great grey kangaroos. There is said to be a white elephant here too, but this is untrue. 'The monkeys are a lot of fun', commented one visitor, 'but when they throw the snakes out for "exercise", stand well back!' Admission to the zoo is 10B and it is open 9 a.m. to 4 p.m. except Sunday. Many backpackers drop in here on a No. 17 bus from Banglampoo.

Suan Pakkard Palace is located at the other end of Si Ayutthaya Rd from the Marble Temple, a 30B *tuk-tuk* ride from the zoo. Built by Prince and Princess Chumbhot of Nagara Svarga, this 'palace' is actually a large compound containing six traditional Thai houses transported from historical locations around the country to their present site. Lovingly restored, they house a unique collection of art and artifacts, some over 5,000 years old. Viewed from the garden, the Lacquer Pavilion, with its classical lines, two-tone roof and gold-embossed walls and windows – is one of the most beautiful original buildings still in existence in Thailand. Suan Pakkard is open 9 a.m. to 4 p.m. (closed Sundays) and admission is 50B. English-speaking guides are available at the entrance.

Day Three
The **Red Cross Snake Farm** on Rama IV Rd (corner of Henri Dunant Rd) is the world's second-largest snake farm, established in 1923 to produce vaccines and sera which are used in the treatment of snake bites. Admission is 40B (extra 10B for use of camera) and 'venom extraction demonstrations' take place at 11 a.m. and 2 p.m. daily.

Move on to **Jim Thompson's Thai House**, located at the end of Soi Kasemsan 2, off Rama I Rd. This is a traditional Thai building (actually six old houses) containing one of the finest collections of Oriental art in Thailand. It was put together by Jim Thompson, an American who settled in Thailand after the Second World War and who did much to revitalise the Thai silk industry. After his mysterious disappearance in 1967 (whilst on holiday in the Cameron Highlands, Malaysia) his house was turned into a private museum. Art *aficionados* will love this place which is full of (now priceless) antiques and curiosities. The house is open to the public from 9 a.m. to 5 p.m. (closed Sunday) and the 80B admission includes an hour-long guided tour. (**Note**: if visiting by taxi or *tuk-tuk*, make sure they do not take you to J T Silk House by mistake!)

A 30B *tuk-tuk* ride away is **Wat Traimit**, near Hualamphong railway station on Traimit Rd. This temple is famous not for its architecture, but for the solid-gold Buddha, 3 m high and weighing 5.5 tonnes, which resides in a small private chapel. The Golden Buddha is in the simple, unadorned Sukhothai style and dates to around the thirteenth century. You can view it between 9 a.m. and 5 p.m. daily and admission is free.

Finish the day with a stroll round **Chinatown**. The best place to start exploring is Song Sawad Rd, although most of the action centres on the Yaowaraj Rd area. Your walk will take you past several of the largest gold shops in Thailand. Everything is painted red, as the Chinese believe this is a lucky colour. Red also highlights the thousands of gold chains hanging behind the counters. There is an amazing array of goods on display at hundreds of small stalls lining the street. Sample some Thai and Chinese sweets, or pick up some fresh fruit to nibble at as you go. Wander down some of the sidestreets and you will find shops selling dolls, toys, fabrics, paper lanterns, curios and antiques. The atmosphere in Chinatown is fast, furious and fun. You are in Bangkok, but it could just as well be Hong Kong, Singapore or Shanghai!

Day Four

If you have time, take a set tour to **Ancient City**, 33 km south east of Bangkok. Here you can see the best of Thailand in one place. It is the biggest open-air museum in the world. All the main architectural highlights from around the country are represented, including a fourteenth-century Ayutthayan palace (the original of which was destroyed 200 years ago), replicas of several major wats and a reconstructed floating market. If you want to see a modern **Floating Market**, do not go to the one in Bangkok. I saw exactly five boats selling fruit, ten selling flowers to tourists, and about 500 tourist boats! For any chance of seeing an authentic floating market, take the 6 a.m. Chao Phya express boat to Prannok Rd pier, a *tuk-tuk* to the Southern Bus Terminal and a No. 78 bus to **Damnoen Saduak**, the alternative floating market, 104 km out of Bangkok. Turn up around 7.45 a.m. and you will see the final preparations of food, etc., without telescopic lenses blocking your view. After 9 a.m., when all the tour boats arrive, the women in the boats are busier fighting off the waves of tourists than in selling their produce. The two best markets are on either side of the Damnoen Saduak

canal. Hire a boat (180-250B per hour) to see them.

ENTERTAINMENT

Traditional Thai dancing takes place at the **National Theatre** (next to the National Museum) every Saturday and Sunday and every last Friday of the month. Tickets cost 30B or 40B and shows start at 5 p.m. on Fridays, at 10 a.m. and 2 p.m. (two shows) at weekends. **Baan Thai** restaurant (tel: 3913013), at Soi 32 Sukhumvit Rd, is a good place to experience a traditional Thai meal and dancing at a cost of 250B. The only problem is that the restaurant seats about 200 people and at least 190 of them arrive on coaches from the tour hotels, so it can be difficult to see the dancing through the bank of video cameras. Nevertheless, it is a great place to catch some Thai culture if you are short on time and the food is good. Classical dance is also well staged at the **Oriental Hotel**, every Thursday and Sunday at ll a.m., in the Riverside Garden, cost 100B, but, again, it is chock-a-block with photographers and very touristy. **Silom Village** on Silom Rd offers free Thai dancing from 8 p.m. nightly, and delicious food. Arrive early and get a seat near the stage. In Siam Square area, the **Indra Regent** and **Siam Inter-Continental** hotels both offer classical dance shows which are included with the cost of an evening meal.

Thai boxing, a very popular event in Bangkok, is best seen (if you like blood sports) at **Ratchadamnoen Stadium** on Ratchadamnoen Nok Ave., next to the TAT tourist office. Bouts take place from 6 p.m. to 10 p.m. every Monday, Wednesday and Thursday and from 5 p.m. on Sundays. Seats cost 80 to 200B and if you want to see all the knees, elbows and rabbit-punches going in at close range, you will need a ringside seat (and a paper bag).

Many of the larger hotels have discos and nightclubs, but most of Bangkok's (rather seedy) nightlife is concentrated in the three parallel streets of **Patpong** on Silom Rd. Whether you are after an ice-cold beer, a sizzling steak, a steamy show, or that perfect dry Martini, you will find it in Patpong. **Peppermint**, a French-style bistro on Patpong l, has half-price drinks from 7 to 9 p.m. and there is strictly standing room only from ll p.m. to 4 a.m. It is the best early early morning scene, where *everybody* goes after **Rome Club** on Patpong 3 closes. Rome is a popular disco, with a very professional transvestite cabaret at l a.m. nightly. **Harry Bar**, also in Patpong 3, has an equally good cabaret show but is more obviously gay. **Superstar**, the biggest go-go bar in Patpong, offers the latest videos (headphones supplied), a big menu (steak and mushroom pie, pork chops, etc.), draught beer at the open-air bar and 40 leggy dancers inside. Upstairs, the glittery Superstar Disco is packed until 3 a.m.

An increasingly popular variation on the go-go theme is the 'sexotic' show. Upstairs bars like **Lipstick** (Patpong l) and **Cleopatra** (Patpong 2) are fun and safe. Steer clear of touts on the street pushing special shows – the bill for a beer may come to US$30! Straight places have a sign outside saying there is no cover charge and telling you the price of a beer (normally 50B). Besides the 'normal' nude dancing (often little more than a dozen nubile teenagers standing and chatting on the stage in their birthday suits), 'sexotic' performers defy the accepted limits of human anatomy, opening bottles of soda, writing poems and skewering balloons with blowpipes – all no hands!

Not everybody goes to Patpong to drink, dance and ogle naked ladies. Excellent dining, no matter what your tastes are, is just a few steps away. **Mizu's Kitchen**, still going strong after 15 years, is always packed for lunch and dinner. Forgive the shabby exterior. Inside, the red-checked tablecloths are well darned, and a sizzling T-bone steak costs only US$3, a three-course dinner, with dessert and coffee, just US$5. A great favourite among ex-pats, the **Thai Room** (Patpong 2, near the Roxy Bar) serves the best Mexican food in the area. Cool and quiet, this is where you will find locals browsing through the Sunday papers over breakfast. **Roberto's**, in Patpong 2, offers excellent Italian fare (lasagna is the speciality) and a good selection of wines. Right next door, **Bobby's Aroi Dee** opens at 6 a.m. for breakfast and pastries. Through Patpong carpark, you will find **Bobby's Arms**, with genuine British pub food and atmosphere, and (from 8 to ll p.m. every Sunday) lively trad and Dixieland jazz. For more mundane tastes, there are **Kentucky Fried Chicken**, **Mr Donut** and **McDonald's**, all at the Silom Rd entrance to Patpong. Two bookstores, **Bookseller** and **Siam Drug**, stock the latest bestsellers, fashion glossies, foreign dailies and coffee-table tomes. Air-conditioned and quiet, they are the ideal escape from Patpong's noise and hype.

When you have had enough offers of fake Cartier watches, preserved scorpions, 'sandwich' massages and child prostitutes, it is time to leave Patpong and check out the ex-pat clubs in nearby Soi Sarasan, a tiny cross-street running between Wireless Rd and Ratchadamri Rd. **The Blues Bar** is really nice (once you get past all the stares – there are very few Europeans here) and you will have a great time. This is a Thai joint, full of fashion models and movie stars and very trendy. Next door, the **Brown Sugar**, is packed with resident ex-pats and boutique/hotel people. You will meet some interesting people here. This place has really good jazz-jamming sessions on a Tuesday night.

Soi Cowboy, the small bar street behind Sois 21/23 Sukhumvit, is something of an 'easy man's Patpong'. It has no loud music, girlie shows or hard-sell touts, just a selection of quiet and friendly ex-pat bars, cocktail lounges and coffee shops. Popular bars at the moment include **Jukebox**, **Tilac** and **Ruby Star**. A great Dutch-British pub is **Lord Mike O'Henry** in Soi 23, with first-rate European fare, cheap draught beer, bar games and soothing classical sounds.

Two other discos recommended by travellers are **Flamingo** at the Ambassador Hotel (100B Saturday night, two free drinks) and **Freak Out** at Silom Plaza (90B weekdays, one free drink; 180B Friday/Saturday, two drinks).

Warning: the main 'entertainment' on offer in Bangkok is sin and sex. If AIDS is going to explode anywhere in the world, it will explode in Patpong. Recent statistics suggest over a third of all male tourists to Thailand have spent time with a prostitute. They have all been dicing with death, and if they lost, they have taken the consequences back home to their partners.

SHOPPING

Bangkok is the bargain basement of South-East Asia. You can save, and spend, a fortune here. The best traditional buys are silk, gems, jewellery, wood carvings, antiques, handicrafts and made-to-measure clothes. More recently, Bangkok has been doing a roaring trade in fake designer goods: clothes, perfume, bags, accessories, lighters, watches and T-shirts. There is no clearly defined downtown and shopping areas are scattered throughout the city. Check Chinatown for gold jewellery and antiques, Silom for silk, Sukhumvit for leather and made-to-measure suits, Siam Square for high-fashion clothes and Banglampoo for hilltribe handicrafts. General markets like Pratunam (at the corner of Rajaprarob and Phetburi roads) and the Weekend Market (at Chatuchak Park, in front of the Northern Bus Terminal) sell just about everything. The night market at Patpong has the cheapest fake watches ('Date-Day' Rolexes at 500B, waterproof ones at 1200B, bargain hard) and the best range of pirate tapes I have come across in Thailand. Along Sukhumvit Rd, I've seen Dunhill, Cartier, Gucci, Boss, Puma, Playboy, Nike and Lacoste socks, all on one stall, and all at 50 pence a pair. The quality is generally very good

– your friends back home will never know the difference!

Most goods are bargainable. The only places which do not discount are leading department stores and a few fixed-price shops. Every tourist area of Bangkok has a department store and they very often give better prices than high-street boutiques and shops – even after haggling. **Siam Shopping Centre**, on Rama IV Rd, is 'boutique city', with four floors of fashion clothing, jewellery and souvenirs. **Central Department Store** at 306 Silom Rd and **New World Department Store** in Banglampoo are less à la mode but have a better selection of general goods. All Thais go shopping on a Sunday, which is their one day off work and all the department stores (and many shops) stay open till late. Areas like Chinatown and the new Night Bazaar (cum Weekend Market) opposite Sukhumvit Soi l, turn into a vast, sprawling, frenetic free-for-all with goods exchanging hands at rock-bottom prices.

Wherever you shop, always take your time and compare prices before buying. Do not respond to a hard sell (walk out if you feel the pressure coming on) and bargain 20 to 50 per cent off the first asking price in shops and on street stalls. Above all, avoid touts, taxi drivers and 'students' wanting to take you to recommended shops – you will *always* pay commission to them. Before you start serious shopping, nip down to the nearest street market and get yourself a strong lightweight 'expanding' (three in one) bag – Silom Rd does a good range, starting at around 280B apiece (bargain hard). Use this to hold any travel purchases (and unwanted luggage) and leave it in store in your Bangkok hotel while you venture further afield – this saves carting lots of excess weight around South-East Asia! Keep in mind that receipts should be obtained for everything you buy. Certificates of guarantee are especially important for jewellery and gemstones. If you use credit cards, make sure the shop does not add an extra surcharge to your purchase.

Thai Silk is internationally famous, but beware of being fobbed off with inferior merchandise. To test silk, ask for a scrap of the fabric and burn it. Only silk smells like burnt hair and the ash powders away like cigarette ash. If you are left with an amorphous black blob with a burnt plastic odour, cancel your order! The quality of silk depends a lot on how it has been treated. Good silk is oiled before tailoring. This preserves it, and prevents creasing (especially applicable to suit silks). You need four-ply silk for a suit, three-ply for a light skirt, two-ply for a dress shirt and one-ply for a regular shirt. Silks can cost anything from 200B to 350B per metre, depending on quality

and weight and while you can buy cheaper in Chiang Mai, the same materials would cost two or three times as much in London. Few people can afford the high prices charged at **Jim Thompson's Silk House** on Surawong Rd, but you will not find such quality or such a range of original designs anywhere else. **Julie Thai Silk** at 1279 New Rd (for women) and **Intersuit** at 1212 Silom Rd (for men) have much cheaper silk and can make up suits, dresses and jackets very quickly. They both charge slightly more than other tailors, but their fabric choice is good and their seamstresses have more idea of fashion than many others. Despite their '24-hr service' claims, you really must allow three to four days and insist on a fitting. Also ask for clothes to be fully lined – it rarely costs extra!

Bangkok is *the* place to buy **jewellery** and **gemstones** especially rubies and sapphires). You must bargain, however, and you must go to recognised TAT-licensed jewellers (look for the logo in the window). If you buy anywhere else, take your purchase to one of these TAT-recognised places and get a valuation immediately. If you find you have been stung, go back to the shop and threaten to demonstrate on the street outside until they change the stone or give your money back – it works! The best place I have come across (fairly priced, a good selection of stones, rings, jewellery, all purchases certificated) is **Bangkok Jewellery Co Ltd** (Factory) at 577-583 Bantadthong Rd, near Charoen Pol Market, Patoomwan (tel: 2153214).

Antique buying can be a risky business as a great many fakes are peddled in Bangkok. Stick with reputable dealers and always insist on a certificate of authentication. **River City Shopping Complex**, next to the Royal Orchid Sheraton Hotel, has quality goods and is especially good for antique dealers on the third and fourth floors. It also has an antique auction on the first Saturday of each month. Popular buys include old temple bells, lacquered boxes, chests and cabinets, bronze cutlery and works of art. Before paying out any money, make sure that what you are buying is not classified as part of the national heritage – the export of Buddhas and *garudas* for souvenirs is, for example, officially banned.

ACCOMMODATION/FOOD

Apart from Singapore, Bangkok offers the best choice of restaurants (Thai, Korean, Chinese, Indian, Japanese and European) and the best range of accommodation (cheap guest houses to international-class hotels) in the Orient. With regard to big hotels, rooms are in short supply from October to April (high season, book ahead) and cheapest from May to September (low season, bargain for discounts). All tariffs listed below are subject to additions of ll per cent government tax and 10 per cent service tax. Restaurants featuring Thai food divide into two categories: those which include entertainment (classical dancing, etc.) and those which do not.

SILOM-SURAWONG

This is probably the most 'central' area in Bangkok. It is close to the Chao Phya River (convenient for sightseeing) and has a number of shops, restaurants, banks and hotels. The big GPO is here and so are major entertainment centres like Patpong and Silom Village. Silom is a particularly good base if you are on your way out of Thailand. All the major airlines are nearby, which is useful for arranging your flight home. The cost of living is high, however, and there is a serious shortage of budget-class accommodation.

Silom's classic **Oriental Hotel** (tel: 2360400), at 48 Oriental Ave., is more of an institution than a hotel. Even if you cannot afford to stay (and with rooms from 3800B, few can) it is *de rigeur* to drop in for evening cocktails on the terrace and watch the sun going down over the river. For a special occasion, try a Siamese buffet lunch (12 to 2 p.m.) at the **Sala Rim Naam** across the river from the Oriental – all the delicious Thai dishes you can eat for 200B per head. Two more modern hotels, both with rooms from 3400B and many facilities, are the **Dusit Thani** at 946 Rama IV Rd (tel: 2331130) and the **Shangri-La** at 89 Soi Wat Suan Phu, New Rd (tel: 2367777). The first-class **Manohra Hotel**, at 412 Suriwongse Rd (tel: 2345070) is excellent value for money, with an indoor pool, a rooftop garden and comfortable air-conditioned rooms from 1000B single, 1200B double. Its **Buttercup** coffee shop does a fine buffet lunch from ll a.m. to 2 p.m. daily for 120B plus 10 per cent service tax.

Swan Hotel (tel: 2338444), at 31 Custom House Lane, New Rd, is a good mid-range bet. It has a quiet, central location, an air-conditioned coffee shop, a good pool and cosy rooms from 300B fan, 400B air-conditioned. If full (and it often is), try **River View Guest House** (tel: 2358501) at 768 Soi Wanit 2, Talad Noi, near the River City shopping complex. This is a new place, very pleasant, with air-conditioned rooms from 380B. If you can get it, Room 41 has fantastic views over the river.

Economy hotels start with the **Niagara** (tel: 2335783) at 26 Soi Suksavithaya, Silom Rd. It is a bit rundown, but has a small restaurant, an overseas phone and spacious fan rooms (double-bedded, with balcony) at 210B. The air-conditioned rooms (360B) are, however, disappointing. If you are on a budget, you must stay at **TT Guest House** (tel: 2363053) at 138 Soi Wat Mahaprhutharam. To get there, walk down Thanon Phraya (between Sois 37 and 39 New Rd), and take the first turning left. TT is to my mind the best guest house in Thailand. It has all sorts of useful services: bus/rail ticket service, post-box, laundry, baggage store, TV lounge, cheap restaurant, good noticeboard, free information and delightful staff. Rooms are clean and quiet and cost 100B single, 120B double. There are also a few 90B rooms in the old 'wooden house', and a fan-cooled 50B dormitory. This place is run by helpful young Sukhum, who is really tuned into travellers' needs. His brother Mongkon runs the new **TT 2 Guest House** in Soi Sawan, off Si Phraya Rd (opposite the old *Daily News* building), offering the same excellent services and rooms from 100 to 120B.

Finding somewhere to eat in Silom is no problem. **Maria Bakery**, just below the GPO on New Rd, is a peaceful little breakfast spot, ideal for reading letters (or writing them) over a croissant and a cup of coffee. Two other air-conditioned places offering cheap Western breakfasts are **Jimmy Bakery** near Swan Hotel and **Kew Gardens Pub** opposite Manohra Hotel. Down an alleyway opposite the GPO is **Pak Muslim**, a great little Indian restaurant with a very limited menu but fantastic food – the 50B chicken *birianis* are particularly good. **Himali Cha Cha** on New Rd has slightly more expensive Indian fare and is just as popular. **Phra Khai**, attached to the New Fuji Hotel on Suriwong Rd, offers set Thai and vegetarian dinners at 99B – not bad value, but it is best to eat à la carte in a group. Japanese food is very affordable at **Akamon** at Victory Hotel, Silom Rd. **Wing-On**, at 913-5 Silom Rd, does nicely presented Chinese food and **Whole Earth** at 93/3 Soi Langsuan, Ploenchit Rd, is a relaxing vegetarian restaurant with acoustic guitar downstairs and videos upstairs. **Silom Plaza Hotel**, Silom Rd, has two floors of bars, discos and coffee shops. Here you will find **Thank God It's Friday**, with Thai-European three-course meals at 180B, and live jazz on Friday and Saturday nights.

SUKHUMVIT

Sukhumvit Rd is strictly for rich kids and shoppers, who like its ritzy hotels and restaurants, its fashion boutiques and tailors and its high-octane street action. Sightseeing is a real problem, however, as most of Bangkok's temples are over an hour away by taxi. The top hotel is the stylish **Landmark** (tel: 2540404) at 138 Sukhumvit Rd, with rooms from 3000B single, 3200B double, and a good buffet lunch (all you can eat for 260B net) from ll.30 a.m. to 2 p.m. Across the road, the **Ambassador** (tel: 2540444), at 17l Sukhumvit Rd, is a vast complex with seven restaurants, five coffee bars, a disco on the seventh floor and classy rooms from 1694B single, 1936B double. Moderate hotels on Sukhumvit Rd include **Quality Inn** (tel: 2544783) on Soi 19 with one-price rooms at 750B net, a snooker hall and 24-hour service, **Windsor Hotel** (tel: 2580160) down Soi 20, with single/double rooms from 1500/1800B and a great buffet lunch (99B net), finally **Mermaid's Rest** down Soi 8, with a small pool, a cosy beer bar and homely rooms from 125B fan, 250B air-conditioned. Cheaper places are **Ruamchitt Mansion** behind Soi 15 (150 to 400B), **Miami Hotel** down Soi 13 (150 to 500B), **Crown Hotel** in Soi 12 (250 to 500B) and **Atlanta** at the bottom of Soi 2 (150 to 390B).

Danish Bakery at 591/8 Sukhumvit is typical of Sukhumvit's many classy cake shops. It is air-conditioned and full of yummy cakes and other treats. **Wattana** on the corner of Soi 18 is an ice-cream palace, with value-for-money continental breakfasts and set lunches. At the **Seafood Market & Restaurant**, 388 Sukhumvit Rd, opposite Soi Asoke, you can select your own fresh seafood and vegetables. Tandoori chicken and fish (and other north Indian specialities) are good at **Moghul Room** in Soi ll, near the Ambassador Hotel. Traditional Thai cuisine (and an impressive selection of wines) can be found at **D'jit Pochana**, 60 Sukhumvit, Soi 20. The **Ambassador City Food Complex**, Ambassador Hotel, is the place to pick and mix from over 30 different foodstalls – Thai, Chinese, Japanese, European and Korean – at around 20/30B per dish. A very reasonably priced restaurant is **Cabbages & Condoms** down Soi 12. It is run by Thailand's planned parenthood group, and the profits go to various projects. They have quite a selection of keyrings and T-shirts promoting (yes, you guessed it) condom use. All that aside, it is a pleasant place to eat and your money goes to a good cause.

SIAM-PRATUNAM

This is probably the least pleasant area to stay in Bangkok, despite the good shopping and entertainments. What accommodation there is is expensive and the traffic is dense. The **Siam Inter-Continental Hotel** (tel: 2530355), at 967 Rama I Rd, is the single oasis from the noise of the city, with 10 hectares of gardens and many recreations. Even if you cannot afford a room here (from 2600B) it is worth stopping by for a lunch buffet. For only 120B (plus taxes) they serve up prawns, mussels, crab, raw fish, wonderful desserts and much much more. Tea and coffee are included, but watch out for expensive alcoholic drinks! Also recommended is the 300B dinner-dance at the **Indra Regent Hotel** (tel: 2511111), 120/126 Rajaprarob Rd. Rooms start at 2100B and there is a good pool and a shopping arcade. Cheaper offers of accommodation are close together near Jim Thompson's House. **Krit Thai Mansion** (tel: 2153042) at 931/l Rama I Rd has a 24-hour coffee bar, free newspapers in the lobby and quiet rooms at 800B single, 1000B double. **Muangphol Building** (tel: 2153056) at 931/8-9 Rama I Rd is a very safe place, with one-price rooms at 450B. Next door is the **Star Hotel**, run by a friendly family, with air-conditioned rooms (hot water, phone, etc.) from 300B. Opposite the Star, the brand-new **A-One Inn** (tel: 2153029) charges 350B for bright, well-furnished air-conditioned rooms – as advertised, it's a real home from home.

For cheap eats, go to **Tokyu Food Centre** at the corner of Rama I and Phyathai Roads. There is a bakery-restaurant on the first floor, a food plaza and supermarket on the fourth floor and an international food hall (a vast array of 20-40B dishes) on the sixth floor. Behind Siam Center is **Kloster Bier Garden**, a good evening hangout with draught Kloster beer and tasty Thai snacks. Opposite Siam Center are two **Scala** restaurants specialising in seafood. Anyone in urgent need of Western fast-food should go straight to the Meridien President Hotel on Rama I Rd, where they will find **McDonald's, Pizza Hut, Kentucky Fried Chicken** and even a **Svenson's** ice-cream palace.

BANGLAMPOO

Banglampoo, along with its 'freak street' of Ko-Sahn Rd, is the main backpackers' enclave. Here there are many budget guest houses, travel agents, visa-photo shops, video bars and great little restaurants. Ko-Sahn Rd is where to eat Western food, buy hippie and hilltribe clothing, book cheap travel, look out for second-hand books and pirate cassettes and meet other travellers. Like Silom, this area has the advantage of being very central for most of Bangkok's major sights. It is also very economical. Rooms at most guest houses are around 50/60B for a single, 80/100B for a double. Current favourites in Ko-Sahn Rd include **CH** (with currency exchange and 24 hour video restaurant), **VC** (popular food, good noticeboard), **Good Luck** and **160** (quiet, out of the way), and **Bonny's** (a firm favourite). Down an alley behind **New Nith Charoen** (upmarket rooms at 150B) are **Sunee Porn** and **Lek** (clean, friendly) and the luxury **Vieng Thai Hotel**

(720B single, 820B double, nice pool, student travel office). **Sweety Guest House**, a one-minute walk from the bottom of Ko-Sahn Rd, is at 49 Ratchadamnoen Rd. It is a snug, secure place with one-price rooms at 80B, cheap massage (80B/hour), laundry, travel service, baggage store, etc. Nearby, at 2 Ratchadamnoen Rd, the **Royal Hotel** (tel: 22291ll) caters for travellers who have had enough of budget room bugs, noise and squalor. One night of air-conditioned comfort costs 557B, but does wonders for the morale! At the other end of Ko-Sahn Rd, across Chakrabong Rd and behind the temple, **Peachy Guest House** at 10 Phra Athit Rd (near the Unicef building) is quite the best deal I have found in Banglampoo. Rooms are 75B single, 120B double, and they are large, clean and very livable in. Ask for one on the middle floor, away from the noisy street. If it is full, stroll over to **New Siam** or **Rose Garden**. Or walk for 10 minutes from Banglampoo to **Chan** at 42 Samsun Rd (near Phra Singh Rd). This is a sleepy out-of-the-way guest house, run by friendly, informative people, with a 30B dormitory and spotless rooms for 80B.

SOI NGAM DUPHLI

This road, just off Rama IV Rd, is another big travellers' centre. Well located for Silom, Patpong, Siam Square and the foreign embassies, it has a more 'Thai' feel to it than Ko-Sahn (which is just a sea of European faces), but is rather more seedy. In Soi Ngam Duphli you will find the old Vietnam R&R hangout, the **Malaysia Hotel** (air-conditioned rooms from 312B single, 396B double, pool, 24-hour coffee shop/video bar). There are also worthwhile cheapies like **Anna** (80 to 100B) and **Sweet House** (60 to 250B, with restaurant, videos, games, cheap beer and breakfasts).

In Soi Si Bamphen, the road running across Soi Ngam Duphli, you will find the dilapidated **Boston Inn**, with fan rooms for 190B, and **Freddy 2** with a breezy outdoor restaurant, security lockers, luggage deposit, good noticeboard and clean rooms from 70B. To escape the noisy traffic, go down the small alley before Freddy 2 and take rooms at peaceful **Sala Thai** (from 120B) or **Madame** guest house (from 60B). For eats, try **Blue Fox** opposite the Malaysia Hotel (well-stocked bar, Western food, jukebox, open till midnight) or nearby **Lisboa** restaurant (Mexican fare and pizzas). There is lots of good street food on offer (*satay, kai yang*, etc.) together with the usual travellers' diet of chips, *lassis* and banana pancakes. Try to sample everything.

KANCHANABURI

Only 130 km from Bangkok, Kanchanaburi is a very pretty area with good rafting, nice walks and interesting topography. If you want to see some real Thai countryside (caves, jungles, waterfalls and rivers) and don't want to go all the way north to Chiang Mai, this is where to come. Situated at the junction of three rivers (the Kwai Yai, the Kwai Noi and the Mae Klong) the town was originally founded by Rama III as a defence against Burmese invasion over the Three Pagodas Pass. Today, it is best known for its associations with the Second World War. From here, in 1942, the Japanese army began constructing the infamous 'Death Railway', a 415-km strategic line linking Thailand with Burma. By October 1943, when the rail link was completed, some 100,000 Asian labourers and 16,000 Allied prisoners of war had perished, mostly through forced labour, starvation and disease. Every year, for a week commencing at the end of November, the Allied bombings of the Death Railway in 1945 are commemorated in a spectacular Sound and Light Show, using the world-famous bridge over the River Kwai as a backdrop.

ARRIVAL/DEPARTURE

Rail

It is still possible and well worth the trip, to travel the Death Railway from Bangkok Noi station (on the Thonburi side of the Chao Phya River) all the way to Nam Tok. Two trains leave Bangkok Noi daily, at 8 a.m. and 1.50 p.m., and they make stops at **Nakhom Pathom** (worth a short detour, to see the famous Phra Pathom Chedi) and at Kanchanaburi, before continuing on over the Kwai Bridge to Nam Tok. The one and a half hour ride to Kanchanaburi costs 29B. Trains back to Thonburi from Kanchanaburi leave at 8.03 a.m. and 2.29 p.m. daily.

Road

From Bangkok, take a boat up the Chao Phya River (5B) to Prannok Rd pier (one stop below Bangkok Noi railway station), then a 20B *tuk-tuk* to *either* the air-conditioned or non-air-conditioned terminals of the Southern Bus Station. Ordinary buses to Kanchanaburi take three hours and cost 28B. Air-conditioned buses take only two and half hours and cost 53B. Again, there is the option to get off halfway, at Nakhon Pathom, the oldest city in Thailand, to see the highest Buddhist monument in the world, the 127-m-high Phra Pathom *Chedi*. From Nakhon Pathom, you can pick up bus No. 81 from the east side of the chedi to travel on to Kanchanaburi.

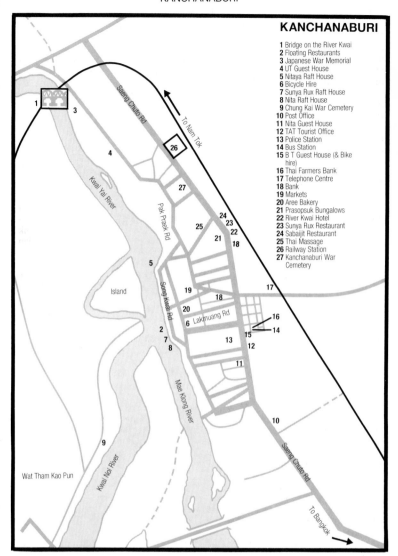

KANCHANABURI

1 Bridge on the River Kwai
2 Floating Restaurants
3 Japanese War Memorial
4 UT Guest House
5 Nitaya Raft House
6 Bicycle Hire
7 Sunya Rux Raft House
8 Nita Raft House
9 Chung Kai War Cemetery
10 Post Office
11 Nita Guest House
12 TAT Tourist Office
13 Police Station
14 Bus Station
15 B T Guest House (& Bike hire)
16 Thai Farmers Bank
17 Telephone Centre
18 Bank
19 Markets
20 Aree Bakery
21 Prasopsuk Bungalows
22 River Kwai Hotel
23 Sunya Rux Restaurant
24 Sabaijit Restaurant
25 Thai Massage
26 Railway Station
27 Kanchanaburi War Cemetery

TOURIST SERVICES

The TAT tourist office (tel: 511200) is in Saeng Chuto Rd, just up from the bus station. It is a small efficient outfit, open 8.30 a.m. to 4.30 p.m. daily. Further down the same road is the post office, where you can make overseas phone calls. For money changing, go to the Thai Farmers Bank or Thai Military Bank at the bus station. For flight reservations and sightseeing tours, try TCS Travel on Saeng Chuto Rd, below the big River Kwai Hotel.

SIGHTS

Sightseeing is much cheaper (and more enjoyable) by bicycle than by *songthaew* or *samlor*. Several places, including guest houses, hire out bikes for around 20B a day. *Songthaews* charge 3B place-to-place and ask 200B (one to six persons) to go sightseeing for three to four hours. *Samlors* charge 80B (fixed rate) for a standard four-hour tour of the local sights and a few of them have good English-speaking drivers. Suzuki, near the bus station, rents out motorbikes (200-300B per day) for out-of-town touring.

There is enough in and around Kanchanaburi to keep you busy for a week. Most people start with a bicycle tour of the town and its surroundings. Set out early (to avoid the heat), go down to the floating restaurants, cross over the river by ferry and cycle 20 minutes to **Wat Thum Khao Pun**, an interesting cave-temple housing a glitzy underground Buddha. Just before the temple is **Chungkai War Cemetery**, one of two in

41

Kanchanaburi. Here are buried 1,740 soldiers, sailors and airmen. For a better idea of wartime conditions, go back across the river and cycle up the hill to **Jeath Museum** which contains photographs and articles belonging to Japanese and Allied soldiers. The museum itself is built of bamboo and is modelled after the prisoners' living quarters. The name Jeath comes from the initials of the countries involved in the building of the Death Railway – Japan, England, America and Australia, Thailand and Holland. From the museum, cycle up Saeng Chuto Rd to **Kanchanaburi War Cemetery** containing 6,982 more Allied graves. Continue up Saeng Chuto Rd and turn left down New Zealand Rd (just before the railway line) for the **Japanese War Memorial**, built by the Japanese to honour their own dead. Just up from the memorial, the present **River Kwai Bridge** resembles, but is not, the original wooden bridge built by Allied POWs. That bridge was destroyed on 13 February 1945 by US Airforce bombers. Walking across the bridge is not as safe as it could be because of the Thai motorbikes ripping down the narrow plank walkway at 30 kmph! But the bridge is a good place to be around sunset, as it is very picturesque. Close by, just past the railway museum, is a small Peace Temple built by a Japanese ex-serviceman as an act of reconciliation. The bronze temple bell was bought with money collected by a British ex-POW at a London Unitarian church.

If you visit the bridge in the morning, you can pick up the 10.30 a.m. train from Kanchanaburi to the village of **Nam Tok**. This is a scenic, sometimes hazardous, two-hour ride along the Death Railway, costing 15B one-way. During the Second World War, Nam Tok was the station for Tha Soa (Tarsau), a Japanese POW transit camp. The rail link from Nam Tok to Burma has gone and sturdy trees now grow in the cuttings dug at the cost of so much suffering and so many lives. At Nam Tok station you can take a 5B *songthaew* (or walk 2 km) to **Kao Phang Waterfall**, for a splash or a swim. Behind the waterfall, another 2-km stroll takes you to the recently discovered **Cave of God**, buried deep in the jungle. The path leading there is easy to follow. From the main road below the falls, buses run back to Kanchanaburi (45 minutes) for 23B.

A much better waterfall than Kao Phang is **Erawan**, 65 km from Kanchanaburi. To make a day of it, get the first bus out there at 8 a.m. – it is two hours to Erawan (17B), then a 2-km walk (or 3B minibus ride) to the National Park. Pay 3B entrance to the park, then climb two hours (at leisure) up through seven tiers of waterfalls. The scenery is pretty, there are lots of exotic birds and butterflies,

and you can go swimming in several plunge pools on the way up. Note that the last bus back to Kanchanaburi leaves at 4 p.m.

Raft trips from Sunya Rux in Saeng Chuto Rd are still great fun. They include bongo drums, Thai-style water-skiing (no skis), diving, floating behind the rafts in tubes, boogying to Madonna, and lots of good food. The popular one-day trip up the Mae Klong River costs 200B (plus 100B for two meals) and takes in a couple of worthwhile temples and viewpoints. The two-day trip up to the Burmese border is 500B per person and includes all meals. The main event, the four-day jungle trip, costs between 1000 and 2000B per person and is, according to one report a 'total experience'. Sunya himself is a great host, a good cook and an all-round entertainer. He offers raft trips all year round, but they are best between the months of November and April.

Three Pagodas Pass is a border town between Thailand and Burma. It is mostly under the control of Mon rebels, who have proclaimed an independent state there. The Three pagodas themselves are rather disappointing – they are only about 2 m high apiece – but the landscape is really beautiful. From Kanchanaburi, take bus No. 8203 to Thongphaphum (80B, three hours), then a second bus on to Sangkhlaburi (two and a half hours). Stay overnight in Sanghklaburi (one hotel, 90B single, 100B double). In the morning, find a pick-up (100B return) that goes to Three Pagodas Pass; it should return about 12 noon, in time to catch the 1 p.m. bus back to Kanchanaburi. If you want more than a morning at the pass, you will have to stay a second night in Sangklhaburi. Sometimes it *is* possible to cross over into Burma, but check first with TAT before you try it – the current situation in Burma is volatile, to say the least.

SHOPPING
The best buys are blue sapphires from the nearby mines at Bophloi. If you have a good eye, you can get bargain prices at **Jumlas** jewellers, 160-169 Kanchanaburi centre, behind the TAT office. If you cannot trust your own judgement, drop in on Sunya (cf. above) for advice. He has never cheated a tourist yet.

ENTERTAINMENT
Kanchanaburi's top nightspot is the **Raft Disco** at River Kwai Hotel. It is open 9 p.m. to 2 a.m. nightly and the 100B admission includes one free drink. Sunya can give directions to another (much better) local disco. He can also arrange traditional Thai massage from 'old girls' (i.e. no hanky-panky) for just 60B an hour.

ACCOMMODATION

On arrival, do not believe *samlor* drivers (who lie in wait for tourists at the bus station) when they say the hotel or guest house of your choice is 'closed'. All they want is to drive you to an accommodation of their choice, which gives them a big fat commission.

Kanchanaburi's one claim to luxury is the **River Kwai Hotel** (tel: 511184) at 284/3-16 Saeng Chuto Rd, with rooms at 545B single, 641B double (net), pool, coffee shop, disco, health club, etc. It has a wonderfully cool air-conditioned lobby, worth flopping in (even if you are not a resident) after a hard day's sightseeing! Across the road, **Prasopsuk Bungalows** offer quiet, clean rooms with tiled bathrooms for 80/90B fan or 150/200B air-conditioned. There is a cheap open-air restaurant here and also a smart air-conditioned coffee shop with live music nightly. **VL Guest House**, next to Prasopsuk, is a brand-new place with bright, cheerful rooms from 100B fan to 250B air-conditioned. It is the best guest house in town – all rooms have bathrooms attached. **Sunya Rux** (tel: 513868) above the River Kwai Hotel, has a few rooms at 50B. They are simple, but clean, with fans and big double beds. Sunya's new idea however, is 'moving beds'. As one guest enthused: 'Okay, you can spend a night on the water here in one of a dozen houseboats, but how many of them move once you're on board to a quiet little estuary away from the nightclubs and live bands of the noisy floating restaurants? If you want a peaceful night's sleep in comfort, this is the way to do it – no mosquitoes, plenty of fresh air and the scenery is fantastic. The rooms have luxury 20-cm sprung mattresses and are well-decorated. Each raft-house costs 150B a night and sleeps up to four people in two double-bedded rooms.'

Also worth a try is the new **River Guest House** (tel: 512491) with clean, adequate huts right on the river (40B single, 70B double), spotless toilets, good food, friendly people and a first-rate view of the Kwai Bridge. Superior raft-houses like **Kwai Yai Garden Resort** (tel: 511261), 2 km from the Kwai Bridge, charge between 450 and 700B per night – contact TAT for a full listing.

FOOD

Go to the floating restaurants for a cool beer at dusk and to watch the sunset. You can stick around for a romantic candle-lit supper here, but it is a bit chancy. Dishes are washed in the river water and several people have complained of stomach bugs. For a high-class meal, try the **River Kwai Hotel**. It is a little expensive, but the food is superb. **Sunya Rux** restaurant does the best travellers' fare in town and the best fish dishes too. There is some wonderful food on the 'spicy' menu – items like venison, bird and frog curry, prepared in 'older Thai style'. Most people order 'no-spicy' favourites like sweet-sour vegetables and grilled river-fish. **Sabaijit**, just up from Sunya's, offers cheap and popular Chinese food: noodles, fried rice, stuffed egg roll, seafood and salads. Near the market, **Aree Bakery** has great cakes and ice-cream, and proper home-style breakfasts too.

KOH SAMET

This island comes as a pleasant surprise to many travellers, especially since the beaches are so clean and the water so deep and good for swimming. The best thing about Samet is its refreshing mix of Thais and Westerners. There is not the Samui kind of situation of Westerners taking over an island. This is still primarily a Thai resort and let us hope it stays that way. Videos are creeping into the restaurants and motorbikes are starting to rip along the beaches, but Samet still has a long way to go before it becomes another Pee Pee island or Koh Samui.

Accommodation is mainly cheap beach huts (50 to 150B) strung along the north-east coast. These usually contain just a mattress, a mosquito net and (sometimes) an attached bathroom. All accommodation is half-price in the low season and more than normal price at weekends and on Thai public holidays. You can often get 50B or more off the cost of a room by asking for the local (Thai) price and further reductions are possible if you stay three days or more. Some places hire out tents on the beach, but they are hot and stuffy. As for food, there is a great deal of it and it is generally of a high standard. On the Thai beaches (Diamond and Ao Wong Duan), there are several food stalls at the back of the beach, so you do not have to eat at expensive Western restaurants attached to bungalows. Also, people walk up and down the beaches with cheap snacks (barbecued chicken on sticks, etc.) and ice-cream. Massages (around 100B an hour) are offered on the beach also.

It is still wonderfully quiet on Samet; most times the only sounds to be heard are the gentle sounds of the sea. Many places now have electricity, at least between 6 p.m. and 6 a.m., but it is still advisable to carry a torch/flashlight at night. It is also a good idea, after dark, to cover yourself with mosquito repellent. The one drawback to Samet – the main reason the developers have kept away – is malaria. It is difficult to catch, but do take all necessary precautions. If you develop symptoms (cramps, fever, etc.), go straight to Sue Wild at Naga bungalows for help.

The island still suffers from water shortages, especially from November to February. During these months having a shower can be a real problem. Lots of travellers come then though because a big advantage of Koh Samet is that it is dry and pleasant when Koh Samui is having its worst rains.

ARRIVAL/DEPARTURE
From Bangkok, minibuses go direct to Samet in four hours (120B one-way) from various guest houses in Banglampoo or Soi Ngam Duphli. Alternatively, it is a three-hour, 62B, bus ride from the Eastern Bus Terminal in Bangkok to Ban Phe, then a 40-minute, 20B boat over to Samet island. Boats leave at regular intervals (as and when full) and they go either to Na Darn or Ao Wong Duan. At Na Darn, which is closest to the cheap accommodation, *bemos* meet you off the ferry and run you down to the beach of your choice for 10B.

THE BEACHES
Sai Kaew (Diamond)
Working south from Na Darn, this is the first beach you will come to. Like most of Samet's beaches, it has crystal-clear waters and some of the whitest, cleanest sand in Thailand. **Diamond** is the best operation, with basic huts at 70B, nicer bungalows at 250B, a good beach-front restaurant, boat trips around the island (every Wednesday, 120B per person), currency exchange, airline confirmations, Bangkok bus bookings and a very relaxing atmosphere. Most people eat here, or at **Toy** bungalows further down. Toy is a lively place, with a video, friendly staff and exceptionally good food. Enquire about glass-bottom boat trips here; hire windsurfers/catamarans at **Ploy Thaloy** next door. Windsurfing is best around April, the crossover month between the dry and wet seasons. The new **Seaview** operation has a popular restaurant with saucy cocktails (e.g. 'Orgasm' and 'Multiply Orgasm') and primitive but fun discos every Tuesday and Friday night.

If you want to stay with other Westerners, go to **Naga** bungalows between Sai Kaew and Ao Phai (near the concrete mermaid). Sue and Toss, the friendly English-Thai owners, offer Western food (brown bread, cookies, cakes, etc.), Western sounds (great jazz tapes) and lots of Western-style facilities, including a library and a supply shop. Most bungalows are 60B single, 80B double, but a few have electricity and cost 100B.

Ao Phai
This beach is being built up and cheap places to stay are vanishing fast. **Ao Phai** bungalows are still good value. 70B buys

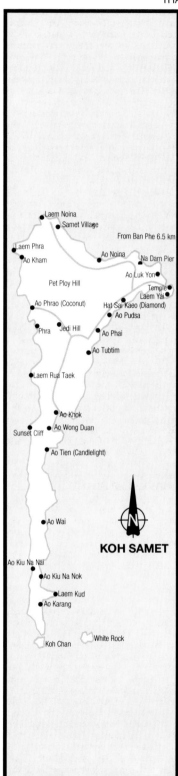

Laem Noina
Samet Village
From Ban Phe 6.5 km
Laem Phra
Ao Kham
Ao Noina
Na Darn Pier
Ao Luk Yon
Pet Ploy Hill
Temple
Laem Yai
Ao Phrao (Coconut)
Hat Sai Kaeo (Diamond)
Ao Pudsa
Phra
Jedi Hill
Ao Phai
Ao Tubtim
Laem Rua Taek
Ao Khok
Ao Wong Duan
Sunset Cliff
Ao Tien (Candlelight)

Ao Wai

KOH SAMET

Ao Kiu Na Nai
Ao Kiu Na Nok
Laem Kud
Ao Karang

White Rock
Koh Chan

you a cosy little hut on stilts with electricity, mosquito net and a verandah. Superior chalets, with fan, shower and toilet, cost around 250B. **Seabreeze** has a water-sports centre, a useful travel service, swish bungalows for 250B (tiled bathrooms, big double beds, fan, etc.) and two-person tents at 100B. **Samed Villa** charges 200/300B and is run by a friendly Swiss-Thai couple. Food is good at **Nop's Kitchen** and **Silver Sands** has a disco every Saturday night with a BBQ, music and dancing.

Ao Pudsa

Another nice beach, rather crowded at weekends. **Tubtim** bungalows are the best deal at 150B, with fan and shower. **Pudsa** restaurant offers day boat-trips round the small islands within the Koh Samet National Park at 150B per ticket, inclusive of fresh fried fish with rice on the beach, plenty of fruit and water and fishing/snorkelling gear.

Tantawan

At the bottom of Tubtim beach, the road splits. Take the lower path for **Nuan Kitchen** (very secluded, own little rocky beach, bungalows at 80 to 150B) or walk over the hill to Tantawan beach. Here you will find expensive accommodation, a small scuba-diving school and the cheap **Bamboo Restaurant** offering novelty snacks (try 'potato salad Vienna warm style') and boat trips to **Tha Lu** island for snorkelling and fishing, every Monday and Friday, 150B per person.

Ao Wong Duan

This is the main Thai beach, touristy and polluted. The sole surviving budget outfit is **Seahorse**, with 150/200B bungalows, overseas telephone, money exchange, travel service, scuba-diving, and glass-bottom boat tours (9 a.m. to 12.30 p.m., 200B per person). If you have money to spend, try **Wong Duan Resort**. There are nice chalets at 300B (400B at weekends) and a classy restaurant.

For peace and quiet, go south of Ao Wong Duan to Ao Thian beach (primitive but cheap) or walk for 20 minutes across the mainland from Ao Phai to Ao Phrao (Coconut Bay) on the other side of the island. Ao Phrao has low-price accommodation and amazing sunsets. Even here, however, it gets busy at weekends.

CHIANG MAI

Thailand's second largest city is located at the foot of majestic Doi Suthep mountain, 700 km north of Bangkok. On the banks of the Ping River in a fertile plain ringed by heavily forested hills, Chiang Mai is often called called 'The Rose of the North'. It dates back to 1296,

has a population of 160,000, and is noted for the beauty of its women, cool invigorating climate and nearby hilltribes. Its unique customs and culture owe much to its mountainous situation; until the late 1920s it was virtually cut off from Bangkok. Founded by King Mengrai as the capital of the fast-expanding Lanna Thai (One Million Rice Fields) kingdom, Chiang Mai enjoyed two centuries of power and influence as the principal city of the north before being captured by the Burmese in 1556. It was liberated by the Thai King Taksin of Thonburi and slowly (but inevitably) came under the central control of Bangkok.

Today Chiang Mai is famous for its hilltribe treks, ethnic handicrafts and more than 300 temples. Despite escalating tourist development, it is still a small, relaxed and easy-going city with few of the pressures of Bangkok. The people are friendly, the air is cool and there is enough to see and do to keep you busy for a week or more. Chiang Mai is half as noisy and polluted as Bangkok, and Chiang Rai, further north, is half as noisy and polluted as Chiang Mai. That is where to go to visit the famous Golden Triangle (the old opium-dealing centre) and to really get away from city life.

Chiang Mai, and the north generally, has its high season from December through to February. By March, a lot of travellers are drifting towards the southern beaches, but several return for the big Songkran (water-throwing) festival of 13-15 April. This is a lot of fun. Though it is a nationwide event, it is always best in Chiang Mai!

ARRIVAL/DEPARTURE

Air

There are now six flights a day between Chiang Mai and Bangkok. The short one-hour flight costs 1275B by day and a little less by night. Chiang Mai's airport is 5 km out of town, around 30B by *tuk-tuk* or 60B by taxi.

Rail

From Bangkok, there is an express train at 6 p.m., arriving at 7.05 a.m. and a special express at 7.40 p.m., arriving at 7.55 a.m. There are three rapid trains daily, at 6.40 a.m., 3 p.m. and 10 p.m., but they take a long 15 hours to Chiang Mai. On the express trains, you can get second-class tickets for around £10, inclusive of sleeper charge. The rapid trains are third class only and tickets cost 15lB. From Chiang Mai, express trains return to Bangkok at 5.25 p.m. and 7.10 p.m. and rapid trains at 6.30 a.m., 4.05 p.m. and 8.45 p.m. Tickets should be booked at least a day ahead, either at the rail station, or from hotels/travel agents.

CHIANG MAI

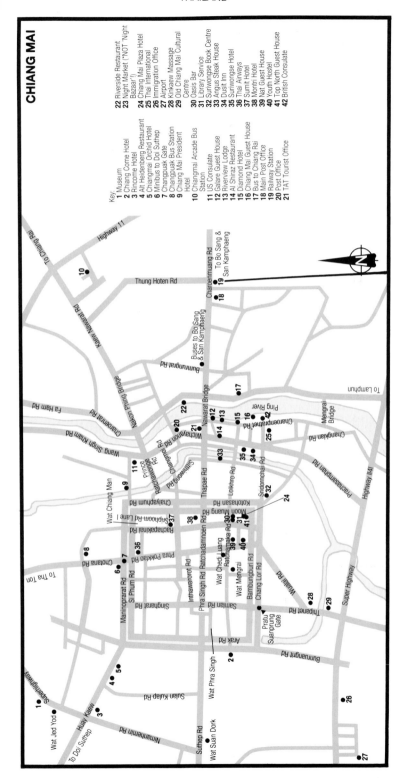

Key:
1 Museum
2 Chiang Come Hotel
3 Rincome Hotel
4 Alt Heidenberg Restaurant
5 Chiangmai Orchid Hotel
6 Minibus to Doi Suthep
7 Changpuak Gate
8 Changpuak Bus Station
9 Chiang Mai President Hotel
10 Chiangmai Arcade Bus Station
11 US Consulate
12 Galare Guest House
13 Riverview Lodge
14 Al Shiraz Restaurant
15 Diamond Hotel
16 Chiang Mai Guest House
17 Bus to Chiang Rai
18 Main Post Office
19 Railway Station
20 Post Office
21 TAT Tourist Office
22 Riverside Restaurant
23 Night Market ("NOT 'Night Bazaar'!)
24 Chiang Mai Plaza Hotel
25 Thai International
26 Immigration Office
27 Airport
28 Kinkaew Massage
29 Old Chiang Mai Cultural Centre
30 Oasis Bar
31 Library Service
32 Suriwongse Book Centre
33 Angus Steak House
34 Dusit Inn
35 Suriwongse Hotel
36 Thai Airways
37 Sumit Hotel
38 Montri Hotel
39 Nat Guest House
40 Youth Hostel
41 Top North Guest House
42 British Consulate

Road

Buses from Bangkok's Northern Bus Terminal take eight to nine hours to Chiang Mai and cost around 180B non-air-conditioned, 250B air-conditioned. Several tour buses make the Bangkok-Chiang Mai run and charge a little more. The **VIP** bus is definitely the best bet at 275B, offering a hostess, a lunch-box of chicken drumsticks, cokes and cakes, a video and well-spaced seats (fully reclining, lots of leg room and comfortable). In Bangkok seats on this bus are sold in Banglampoo and Soi Ngam Duphli. In Chiang Mai the main agent is Sombat Tour at the bus stand opposite Dusit Inn Hotel. Most buses going back to Bangkok leave in the morning, around 8 or 9 a.m., from the Arcade terminus 2 km out of town. If you are flying out of Thailand and do not wish to return to the capital, you can ask to be put off at Don Muang airport, which is en route.

TOURIST SERVICES

There is a TAT tourist office (tel: 235334) at 135 Praisanee Rd, just below Nawarat Bridge. It is open from 8.30 a.m. to 4.30 p.m. daily and supplies masses of information. Most travellers come here to enquire about trekking and are given *Travel North* and *Hilltribe Trekking in North Thailand*, two useful monthlies. Also good are freebies like *What's On, Where to Go* and *Welcome to Chiang Mai & Chiang Rai*. TAT issues a very comprehensive city map and Nancy Chandler's 60B map is worth having, but if you are going sightseeing by motorbike or by bus, you will need a tourist map of Chiang Mai (40B), which marks bus routes. A big selection of maps, guides and second-hand books is available from D K Book House on Ta Pae Rd and the Library Service at 21/l Ratchamankha Soi 2, near Oasis Bar, Moon Muang Rd.

The GPO on Charoen Muang Rd (east of Nawarat Bridge) is open from 8.30 a.m. to 12 noon, 1 p.m. to 4 p.m. weekdays, until 12 noon on weekends. The smaller (more central) post office just above Warorot market is closed on Sundays. Overseas phone calls can be made at the main GPO (24 hours) or at the International Telephone Service, 44 Seedorn-chai Rd (9 a.m. to 10.30 p.m.). The Immigration Office, for visa extensions, is off Highway 1141 near the airport. After the banks close, change money at Krung Thai Bank Exchange on Ta Pae Rd (open till 6 p.m.) or Bangkok Bank Exchange at the Night Bazaar Plaza (open till 10 p.m.).

SIGHTS

The first thing to do, if you are up here to see the hilltribes, is to book a trek. While that is coming together (it usually takes two to three days) you can visit the temples, the markets and the handicraft centres. Getting around Chiang Mai is pretty easy. The old thirteenth-century city, with its moat and few remnants of thick walls, is small and compact, ideal for exploration by bicycle. Trips further afield can be tackled by motorbike. Several places along Moon Muang Rd hire out cycles (20-25B/day) and motorbikes (100-250B/day), or you can enquire at your hotel/guest house. Self-drive car hire is around 1200B a day through Avis (tel: 221316) or Hertz (tel: 235496), a little cheaper through M Tour (tel: 251500) or Suda Car Rent (tel: 210030). *Songthaew* minibuses are 5B a ride (although you have to know exactly where you are going) and man-powered *samlors* will take you as far as the National Museum on the superhighway for about 30B return. Motorised *tuk-tuks* should charge 10B for short hops, 20B for long ones. In practice, they double their prices when traffic is heavy (i.e. after 4 p.m.).

If you want to see a lot in a short time, it could be worth hiring a *tuk-tuk* for the day. They ask around 350B and if there are two or three of you, you can share costs. The best 'deal' by *tuk-tuk* is to the crafts villages of **Bo Sang** and **San Kamphaeng**, some 12 km east of Chiang Mai. Since the drivers get appearance money for every place you visit, they will happily take you around for a whole morning for just 50B! Most of the factories have good workshop layouts (where you can see the working processes) and they are usually open 9 a.m. to 5.30 p.m., closed Sundays. Ask to go to **Shinawatra Thai Silk** (tel: 331950) which sells high-quality handloom silk – fabrics from 260B (two-ply) to 390B (four-ply) per metre, patterned kimonos at 1800B, ladies' silk jackets from 1000B, scarves from 350B and cheaper cotton materials from 90B a metre. Men can buy a double-breasted silk suit, lined and interfaced, for just £90 and fitted and made up in only three days. **Chiangmai Sudaluk** (tel: 331489) deals in beautifully carved teakwood and rosewood furniture – secretary tables from £1300, mini-bars from £1350, solid teak bureaux from £80 and complete rosewood coffee-table sets, inlaid with mother of pearl, for £6000 (all prices inclusive of packing, shipping and insurance). Popular low-price buys include laughing Buddhas and lacquered elephants. Nearby **Na Na Phan Silverware** (tel: 331534), has rings, necklaces, brooches and earrings (100 per cent silver), bowls, tea-sets, cutlery (80 per cent silver, 20 per cent nickel), blue sapphires (from 400B per carat) and hilltribe jewellery. Expect a 50 per cent discount on all labelled goods – *before* you start serious haggling! As elsewhere, your bargaining power is strongest when you buy a few pieces, rather than just one or two. **Laitong Lacquerware** (tel: 331178) is a bit pricey, but, as with the silver, you know the quality is good – most pieces here have at least seven coats of lacquer and will not chip or crack. **Bo Sang Umbrella Village** (tel: 331566) sells a wide range of attractive souvenirs: umbrellas from 140B, lampshades from 30B and gaily painted fans from 60B. For a small fee, artisans will daub your purse, wallet or bag with a dramatic Chinese dragon or peacock.

At the crossroads of many cultural realms, Chiang Mai's temples bear the imprint of Burma, Laos, Lanna Thai and Haripunchai, as well as the mainstream Thai influence from the Ayutthaya era. Within the city walls there are three major temples, all quite close to each other. At the junction of Samlan and Phra Singh roads, **Wat Phra Singh** was begun in 1345 and finished around 1600. Controversy still surrounds it. Some claim its main Singh Buddha image originated from Ceylon (Sri Lanka), but it doesn't look particularly Ceylonese and is identical to two other images, one in Bangkok and one in Nakhon Si Thammarat. **Wat Chedi Luang**, on Phra Pokklao Rd near the intersection with Rajmankha Rd, has a massive, partially ruined *chedi*, commenced in 1401, enlarged to a height of 86 m in 1454, damaged by earthquake in 1545 and presently being restored. The eastern niche is said to have contained Thailand's most sacred object, the famous Emerald Buddha. In the north-east corner of the old city, near Sumit Hotel on Ratchaphakhinai Rd, **Wat Chiang Man** is the oldest extant temple in Chiang Mai. Once the residence of King Mengrai, it contains a 10-cm-high Crystal Buddha, thought to have come from the Lopburi area 1,800 years ago.

Wat Jed Yod sits out on the superhighway, north west of town. Famous for its likeness to the Bodhgaya shrine in India, this attractive temple was built over 500 years ago to commemorate 2,000 years of the Buddhist era. Its name comes from the seven brick spires on the roof, or some say from the seven weeks Buddha spent in Bodhgaya after his enlightenment. A short walk down from Wat Jed Yod is the small but interesting **National Museum**, open from 9 a.m. to 4 p.m. Wednesday to Sunday, admission 10B. Returning south down Nimmanhemen Rd, cycle (or direct your *tuk-tuk*) to **Wat Suan Dork** on Cherng Doy Rd. In the fourteenth century, this 'Flower Garden Monastery' was the Lanna Thai kings' pleasure gardens. Later, it became their cemetery. Wat Suan Dork has a large number of whitewashed stone stupas housing their ashes. The central stupa is said to contain a Buddha relic which

arrived here on the back of a white elephant. The same jumbo wandered on until it stopped (and died) up on Doi Suthep. The hill's famous wat, **Wat Prathat**, was consequently built there. A pilgrimage to this temple is more or less obligatory. *Songthaews* charge 35B to Doi Suthep from Chang Phuak (White Elephant) Gate on Manee Noparat Rd (north wall of the moat). The temple itself is nothing special, but early morning views from it are superb.

If you want to see something completely different, visit the newly discovered ruins of **Wat Mengrai** south of Chiang Mai. Turn up at 8.30 a.m. and look out for a German guide called Milos. He was one of the archaeologists who excavated the site and for 150B he will give you a full rundown on the place, plus any other tourist information you may want. Wat Mengrai is about 700 years old. It was covered by sand during floods, and (to date) they have only excavated some 28 probable temple areas there. 'You don't have to be an archaeological buff to enjoy Mengrai,' wrote one visitor, 'it is fascinating stuff! Milos gives you a great tour, then takes you back to his house for concentrated information on what to do and see and how to see it in northern Thailand. It is a perfect introduction to the traveller who's never been to that part of the country. He'll even store your pack in his house for free while you traipse off following his suggestions for travel.'

TREKKING

The Northern Highlands around Chiang Mai are home to some half-million hilltribe people, members of six major groups. The largest group is the Karen, who originated in Burma and who began settling in Thailand several centuries ago. The less populous tribes – the Meo, Lahu, Yao, Akha and Lisu – are descended from Chinese and Tibetan Mongols and only began arriving in Thailand during the last century. Each of the hilltribes has its own customs, costumes, crafts and religious practices. If you are trekking out to see them, a prior visit to the Tribal Research Centre at Chiang Mai University (5 km out of town) is a must. There is an excellent library here, open 8.30 a.m. to 12 noon, 1 p.m. to 4.30 p.m., closed weekends.

Before booking your trek, consider the following. Over the past ten years, the Thai government has made poppy eradication a top priority. The general effect of this on the hilltribes, suddenly deprived of opium and encouraged to grow substitute crops (mainly vegetables) instead, is critical. At present, most of their income comes from selling craft goods and (illegally produced) opium to tourists. The arrival of tourism has not exactly been a boon to the hilltribes. Since the tourists have come to the villages to smoke opium, most of the men in the villages no longer work, because the sale of opium is much easier than working in the jungle. Nowadays, most of them just smoke and sleep. Also, the villages are losing their customs, cultures and ability to produce traditional clothing quickly. Most of the younger generation have no knowledge (or interest) in producing handicrafts. Overexposure to tourists has left them dangerously dependent on Western money and Western luxuries. If you must take presents for the hilltribe people, give something practical and constructive like thin rope, needles and thread, even a torch, in return for them doing you a favour. Don't give something for nothing, otherwise the children will start expecting it. Giving some antiseptic and fungal creams to the headman is fine, as his village may only see a doctor once in six months.

The trekking situation is becoming increasingly competitive, with over 100 agencies operating out of Chiang Mai. Most charge 250B per day, inclusive of guide, transport and food. If you want elephants or river-rafting, that will be 250B apiece extra. The average cost of a three-day trek is therefore in the region of 1250B. I checked quite a few agencies and came to the conclusion that you get what you pay for. If you pay only 900B, do not expect the perfect trip; there are many stories going around about guides not speaking English, getting lost all the time, etc. The treks all go to 'non-tourist areas which we have just opened last week'. It is worth paying a little extra for a quality trek from a reliable agency like Singha Travel at 277 Ta Pae Rd – great five-day four-night trips at 2000B, which go to the area near the Burmese border, or even into Burma itself. Now that the north (around Chiang Rai) has become overtrekked, many of the Chiang Mai agencies are sending treks westward (around Pai) or north west (around Chiang Dao). In the high season (December to February) you will often have to 'share' the villages en route with other trek groups. In the low season, this is not so much of a problem. Good trek companies come and go and your best recommendations will always come from speaking to other travellers. People still speak well of Aiyaret Tour, 422 Ta Pae Rd (tel: 235396) – a bit pricey, but the guides are good, there are no other tourists around, and you really feel you are in the jungle. New Daret's Guest House has popular treks, run by a chain-smoking guide (Pom) who 'hates hills'. The Youth Hostel has a positive feeling for the local people and has a very good relationship with the villages.

Treks, with elephants and rafting, are 1300B for three to four days – about as cheap as you will find without losing quality! Whoever you go with, *don't* leave valuables (especially credit cards) with agencies for safekeeping; there have been too many reports of theft. Travel light (take just a change of socks, T-shirt, underwear, a towel, swimming costume, hat, a camera, film and torch) and do not bring too much money. You can leave your gear behind at your hotel in Chiang Mai.

EXCURSIONS

It can be much cheaper to start your trek from the **Chiang Rai** area than from Chiang Mai, and you will not have to spend a lot of time in a car travelling to the trek start point. Many travellers use Chiang Rai as a jumping off point for the **Golden Triangle**, the famous opium-producing centre, and various places of interest along the Burma/Laos border. Green buses (No. 166) go to Chiang Rai half-hourly from the stop at Nawarat Bridge in Chiang Mai. The three to three and a half hour trip costs 47B, or 66B with air-conditioning. An increasingly popular way of going to Chiang Rai is boat/raft trips down the Kok River from **Tha Ton**. Orange buses (No. 1231) run regularly to Tha Ton from the bus station north of Chang Puak Gate in Chiang Mai. At Tha Ton, stay at **Thip's Travellers House** – 30B a person, great food and a relaxing riverside situation. Mrs Thip is a first-class business woman, but she knows how to take care of travellers. She can arrange good local treks and river-raft trips (September to February) to Chiang Rai. The boat trip from Tha Ton to Chiang Rai is scenic, but expensive – 160B on the big boat (leaves 12.30 p.m. daily) and 1600B for eight people on your own longtail boat. You can stop at the villages (Akha, Karen, Lahu) along the way and also at an interesting cave wat near Chiang Rai, or you can opt to go straight to **Chiang Saen**, 60 km past Chiang Rai, on the Mekong River which separates Thailand and Laos. Here, you can see the sunrise over Laos and catch glimpses of the people on the other side if you get a room with a 'view' at **Gin's** or **Siam** guest houses overlooking the river. Chiang Saen is pretty quiet and by far the best place from which to explore the Golden Triangle. Take a bicycle/motorbike 10 km north to **Sop Ruak**, the place where Thailand, Burma and Laos meet at the confluence of the Mae Khong and Ruak rivers. Enjoy the views from the hilltop temple, then travel on 30 km to **Mai Sai** at the Burmese border. Here stay at **Mae Sai** or **Northern** guest houses, try the seafood at **Rim Nam** restaurant near the bridge, and shop for Burmese gems and handicrafts at **Meang Lai Antique Shop**. From Mae Sai, take directions to nearby **Cheng Dao Cave Temple** (full of carved Buddhas, stalactites and snakes) and, a little further on, the **Monkey Temple.** South of this, a junction leads the way up to **Doi Tun**, the highest peak in northern Thailand with a tenth-century *chedi* at the summit. Halfway up the mountain, 7 km from the main road, is **Akha Guest House**, with cheap rooms, cosy campfire meals in the evenings, unforgettable sunsets and great hilltribe walks. Drive down to **Mae Chan**, 34 km south of Mae Sai and check out the colourful covered market.

From here, it is a 15-km drive (or 10B by pick-up truck) to **Laan Tong Lodge**, a marvellous little place set on a scenic creek, surrounded by seven hilltribes and several villages. Stay at the 'hilltribe bungalow' of your choice (30 to 80B) and enjoy fishing, swimming, trekking and superb vegetarian fare. If travelling by motorbike (you will need a powerful one of at least 125cc), take a ride up to **Doi Mae Salong**, 36 km north west of Mae Chan for fantastic scenery, handicraft bargains at the **Hilltribe Welfare Centre** (20 km out of Mae Chan) and a remote Kuomintang settlement, **Santi Kiri**, just 3 km from the Burmese border. This is where the families of the 93rd (Kuomintang) Regiment fled after the 1949 revolution in China.

Sample a 'gourmet' meal at the highest restaurant in Thailand, take in the breathtaking views, stay (if you can afford it) at **Mae Salong Resort** for 400B a night and then drive back down to **Chiang Rai**. Here try **Boon Young** guest house, 1054 Sanambin Rd, with dormitory beds from 30B, single rooms from 40B, doubles with shower from 70B. It is pleasant, relaxed bungalow-style accommodation. If you are trekking out of Chiang Rai, go to **Lek's** guest house (Dang is a great host, try the snake curry) or to **Chat House** near the Kok River pier. Both places also supply good information and hire out motorbikes. The best mid-range accommodation is **Maekok Villa**, 445 Singhakai Rd (tel: 311786) and **Wiang Inn**, 893 Phaholyothin Rd (tel: 711543), has a pool and air-conditioned rooms from around 500B. Most people try a meal at **Haw Nalika** (yummy Thai food) near the clocktower or **Golden Triangle** (steaks, grills, etc.) in Phaholythin Rd.

Note: **Pai** is three hours north west of Chiang Mai (50B bus from Arcade bus station). It is a small town in a lovely mountain setting, which is very unspoilt. Stay at **Duang** guest house, eat at **Pai in the Sky** and do not miss the hot springs early in the morning. It is a good place to trek from too.

SHOPPING

With the exception of hilltribe handicrafts and copied watches, Bangkok has a much better shopping than Chiang Mai and a much better selection of goods. The main focus of shopping in Chiang Mai is the huge, sprawling **Night Bazaar** in Chang Klang Rd, which runs from around 6 p.m. to midnight daily. It has two central buildings: the **Chiang Mai Plaza**, a three-storey covered area in mock northern style and **Ying Ping Bazaar**, an old-style covered market reserved for the hilltribes. The Plaza sells mainly fake designer clothes and shoes, attractive handpainted fans (in the basement) and luxurious silk robes (on the second floor). Outside, on the street, you can buy copy watches cheaper than anywhere else in Thailand. For 275B apiece I got a Rolex and a Dunhill and both of them, to my surprise, are still working. The Ying Ping bazaar sells the full range of hilltribe produce: Karen shawls, Akha head-dresses, Mon jewellery, Meo silver belts and chains, antique Buddhas, painted fans, wooden cowbells, lacquered rice-whisky cups, Lawa wallet and letter containers, crossbows, wickerwork fishing traps, opium weights and pipes, dance masks and musical instruments. The most popular buys are embroidered hilltribe jackets and beautiful quilted bedspreads in tribal designs. For the best bargains, turn up in the early afternoon as this is when the hilltribe folk drop off their fresh produce.

Note: silver, silk and lacquerware should be bought at the Bo Sang craft factories out of town (cf. Sights). Prices are higher than at the Night Market, but quality is far superior.

ENTERTAINMENT

The most relaxing massage in town is given by **Rinkaew Povech** at 183/4 Wualai Rd, in the *soi* next to the Old Cultural Centre. This is an authentic (no funny business) Thai massage at 150-200B per hour, an excellent way of winding down after a hard day's sightseeing. The **Chiang Mai Centre for Traditional Massage** at 33/30 Sirimungklajan, charges 2000B for a six-lesson course in massage – to book, call Sombat Tapanya (tel: 221122, ext 5422) from 9 a.m. to 4 p.m. One-month meditation courses are given at **Wat Rampong** temple. No costs, just donations. To get there, take a No. 1 bus to Talad Payom market, then a 4B *tuk-tuk* (set route) to the temple. If you fancy a swim, you can use the pools at the **Anodard, Prince** and **President** hotels for 20/25B per day. Bowling is fun at the alley opposite the Chiang Inn Hotel. The balls are cracked, but they still work!

Chiang Mai has a very lively nightlife of discos, bars, nightclubs and coffee shops. Two popular discos are **Plaza** at Chiang Mai Plaza Hotel and **Club 77** at Orchid Hotel. Friday night is for dancing and admission is 70-90B with one free drink. The **Riverside** at 9-11 Jarernrasd Rd, opposite Chinda Hospital, is a hot nightspot. It is not noted for its food, but it has a good location on the river and great jazz/folk music. **Oasis Bar** at 27 Moon Muang Rd is a friendly ex-pat bar with live music downstairs (9 p.m. to midnight) and a video lounge upstairs (movies 7-9 p.m.). **Blues Bar** near New Daret's Guest House has just about the best collection of blues and R&B in Thailand. If you are in the night market and want to take a break from shopping, try **Jack's** and **Marlborough**, two snug little bars on the ground floor of the Plaza.

ACCOMMODATION
Good guest houses in the 250 to 500B range are **River View Lodge** (tel: 251109) at 25 Charoenprathat Rd and **Top North** (tel: 213900) at 15 Moon Muang Rd Soi 2. Small hotels like the **Anodard** (tel: 211055), 57 Ratchamankha Rd, the **President** (tel: 251025), 226 Vichayanon Rd, and the **Prince** (tel: 236396), 3 Taiwang Rd, overlap into that price range – they are in the 400 to 700B league, with pools, coffee shops and air-conditioned rooms. The **Suriwongse** (tel: 236733), **Dusit Inn** (tel: 236835) and **Chiang Inn** (tel: 235655) are the big 'night market' hotels – located respectively at 110, 112 and 100 Changklan Rd. All three have pools, restaurants, coffee shops and nightclubs/discos. Rooms start at around 900B single, 1000-1200B double. The most expensive hotel is the **Chiang Mai Plaza** (tel: 252050) at 92 Sridonchai Rd – it has a nice location, all mod cons and rooms for 1400B single, 1600B double. To my mind, the best upmarket buy is **Diamond Hotel** (tel: 233947), 33/10 Charoenprathat, Rd. It is about 600B for an air-conditioned double and you can ask for a discount out of season. Their coffee shop offers good food, well served at reasonable prices.

Cheap guest houses cost between 60 and 100B a night and for that you should be able to get running water in your room, a shower and a toilet. Air-conditioned rooms start at around 150/180B. If you come during the rainy season (June to October) you will find hotel costs at their lowest, only 40 per cent of posted prices. The rainy season is one hour of rain and two days of sunshine! April and May are the hottest months, but every night is cool and comfortable – you really do not need air-conditioning in Chiang Mai.

There are now over 100 cheap guest houses to choose from and nearly every traveller you meet will be able to recommend a different one. A few current favourites are **S P Court** at Soi 7 Moon Muang Rd (80-180B), **New Daret's** on the other side of the gate from Daret's Inn (80-100B), **Lek House** at 22 Chaiyaphum Rd (70-80B), **Nat** at 7 Prapokklao Rd (100-120B), **Rose** at 25 Ramwithi Soi 1 (80-100B) and **Pun Pun** at 321 Charoen Rat Rd (40-60B). The 'three free nights accommodation' promised by Bangkok bus operators is often in bug-ridden filthy hovels like **Noi** or **Camp of Troppe** – backpackers, beware!

Note: all rates for big hotels are subject to additions of 11 per cent government tax and 10 per cent service charge.

FOOD
The definitive eating experience in Chiang Mai is a Khantoke dinner at the **Old Cultural Centre**, 185/3 Wualai Rd. Here you can enjoy a succession of small-bowl northern dishes while watching a delightful programme of traditional dance. This is a fine opportunity to see a number of hilltribes and to study the differences in their appearance and costume. Shows start at 7 p.m. nightly and tickets (200B) are sold in hotels, at travel agents and on the street so you should have no trouble in buying one.

Chiang Mai has any number of good restaurants, many of them ranged along Moon Muang/Ta Pae Roads or in the Night Market. A personal favourite of mine is the **Bierstube** at 33/64 Moon Muang Rd. It specialises in German food, but also has Chinese and Thai fare. Come here for the best hot dogs, home fries and sausages in town. Another place I like consistently is the **Nang Nual** seafood restaurant at 27 Koa Klang Rd, Nong Hoi. It is particularly famous for its king lobster (600B per kg, serves four) and is most pleasant in the afternoon (between 4 and 7 p.m.), which is before the tour groups arrive. For pastas and pizzas (and a wide range of Italian wines), try **Hungry Horse** at 31 Moon Muang Rd. **Ban Rai Steak House**, next to Wat Chiang Man, offers steaks, grills and popular European-style cooking. The best Chinese restaurant is **Chinatown Suki** at 147/13-15 Chang Klang Rd – well-known for its *sukiyaki* and seafood. Two good Indian-Pakistani restaurants are **Al Shiraz** opposite the Night Market Plaza and **Ali Baba** at the end of the night market, near TAT. For northern Thai food, check out **Aroon Rai** at 43/45 Kotchasarn Rd – get a group together and order the maximum number of dishes. Go vegetarian at **Whole Earth** on Si Dornchai Rd, past the Chang Klang intersection and order a big bowl of Chiang Mai's famous noodles (only 8B) at **Khao Soi Lam Duang** on Charoen Rat Rd, near Je T'Aime Guest House. If you like cheap snacks, there is excellent street food all over town: hot dogs, burgers, chicken drumsticks and spicy sizzling *satay*.

SUKHOTHAI – LOPBURI – AYUTTHAYA

Visit these three ancient capitals on your way south from Chiang Mai to Bangkok.

SUKHOTHAI

Sukhothai is famous for two things: it was the capital of the first Thai kingdom in the 13th century and it is the place where Loi Krathong, Thailand's loveliest festival – is celebrated most spectacularly each year (October/November). The name Sukhothai means 'Dawn of Happiness', and it was here that the first distinctively Thai state emerged at what had been an outpost of the Khmer empire ruling from Anghor. In 1238, having already captured **Si Satchanalai**, a royal town 55 km to the north, two rebel princes seized Sukhothai from the Khmer and proclaimed an independent Thai state. Under King Ramkamhaeng, the son of one of these princes, Sukhothai's influence stretched as far south as Nakhon Si Thammarat, to Vientiane in Laos and Pegu in south Burma. During Ramkamhaeng's short 19-year reign (often referred to as the golden age of Thai history) Theravada Buddhism from Sri Lanka was adopted and codified, while Brahman elements from the Khmer empire were integrated into the kingdom's socio-religious life and court rituals, much of which remain today.

As Buddhism flourished, so did art and architecture. The distinctive bell-shaped *chedis* of many of Sukhothai's temples show a clear Singhalese influence, in contrast to the Khmer forms of rounded towers (*prangs*) which are best seen in **Wat Sri Sawai**. The lotus-bud *chedi* of **Wat Mahathat**, a unique Sukhothai development, was built to enshrine Buddha relics brought from Sri Lanka. King Ramkamhaeng is also credited with inventing the Thai system of writing by revising the various forms of Khmer, Mon and south Indian scripts.

Sukhothai's glorious rule was short, lasting a brief 140 years before it was annexed by the rising new power of Ayutthaya in 1379. In 1833 a monk, later to become King Mongkut of the present Chakri dynasty, discovered a stone tablet among Sukhothai's by then jungle-clad ruins. Its long inscription set out the main achievements of King Ramkamhaeng's reign and led to a renewal of interest in this period. Attempts at restoration were only begun in 1953, however, and it took until the late 1970s for the site, spread over 70 sq km and containing some 200 places of significance, to be fully identified. Today, 'Old' Sukhothai, some 12 km from the new town, has been redesignated an Historical Park, with over 210 hectares of landscaped trees and shrubs and restored ornamental ponds, lakes and canals.

The best place to start a tour of Sukhothai is at the **National Museum** (open from 9 a.m. to 4 p.m., closed Monday/Tuesday), just outside the city moat. The sculpture, art, pottery, weapons and artefacts here will give you an idea of the skilful heights reached by this fourteenth-century culture. There is also a replica of Ramkamhaeng's famous stone inscription and a detailed scale model of the old city which is useful for orientation. Within the massive city walls (2000 by 1600 m) are **Wat Mahathat** and the **Royal Palace**. The temple is Sukhothai's best, with over 200 religious structures, including 98 stupas of various shapes, a huge lotus-bud *chedi*, and numerous stucco Buddha images. The seated Buddha figures among the *viharas* (monasteries) are some of the most beautiful at the site. To the north of Mahathat is another impressive temple, **Wat Si Chum**, with a superb example of Sukhothai art: a monumental stucco-over-brick Buddha image in the attitude of subduing *mara* (opposing forces or beliefs). The enclosing *mondop* walls are 3 m thick and the Buddha is 11.3 m wide from knee to knee.

To explore Sukhothai fully takes at least two or three days, as its many monuments are scattered far and wide, including wats and dams in the hills to the west and a celadon factory to the north which was recently excavated by the Fine Arts Department.

Sukhothai is five hours by air-conditioned bus (84B) from Chiang Mai. If you get the 8 a.m. bus there on your way south, you will have time for a good look around Old Sukhothai the same afternoon. Cheap and friendly guest houses in the new town, like **Number 4** at 234/6 Jarodwitheethong Rd, **Yupa House** at 44/10 Pravetnakorn Rd (across the bridge, overlooking the river) and the brand-new **Sri Kalaya** (1 km out of town, on the ring road), hire out bicycles and motorbikes on which to visit the old city. The mid-priced **Chinawat Hotel**, 1-3 Nikorn Kasem Rd, has minibus daytours round the ruins for 200B each. The next morning, you can catch a bus (18B) to **Si Satchanalai** and hire bikes there for the day. It is similar to old Sukothai – better in some ways since the temples have not been renovated – and 5 km north there is a very good kiln excavation with a brand-new museum built over it. This is far superior to any excavation presentation I have seen in in Europe and definitely worth a look.

If you are short on time, the night bus down to Bangkok from Sukhothai (dep. 10.45 p.m., arr. 6 a.m.) is very comfortable. Otherwise, get a bus to Phitsanoluke (one hour, 15B) and take the 9.14 a.m. train south to Lopburi (five hours).

LOPBURI

Lopburi is the poor relation of Thailand's temple towns. It gets far fewer visitors than Sukhothai or Ayutthaya. Nothing remains of the original fourth-century Lavo civilisation and all that is left of the tenth Khmer capital which replaced it are a few crumbling old temples with looming *prang* towers. Nevertheless, this is a friendly little town with some nice bakeries and ice-cream parlours and a particularly good guest house. This is the **Travellers Drop-In Centre** at 34 Wichayen Rd, Soi 3 Muang, run by a young English teacher called Richard. If you help out with his lessons to Thai students, he will put you up overnight (clean 50B double rooms) and will arrange all your sightseeing. Places to visit include the **National Museum** in the king's palace (open from 9 a.m. to 4 p.m., closed Monday/Tuesday), **Phaulkon's House**, home of the Greek advisor to King Narai during Ayutthaya's heyday and **Nartasin School of Art**, a well-known centre of classical Thai dance and music. If you are not staying over, you'll just have time to visit **Wat Phra Sri Ratana Mahathat**, a large twelfth-century Khmer shrine opposite the railway station and **Phra Prang Sam Yod**, Lopburi's famous 'Three Pagodas' landmark (400 m walk away), before catching the 5.55 p.m. train on to Ayutthaya. This train arrives at 7.07 p.m. and continues on to Bangkok, arriving there at 8.30 p.m.

AYUTTHAYA

Ayutthaya was the capital of Thailand from 1350 until it was sacked by the Burmese in 1767. The Burmese did such a good job on it that it is still impossible, despite recent renovations of its temples and monuments, to visualise the city's original splendour. Situated on an island at the junction of three rivers, it was once a major trade centre and one of the wealthiest cities in Asia. A day trip is quite sufficient to see the various sights. The land is flat, so cycling is easy. Get a *samlor* from the train station to **B J Guest House** at 16/7 Naresuan Rd. They really make you feel part of the family here and Mr Hung and Nu (who run it) will mind your bags while you go sightseeing. Touring the ruins by bicycle (30B from B J's) is a much better idea than hiring an expensive *tuk-tuk*. Bear in mind that for every historical site you visit (each one covers several acres, so you can spend quite a bit of time walking round just one) the entrance fee is 20B and there are about eight different sites to see. If you are on a budget, do a little research first and decide which ones sound most interesting or appealing. Alternatively, when you cycle round you can see which ones look particularly good. Ayutthaya could be expensive for the budget traveller.

The ruins are best visited in the cool of the early morning. Start out at **Chao Sam Phraya Museum** (open from 9 a.m. to 4 p.m., closed Monday/Tuesday) near the centre of town, which sells a good 20B map-guide. Off the island, visit the massive ruined *chedi* of **Wat Yai Chai Mongkol** to the south east, then (close by) **Wat Phanom Choeng** with its 19-m-high seated Buddha, the largest extant Buddha image in Ayutthaya. Walk down to the river pier and take a two-hour river trip (300B, share costs in a group) to **Wat Chai Wattanaram** and **Wat Buddaisawan**, two evocative old temples with Cambodian-style *prangs* situated on the water's edge. Or cycle up to the causeway (near the railway station) and cross onto the island for **Wat Phra Ram** and **Wat Mahathat** (climb the central *prangs* for nice views) and **Wat Na Phra Mane** (the only temple left untouched by the Burmese in 1767, housing Ayutthaya's most beautiful surviving Buddha image). Don't expect too much of the ruins – they are pretty ruined. If you can afford a guide (100B an hour, ask around at the railway station) he will help to make them come alive for you. If you are interested in antiques, there are some fascinating 'pot shops' close to the royal palace, full of treasures from the ancient sites of Ayutthaya, Sukhothai and Sawankhalok. They are much less touristy (i.e. less expensive) than the antique shops in Bangkok or Chiang Mai.

Many people seem to go to Ayutthaya on a day trip from Bangkok. Shoestringers take one of several daily trains from Hualamphong station (15B, one and a half hours). Moneyed travellers favour the deluxe boat tour from the Oriental Hotel – 850B, including a buffet lunch and an air-conditioned coach around the former capital's ruins and **Bang Pa In** Summer Palace. If you are on your way south to Bangkok by train, Bang Pa In is one stop down the railway line from Ayutthaya (3B) and well worth a detour. Take a 2B *songthaew* from the station to the palace (open from 8.30 a.m. to 3.30 p.m., closed Monday and Friday), see the priceless collection of jade and porcelain in the **Phra Thinang Wehat Chamrun** (the 'Peking Palace' inside the summer palace) and admire the picture-postcard Thai pavilion in the the middle of the lake. If you have time, take a cable-car ride across the river to **Wat Niwega Thamprawat**, a Buddhist temple built in the style of a European Christian church by Rama V.

HUA HIN

Thailand's oldest beach resort has cheap clean hotels, friendly little bars and restaurants, breezy wide streets, relatively few tourists and a cheerful seaside atmosphere. Over the past few years, it has escalated from a quiet fishing village and Thai weekend holiday spot to an international-style resort, but it is still one of the most peaceful and pleasant centres of the south. Hua Hin built its reputation as a quiet, conservative escape from Bangkok (230 km north) and it has tried to maintain that image, so do not expect any Samui-style discos and beach parties here. This is essentially a place to wind down and relax. Between noon and 3 p.m., which is siesta time, there is hardly a soul out of doors. The beach is nothing special, but the sea is good for swimming and you can take pony rides on the sands. Rama VII (1925-35) built his summer residence at Hua Hin (still used by the royal family) and there are lots of old-fashioned hotels and buildings dotted around town. The surrounding scenery is beautiful and the local countryside is well worth touring by motorbike. Hua Hin is presently at a very nice stage of development, with a good blend of Thai and European food and facilities, a prestigious 18-hole golf course and a full range of water-sports. Expect this place to change rapidly in the next few years and get there before it does.

ARRIVAL/DEPARTURE
Rail
There are eight trains daily from Bangkok (four hours, 92B second class, 44B third class) and four trains a day from Hat Yai (13 hours, 244B second class, 116B third class). The 6.54 p.m. train from Hua Hin goes direct to Butterworth (777B first class, 363B second class). You can book tickets in advance (advisable) from the stationmaster's office, open from 8.30 a.m. to 4 p.m. weekdays, 8.30 a.m. to 12.30 p.m. Saturdays.

Road
Buses from Bangkok's Southern Terminal cost 41B ordinary, 74B air-conditioned, and they take just three to three and a half hours on the new highway. Leaving Hua Hin, the air-conditioned bus stand to Bangkok is in Srasong Rd. Buses to Samui and Krabi leave from the stand opposite Subhamitra Hotel, on the junction of the main road. They cannot be pre-booked, you just hop on if a seat is available.

TOURIST SERVICES
The Municipal Tourist Office (tel: 512120) at 114 Phetchkasem Rd is open from 8.30 a.m. to 4.30 p.m. daily. Staff are helpful and there is a wealth of printed information. The post office in Damnernkasem Rd is open from 8.30 a.m. to 4.30 p.m. weekdays, 9 a.m. to 12 noon weekends. The adjoining telephone office is open for overseas calls from 6 a.m. to 10 p.m. daily. After the banks close, you can change money at the currency exchange counter at Bank of Ayudhya, Phetkasem Rd, open from 8.30 a.m. to 6 p.m. daily. Western Tour, opposite Sirin Hotel, handles all southern-bound bus bookings and local sightseeing tours by bus or taxi.

THINGS TO DO
The beach is nice, but very narrow. When the tide comes in, it simply disappears. The sea can be a bit rough for swimming and it is worth a stroll along the sand before bathing to check for jellyfish. Swimming is particularly dangerous at high tide, when you cannot see the (sharp) submerged rocks. Walk down to **Miss Pou's** food stall on the beach, just past the Sofitel Hotel and you will be safe. Miss Pou is a friendly soul, who cooks good food, sells beers and cold drinks and lets you pay 'on the slate'. Unlike many other places, she does not charge for deckchairs and umbrellas. Horse-riding on the beach is 200B an hour and you do not need a pony-man.

Hiring motorbikes is a good way of getting out of town for the day. Try the rank on Phetkasem Rd, near Subhamitra Hotel – 150B/day for mopeds, 200B/day for big roadbikes. Check brakes and fuel before setting off and wear long trousers and trainers for safety. Head down Phetkasem Rd (past Royal Garden Resort) to Prachuap. After 15 minutes, you will come to a hilltop temple on the coast, just below Prachuap. This has a large white standing Buddha, facing out to sea and loads of monkeys. Walk up the steep stairway (via the Buddha) for excellent views of the coastline. Further on down the highway, 13 km out of Hua Hin, you will come to **Ban Khao Tao**, a small fishing village with a wide sweep of silk-soft sand, mirror-calm sea, pretty lagoons and excellent seafood. Try Disco Crabs and Yum Shrimps at friendly **Haad Khao Tao** restaurant. On the drive back, about 4 km out of Hua Hin, call in on **Khao Takiab** – an attractive hill temple with high bell-towers, little wooden outhouses and lots of sleepy dogs, plaster Buddhas and lotus ponds. The monks are friendly, and there is fine photography from the *bot* pavilion. The nice beach you can see from the top is **Suan Son**, a much better bet for swimming than Hua Hin. From the foot of Takiab, you can hire a small boat over to **Sing Toh Island** for fishing (if you have tackle) and swimming. **Khao Krilas**, close to

Hua Hin railway station

Takiab, is set inland with a Buddhist temple on the top. If you have not the money or inclination to hire a motorbike, take a local bus to Prachuap (from opposite the Rern Thong Garden Restaurant) and get off at Suan Son or Takiab. In the evening, stroll down to the pier at Hua Hin and watch the fishing boats bringing in their catch.

ENTERTAINMENT
A round on the world-famous Royal Golf Course costs 150B green fees (250B at weekends), 100B caddy and 300B club hire. Contact Royal Garden Resort to arrange a game. This hotel also offers tennis (100B/hour), windsurfing (150B/hour), catamarans (350B/hour), sailing boats (250B/hour), waterskiing (300B per 10 minutes), parasailing (350B per trip) and free indoor games. The sea at Hua Hin is a little rough for water-skiing, but it is ideal for sailing and windsurfing, especially in November. The best all-round month for water-sports is January.

There is not much in the way of night-time entertainment, but the **Satchmo Club** at Hotel Sofitel has live jazz every evening between 7 p.m. and midnight. The **Royal Garden Resort** offers a 'jungle music disco' nightly and the **Friendship** restaurant lays on a special menu at 250B every Wednesday, which includes Thai classical dancing at 9 p.m.

A popular meeting point is the **Snack House** near the night market. It has snooker, cheap draught beer, and great taped music – best of all, it is open till late.

SHOPPING
Sumon Thai Silk at 2786 Mitrafab Rd is a good place to shop for souvenirs, soft furnishings and Thai silk products. It has the cheapest (and best) tailor in town and can make up suits in 24 hours. **Khomapastr Textile Shop** at 218 Phetkasem Rd sells the full range of Hua Hin's hand-printed cottons – many unique designs at very reasonable prices.

ACCOMMODATION
Film buffs will recognise **Hotel Sofitel Central** (tel: 512021), 1 Damnoenkasem Rd, as the Hotel Le Phnom in the film *The Killing Fields*. It offers colonial-style villas from 1600B, a nice outdoor pool, large landscaped gardens and quaint topiary full of clipped elephants, dogs, ducks and peacocks. The international-class **Royal Garden Resort** (tel: 511881), 107/l Phetkasem Rd, lacks character but compensates with superb food, many recreations and a breezy seafront location. Rooms start at 1500B and are stylish and modern. Get one on the sixth or seventh floor, with sea views. Also recommended is the new **Sirin Hotel** (tel:

55

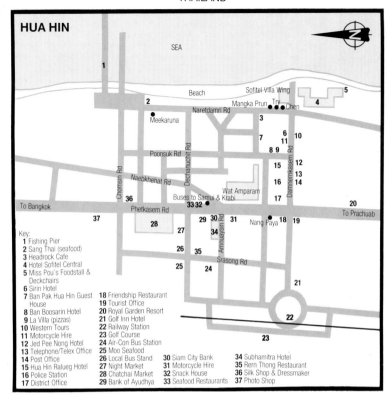

HUA HIN

SEA

1 Fishing Pier

Beach

Sofitel Villa Wing

5

2

Mangka Prun ● Try

Chen

4

Naretdamri Rd

3

Meekaruna

6

Poonsuk Rd

7

11

10

8 9

15

12

13

Naebkhehat Rd

16

14

Wat Amparam

17

36

Buses to Samui & Krabi

20

To Bangkok

33 32

Phetkasem Rd

37

28

29

30

31

Nang Paya 18

19

To Prachuab

27

34

26

35

Srasong Rd

25

24

21

22

23

Key:

1 Fishing Pier
2 Sang Thai (seafood)
3 Headrock Cafe
4 Hotel Sofitel Central
5 Miss Pou's Foodstall &
  Deckchairs
6 Sirin Hotel
7 Ban Pak Hua Hin Guest
  House
8 Ban Boosarin Hotel
9 La Villa (pizzas)
10 Western Tours
11 Motorcycle Hire
12 Jed Pee Nong Hotel
13 Telephone/Telex Office
14 Post Office
15 Hua Hin Ralueg Hotel
16 Police Station
17 District Office

18 Friendship Restaurant
19 Tourist Office
20 Royal Garden Resort
21 Golf Inn Hotel
22 Railway Station
23 Golf Course
24 Air-Con Bus Station
25 Moo Seafood
26 Local Bus Stand
27 Night Market
28 Chatchai Market
29 Bank of Ayudhya

30 Siam City Bank
31 Motorcycle Hire
32 Snack House
33 Seafood Restaurants

34 Subhamitra Hotel
35 Rern Thong Restaurant
36 Silk Shop & Dressmaker
37 Photo Shop

511150) in Damnoenkasem Rd, with a great Thai-Japanese seafood restaurant and split-rate rooms (beautifully appointed, with air-conditioning, video, fridge, hot water, etc.) at 990B weekends, 590B weekdays. All the above hotels cater mainly for Thai weekenders and offer generous discounts during the week.

Lots of good mid-range accommodation has appeared lately. **Ban Boosarin** (tel: 512076), at 8/8 Poonsuk Rd, is a quiet family-run hotel offering smart deluxe twin beds for 550B (only 500B if you stay a week) and excellent service. Every room is fully furnished, with air-conditioning, TV/video, hot and cold showers, telephone and private balcony. **Subhamitra Hotel** (tel: 511208) attracts mainly couples and well-heeled back-packers. It has good security, a laundry service and a nice little restaurant. Fan-cooled rooms (modern and very clean) go for 180B single, 200B double. Air-conditioned rooms have hot water and cost 300B. **Hua Hin Ralueg Hut** (tel: 511940), at 16 Damnoenkasem Rd, is an old hotel with mostly old rooms (comfortable) at 150B and a few newer chalets at 350B fan, 450B air-conditioned.

Budget places include **Gee Guest House**, across the road from the Ralueg. This is a friendly travellers' hangout, with clean 100B rooms, a small restaurant, a long-distance phone, a laundry service and cheap breakfasts. The only problem is the all-night video – get a room as high up as possible. **Ban Pak Hua Hin Hotel**, behind Sirin Hotel, is a quiet, comfy option with rooms from 150B fan, 250B air-conditioned. Travellers like it, despite the diffident staff. A few cheap guest houses are appearing now along Dam-noenkasem Rd. Try **K Dang's Place**, run by a friendly lady, with single rooms for 130B, doubles for 260B. As elsewhere, haggle for discounts – it often works!

FOOD

Hua Hin has a very busy, extensive night market in Chowsin Rd, offering fruit and vegetables, copy watches, pirate tapes, (very) loud beach shorts and a host of cheap food stalls. You can dine out here on all manner of tasty snacks: seafood, omelettes, *rotis, sate,* even waffles and kebabs! The night market starts up early, around 6 p.m. and it has a couple of good seafood restaurants. One is **Moo Sea-food**, a pleasant place where you sit outside, with an interesting menu: boiled serpent, crab jaws with 'powder', soya 'bear' hotpot and 'hundred years of old egg'! The cook is a wizard with the wok, a real class performer and great fun to watch.

The best place to try Hua Hin's famous seafood is **Sang Thai** restaurant down at the pier. Get a seat on the top level though, so that the seabreeze wafts away the smell of sewage! If you can afford it, the seafood at Royal Garden Resort's **Market** restaurant is pretty special – do not miss the lobster thermidor.

The big evening hangout area is Damnoenkasem Rd, often termed the Khao-San Rd of Hua Hin. It is like a mini-Bangkok all pushed into one street, with videos (mainly bland American violence films), girlie bars, pizzerias, German *biergartens*, snooker and psychedelic hippie clothing. Here, the **Headrock Cafe** does great toasted sandwiches and has an imaginative dinner menu from 6 p.m. onwards. There is a fine selection of seafood at **Try Restaurant**, good sounds and cheap beer at **Jellyfish Pub** and live Thai-style music at **Country Bar**. Elsewhere, **La Villa** in Poonsuk Rd is *the* place to go Italian: carbonara, spaghetti, seafood and a great selection of wines. If you are pining for home cooking, **Friendship Restaurant** in Damnoenkasem Rd does a great T-bone steak (150B) with all the trimmings.

KOH SAMUI

Regardless of fads, Koh Samui remains Thailand's top island destination. It is often criticised for being full of hippies and yuppies, but full it certainly is not. Even in the so-called high season, there are vast stretches of dazzling white beaches with scarcely a visitor in sight. This is the good thing about Samui – it's so big, it doesn't really matter that there are so many tourists about. You can still find lots of quiet bits which are just like they were ten years ago. Further, while the rest of Thailand is now overrun by long-haul package tourists, the difficulties of getting to Samui and the absence (until recently) of large hotel developments, have protected it from exploitation.

This said, the island has really cleaned up its image of late – gone are the days of hash cookies, magic mushrooms and psychedelic beach parties. You have to look really hard to find the old 'freaky' atmosphere now and many younger travellers go to neighbouring Phangan instead. Those who remain are an entertaining mix of beachcombing backpackers, ageing drop-outs and trendy jet-setters in search of a laidback lifestyle in a Robinson Crusoe setting. One or two can afford the few upmarket beach bungalows on the island. The rest head for the cheaper huts, which are often equipped with little more than a bed and a mosquito net. It is these 'back to nature' resting places that still capture the spirit of the Samui first discovered by intrepid shoestringers over 15 years ago.

The largest of 80 or so islands off the west coast, Koh Samui is about 16 km from north to south and just a bit more from east to west. The whole hinterland, which rises steeply to around 600 m in the centre, is just one vast coconut plantation. A well-surfaced ring road runs round the island, connecting the main town of Na Thon to the major beaches. Samui's tourist season runs from mid-November to around the end of March. From April to late June is dry and hot, often uncomfortably so. The rest of the year can be wet and windy, although you might be lucky and have fine weather in September/October. Off season, you can bargain yourself 50 per cent discounts on most bungalows because they need the business.

ARRIVAL/DEPARTURE
Koh Samui is 84 km from Surat Thani (the nearest coastal town) which is itself 650 km from Bangkok and 298 km from Hat Yai. There are three ferries daily between Ban Don pier (Surat Thani) and Samui island. The two-hour crossing costs 80B one-way. A slow night ferry boat, for those who don't want to stay over in noisy Surat Thani, leaves Ban Don at 9 p.m. and reaches Samui six hours later.

Air
In mid-1989, after several false starts, Samui's airport finally opened. Bangkok Airways is offering three flights daily from Bangkok (1550B) and one flight a day from Hat Yai.

Rail
The daily 7.20 p.m. express train from Bangkok arrives in Surat Thani at a convenient time (6.34 a.m.) for the early morning ferry over to Samui from Ban Don pier. Combination train-bus-ferry tickets (400/430B, with second-class sleeper berth) are sold at the advance booking office of Hualamphong station. The 2.55 p.m. and 4.53 p.m. express trains from Hat Yai arrive in Surat Thani in good time for the night ferry to Koh Samui. If you miss this, stay overnight in Surat Thani at **Surat Hotel**, 431/1-2 Chonkasem Rd (80-160B) or **Siam Thani Hotal**, 180 Surat-Phunphin Rd (330-700B).

The 3 p.m. ferries out of Samui (Na Thon) connect with the 6.54 p.m. and 8.12 p.m. express trains back to Bangkok, which get there at 6.10 a.m. and 7.05 a.m. respectively. A free bus service is provided from Ban Don pier to Phun Phin rail station, 14 km out of Surat Thani.

Road/Sea
Travel agents in Bangkok, Krabi and Hat Yai offer cheap combined bus/ferry tickets to Samui via Surat Thani (see re-

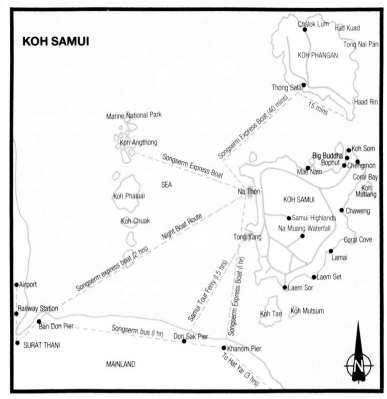

KOH SAMUI

levant sections for more details). The VIP bus from Bangkok (320B) is particularly luxurious with waisted reclining seats, frilly pillows and a tartan bedspread! A stewardess in a white silk suit passes up and down the bus handing out dinner boxes – the mandatory chicken drumstick and Pepsi. This bus leaves Bangkok early in the morning and arrives at Samui 11-12 hours later.

Songserm Travel and Highway Travel, both on the jetty road at Na Thon, are the two main agents on Samui for confirming air tickets and for booking onward transport. They sell the cheapest combined bus/ferry tickets to Bangkok (280B), Singapore (550B), Kuala Lumpur (500B), Penang (400B) and Krabi/Hat Yai (200B).

TOURIST SERVICES

People drop into Na Thon to change money, to confirm flights, to book transport, to buy film and supplies and to phone home. Na Thon is a small bustling town of three parallel roads. The back road (where *songthaews* go to and from the beaches) has a supermarket, a big Siam Bank, a Kodak 23-minute film processing shop, a burger bar (**New York Grill**) and a great Indian/Pakistani restaurant (**Shah B-O Roze**). The middle road has **Buayen's** bookshop (best selection of second-hand books and pirate

tapes), **Samui Divers** (best scuba-diving outfit), a vegetarian restaurant, a great Italian restaurant (**Fountain**) and a popular burger joint (**Bird in the Hand**). On the jetty road, you will find the post office, several travel agents, two 100/120B hotels (**Palace** and **Samui Bungalow**) and lots of stalls selling à la mode Samui T-shirts. Most of this stuff, incidentally, comes from Bangkok!

If you're staying at Chaweng, you don't need to go into Na Thon. **J R** bungalow has an overseas phone and a small post office. **Chaweng Supermarket**, next to the Beach Club disco, has a Songserm office, a Siam Bank counter and cheap beer/supplies.

GETTING AROUND THE ISLAND

Songthaews go everywhere round the island for 10 to 20B per ride. They don't, however, connect the two main beaches, Chaweng and Lamai. To get from one of these beaches to the other, you have to go into Na Thon first. *Songthaews* stop running around 7 p.m., so if you want to hit the discos at night you will probably want to hire a motorbike or jeep. Alternatively, hitch a lift from a passing vehicle – it's quite easy.

You can hire motorbikes all over the island. The prices are pretty much standard (150B for a moped and 200B for a big trial bike) and you can haggle for discounts in the off season or if you take it out for a few days. Do take your vehicle for a test run before paying any money, however, as some of them are past their best. The same goes for jeeps, which cost around 500B per day, again less if you are prepared to bargain. Rental rates are cheapest in Na Thon, where reliable places like Sirivait, 91B Back Rd, have mopeds from 130B/day, big bikes from 160B/day and jeeps from 450B/day. Be *very* careful driving round Samui. The main ring road running around the island is very safe, but the small connecting roads between the beaches are most definitely not. Just look at all those *farangs* with banged-up knees and elbows!

A one-day bike/jeep tour of the island is a must. From Na Thon, drive south down the ring road for about ten minutes until a turning (unsigned) on your left appears. Drive 1 km down this path, then make the steep ascent by foot (40 minutes) to **Samui Highlands**, the highest point of the island with a rip-off cafe (20B for a 'real mineral water' shower!) and, ten minutes' walk above this, amazing coastline views. A little further south is **Na Muang Waterfall**, 2 km inland from the main road, where you can enjoy a cool dip beneath the rushing falls. At the southern tip of the island is **Laem Sor**, with a small mustard-coloured pagoda on the water's edge ('Please dress politly. Welcome only people dress'). Stop here for lunch at **Diamond Villa** – lovely beach, marvellous food and great snorkelling/fishing off the nearby island. A little way east, **Laem Set** has another old pagoda and **Laem Set Inn**, where the English owner, Bill Parry, puts up 'discriminating guests only' and ferries them to the coral reefs offshore. If you have any appetite left, he'll do you a dinner of grilled local tuna in a tamarind and chilli sweet-sour sauce and pancakes with Samui honey. Like Diamond Villa, this is another off-the-beaten-track option in a paradise setting. Just below Lamai beach, **Wonderful Rock** (look out for 'Hinta-Hinyai' sign on the right of the main road) is a good place to be at sunset. It is actually two rocks, Grandfather and Grandmother, which appear in all their phallic glory at low tide. **Coral Cove**, between Lamai and Chaweng beaches, has loads of beautiful coral in the small bay, but shallow water makes snorkelling dangerous after noon. The best time to visit is around full moon, when the tide is high. Finish your tour at **Big Buddha**, north of Chaweng Bay, where the 12-m-high Buddha seated on the hill is a picture-postcard silhouette at sunset.

Several agencies in Na Thon sell the 150B day-trip to **Ang Thong National Marine Park** north west of Samui. This is an archipelago of 49 islands featuring clear waters, towering limestone rock masses and virgin white sand beaches, in many ways much nicer than Samui. Tours make diving stops in secluded lagoons and visit Thale Noi on Mae Ko, which is a delightful saltwater lake.

Koh Phangan, a short boat ride north of Samui, is a worthwhile side-trip. This island is nearly as big as Samui and is completely different. It is more primitive, more rugged and it has more mosquitoes. It really is like Samui ten years ago. Accommodation is generally spartan, mainly 50B dogs' kennels on stilts, but they are building nicer bungalows now, in the 200/250B range, with bathrooms. The food is less interesting than on Samui, (expect the basic two rice dishes and fish), but is good none the less. The island itself has a real hippie feeling to it, which attracts all the young people who missed out on that era and who want to see what it was like. Anything goes on Phangan – nudism on the beaches and every kind of drug imaginable. The generators cut out at 9 p.m. and after that you either go to the disco, or hang out with your friends, watching the stars, playing guitars or getting stoned. All that is going to change when the new road opens up Haadrint (the most popular beach, currently isolated). Then this whole psychedelic scene will have to transfer to another part of the island. This aside, Koh Phangan will always be a backwater of Koh Samui. It is very unlikely ever to replace it, or to get overdone.

The main boat to Phangan goes from Na Thon. This is the twice-daily Songserm speedboat (70B, 45 minutes) to Thong Sala, the main village on the island. Thong Sala itself is a dump, with little to recommend it. Most people get direct boats to Haad Rin Bay from Bophut (dep. 9.30 a.m. and 2 p.m., 50B, 45 minutes) or from Mae Nam (dep. 2.30 p.m., 50B). If you go to Thong Sala, take a 5B boat-trip down to Haad Rin, or, when the new road is built, a taxi. You can now go direct from Surat Thani to Koh Phangan on the night ferry from Ban Don.

Right now, the hottest spot on Phangan is **Haad Rin Bay**. The east side is full of hippies and nudists but it has fantastic sand, sea and swimming. **Sunrise** has spacious bungalows at 80B, cheaper ones (further back) at 50B. The bathrooms are clean and the food is good. **Haad Rin** has nice people, livable huts from 30 to 80B, and T'ai Chi courses at 650B per week (four hours a day, five days a week). West Haad Rin is quieter and has great coral, but is not swimmable. **Lighthouse** has the finest views, **Sunset** the freshest seafood, and **Sooksam** the top vegetarian restaurant. The best disco on the island is Haad Rin's **Casablanca**, which is small, completely open-air and very laidback, much like the Arabian on Samui used to be in the good old days before it became too popular!

Haad Rin is the nicest beach because you get the sunrise and the sunset just by walking for a few minutes from one side of the bay to the other. There are other beautiful bays all along the east coast which are as yet completely undeveloped. **Thong Naay Paan**, for example, is a magical bay with hardly a bungalow on it. It is a 40B boat ride from Haad Rin and **Chitchat Wonderland** (30B) is the place to stay. Then, on the north side, there is beautiful **Bottle Beach**, a two-hour walk from Thong Naay Paan, with only 25 bungalows on the entire bay. **Coral Bay**, at Haad Khom, on the northern tip of the island, has the best snorkelling on Phangan. Try **Mr Tu's** bungalows – very cheap and run by a nice family. In nearby Chaloklum Bay, **Fanta** is a quiet, comfortable option with 40 to 60B huts, excellent food, good swimming, coral and sunsets. To the south, you can walk or take a boat from Haad Rin to laidback **Banta-I Beach** – poor swimming (water too shallow) but great snorkelling off the reef. Stay at **Mac Bay Resort** or **Lee's Gardens**, both with newly built huts from 50 to 100B and excellent food.

Transport on Phangan is still primitive. To get around, you can rent jeep-taxis or motorbike-taxis, but the roads are scary. The best way to tour the island is by boat, which hops from beach to beach. Again, that's going to change; as more money comes in, they will start paving some roads and things will be much better.

Koh Tao, three hours by boat from Phangan (Thong Sala or Coral Bay), is a craggy little island of huge towering cliffs, dense forests and lush palm plantations. It has the best diving in the region (bring your own equipment over from Samui) and is definitely the place to go in December-January, when tourist crowds overrun Phangan. Koh Tao has bungalows at the jetty, some more on the other side of the island and still more strewn along the beach. **Ochai's** is one of these, a 2-km walk down the beach from the jetty. The beaches on the east coast are secluded but rocky. Those in the south, around **Hope** bungalows, are situated in a very pretty area. Several new places will be opening here in 1990. There is no transport on the island – you walk everywhere. A series of neat little sandbars run out from the east coast to other islands. The best of these is **Koh Nan-gyuang**, an easy boat ride (115B) from the village in Koh Tao. This tiny island has two bungalows and excellent snorkelling.

BEACHES

Samui has beaches to suit every taste and pocket. The two most popular beaches, Chaweng and Lamai, have the nightlife and the best range of accommodation. Unfortunately, they have the crowds too. There is a lot to be said for staying at a quieter beach, like Bophut or Maenam and travelling into the action from there. Wherever you stay, the big activity on the beaches, after sunbathing, snorkelling and an afternoon siesta, is checking out the videos playing at the various bungalows. It's hard to get sense out of anyone after dark; they all turn into video vegetables! On the beach, you can do all your shopping lying flat on a towel. The offers range from 10B for coconut milk and munchies, 50-200B for hammocks, gems and beach attire, Thai massage for 100B an hour and 200-250B for fortune-telling. It's just like Bali, but without the hassle!

Chaweng is the biggest beach on the island, curving in a broad crescent of sand for about 3 km, backed by coconut palms and pounded by white surf. Water sports here include windsurfing, snorkelling, fishing trips and even water bikes which rent out for around 150B per 15 minutes. The top end of the beach, near Matlang island, is the quietest and least developed part, mainly because the water is so shallow. **Moon** and **Matlang Resort** have nice bungalows with mosquito nets, attached bathrooms and verandahs from 100/150B, also restaurants with videos, cocktails and fresh seafood. Further south, on the main strip, a few nice upmarket places – with hot showers and air-conditioned rooms, are **Pansea**, **Tropicana** and **Imperial Samui**, from around £30 a night. The Imperial has a pool on the beach (who needs it?) and the Tropicana features a good live Thai band from 7 to 10 p.m. Cheaper favourites include **Amanda** (great beach location), **Coconut Grove**, **Lucky Mother** (trendy bungalows and music at the bar), **Best Beach** (best 'no-name' seafood on Chaweng), **J R's** (try a shark steak), **Munchies** (lovely chalets, pity about the Thai hookers) and **Lotus** (everybody who's anybody has breakfast here). The well-rated **New Star** bungalows are at the bottom of Chaweng Noi bay, on the way to Coral Cove. **Coral Cove** itself has very livable huts/chalets from 50B to 300B, plus an excellent restaurant.

All three of Chaweng's discos, the **Fiesta**, the **Black Cat** and the new **Beach Club**, are in the centre of Chaweng Yai beach, between Pansea and Arabian bungalows. All three run nightly, and the Fiesta is the most popular. Just above Pansea is Chaweng village, with **Colibri** restaurant (great pizzas, French bread sandwiches and ice-cream) and below this, on the beach, **Bodgett & Scarper** bar (regular beach parties in the true Samui tradition). The hotspot bar at Chaweng is **Reggae Pub** near Fiesta disco, offering free peanuts and cheap drinks. Everybody shakes your hand when you walk in as though they have known you for years! It's always full.

LAMAI

Lamai generally gets poor reports nowadays. It reminds people of a mini Patpong, with its host of bars, discos and Thai girls. This said, the southern end of the beach is still quiet and pleasant, with clear deep water and good snorkelling round the rocks. Stay at **Whitesands** (40B), **Nice Resort** 1 (50-200B), **Rocky** (80-200B), or **Palm** (80-250B). The newly built **Mui** bungalows at the north end of Lamai are clean and functional, with fan/shower/toilet, hot water, mosquitoproof windows and a verandah, for 80B or (slightly larger, with ceiling fan) 100B. Staff are very friendly and the beach is fine for swimming.

Lamai village has Thai boxing, video bars, cafe-restaurants, and the **Flamingo** disco (surely Samui's best) which rocks on every night to around 4 or 5 a.m. One really cool cafe, about 4 km out of Lamai, is **Beverly Hills Cafe** between Ao Tang-Ta-Kien and Coral Cove. It overlooks most of the island and coastline and serves quality Thai and European fare from 9 a.m. to 10 p.m.

Maenam beach is really long and is one of the best for swimming. This is where to come if you don't want to be bothered by anyone – there is no loud music, no motorbikes and there are no taxis blowing their horns. All there is is a small windsurfing school and a small village with good Muslim food. Popular bungalows are **Happy**, **Friendly** and **Silent**, all of which live up to their names.

Bophut beach has the best sunsets on the island. It is even cheaper and quieter than Maenam. It has some pretty nice resorts now and attracts a completely different class of traveller than of old. **Peace** is about the cheapest for accommodation (40 to 250B) and gives lowprice windsurfing lessons. So does **Calm** (80 to 250B) next door. Bophut town is quaint, but the beach has lost a lot of atmosphere.

Big Buddha is on the north coast facing Koh Phangan and tends to be very secluded. **Big Buddha** and **Sunset** bungalows are the current favourites, with value-for-money huts from 30B and choice food. Check out the row of shops below the Buddha statue. One of them, **Farn**, has excellent jewellery from the north, great leather products and is run by really nice people. It's quite possibly the best place to shop on the island.

Chengmon beach, just up from Big Buddha, is getting a bit pricey nowadays but is wonderfully quiet and relaxed. It has a beautiful beach-front, with plenty of palm trees, and the snack bar in the middle serves really fresh seafood. At **Chengmon** bungalows, accommodation ranges from old shacks with double beds and mosquito nets at 50B to swish new chalets with attached bathrooms for 250B. The one luxury option, **Chengmon Village**, caters to the yuppie crowd and is, at 500-800B, very expensive.

KRABI

As Koh Samui becomes increasingly commercialised, nearby Krabi is attracting visitors looking for untouched beaches and beautiful natural scenery. Krabi province contains 130 islands, many of which are worth exploring by daily boat tours. Especially interesting for snorkelling are Pee Pee and Chicken islands, with calm lagoons filled with multi-coloured fish and coral under dramatic cliffs. Krabi town itself is a small, charming travellers' centre with lots of laidback cafes, restaurants and ice-cream parlours. It is a very relaxing spot – but get there soon. Already there is talk of turning Krabi into the biggest international seaport in Thailand. If this happens, its brief tourism heyday may soon be over.

ARRIVAL/DEPARTURE
Air
The airport is ready and will shortly accept flights from Bangkok and Hat Yai.

Road
Krabi is 814 km south of Bangkok, only 12 hours away by VIP bus (the most comfortable option, with reclining seats, video and meals; tickets sold in Ko Sahn Rd). From Talaat Kao village, where all Krabi-bound buses stop off, it is a 5-km (3B) ride by *songthaew* into town. Seats on the VIP bus back to Bangkok (350B) are sold by Lignite Tour. The bus leaves every other day from behind Vieng Thong Hotel. The regular air-conditioned buses (310B, 13/14 hours) leave daily from Talaat Kao village. From the same place, local buses go half-hourly to Surat Thani (60B, four hours), for Koh Samui. Most people, however, buy the combined bus-ferry ticket to Samui from agencies in Krabi town. These tourist buses leave twice daily, at 11 a.m. and 2 p.m. At Surat Thani, there are several travel agents (the bus always stops at one or the other) where you can confirm flights or book onward travel by air-conditioned bus or plane to Bangkok, Chiang Mai, Hat Yai, Singapore, etc. The last buses out of Surat Thani for Samui leave around 3.30

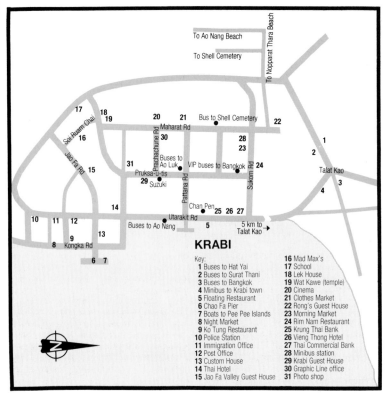

KRABI

Key:
1 Buses to Hat Yai
2 Buses to Surat Thani
3 Buses to Bangkok
4 Minibus to Krabi town
5 Floating Restaurant
6 Chao Fa Pier
7 Boats to Pee Pee Islands
8 Night Market
9 Ko Tung Restaurant
10 Police Station
11 Immigration Office
12 Post Office
13 Custom House
14 Thai Hotel
15 Jao Fa Valley Guest House
16 Mad Max's
17 School
18 Lek House
19 Wat Kawe (temple)
20 Cinema
21 Clothes Market
22 Rong's Guest House
23 Morning Market
24 Rim Nam Restaurant
25 Krung Thai Bank
26 Vieng Thong Hotel
27 Thai Commercial Bank
28 Minibus station
29 Krabi Guest House
30 Graphic Line office
31 Photo shop

p.m., so you will need to take the morning bus out of Krabi if you want to make Samui the same day. The 3.30 p.m. buses connect with the 5 p.m. ferry from Donsak (one and half hours' drive from Ban Don) over to the island. The trick is to avoid having to stay in noisy, depressing Surat Thani overnight. While waiting to escape, take a stroll down to the riverfront (near the bus-stand), which has some good food stalls and cool river breezes – nice sunsets too! In Krabi town, two reliable travel agents are Chan Phen (tel: 612004) at 145 Oootarakij Rd and Graphic Line, next to Amata restaurant. They sell seats on air-conditioned buses to Hat Yai (145B), Penang (380B), Singapore (490B), Kuala Lumpur (435B) and Koh Samui (200B).

TOURIST SERVICES
There is no tourist office, just a lot of 'tourist information centres' selling bus/boat tickets along with refreshments and ice-cream. Mrs Lee at the Chan Phen Coffee Shop, opposite the jetty, is about the best source of information at the moment. If you are staying at Rong's Guest House, she will provide free transport there. A very well-researched map of Krabi town, Krabi area and Pee Pee Islands is sold all over town for 35B.

From 8 a.m. to 8 p.m., you can make overseas phone calls (60B per minute to most foreign countries) from the post office, which is open from 8.30 a.m. to 4 p.m. weekdays, 8.30 a.m. to 12 noon Saturdays. Many guest houses and travel agents have an IDD telephone facility, but they charge 30B for the service.

The Thai Commercial Bank, a few doors up from Chan Phen, is open from 8.30 a.m. to 6 p.m. daily. It is the best place to change money. Krabi Travel Tour, 36 Pattana Rd, has a large selection of English books for sale and hire.

SIGHTS
There are a few inland sights worth exploring by bus or motorbike before hitting the beaches. The **Shell Cemetery**, 20 km west of Krabi, is a 75 million-year-old fossilised shellbed, best seen at low tide. Check timings with Mrs Lee. **Than Bokkharani Arboretum**, a short walk from Ao Luk, 46 km north, is a botanical garden of trees, streams and brooks, with tropical fauna and a waterfall (most pleasant from November to May, avoid busy weekends). **Wat Tham Sua**, a few kilometres north of Krabi, is south Thailand's most famous forest wat, where 300 or so monks and nuns lead an ascetic life in cliffside caves (kutis) or in primitive huts buried in the dense jungle. The wat is set in a deep valley enclosed by towering limestone crags. A walk up the stone steps brings you to a high plateau

with fine views down into the valley. Local buses to all the above destinations, as well as **Noppharat Thara Beach** (a quiet 2-km-long beach 18 km north west), leave from Krabi town – one-way fares are 10-15B. If you want to see everything in a day, hire a motorbike from Suzuki on Pruksa-u-tis Rd.

BEACHES

Ao Nang, a 15B minibus ride from Krabi town, is a nice long white-sand beach with good swimming and snorkelling. **Ao Nang Villa** has a range of bungalows from 80B to 310B. Nearby **Peace** is of similar quality and charges 150B to 300B. **Princess Garden**, up the hill road behind Ao Nang Villa, has forest-style huts from 50B to 150B and a cosy restaurant. The big **Krabi Resort** is an ugly concrete block with rooms/bungalows at 660B fan, 1300B air-conditioned. It has a disco, pool, water-sports and an expensive (but pleasant) restaurant. The latest news is that they are digging a tunnel from Ao Nang through to neighbouring **Pai Plong** beach, where **Club Med** is expected to set up shop soon.

Ao Phra Nang, a 20B boat trip from Ao Nang (or 30B by boat from Krabi town), is the most popular beach, probably because of its secluded situation, peaceful atmosphere and scenic surrounding cliffs. Actually, it is three beaches in one, all within easy walking distance of each other. **Joy** beach has the famous **Princess Cave** (home of a heavenly princess who protects local fishermen) and basic huts for 50/60B; **Rai Lee** beach has better bungalows with shower/bath and electricity from 80B to 150B; and **Ao Nam Mao** beach offers a range of accommodation from 50B bamboo huts (containing only a mattress and mosquito net) to smart 150B chalets. The older operations, life **Cliff** and **Pine**, set deep in the forest, are no longer favoured.

ISLANDS

Koh Pee Pee, the twin pearls of the south Andaman sea, lie some 40 km offshore from Krabi. With clear blue waters, spectacular scenery, fantastic coral and interesting inland walks, they remain, despite the tourists, as close to paradise as one can reasonably expect to find. Pee Pee Don, the larger island, has the accommodation (mainly ranged on either side of Don Sai bay) and is gently undulating, with many beautiful beaches and viewpoints. Pee Pee Le is mainly rocky with towering cliffs. It is famous for its birds' nests, which are collected (at much risk to life) from the top of the sheer crags. Birds make their nests from saliva, mixed in with twigs and feathers. The first three nests they make are collected and sold to Chinese res-

taurants. The third nest is the most valuable, since the exhausted bird has to produce blood as well as saliva to make it. The Chinese prize 'third nests' for their medicinal and aphrodisiac properties and pay up to 30,000B per kilo for them!

Pee Pee is not overcrowded, but the limited accommodation on the Don always seems to be full. To avoid disappointment, it is a good idea to book ahead from Krabi. If you cannot do this, pay a little extra and get the early-morning express boat (around 9 a.m., 125B) out to the island. It arrives at Don Sai before all the slower boats and gives you time to find a bungalow in a nice situation. Always be first off the boat. If you are in a group (best), leave one person to mind the bags while the rest of you sprint up and down the beach looking for a bungalow. Still better, hop on a taxi-boat (10B) from the Don Sai pier out to the less crowded beaches. This taxi-boat service connects all the major beaches and is the most convenient method of beach-hopping. Avoid busy weekends, the Thai holiday season (mid-March to mid-May) and the New Year as accommodation is particularly difficult to find then and many people end up sleeping on the beaches. The beach is *always* full on the main strip (near Don Sai village) and most travellers head straight out to Viking and Long Beaches, at present the two least touristy places to stay. During the rainy season (mid-April to mid-October) most bungalows close down and few boats make the crossing from Krabi.

Over the past couple of years, Don Sai village itself has mushroomed into a busy little tourist town of shops, travel agents, cafes and seafood restaurants. Here you can buy boat tickets, confirm flights, watch videos, exchange books, make overseas phone calls and change money. By the (polluted) pier is **Pee Pee Cabana**, with luxury bungalows at a flat rate of 500B and a European-style restaurant. Right next to the cliff, below the Cabana, is **Donsai Village**. This is the new air-conditioned operation, with swish chalets at 1100B and all mod cons. Ten minutes' walk up the beach from Don Sai pier is **Andaman**, a friendly outfit with good food and bungalows from 100 to 250B. Past this, the small **Viking** beach has nice (if dinky) huts for 70B. Further on, **Pee Pee Paradise Pearl** has a great restaurant, but is no longer a pleasant place to stay as the staff are unfriendly and the bungalows are overpriced at 130 to 280B. Ten minutes away (walk to the end of the beach, up a steep hill path and down the other side) is **Ma Prao Ton Deao** (ex-**Funnyland**) with well-priced chalets at 100/150B and amazing food: French cheese, wine, continental specialities, etc. Just up from the Paradise Pearl is a series of basic 90B huts with electricity, communal toilets and showers. This is **Long Beach**, the best beach (say some) since the coral is only 10 metres offshore, great for snorkelling.

Most places organise boat-trips around the Don and out to the neighbouring island of Pee Pee Le – 600B full day, 400B half-day, per boat. Since there is never any difficulty in getting a boatload of six to eight people together, this works out pretty cheap. Snorkelling equipment and food should be included. The full day trip is best: spectacular scenery, looming cliffs, bone-white beaches, crystal-clear waters and diving stops to see beautiful fish and coral. Back on the Don, the easiest path to the 'viewpoint' (for fine views of the island interior and the twin half-moon bays) starts behind Charlie bungalows – go through the rice-fields and follow the markers. Sunsets are best seen on the west coast. Take an afternoon stroll down the back of Lo Da Lum bay, climb over a few rocks and you arrive at **Camel Rock**, a delightful little beach with fine coral. **Lana Bay**, or sunset point, is just past this, a total of 20 minutes' walk from Charlie's. Parasailing and water-skiing take place on either Lo Da Lum or Long Beach, depending on the tide. Scuba-diving is best arranged with Jerry at Lemhin bungalows, just above Andaman.

Koh Lanta, 68 km south of Krabi, is quickly catching on as an alternative to touristy Pee Pee. It has an interesting landscape, beautiful sea, rocks for snorkelling and gentle sandy beaches going out into the water for miles. If you want to be on your own, it is just perfect. To get there, catch a minibus from Krabi to Hua Hin pier (very dusty ride, sit at the front, 25B), then a longtail boat over to Lanta Noi (wear thongs, you have to wade on the other side, 5B), then a motorcycle-taxi (20B) or minibus (10B) across the island, then a longtail boat to Lanta Saladan village at the top of Lanta Yai (9B), then a motorcycle-taxi from the village (10B) or walk 2 km to your right, along the beach, to **Kaw Kwang** or **Lanta Villa** bungalows. The total journey time from Krabi to Kaw Kwang is about four hours. Both bungalows charge 80 to 120B and are close together at the north-eastern corner of Lanta Yai. Travellers rave about them and about the long crescent beach and secluded bays. Others hop on a motorbike (30B) at Saladan pier and go to **Marine Hut** bungalows. These are really nice, especially the big family-size chalets (80B) with attached bath and writing desk. The smaller 50B bungalows are good value too. As for the restaurant, it serves just about the best food I have had in Thailand. Ten metres away from Marina,

there is a 2-km-long beach without a soul on it – real picture-postcard stuff. The big thing to do at Lanta Villa, by the way, is three-day jungle treks. Near Lanta and another nifty escape from Pee-Pee's crowds is **Jammu Island**, with more fine beaches and cheap accommodation. It is only one hour by boat from Saladan pier.

Most bungalows at Ao Nang and Ao Phra Nang organise boat trips to offshore **Chicken** and **Poda** islands, for fantastic coral-diving, fishing and snorkelling.

WILDLIFE

The following report on wildlife localities in the Krabi area comes from David Pearce (UK), to whom many thanks.

Southern Thailand and in particular the Krabi area offers a variety of sites for observing wildlife in a diversity of habitats from offshore islands to coastal mangroves and inland forest.

On the western boundary of Krabi town is an area of secondary and scrub mangrove which holds several species of birds scarce or absent from the good mangrove on the river. Best visited early morning or evening, it can easily be found by leaving town on the road opposite Sukhorn Rd to the T-junction, turning left and walking 250 m, then right down a long dirt track past the large mast on the right; the track continues to the river north of the port.

Boat trips out into the mangrove on Krabi River opposite the harbour can be arranged with local boatmen in the town and provide an interesting insight into mangrove life and its tidal existence. Observers with a keen eye should see several species of kingfisher plus sunbirds, the occasional woodpecker and elusive crab-eating macacques. Whilst on the river, white-bellied sea eagles can often be seen soaring above the karst formations just north of the town.

South on the river from Krabi are areas of mud and sandflats exposed at low tide to reveal feeding areas for wading birds and terns, the latter often sitting on fishing nets strung out across the river. Continuing downriver by boat, you can visit Pee Pee islands, 42 km further into the Andaman Sea, where the primary objective is to see flocks of frigate birds and terns, both on the crossing of the Andaman Sea and off the islands themselves. Pee Pee Don supports a small bird population but increasing tourism to the island poses problems for its wildlife.

About 20 km north of Krabi is an area of forest amid plantations of rubber, easily reached by pick-up en route to Ao Luk. An early morning start here (before the heat intensifies) will reveal various forest birds, reptiles and endless species of insects and butterflies, all visible from

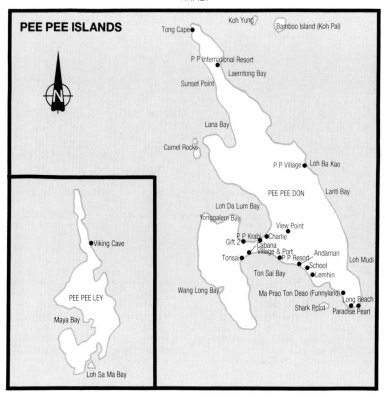

PEE PEE ISLANDS

the track through the forest. This begins next to the 20 km post, opposite some large rock formations.

Species obviously vary with the time of year, especially birds, but there is something to see throughout most months for the keen and interested observer. Looking on the debit side, the Krabi area, like much of Thailand, has not escaped progressive development and many of the surrounding areas are being deforested to make way for the escalating palm oil and rubber industry, a large part of the Thai economy and export trade. Faced with this and with increasing pollution, population and tourism, the future of wildlife and its respective habitats is now delicately balanced and so prospective visitors to any wildlife sites would be well advised simply to appreciate their beauty, respect their habitat and show concern for the local environment whilst enjoying the fascinating spectacle.

Further information on the local wildlife can be obtained from Rong's Guest House. There is a good ornithologists' book here, giving directions to the best viewing spots.

ENTERTAINMENT
Thai-style boxing should take place every Tuesday night (100B) at the boxing stadium near the market, but it does not always happen. The Matura nightclub at Mataraj cinema is 80B admission (one free drink), but it is unpopular.

ACCOMMODATION
Krabi's only high-class accommodation is the **Thai Hotel** (tel: 611122) at 7 Isara Rd, with a good restaurant, an overseas calls booth and a 'permanent' 20 per cent discount on room tariffs (200-260B fan, 320-360B air-conditioned). The less clean **Vieng Thong Hotel** (tel: 611288) at 155-7 Uttarakit Rd has fan doubles from 140B (one bed) to 200B (two beds) and air-conditioned rooms at 360B.

There are a number of cheap, friendly guest houses in town. **Mad Max** on Chao Fa Rd (near the Court House) is a traditional Thai house in a quiet part of town. Charges are 30B a person or 50B a room. The manager is a nice man, with lots of information and an awesome music collection. **Lek House** at 86 Isra Rd (near the temple) is a cosy family-style house with dormitory beds at 30B, double rooms at 60B and a small garden. Don't confuse it with Lek Guest House (an imposter and part-time brothel) on the opposite side of the road. **Rong's** at 17 Maharaj Rd, a few minutes' walk out of town, is a spotlessly clean place in a quiet, relaxing palm-grove setting. Mr Rong is a charming, informative host, who goes out of his way to help travellers. His rooms are 70B single, 90B double and the two new bungalows with bathrooms attached (120B) are worth the extra cost. Useful facilities include cycle rental, use of kitchen and free baggage store.

FOOD

The small night market below the pier offers a large variety of cheap snacks. Here you will find **Kotung** restaurant, famous for its seafood. **Rim Nam**, near Rong's guest house, serves authentic Thai food at low prices. So does **New Ros Dad**, just along from the Maharaj cinema. **Sukiv I**, opposite the Maharaj, is popular for continental breakfasts, beer, snacks and ice-cream. **Parkway Cafe**, at the Thai Hotel, is the place to enjoy Western-style fare (steaks, grills, etc.) in romantic, low-lit surroundings.

HAT YAI

Hat Yai is the south's principal city, with a bustling night-life, the cheapest shopping in Thailand and international-class accommodation and restaurants. Though mainly used as a one-night stopover, it is worth sticking around longer to take in the multi-cultural cosmopolitanism of the place which has a very special atmosphere. If coming up from Malaysia, Hat Yai is a good introduction to Thailand – really lively! The street food is top rate and you can walk around the markets for hours.

ARRIVAL/DEPARTURE
Air

Hat Yai is connected by air with Bangkok (three flights daily, 1760B) and with Penang, Kuala Lumpur and Singapore. Thai Airways run a minibus service from Hat Yai airport to the city centre (30B), or you can take a share-taxi (120B per load).

Rail

Express trains leave Bangkok daily for Hat Yai at 2 p.m. and 3.15 p.m., arriving at 5.48 a.m. and 7.05 a.m. respectively. Basic fares are 664B first class, 313B second class, 149B third class. From Hat Yai, the 2.55 p.m. and 4.53 p.m. express trains take five hours to Surat Thani, 12/13 hours to Hua Hin and reach Bangkok at 7.05 a.m. and 8.35 a.m. respectively.

For east-coast Malaysia, go to Sungai Kolok by train (dep 4.52 a.m. and 6.05 a.m., 42B third class, three and half hours), by air-conditioned bus (dep. 7 a.m., 9.30 a.m., 1 p.m. and 3 p.m., 77B, three hours), or by share-taxi. At Sungai Kolok, take a rickshaw/motorbike to Thai immigration, then walk into Malaysia.

For west-coast Malaysia, take a local bus down to Padang Besar (13B, one and a half hours) or catch the 7.20 a.m. express train (42B, three and half hours) from Hat Yai Junction. From the Thai border post at Padang Besar, you can stroll over to Malaysia to claim the second half of a double-entry visa (if you want to re-enter Thailand) or stay on the train for Butterworth (second class only, 120B), arriving at 12.10 p.m.

Road

Buses from Bangkok's Southern Bus Terminal cost 339B regular (14 hours) and 187B air-conditioned (15/16 hours). There are several travel agents in Hat Yai, offering air-conditioned buses to Bangkok (350B), Butterworth (200B, 10 hours), Kuala Lumpur (250B, 12 hours) and Singapore (300B, 16-18 hours). Prices are slightly cheaper if you book direct at the bus terminal in front of the market. Magic Tour, at Cathay Hotel, has a very reliable bus-ticketing service. Their morning express bus to Krabi (200B) takes four hours flat and drops you in the centre of town, right opposite the boat jetty, just in time for the 2 p.m. boat across to Koh Pee Pee. Non-air-conditioned buses to Surat Thani, for Koh Samui, leave at 5.30 a.m., 8.30 a.m. and 11.30 a.m. from the bus terminal (67B, five hours).

TOURIST SERVICES

The TAT tourist office (tel: 243747) at Soi 2, Niphat Uthit 3, is open 8.30 a.m. to 6.30 p.m. daily. It has helpful staff and up-to-date maps and handouts. The GPO is on Niphat Songkhro Rd, open 8.30 a.m. to 4.30 p.m. weekdays, 9 a.m. to 12 noon Saturdays. You can make overseas phone calls here between 7 a.m. and 10 p.m. daily. Banks in Hat Yai are open 8 a.m. to 3.30 p.m. weekdays and some have foreign exchange counters open till late – the Krung Thai Bank, next to Yong Dee Hotel, stays open till 8 p.m. and the Siam Bank, a few doors along, until 9 p.m. If coming up from the south, bring all your spare Malaysian *ringgit* and Singapore dollars to the Yong Dee Hotel – it gives a much better rate than any bank. This is because of the thriving black market in these currencies. Thai Airways has two offices in Niphat Uthit 2 – one for domestic flights (next to New World Hotel), the other for international flights (near Kosit Hotel). Both are open 8 a.m. to 5 p.m. daily.

THINGS TO DO

Wat Hat Yai Noi, located down Soi 26 Phetkasem Rd, on the way to the airport, has a large reclining Buddha – 35 m long and 15 m high – with a big Mona Lisa smile. It used to be open to the skies, but now has an 'umbrella' roof against the rain. The monks at this wat are very

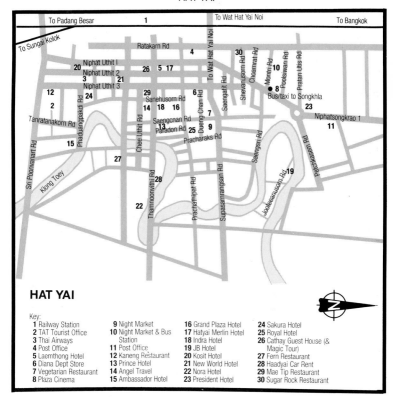

HAT YAI

Key:
1 Railway Station
2 TAT Tourist Office
3 Thai Airways
4 Post Office
5 Laemthong Hotel
6 Diana Dept Store
7 Vegetarian Restaurant
8 Plaza Cinema
9 Night Market
10 Night Market & Bus Station
11 Post Office
12 Kaneng Restaurant
13 Prince Hotel
14 Angel Travel
15 Ambassador Hotel
16 Grand Plaza Hotel
17 Hatyai Merlin Hotel
18 Indra Hotel
19 JB Hotel
20 Kosit Hotel
21 New World Hotel
22 Nora Hotel
23 President Hotel
24 Sakura Hotel
25 Royal Hotel
26 Cathay Guest House (& Magic Tour)
27 Fern Restaurant
28 Haadyai Car Rent
29 Mae Tip Restaurant
30 Sugar Rock Restaurant

famous for their fortune-telling skills. Malaysian and Singaporean visitors flock here in droves to consult them. If you want a reading, turn up before 11 a.m. – and do not worry, they speak English! Wat Hat Yai Noi is a 5B *samlor* ride from the city centre. The big food night market outside the wat is worth a return visit.

The **Southern Cultural Village** is 5 km out of town, inside the municipal park. To get there, take a share *tuk-tuk* (5B) from the stand at the night-hawker centre near the Plaza cinema. Anywhere else, the fare will be 20B or more. The 'village' offers instant culture shows (Thai boxing, cockfighting, ceremonies, dances, etc.) between 4 and 5.30 p.m. daily (except Monday/Tuesday) for 140B. If you book with Magic Tour at Cathay Hotel, they throw in transport for free. Magic Tour also sell tickets for local cabaret and 'go-go' shows and can set up a good straight massage for 100B per hour.

Bullfighting (bull against bull) takes place between 10.30 a.m. and 6 p.m. every first Saturday of the month. Entrance fees vary from 50B to 200B (depending on how long you stay) and the tourist office knows the current venue.

The **Ambassador Hotel** has a good video bar, showing English-speaking movies. It serves cold beer and snacks and is a peaceful, relaxing haven away from the heat and noise of the city. So is **Post Laser Disc** on Thamnoonvithi Rd, which has smaller screens but a better choice of films. Three cinemas, the **Coliseum** in Prachatipat Rd, the **Chaloem Thai** in Suppasanrangsan Rd and the **Hat Yai Rama** in Phetkasem Rd, have English original sound track rooms where you can watch movies before they have been dubbed over for local audiences. If you want more action, you can dance the night away at the **Hollywood Nightclub** in Thamnoonvithi Rd – it is best on Friday, Saturday and Sunday nights.

The fishing port cum beach resort of **Songkhla**, 30 km east of Hat Yai, offers a good day out. Buses go there from the taxi-stand in front of the President Hotel (30 minutes, 7B), or you can take a share-taxi for 12B per person. On arrival, hire a 10B *songthaew* to **Samila Beach** (poor swimming, but great seafood restaurants) or get a 5B orange bus from opposite the Queen Hotel to **Koh Yaw** on the lake, where you can get beautiful cotton fabrics at bargain prices. In Songkhla town itself, visit the **National Museum** on Rongmuang Rd. Converted from an elegant nineteenth-century Thai-Chinese house, it has fine archaeological displays and gives a complete insight into south Thai culture and arts from the prehistoric period of Ban Chiang to the

Rattanakosin period. It is open from 9 to 12 noon and 1 to 4 p.m., except Mondays and Tuesdays. **Wat Matchimawat** on Saiburi Rd is the largest temple in town. Around 400 years old, it houses another museum with art and ancient relics from various southern sites. **Wat Chaimongkhon**, by the railway station, contains an impressive statue of Buddha originating from Sri Lanka. Still in town, you can walk up **Khao Noi Hill** (20 minutes), to see its large white *chedi* and enjoy the views. Then take a stroll along the busy waterfront to watch the fishing boats unloading their catch. If you want to stay in Songkhla overnight, two comfortable hotels are the **Queen** at 20 Saiburi Rd and the **Sansabai** at 1 Pethckeree Rd, both charging around 120/150B for fan-cooled rooms, 250/300B with air-conditioned. The cheaper **Songhkla Hotel** on Vichianchom Rd costs 90/120B and attracts the backpacker crowd. Western-style breakfasts are good at **Fern Bakery**, 53 Petchkiri Rd and **Buatip Restaurant**, a few doors along, serves delicious seafood. After 6 p.m., a popular food night market starts up along Vichianchom Rd.

SHOPPING

Santisuk Market is probably the biggest open black market in Thailand. It is full of cheap goods (hi-fi, watches, cameras, etc.) smuggled in from Singapore. In the evening, there is another market at the top of Niphat Uthit 2, selling inexpensive fashion clothes. General shopping is best at department stores like **Diana**, **Ocean** and **Expo**, at the junction of Niphat Uthit 3 and Duangchan Rd.

ACCOMMODATION

Hat Yai is a business town with business prices. Hotel tariffs are highest at weekends, when all the Malaysians and Singaporeans roll in; during the week, you can often negotiate 20 per cent discounts. Two recommended first class hotels are **JB** (tel: 234300) at 99 Jootee Anusorn and **Regency** (tel: 234400) at 23 Prachathipat. Both are centrally located, with comfortable air-conditioned rooms around 650/750B and several facilities. The Regency has an overseas phone service and the JB has a pool. A small step down is the **Montien** (tel: 245399) at 120-124 Niphat Uthit 1, with well-equipped rooms from 532B. Right next door, the cosy **King's Hotel** (tel: 243966) has rooms with air-conditioning at 240B single, 320B double. The **Pacific** (tel: 244062) at 149/l Niphat Uthit 2 charges 150B for nice quiet fan doubles, or 250B with air-conditioning. A couple can even use an air-conditioned single (150B) because the beds are so big! **Prince Hotel** (tel: 243160) at 138/2-3 Thamnoonvithi has clean rooms with shower/bath and free soap/towels at 120B single, 200B double. If you want air-conditioning, it is 50B extra.

Cathay Guest House (tel: 243815) at 93/1 Niphat Uthit 2 is, as it advertises, the travellers' centre in Hat Yai. Rooms go from 80 to 120B (dormitory beds 50B) and the TV lounge has a casual family atmosphere. The 22B Western breakfast is the cheapest in town, and the upstairs noticeboard is full of useful tips from other travellers. If full, Mr Jit or Mrs Kanya can direct you to a budget Chinese hotel nearby. **Angel Guest House**, at 127 Thamnoonvithi, has modest rooms for 100B, a small restaurant and a travel service.

FOOD

Hat Yai comes into its own after dark, when the whole town turns into one big night market. There are night hawker centres dotted all round the city, but the biggest and best food scene is up at the bus-station near the Plaza cinema. Here you can experiment with a wide range of Thai snacks at around 10-15B per dish. **Mae Tip II**, 180 Niphat Uthit 3, is a pleasant garden restaurant serving tender BBQ beef, perfumed chicken wrapped in banana leaves and tangy banana flower salad. It also does very good seafood. Two worthwhile Muslim restaurants are **O Cha** opposite **King's Hotel** and **Muslim Ruby** at 59/3 Rattakarn Rd. For European fast-food, burgers and cakes, try **Sugar Rock** at 114 Thamnoonvithi or **Boat Burger** opposite Kosit Hotel. Close to the Sakura Hotel, the **Crest** and **Black Canyon** coffee houses offer a large variety of hot and cold coffees all day long, as well as ice-cream, soothing music and a relaxed atmosphere. The **Old Time Pub** upstairs from the Black Canyon is a quaint little pub, very quiet, with music videos.

Peninsular Malaysia

Malaysia offers endless choice. Depending on where you go you will enjoy long sandy beaches, lovely coral reefs, lush tropical jungles, idyllic islands, city bustle and village stillness. There is not much in the way of culture or history, but the people are friendly, the scenery beautiful and the travel easy and comfortable. Unlike Thailand, which has had a tourism industry for 30 years, Malaysia's tourism is only five years old – and you can see the difference. Thailand runs a very slick operation now and a lot of travellers miss all that glitz and glamour when they come to Malaysia – there is nowhere to watch videos like they do on Koh Samui! On the plus side, especially if you hit the east coast, there are unspoiled beaches, untouristy villages and uncrowded towns with a lot of traditional atmosphere still clinging to them. If you want challenge, go to the hill stations and national parks of the interior, or to remote islands, like Tioman or Perhentian which are only now opening up.

If you have just come from Java and are pining for home comforts, visit the west coast. This has most of the Malay towns and population, and also the high-class hotels and facilities. There is less to see and enjoy here, but a lot more people speak English and it is far easier to get around. Many Asian countries encouraged tourism before they could cope with it, but Malaysia seems well prepared. 1990 is 'Visit Malaysia' year and there is an event going on in all 13 states on every day throughout the year.

THE LAND

Bordered on the north by Thailand, the long 'leg' of peninsular Malaysia extends for some 700 km southwards to the small island of Singapore. The country is in the tropical zone, but includes hot, humid lowlands and cool highlands. Some 70 per cent of the 134,680 sq km of land area is covered by tropical rain forests that abound with an enormous variety of plant and animal life.

Crossing over into Malaysia from Thailand, you do not see much of a difference at first. Then, after the first few miles, you leave behind the paddy fields and come across the Malay *kampongs* (little villages) and (a startling difference) the 'personal' car. The average Malay is a lot wealthier than his Thai counterpart – he can afford to sit around drinking beer (even at £1 a bottle) and he can afford a Japanese car. Malaysia's economy went into steep decline in the mid 1980s, when the prices of its main

three commodities – rubber, tin, and palm oil – went down. Since then, it has staged an impressive comeback. The AIDS disaster, for instance, caused a resurgence in the rubber trade, because condoms are one of the few things made of natural rubber. Tin has also achieved some stability, but Malaysia has put most of its money into palm oil. When you get into Malaysia proper, all you will see for mile after mile is palm plantations. What you will not see is much food production. There is the usual presence of fruits like banana and coconut which can grow anywhere, but there is not the concerted effort to grow food that you see in Thailand. More and more people are abandoning the fields and the farms and are moving into the cities looking for work and money.

The shoreline of peninsular Malaysia's east beach has a scattering of pretty offshore islands, while its western shores are sandy, though not as spectacular. More and more visitors are getting into Taman Negara, the national park, since it became more accessible and they are also heading for places in the interior like the Cameron Highlands. Most visitors come to Penang, but since 1985 backpackers have favoured the east coast route, entering the peninsula at the small border town of Kota Bahru, just one hour from the Thai border. Like north Thailand, east Malaysia is where the culture is, and where the giant leatherback turtles come ashore each year, between May and September to lay their eggs in the warm sand.

CLIMATE

Temperatures in Malaysia range from 70-90°F (21-32°C) in the lowlands, to as low as 61°F (16°C) at night in the highlands. Rain is possible throughout the year, but the main rainy season is from October to March, when monsoon winds bring heavy downpours to the east coast. The peak tourist season is April to August, when the weather is at its best. The two months to avoid are November and December, when it rains day and night. Then humidity averages 85 to 95 per cent.

HISTORY

In sharp contrast to Thailand, the Malay peninsula has always been either partly or wholly under foreign rule. From the seventh century AD, the country was controlled by the powerful Srivajaya kingdom of Sumatra. In 1403 Paramesvara, a Sumatran prince, established himself at Malacca, which soon began to

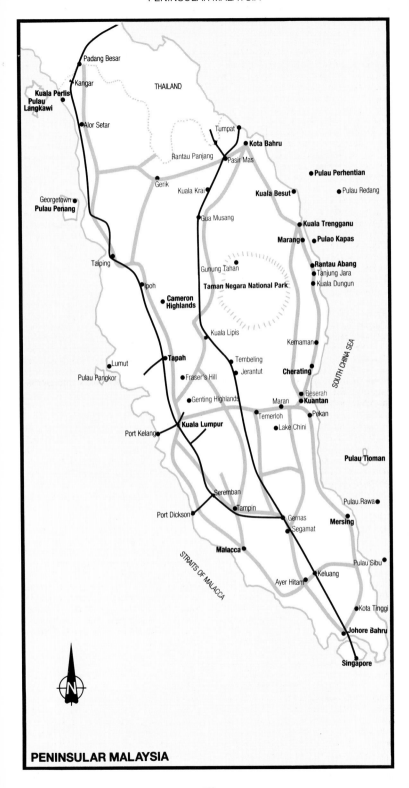

PENINSULAR MALAYSIA

predominate as a sea power. Islam took a foothold on the peninsula when Malacca was converted in the fifteenth century.

The Portuguese first came to the Malay states in 1509 and seized Malacca in 15ll. The Dutch arrived on the scene in 1641, taking Malacca from the Portuguese and founding the East India Company. Captain Francis Light landed at Penang in 1786, giving the British their first outpost. In 1824, a treaty was signed which left Nias and Sumatra to the Dutch and Malacca in British hands. From 1874, a series of treaties and agreements signed by local Malay rulers quickly brought the rest of the peninsula under British control. To smoothen the process of colonisation, the British divided Malaya (as it was then known) into three administrative areas, namely the Federated Malay States, the Unfederated States and the Straits Settlements. After independence from Britain in 1957, Malaya was joined, in 1963, by the north Borneo states of Sarawak and Sabah, and became Malaysia.

PEOPLE AND RELIGION
Ethnically and culturally diverse, the 13 million population of the Malay peninsula is part Chinese (36 per cent), part Malay (47 per cent) and part Indian (12 per cent), with members of various proto-Malayan tribes forming a tiny minority. The natural-born Malays have chocolate-brown skins and lovely slicked-back, straight hair. They are easy to recognise, although the Tamils (part of the Indian group) look quite similar. The Chinese are successful businessmen. That has caused big problems because they don't give the Malays jobs in business and in return the Malays will not let them hold high-ranking official posts in the army, police and civil service. The two races live together in delicate but superficial harmony. The Chinese are concentrated on the west coast (especially in business centres like Penang and Kuala Lumpur), while the east coast is over 90 per cent Malay.

Religion is another problem area. The official religion is Islam, but other religions are widely practised. Nearly all Malays are Muslim, the Chinese are Buddhist and the Indians are Hindu or Buddhist. In Malaysia, you have the curious situation of a Muslim society which demands that women cover themselves up in public and, working against this, Chinese girls who go out jogging every morning in skimpy shorts and T-shirts! Malaysia has a very relaxed Muslim code, at least on the west coast. The east is far more strict and you will have to be more careful in observing religious customs. When visiting a mosque, women must cover their heads, men must wear long trousers (or rent a

sarong) and everyone must remove their shoes. Elsewhere, women can avoid offence by covering up their shoulders and wearing dresses cut no higher than the knee. On the whole, Malays are just as friendly as the Thais, although as Muslims they tend to be rather more reserved and less smiling.

VISAS
The standard visa issued on arrival is for one month only. A two-month extension is easy to obtain on application to any immigration office in the country. A second extension of two months is also possible, on payment of MS$5. Anybody wishing to stay over five months must hop over to Thailand, Singapore or Indonesia, and then re-enter. For up-to-date information on visas, contact the Malaysian embassy (tel: 01-235 8033) at 45 Belgrave St, London SWl, which is open from 9.30 a.m. to 12.15 p.m. weekdays.

DOMESTIC TRANSPORT
Air
Air service in Malaysia is provided by MAS (Malaysian Airline System) which flies to all major cities in the country. The airport tax for domestic flights is MS$3, for international flights MS$15 and for Singapore MS$5. All tickets issued in Malaysia have airport taxes automatically added.

Rail
Malaysian trains are modern, cheap and comfortable. The main rail line from Singapore to Butterworth connects with the international express from Bangkok. These trains include air-conditioned first-class coaches and cabins, as well as sleeping berths. A second rail link branches off this line at Gemas, running through Kuala Lipis up to Kota Bahru on the east coast. If you are doing a lot of rail travel, it may be worth buying a Malay Rail Pass, giving unlimited travel on any class (except sleeping berths) at MS$85 for ten days, MS$175 for 30 days. Passes are available from MSL in Kuala Lumpur or any major travel agent in Malaysia. Advance reservation of trains is usually no problem, and timetables are readily available from railway stations or tourist offices.

Road
Most towns and cities are connected by a quick, efficient bus service. Privately owned air-conditioned express buses are often cheaper than public buses. Route information is available in English from tourist information centres. Malaysia's roads are scheduled for great improvements over the next few years. When the North-South highway is completed in 1995, the travelling time to Singapore

from Penang will be cut in half – from 14 hours to only seven and a half hours. Highway 3, which runs up the east coast from Johore Bahru to the Thai border, was resurfaced and streamlined in 1985, making for smoother, faster travel. In addition to buses, most towns and cities now have a taxi station where, as soon as four people are assembled and a destination agreed, off you go! Share-taxis are around twice the cost of buses, but they are quicker and there is often no waiting involved.

LOCAL TRANSPORT
Metered taxis are available in all cities and large towns and drivers generally have some knowledge of English. Taxis may also be hired by the hour. Car hire is cheap (from around MS$120 a day) and can usually be arranged at the larger hotels. The most common and convenient form of local transport is still (apart from in KL) the bicycle rickshaw or trishaw. Fares start at around MS$l per kilometre and should be fixed in advance.

ENTERTAINMENT/SHOPPING
Traditional Malay entertainments, like top-spinning, kite-flying, drum-playing and *silat* dancing, can be seen to best advantage in east coast centres like Kota Bahru or Kuala Trengganu. Best buys in Malaysia include batik materials as well as silverware, brassware, pottery, pewterware, woodcarvings, leather, *kain songket* (fabric with gold and silver woven in by hand, used for formal and festive dresses) and antiques (which require special permission from the National Museum to export). Kota Bahru has the best silver, batik and weaving, Penang the best duty-free shops and hi-fi bargains and Kuala Lumpur the markets, supermarkets and the all-in-one department stores.

ACCOMMODATION
The larger hotels are concentrated on the west coast and many of them have supper clubs, discothèques and bars with entertainment and regular cultural shows. Mid-budget travellers are generally well catered for, with a good selection of MS$15 to MS$25 guest houses in most tourist centres. Economy accommodation is in general inferior to that of Thailand – most cheapies are run by men, which makes for less service and less attention to hygiene. Often, however, you will find Chinese-run places which are, as a rule, spotlessly clean. Rates start at around MS$10-12 per person and for that you usually get a bed, a table, a sink, a chair or two and a ceiling fan. The shower is often down the hall, along with the (squat) toilet. Chinese hotels are prone to noise, but they nearly always have a restaurant downstairs. Couples can save money by asking for a 'single' room, which is likely to have a big double bed. Accommodation is generally most expensive and hard to find during local holidays (March, July and November) and at the Chinese New Year (December).

FOOD
Malaysian cuisine reflects the ethnic mixture – it has been influenced by Indian and Chinese as well as native preferences and is generally spicy. A favourite dish is *satay*, cubes of beef or chicken barbecued and dipped in a hot peanut sauce. Other popular styles of food include Cantonese, Hokkien, Szechuan, Indian, Japanese, Korean, American and European. This gives you a wide choice and for breakfast you can often choose between eggs on toast, noodle soup, vegetables and rice or *rotis* and dal. In Malaysia you can eat well for as little as 25p at a street-stall or bottom-end restaurant, or for as much as £25 at an international-class restaurant. The standard of street-food, as in Thailand, is generally excellent.

Note: Malaysia is hard on vegetarians. Whenever you order mixed fried vegetables, it nearly always has pork and shrimps in it!

MONEY
The unit of currency in Malaysia is the Malaysian dollar (MS$) or *ringgit*, which is divided into 100 cents. Notes are issued in denominations of 1, 10, 20, 50, 100, 500 and 1000 *ringgit*. There are coins of MS$l and 50, 20, 10, 5 and 1 *sen* (cents). At the present time, there are MS$4.50 to the UK£ and MS$2.60 to the US$. Any amount of local and foreign currency may be taken into Malaysia, but no more than 5000 *ringgit* may be taken out of the country.

TIME
Standard Malaysian time is eight hours ahead of GMT.

ELECTRICITY
Electrical current in Malaysia is 220 volts. Transformers are necessary when using American and European appliances.

LANGUAGE
Bahasa Malaysian is the official language, and it is very similar to bahasa Indonesian (cf. p 132). If you are going to be spending any amount of time in the country, it is probably worth learning a little of the local language. Otherwise, you can get by quite well in English as most Malays and Chinese both speak and understand it.

PENANG

Penang (Betelnut) Island is the oldest of what were once the Three Straits Settlements (Singapore and Malacca being the other two). It was ceded by the Sultan of Kedah to the East India Company in 1785 and occupied by Captain Francis Light in 1786. He named the original settlement Georgetown after King George III, and made Penang a free port to attract trade away from the Dutch. This in turn attracted many immigrant traders to the island and it became a melting pot of different races, religions and architectural styles. It is this cultural hotchpotch which makes Penang one of Asia's most popular destinations – most of its half-million population are indigenous Chinese, Indians and Malays who have stamped their individuality on the island's 285 sq km and whose influences can be clearly seen.

With its outstanding natural harbour and international airport, Penang serves as an island gateway to Malaysia. It is also a popular entry/exit point to Thailand. Since the construction of the bridge linking it to the mainland five years ago, Penang has been groomed as Malaysia's prime tourist centre – in 1988 it played host to over one million visitors. It offers beaches, resort hotels, good shopping, a wide variety of cuisines and (in Georgetown) the most authentic Chinatown outside of Bangkok. The people are friendly, the atmosphere relaxed and the cosmopolitan contrasts vivid: here, temples and mosques vie for prominence with Anglican Catholic churches and bustling bazaars and frenetic city life highlight the tranquillity of near deserted beaches. But Penang is no longer the 'Pearl of the Orient' it used to be. The steamhammer blows of property development are sweeping away Georgetown's heritage and turning it into a modern business and administrative centre. At the same time the island's only worthwhile beach, Batu Ferringhi, is being polluted by poor drainage and litter. Most worrying, the Penang Malays are discovering that making cars, air-conditioning units, TVs and radios brings in much more money than tourism. Suddenly the island is developing primarily as a business centre, and tourism is now distinctly low priority. If you want to go to Penang, go there soon before it changes forever.

ARRIVAL/DEPARTURE
Air
Through MAS, Penang has direct air links with Singapore (US$154), Kuala Lumpur (US$64), Bangkok (US$263), Hat Yai and Medan. Via Kuala Lumpur, Penang is linked with Los Angeles, London, Tokyo, Hong Kong and many other major cities round the world. You can get some really good flight deals from the travel agents in Leboh Chulia and from MSL Student Travel (tel: 04-24748) in the lobby of Ming Court Inn Hotel, Macalister Rd. A few sample fares include Bangkok-London £140, Kuala Lumpur-London US$275, and Penang-Los Angeles US$400.

Arrivals at Penang's Bayan Lepas Airport have a 16-km taxi trip to Georgetown (MS$13.50) and it is 36 km to the beach hotels of Batu Ferringhi (MS$20). Yellow bus 83 runs between the airport and Georgetown for MS$1.25.

Rail/Ferry
From Thailand, there is a comfortable daily train leaving Bangkok at 3.15 p.m., arriving at Butterworth around 1 p.m. the next day. The 22-hour journey includes regular food stops and passes surprisingly quickly, especially if you get a good night's sleep. The same train heads back north from Butterworth at 1.35 p.m. daily, arriving at Bangkok at 9 a.m. the following day. Fares are MS$110 first class air-conditioned cabin, MS$61.40/MS$65.90 second class upper/lower air-conditioned sleeper, MS$52.40/MS$56.90 second class upper/lower non-air-conditioned sleeper. To be sure of a seat, make your reservations at least three days ahead from the booking office at the ferry terminal (right-hand side, by taxi stand) in Georgetown. This office is open from 8 a.m. to around 7 p.m. daily and is fully computerised. It is also the best place to arrange train travel to Kuala Lumpur, Singapore and Malacca. There are two express trains daily to Kuala Lumpur, a six-hour trip. The early morning train carries straight on to Singapore.

Off the train at Butterworth, follow the walkway over the bridge to the ferry station. A round-the-clock ferry service operates from Butterworth to Georgetown and takes 20 minutes – have a 20-sen coin handy for the ticket machine. Off the ferry, it is a short walk down into the car-park, where you can get a taxi or a bicycle-rickshaw to your hotel.

Notes: If coming in by train from Thailand, you will have to disembark at Padang Besar, the border town, to check your passport through Thai immigration. When leaving the train, close the window by your seat (to stop thieves helping themselves to bags and valuables) and be *very* careful that nobody slips drugs into your hand luggage – tourists are sometimes used as unwitting carriers by drug smugglers. The station at Padang Besar has a money changer (useful for unloading unwanted Thai currency) and a breakfast cafe. Butterworth railway station has an extremely useful left-luggage facility.

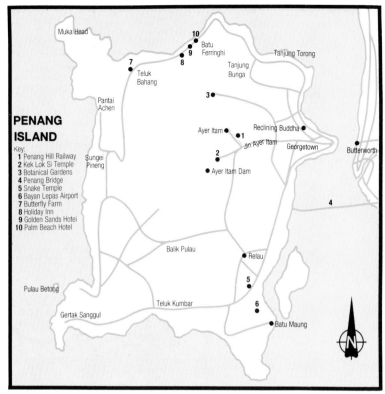

PENANG ISLAND

Key:
1 Penang Hill Railway
2 Kek Lok Si Temple
3 Botanical Gardens
4 Penang Bridge
5 Snake Temple
6 Bayan Lepas Airport
7 Butterfly Farm
8 Holiday Inn
9 Golden Sands Hotel
10 Palm Beach Hotel

Road

From the bus stand by the ferry terminal in Butterworth, you can get buses to Kuala Lumpur (MS$15), Singapore (MS$28-31) and Kota Bahru (MS$18). From the nearby taxi-stand (or from hotels like Hotel Mingood in Georgetown) you can get taxis to Hat Yai (MS$22), Kuala Lumpur (MS$30) and Cameron Highlands (MS$30). Several travel agents in Georgetown sell seats on express buses to Kuala Lumpur and Singapore, as well as the combined train/bus/boat ticket to Koh Samui in Thailand and the twice-weekly (dep. Monday and Wednesday) boat to Medan in north Sumatra.

TOURIST SERVICES

Georgetown has two good tourist offices near the seafront. The TDC office (tel: 04-620066), at 10 Jln Tun Dyed Sheh Barakbah, is open from 8 a.m. to 12.45 p.m. and 2 to 4.15 p.m. weekdays, 8 a.m. to 12.45 p.m. Saturday. It has lots of handouts, helpful staff and a baggage deposit. Just up the road is Penang Tourist Association (tel: 61663) at Pesara King Edward. It is open from 8.30 a.m. to 4.30 p.m. weekdays, 8.30 a.m. to 1 p.m. Saturday and is more geared to backpackers.

The GPO and poste restante is on Leboh Downing, below the clock tower. The immigration office is close by on Leboh Light. There is a handy post office on the ground floor of the Komtar building, and a telephone office on Jln Burma where you can make overseas calls (24-hour service). Most banks are located in Beach St, open from 10 a.m. to 3 p.m. The money-changer at the base of White House Hotel, at the corner of Penang Rd and Jln Sri Bahari, offers a comparable rate without commission or stamp duty. While in Penang, it is a good idea to get a few dollars of your next currency (Singapore dollars or Thai *baht*).

Penang is *the* place on the west coast to apply for (or renew) Thai visas. The Thai consulate (tel: 04-23352) at 1 Ayer Rajah Rd is very efficient and co-operative. The cost of a visa is MS$15 for one month, MS$30 for two months and if you apply before 10 a.m. (with passport and two photos) it will be ready for you at 4 p.m. that afternoon. Several hotels, notably Hotel Mingood, Hotel Golden City and New China Hotel, offer a quick, convenient Thai visa service.

Airline offices in Penang include: Cathay Pacific, AIA Building, 88 Leboh Bishop (tel: 04-620411); Garuda, 41 Aboo Sittee Lane (tel: 04-365257), Malaysian Airlines System, Kompleks Tun Abdul Razak, Penang Rd (tel: 04-621403), Singapore Airlines, Wisma

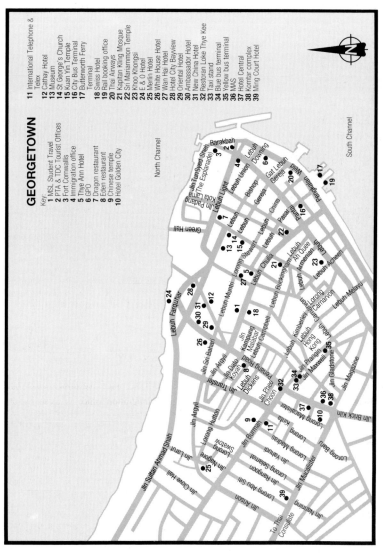

GEORGETOWN

Key:
1 MSL Student Travel
2 PTA & TDC Tourist Offices
3 Fort Cornwallis
4 Immigration office
5 Thye Ann Hotel
6 GPO
7 Dragon restaurant
8 Eden restaurant
9 Chinese temple
10 Hotel Golden City

11 International Telephone & Telex
12 Cathay Hotel
13 Museum
14 St George's Church
15 Kuan Yin Temple
16 City Bus Terminal
17 Butterworth Ferry Terminal
18 Swiss Hotel
19 Rail booking office
20 Thai Airways
21 Kapitan Kling Mosque
22 Sri Mariammon Temple
23 Khoo Khongsi
24 E & O Hotel
25 Merlin Hotel
26 White House Hotel
27 Wan Hai Hotel
28 Hotel City Bayview
29 Oriental Hotel
30 Ambassador Hotel
31 New China Hotel
32 Restoran Loke Thye Kee
33 Taxi stand
34 Blue bus terminal
35 Yellow bus terminal
36 MAS
37 Hotel Central
38 Komtar complex
39 Ming Court Hotel

Penang Garden, 42 Jln Sultan Ahmad Shah (tel: 04-363201); Thai Airways International, Wisma Central, Macalister Rd (tel: 04-23484).

Notes: Penang has something of a reputation for bag-snatching. Leave your passport/travellers' cheques/air tickets locked in a bag in your room, or deposit them at the hotel reception. On the street, wear shoulder bags across the body. Don't accept offers of drugs from trishaw drivers – Penang is also famous as the place where two Australian drug couriers were arrested (and later executed in Kuala Lumpur).

GEORGETOWN

Penang's capital, located in the northeast of the island, is a colourful, compact city of colonial buildings, temples, restaurants and shops, easily negotiable on foot or by bicycle rickshaw. Georgetown still has some character, especially round the Chinese areas with their roadside temples and shrines. The main streets are not for jaywalking (horrendous traffic), but a stroll down the backstreets reveals many small shops dating from the early 1900s, often with carved doorways and windows. These are fine examples of what is known as Straits eclectic architecture, a clever blend and borrowing of Chinese and Malay styles. The Pasar Malam night market and the lively Chinatown district merit a wander. So do the Chinese clan piers along the waterfront and the antique and 'junk' shops of Rope Walk. For quick orientation, hire a trishaw (MS$4 per hour) or a taxi (MS$8 per hour) and take in a few 'set pieces' on a half-day sightseeing tour:

Penang's big landmark, visible from practically anywhere on the island, is the tall **Komtar** building in Georgetown. Most people start their tour here, usually with a cold coffee, an orange juice or a pizza. There are four trips daily (ll a.m., l p.m., 3 p.m. and 5 p.m.) to the top of the Komtar (fiifty-ninth floor) for spectacular city views. Tickets cost MS$3 and are sold at the booth on the third floor.

From the Komtar, drive on to **Fort Cornwallis** by the seafront. When Francis Light established the first British settlement in Malaysia here, he persuaded the locals to clear the dense jungle by firing a cannon loaded with silver dollars into it. The original wooden stockade was rebuilt in stone by convict labour between 1808 and 1810. There is little to see nowadays, except a few rusty old cannon, but you can stroll along the Esplanade and admire the pretty pastel clock tower, built by the Dutch in 1837. Back in town, visit Malaysia's first Anglican church, **St George's**, in Farquhar St. Erected in 1818 by convict labour, it is distinguished by its white columns rising from a marble floor.

The adjoining **Museum & Art Gallery** is open 9 a.m. to 5 p.m. (closed Sundays) and is wonderfully air-conditioned – the ideal escape from the city heat. The history room gives a full rundown of the history of the island and all exhibits, including the showpiece Penang Hill Coach, are well presented and labelled in English. Only a stone's throw away is Penang's oldest and most popular temple, the **Kuan Yin Teng** or Goddess of Mercy Temple, at the corner of Pitt St and Stewart Lane. It was built by the first Chinese settlers in the 1880s and attracts hundreds of devotees daily. They come to burn incense at the shrine and to earn wealth in the afterlife by burning paper-money in the twin burners outside. Between Pitt St and Queen St, you will find **Sri Mariammon Temple**, an ornate Hindu temple constructed in the south Indian style in 1883. The fine carvings above the entrance are especially noteworthy. Walking down Pitt St, turn into Acheen St for the **Malay Mosque**. Of Penang's several mosques, this is arguably the most interesting with its unique Egyptian-style minaret. Round off your excursion with a visit to **Khoo Kongsi**, a Chinese clanhouse in Cannon Square, off Cannon St, off Acheen St. This is a beautiful structure, intricately decorated and very photogenic, which was rebuilt after a fire in 1906 and renovated in the 1950s. Entering the square, you should find a guard seated on the right. Go upstairs to sign the visitors' book, and he will then unlock the gates to the clanhouse. Khoo Kongsi is open 9 a.m. to 5 p.m. daily. Sometimes MS$l is charged, sometimes not.

GETTING AROUND THE ISLAND

Probably the easiest way of touring the island is by taxi and it is not too expensive. Chat to the taxi drivers at the rank outside the Oriental Hotel, on the Penang Rd side, till you find one who understands your needs and who can speak a bit of English; some taxi drivers are actually good guides, who will point out things of interest and can answer any questions you may have. With bargaining, you should be able to negotiate a five-hour tour of the island for around MS$70/80 (share the costs as a group). Give the driver your itinerary, and make sure the final stop is Penang Hill. That way, you are not paying him for sleeping in his car for one and a half hours while you go up the hill and come back down again! If you want to tour Penang on a cheaper basis, you can hire motorbikes from guest houses/hotels at around MS$20 per day or take a MS$18 air-conditioned minibus tour (three and a half hours) from the Continental Hotel or the various agencies along Chulia St. Private car hire can be arranged with Ferringhi Rent-a-Car (tel: 811130), who charge MS$64 per day, inclusive of insurance and unlimited mileage. Hertz (tel: 375914) are not so cheap, but more professional. If you are on a shoestring and have lots of time to spare, you can tour the island by bus. From the terminus on Jln Maxwell, blue buses run north to Batu Ferringhi, Telok, Bahang, etc. and yellow buses run south to the airport, the Snake Temple and the southern beaches. The average point-to-point fare is 50 *sen*, and you can do the whole 80-km round-trip of Penang for less than MS$4.

By taxi/motorbike, it is a short 25-km cruise south of Georgetown to the **Snake Temple** or Temple of the Azure Cloud, dedicated to the Taoist deity Chor Soo Hong. Built in 1850, it is home to venomous Wagler's pit vipers which are kept drugged and harmless by the constantly burning fumes of incense. Don't pay the MS$10 fee to have your photo taken with a pit viper – wait until some other poor soul has a bunch of snakes coiled round his video camera, and take a (free) photo of him instead!

Moving south, the scenery becomes more attractive with vast expanses of banana and palm plantations in the interior, and the odd glimpse of beautiful coastline. The southern beaches, if you can make time for them, are quite pretty – it is a pity there is nowhere to stay. Coming up the west coast, do not miss the **Butterfly Farm** at Teluk Bahang. For many, this is the best 'sight' that Penang has to offer. Here can be seen a spectacular array of butterflies (more than 4,000 specimens from over 120 species), cater-pillers, centipedes, locusts and, in the 'reptile corner', turtles, alligators and scorpions. The largest farm of its kind in the world, it is open from 9 a.m. to 5 p.m. weekdays, 9 a.m. to 6 p.m. weekends. Admission is MS$2, camera charge MS$1, video cameras MS$3.

Nearby is the touristy **Craft Batik Factory**. The showroom is outrageously expensive, but there is a good workshop layout at the back. A few kilometres further north is **Batu Ferringhi** beach, which is pretty much a disaster. Lots of big new hotels have been built along the beach and they have upset the drainage system coming off the cliff and through the woods. Foul-smelling streams which used to drain off elsewhere now run out onto the beach and the once blue sea is now muddy brown. Having said that, if you have the gall to do it, you can swan along to the Palm Beach Hotel or Golden Sands Hotel and, if you look the part and sit on their sun lounges and maybe order lunch, you can use their nice clean swimming pools and 5-star facilities. This way, you might be able to enjoy a few nice hours up on Batu Ferringhi!

If you want to stay over, try the **Golden Sands** (tel: 04-8119ll), a pleasant high-class hotel with rooms from MS$175, two outdoor pools, jacuzzi, four restaurants and a beachfront bar. Budget travellers favour **Ali's Guest House**, next to Palm Beach Hotel, with big triple rooms for MS$8, good atmos-phere, cheap food and fun live music. Ask Ali for directions to the small secluded bay (beautiful beach, much better than Batu Ferringhi) only a 1-km walk back towards Georgetown.

Batu Ferringhi has good water-sports like parasailing and windsurfing, but they are expensive. A less expensive recrea-tion is to hire out canoes, but watch out for strong currents. Ask around before you go swimming – there is a season for (venomous) sea-snakes and for jellyfish. If not on a tour, you can go to Batu Ferringhi by blue bus 93 from Jln Prangin terminal in Georgetown. The 14-km journey takes around one hour and costs 85 sen. Going by taxi costs around MS$12 per load on the way out and MS$10 coming back.

Penang's 30-hectare **Botanical Gardens** are located off Waterfall Rd, below Penang Hill. This is a popular picnic spot, with lots of trees and monkeys and a mini-zoo with orang-utans. You can also go there by No. 7 bus from Chulia St, Georgetown. Nearby Ayer Itam vil-lage has **Kek Lok Si Temple**, reputed to be the finest and largest in South-East Asia. Built around the turn of the century, it is actually a fairly gaudy mixture of Chinese, Thai and Burmese styles, with a seven-storey pagoda of 10,000 Buddhas. If you walk 3 km up the hill, keeping the temple on your left, you will come to **Ayer Itam Dam** with its 18-hectare lake and pleasant views. For even better views from the uplands, take a cable-car ride up to the top of 692-m **Penang Hill**. Cars run every half hour from 6.30 a.m. to 9.30 p.m. and the round-trip fare is MS$3. There is a nice hotel at the summit, where you can savour the cool temperatures and scenic vistas over a meal or a beer. If you have time, try the two-hour walk up Penang Hill from the base. Coming in by bus (No. 7 from Chulia St), ask to get off at Moon Gate (circular light green gate on left) and follow the yellow arrows up the hill, keeping more or less to the left. It is a hard sweaty slog, but worth it (say some) and you can get the cable car down. Less masochistic travellers do it the other way round!

PULAO LANGKAWI

If you want white sandy beaches, clear waters, good coral and cheap duty-free shopping, consider a side-trip to the 99 Langkawi islands ll2 km north of Penang. Quiet and unspoilt, they are suddenly becoming popular, especially with honeymooners wanting to get away from it all. The main island, 30 km off the coast from Kuala Perlis, has an interesting legend attached to it. Mahsuri, a legendary princess, was wrongfully executed here for adultery and laid a curse on the island that it would not prosper for seven generations. When fishermen later came to fish at the island, all they could see were eagles drifting over barren limestone hills and that is how Langkawi (from lang or eagle, and kawi or limestone) got its name. The curse lapsed about 50 years ago, allowing Langkawi to become a big tourist resort. So far, however, only the main island is being developed, primarily with expensive resort hotels.

To get to Langkawi from Butterworth, take the Ebban Express bus (hourly departures from 8 a.m. to 6 p.m.) up to Kuala Perlis. The three-hour trip costs MS$4.85, or MS$6.65 air-conditioned. Ferries from Kuala Perlis over to Lang-kawi run on a regular basis from 8 a.m. to 5 p.m. The crossing takes one hour and costs MS$10 one-way. The ferry drops you at the main town of Kuah, from where you can get a taxi (rates posted at the jetty) or a **Mara** bus to your hotel. Kuah has several good seafood restaurants and one particularly good Chinese restaurant. Cheap accommoda-tion is mainly chalets like **Sandy Beach Hotel** and **Charlie Motel** (MS$15 to MS$45) at Pantai Cenang beach, near the airport, or **Pantai Kok Motel**

(MS$30) at Pantai Kok beach, close to Telaga Tujuh. The brand-new **Pelangi Beach Hotel** (tel: 03-2610393) on Pantai Cenang is a palatial structure with luxury chalets from US$125. The two other big luxury hotels are **Langkawi Island Resort** (tel: 03-788209) in Kuah and **Mutiara Beach Hotel** (tel: 03-788488) at Tanjung Rhu, in the north of the island. Avoid Langkawi at weekends and during the Malay holidays as it gets very busy! If you get tired of lying on a beach, you can hire a bicycle/motorbike to travel round the island, or take a speedboat over to the neighbouring island of Pulau Dayang Bunting, famous for its beautiful lake which is worth a visit.

Notes: MAS has flights to Langkawi from Penang (MS$42) and from Singapore/ Kuala Lumpur. Off the island, you can get a taxi from Kuala Perlis up to Padang Besar (for Thailand) for just MS$10/12 per load. If you are coming down from Thailand, the first major rail stop is Alor Setar, from where you can get a bus/taxi to Kuala Perlis.

ENTERTAINMENT

Georgetown is full of bars, discos, video-game parlours and nightclubs, most of which have appeared over the past few years. Discos are rather pricey, but worth it if you are in town on a Friday/Saturday night and if there is a group of you. Try **Xanadu** disco next to the Malaysia Hotel or **Hotlips** disco (happy hours 6 p.m. to 9.30 p.m.) next to Hotel Continental. Both places charge around MS$8 entrance and the first beer/soft drink is free. Nightspots can be fun, but check them out before paying any money. Decide whether you want a good Filipino band which plays music suitable for dancing or a Malay band playing local tunes which most Westerners cannot easily relate to. A decent group play in the **City Lounge** on the ground floor of the City Bayview Hotel. **Polar Cafe**, just round the corner from Hotlips disco, has live country and western music from 9 p.m. to midnight. **Tiger Bar** at Lumfong Hotel, near Cathay Hotel, has cheap draught beer, a good jukebox, and friendly atmosphere. At **City Snooker Hall**, opposite Eden restaurant, you can play pool/snooker for MS$7.80 per hour. The **Cafe Cinema**, opposite Cris Night Corner and **Rex Cinema**, at the junction of Jln Burmah and Jln Transfer, show English-speaking movies.

Penang's large 18-hole golf course is a MS$10 taxi ride from Georgetown centre. Golf is cheapest after 4.30 p.m. on weekdays, when it is only MS$15 per round. Horse-riding, tennis and watersports are all available on Batu Ferringhi beach.

SHOPPING

Georgetown shopping is good. Prices are a little higher than Singapore, but there is far less hard sell and nastiness. The main shopping areas are Jln Penang, Jln Burmah and Lebuh Campbell. Most shops are open from 10 a.m. to 10 p.m. Watches, cameras, hi-fi equipment, sunglasses and beach clothes are inexpensive and local products like batik, pewterware and pottery are popular souvenirs. Most items have marked prices, but you can generally bargain down 50 per cent. The Komtar building has stacks of boutiques and fashion/ clothes shops on the first to fifth floors, and the local street market outside sells fake watches, T-shirts and perfumes at rock-bottom prices. You can pick up a bottle of Chanel No 5 Eau de Toilette (£18 in London) for less than £3 here, and while the perfume itself is obviously inferior, the packaging is excellent! There are a number of duty-free shops in Penang, including the TDC Duty-Free Shop at Komplek Tun Abdul Razak and the Komtar in Penang Rd. The street stalls along the Batu Ferringhi beach strip do a cheap line in watches, shirts and Bali-style sarongs.

ACCOMMODATION

Most visitors choose to be near the main attractions of Georgetown and the northern beaches. Most of the 4- and 5-star international hotels are located out at Batu Ferringhi. Georgetown's only 4-star hotel is **Shangri-La Inn** (tel: 04-622622) in Magazine Rd, with rooms from MS$140, pool, health club, business centre and Western and Chinese restaurants. The other high-class favourite is the **Eastern & Oriental Hotel** (tel: 04-375322) at 10 Farquhar St. The E & O is without a doubt the unchallenged 'grande dame' of Penang's hotels and a symbol of its colonial history. It lacks mod cons, but compensates with old-style rooms from MS$125, pool, grill and seafood restaurants and lots of traditional touches, including a manually operated lift and a veteran lift 'boy' who has been there for the last 34 years of the hotel's 104-year-old existence! Across the road, the recently refurbished **City Bayview Hotel** at 25A Farquhar Rd has very well-priced rooms from MS$60 and also a pool, business centre, disco and revolving rooftop restaurant with panoramic views over Georgetown.

The friendly and clean **Oriental Hotel** (tel: 04-24211) at 105 Penang Rd is a good mid-range bet. Rooms start at MS$53 and have hot showers, bathtubs and air-conditioning. The higher you go, the better the views. Down the backstreets, you will find **Hotel Mingood** (tel: 373411) at 164 Argyll Rd, and **Hotel Golden City**, at 12 Lerong Kinta, off Rex Cinema.

Incense sticks at Chinese temple, Penang

Cathay Hotel

Both places have spacious air-conditioned rooms from MS$46, restaurant-coffee shops and travel services. The Mingood has the better rooms – super-comfy Duplex mattress beds, TV with in-house videos, etc. The **Cathay Hotel** in Leith St is still popular, but the attractive old-colonial façade cannot conceal the rather basic, disappointing rooms, now overpriced at MS$27.60, or MS$30.60 with air-conditioning. Better value is the next-door **Waldorf Hotel** with friendly staff, coffee-shop/restaurant and cosy air-conditioned rooms at MS$27 single, MS$34 double. A couple could easily use a single room as the beds are so big!

Budget lodges are concentrated down Lebuh Chulia, Lebuh Leith and Love Lane. The ever-popular **Tye Ann**, at 288 Lebuh Chulia, has clean fan-cooled rooms at MS$ll, dormitory beds at MS$4.50 and a marvellous little restaurant. If you want cleaner toilets, try the **Swiss Hotel** or the **Eng Aun** along the same road. Both have rooms from MS$10/12 and offer good information. The **Yee Hing**, at 302 Lebuh Chulia, offers clean doubles for MS$8.40. There are many reports of it opening and closing, but at the time of writing it is still open. A nice dormitory is in the **Wan Hai Hotel** in Love Lane – only MS$4.40, with a small breakfast included. The best all-round cheapie is **New China Hotel** on Lebuh Leith, with spotless rooms at MS$12 single, MS$15 double, a money-changing/visa service and a coffee shop at the bar.

FOOD

Penang is a gourmet's paradise, with food to cater for every palate – Thai, Korean, Indian, Chinese, Japanese and Malay restaurants stand on every corner. A proliferation of American fast-food joints make it easy to get a Big Mac and chips, but the best meals are still to be enjoyed on the street food stalls. Here, rubbing elbows with the cook, you can make a mix-and-match selection from Indian breads and mutton, Chinese *dim sum* and spring rolls, Malay *satay* and *murtabak* and Penang specialities like *laksa assam* (fish soup with noodles) and *curry kapitan* (spicy chicken curry). Gurney Drive, 3 km east of Georgetown, is one such food circuit. The Esplanade is another. The big night market, which changes location every two weeks, is a third. Ask the tourist office for the current venue. Elsewhere, almost every street junction and corner has food stalls selling seafood, rice and noodle dishes, *laksa*, chicken and curries. The delicacy at the massive food market below the Komtar is sliced roast duck, but check the finger bowl for stray flippers! The **Komtar Complex** is an ever-growing food

palace, located at the base of the Komtar tower. It is Penang's answer to Singapore, with **Kentucky Fried Chicken**, **McDonald's**, **Pizza Hut**, ice-cream parlours and (on the fifth floor) the excellent **Komtar Food Court** – a collection of reasonably cheap Malay, Chinese and Indian food stalls. Also at the base of the Komtar is the **Super Department Store**, purely for those who have done enough hard travelling through India, China, etc. and who have a serious longing for luxuries like Swiss cheese, Australian apples and French wine.

Many people start the day at **Tye Ann**, on the junction of Lebuh Chulia and Chulia Lane. This is a very popular breakfast spot, as well as the unofficial backpackers' centre of Georgetown. Arrive by 8 a.m. at the latest to be sure of a seat and choose from an extensive menu including honey/cheese/bean/egg toasts, banana porridge, bacon and eggs, fruit juices, tea, coffee, etc. Many shoestringers pass over lunch in favour of take-away buns, cakes, pastries and pies from **O G Bakery** in Penang Rd. The end of the day finds them at **Cris Fast Food Night Stall** on the pavement opposite Cathay Cinema in Penang Rd. Open from 10 p.m. to 4 a.m., this has a vast selection of good cheap fast food for the late-night eater. It is the ideal place to head for if you have just emerged from a nightclub, disco or bar.

For a bit of class, visit the revolving restaurant on the sixteenth floor of the **City Bayview Hotel**. This does a good-value Malay buffet dinner from 7 p.m. to 9 p.m. for MS$13 net. The cocktails are special and so are the views. On the ground floor, the **City Lounge** has a happy hour between 4 and 8 p.m., with 25 per cent off all drinks. If you are feeling homesick for Western food, choose the restaurants in the larger hotels, or try steaks, grills, stroganoff, etc. at **Eden Steak House** (tel: 04-377263) in Hutton Lane, off Penang Rd. You can dine very well here for MS$30 per head, inclusive of wine. Indian curry lovers should plump for the **Kashmir** at 105 Penang Rd, in the basement of the Oriental Hotel. Authentic Indonesian cuisine can be had at the **Nasi Padang** at the Hang Chow Hotel Coffee Shop, 5ll Lebuh Chulia. It is the last word in traditional coconut-milk curry. **Loke Thye Kee**, at the corner of Penang and Burmah Roads, is the oldest restaurant in Penang. Try the sweet and sour dishes and enjoy eating out of doors on the breezy verandah. The chef is fond of disembowelling snakes in front of diners – he is a real performer! **Dragon King**, at the corner of Bishop and Pitt Streets, serves delicious *nyonya* food (a mix of Malay and Chinese) at around MS$12/14 per head. Ask the manager to select a menu and arrive before 9 p.m. as this place closes early. Out at Batu Ferringhi, the **Eden Seafood Village** specialises in Cantonese cuisine and has popular evening entertainments.

CAMERON HIGHLANDS

Malaysia's biggest and best known hill station is located some 60 km from Tapah, off the main Kuala Lumpur-Ipoh highway. It was discovered in 1885 by William Cameron, a government surveyor on a mapping assignment. He described the area as a 'fine plateau with gentle slopes shut in by lofty mountains'. At 1500 m, the Highlands have a pleasantly cool climate and attract a lot of Malaysian and Singaporean holidaymakers. They come here to take relaxing forest walks, to visit the tea plantations and to play golf. Travellers drop in for the same reasons and also to break their journey between Penang and Kuala Lumpur. The resort is presently made up of three townships, namely Ringlet, Tanah Rata and Brinchang, in ascending order. Most people stay in Tanah Rata, which is odd since there is nothing much down there. Brinchang, 3 km above Tanah Rata, is a smaller centre with nicer scenery, less action (thus quieter) and better hotels. Times *not* to visit the Highlands are weekends, school holidays (April, August and December) and Chinese New Year (end December) – hotel prices soar by 30/40 per cent then and accomodation is hard to find. Throughout the year, the area is damp and subject to afternoon rains, so bring an umbrella or a waterproof!

ARRIVAL/DEPARTURE

To Tapah Rd, the nearest rail junction, there are two fast trains daily from Butterworth (dep. 7.45 a.m. and 2.15 p.m., four hours) and two fast trains from Kuala Lumpur (dep. 7.30 a.m. and 3 p.m., two hours). From Tapah, the 153 bus runs hourly up to Tanah Rata (MS$l) and to Brinchang (MS$l.30). Or you could ring 05-941555/941257 and have a taxi waiting at the station – MS$30 to Tanah Rata, MS$35 to Brinchang (cheap, if there are three or four of you). Either way, it is a *very* scary ride up to the Highlands – there are 642 corners from Tapah Rd to Brinchang, so have the travel-sickness pills handy!

On the way out, Tapah Rd bus terminal has two express buses daily to Singapore (MS$26/28), Malacca (MS$18) and Penang (MS$9); also regular buses to Kuala Lumpur from 8 a.m. to 6 p.m. (MS$7.50/MS$8.50) and one bus a day to Hat Yai (MS$28). Town House Hotel, Tanah Rata, is the agent for the only daily express bus from the Highlands direct to Kuala Lumpur (dep. 2.30 p.m.,

MS$9.80). Highland Lodge, Tanah Rata, arranges express bus tickets to Hat Yai, Penang, Singapore and the east coast. From Tapah Rd rail station there are two fast trains daily to Butterworth (dep. 9.40 a.m. and 5.10 p.m.) and two fast trains to Kuala Lumpur (dep. ll.29 a.m. and 5.52 p.m.). On arrival in KL, take the subway over to platform 4 to hire a taxi to your hotel (MS$7/8 per load) or walk out of the station and catch a bus.

TOURIST SERVICES

Information on the Highlands is best gathered in Penang or KL. Tanah Rata has a (useless) information centre near the bus-stand, a post office and a Hong Kong Bank (open from 10 a.m. to 3 p.m., slow service). Brinchang has a small post office, but nowhere to change money.

THINGS TO DO

Most people come to the Cameron Highlands for the walks. Within the confines of this largely oak-laurel rain forest is an abundance of flora and fauna unique to this region. Brilliant butterflies and warbling birds accompany you on your jungle jaunts. You will not see many animals up here, or even insects, but there are lots of interesting trees, vegetation and birdlife. Good maps, marking all the local walks, are posted opposite the Friendship Restaurant in Tanah Rata and in the lobby of the Kowloon Hotel in Brinchang. The walks are of varying difficulty. Walks 2 and 8 are hard, walks 3 to 5 are easy. If you want to walk down to Tanah Rata from Brinchang, path 44 is by far the easiest, quickest and prettiest way to do it – stroll down Brinchang hill until you see the golf course, turn left at the junction, walk round the edge of the course till you reach a small roundabout, take the second turning left off the roundabout and follow the river (keeping to the right) all the way down to Tanah Rata. This takes around 40 minutes at a brisk pace.

Another option is walks 3 and 5, starting at House Arcadia (cf. map). This takes you to Tanah Rata in around one and a half hours, gets you further into the actual jungle and finishes at **Mardi** tea factory. The small tea plantation here is worth a quick look. From Mardi, you can return to Brinchang on walk 7, which connects to walks 5, 3 and 2 and brings you out (after two hours' tough hike) at **Sam Poh Buddhist Temple**, where you can give thanks for your survival! Walk 8 is harder still. It takes one and a half hours just to the top of **Mt Beremban** (1,841 m), followed by a straight one-hour descent down path 7 to Tanah Rata. Be warned, you could easily get injured on walks 2, 7 and 8 as they are

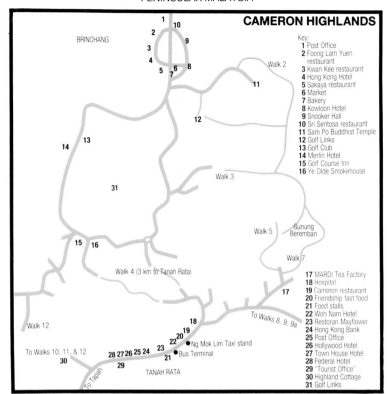

CAMERON HIGHLANDS

BRINCHANG

Walk 2

Walk 3

Walk 5

Gunung Bereman

Walk 7

Walk 4 (3 km to Tanah Rata)

Walk 12

To Walks 8, 9, 9a

● Ng Mok Lim Taxi stand

● Bus Terminal

To Walks 10, 11, & 12

TANAH RATA

To Tapah

Key:
1 Post Office
2 Foong Lam Yuen restaurant
3 Kwan Kee restaurant
4 Hong Kong Hotel
5 Sakaya restaurant
6 Market
7 Bakery
8 Kowloon Hotel
9 Snooker Hall
10 Sri Sentosa restaurant
11 Sam Po Buddhist Temple
12 Golf Links
13 Golf Club
14 Merlin Hotel
15 Golf Course Inn
16 Ye Olde Smokehouse
17 MARDI Tea Factory
18 Hospital
19 Cameron restaurant
20 Friendship fast food
21 Food stalls
22 Woh Nam Hotel
23 Restoran Mayflower
24 Hong Kong Bank
25 Post Office
26 Hollywood Hotel
27 Town House Hotel
28 Federal Hotel
29 "Tourist Office"
30 Highland Cottage
31 Golf Links

very steep and if you slip on the damp steps you could easily drop 6 m in a bad spot! It is a good idea to walk with someone else in case of accident. You will not get lost on your own as the paths are well marked, but you should tell someone where you are going and when you expect to return. Don't set out on any walk after 2.30 p.m. if you want to be sure of getting home before dark. Wear long trousers, long-sleeved shirts and proper walking shoes. Carry some water or fruit juice too – walking can be hot, sweaty work!

The big reward at the end of a hard day's trek is a Devonshire cream tea at **Ye Olde Smokehouse**, a delightful Tudor-style accommodation overlooking the golf course. Look smart though, or you could be turned away. Cream teas are served between 3 and 6 p.m. only. If they say they have run out, it is odds on they do not like the look of your muddy boots!

Of the Highlands' several tea plantations, **Blue Valley Tea Estate**, 18 km north of Tanah Ra, is probably the easiest to get into. To visit, hire a taxi (around MS$14 per hour) and ring ahead (tel: 05-991302) to tell them you are coming. The bigger your group, the more likely they are to give you a decent guided tour. If you are on your own, visit the small **Mardi** plantation instead.

A game of golf on the famous 18-hole course up at Brinchang can be pricey – MS$40 green fees (MS$20 after 4 p.m.), MS$18 club-hire (MS$10 half-set) and MS$4/5 for a caddy. Still, it is a fine course and if you play all day it is possible to get 36 holes in. Long trousers are a must – you cannot play in shorts.

Note: share-taxis run between Brinchang and Tanah Rata for MS$l per head. It is only 50 *sen* by local bus, but the service is infrequent – timings are posted in the Hong Kong Hotel, Brinchang.

ACCOMMODATION/FOOD

The Cameron Highlands have a wide variety of accommodation. The hotels have swimming pools, gyms, squash courts, tennis courts, jogging tracks, ponyrides, discos and restaurant facilities. **Strawberry Park** (tel: 05-951166) is a cluster of condominiums with bougainvillaea-laden balconies from MS$140 to MS$310. It has a perfect situation overlooking the golf course and top-quality (very expensive) food. **Ye Olde Smokehouse** (tel: 05-941214) is the other high-class favourite, with rooms from MS$85 single, MS$95 double. This 50-year-old country inn looks like a Tudor coach house and the interior decor is made up of Victorian antiques. Dining is typically English, with prices to match.

For the budget traveller, Brinchang

and Tanah Rata have many moderately priced hotels and chalets. In Tanah Rata, choose between simple rooms with attached bath (MS$32) at **Town House Hotel** (tel: 05-941666) or much nicer rooms without bathrooms (MS$15/18) at **Federal Hotel** (tel: 05-941777). Both places are in Main Rd, close to the bus-stand. Popular fallbacks in the same street are **Hollywood Hotel** (MS$16 to MS$25) and **Highland Lodge** (MS$10.50 single, MS$13 double). **Paradise Hostel**, eight minutes' walk from the bus-stand, has dormitory beds at MS$5, rooms with bathroom at MS$12 single, MS$15 double, free coffee and tea, use of fridge, indoor games, free laundry, travel tips, TV and library, etc. **Bala's Holiday Chalet**, 1.5 km up from Tanah Rata (on the way to Brinchang) charges MS$5 for dormitory beds and MS$12-35 for rooms. Backpackers like this place, but it is not as clean (or as safe) as it once was. Tanah Rata has some good restaurants: the **Woh Nam** does tea and toast, the **Cameron**, egg and bacon, tomatoes and mushrooms, and the **Mayflower** and **Friendship**, tasty Chinese buffets. **Restoran Kumar**, opposite the taxi rank, cooks great Indian food – as much as you can eat for less than MS$5. Just along from the bus-stand is an arcade of fast-food stalls and an 'ice-cream station'.

Up at Brinchang, the clean, bright and cheerful **Kowloon Hotel** (tel: 05-941366) gives a choice of Asian-style rooms with squat toilet and no bath and Western-style rooms with sit-down loos and a bathtub. All rooms (MS$30 twin, MS$35 triple) are fully carpeted, with hot and cold water. The restaurant prepares delicious Chinese and European food. Set dinners are good value at MS$10 and MS$12, but it is better to eat in a group and order a wide selection of dishes. You can sup beer at the bar till midnight. The next-door **Brinchang Hotel** (tel: 05-941246) bears no comparison, but the rooms (MS$55 double, MS$65 triple) are smart and the staff friendly. This is the best place to try Steamboat (an everything-in-the-pot speciality dish) at MS$8 per head. A few doors along, the brand-new **Parkland Hotel** is Brinchang's one claim to luxury (prices on application). Across the block, **Hotel Hong Kong** offers clean double rooms with hot water and bathtubs for around MS$20. They are so big, they can sleep four people! Downstairs, the restaurant does cheap, filling Western-style breakfasts from MS$2.50. **Kedai Kek Rich Bake,** a good bakery, is below the small market (quite an attraction on Saturday mornings) near Kowloon Hotel. For an inexpensive Chinese-style lunch or dinner, try the **Sakaya, Kwan Yee** or **Foon Yam Luen** restaurants – even with tea or coffee, it is still hard to spend MS$5!

KUALA LUMPUR

The capital of Malaysia, Kuala Lumpur (commonly referred to as KL) is also the largest city in the country, with a population of approximately one million. A cosmopolitan metropolis of busy freeways, soaring skyscrapers and landscaped gardens, it is similar to Singapore but about ten years behind and 20 per cent more humid. It is clean, safe, efficient and the traffic moves, and, unlike Singapore, there is sufficient local colour to interest the foreign visitor. A pleasing blend of the old and the new, KL combines the ultra-modern with the mosques and minarets of its Moorish past. Having developed at a slower rate than its Asian sister cities, it has managed to retain much of its rich architectural heritage. Thus, beside the Western-style shopping malls, luxury hotels and department stores, you can still see the temples, mosques and colonial-style buildings of its indigenous multi-ethnic groups, of which the Chinese (50 per cent), Malays (37 per cent) and Indians (10 per cent) form the majority.

Nevertheless, KL knows it has limited tourist appeal – sights to visit are not its long suit. Travellers enjoy its shopping, fast food and easy-going atmosphere, but because there is nothing of specific interest to see, they mainly treat it as a one-day stopover between Singapore and Penang. To compensate, KL is now building up its infrastructure and cleaning up its rivers in order to become a city of 'leisure'. The whole face of the city is rapidly changing as it gears up for the 1990 Visit Malaysia year. Major construction is going on in the area presently taken up by the cricket pitch, which will shortly become the new focus of the city – an Independence Square of shops, promenades, fountains, lawns, band performances, acrobatic displays, mini-exhibitions and live pop bands. You will soon be able to go down there any day of the week and something will always be happening!

The pulsating urban atmosphere of modern-day KL is a far cry from its rough-and-ready pioneer days when, following its discovery by a band of Chinese tin miners in 1857, it was named Kuala Lumpur or 'muddy river-mouth'. The estuary in question was the junction of the Gombak stream and the Klang river and if today you stand on the Market St bridge in the centre of town and look upstream towards the mosque, you are looking at the spot where it all began. These days, KL bristles with the confident towers of an independent and rich Malaysia – money from here, gleaned mainly from import-export and international trade, is buying up Australia and building top hotels in half a dozen countries. Clean and progressive, this city is nothing like the Third World backwater most Westerners seem to expect – it certainly puts London to shame!

ARRIVAL/DEPARTURE
Air
KL is the main international gateway to Malaysia and is, like Singapore and Penang, a good place to buy discounted air tickets worldwide. Sample one-way fares from MSL Student Travel (tel: 03-3989722), 1st Floor, South East Asia Hotel, 69 Jln Haji Hussin, include KL-London for MS$2500, KL-Sydney for MS$1500 and KL-New York for MS$1700. MAS offer domestic flights from KL to Singapore from MS$98, to Langkawi from MS$112 and to Penang, Kuantan or Kota Bahru from MS$61. There are only two flights a week to Bali (one MAS and one Garuda) both around MS$700 one-way. MAS have their main office (tel: 03-2610555) in Jln Sultan Ismail and a less busy desk (tel: 03-2936759) on the third floor of the Pan Pacific Hotel.

KL's Subang International Airport is 20 km from the city centre. On arrival here, walk out of the airport and up the stairs for a No. 47 bus (hourly service from 6 a.m.) which takes 45 minutes to the Klang terminal on Jln Sultan Mohamed. The fare is MS$1.20. A taxi to your hotel will cost MS$15-18. Buy a coupon at the airport booth.

Rail
Kuala Lumpur has one of the great railway stations of the world – an 'Arabian Nights' fantasy with more minarets than a Disney artist would find tasteful. It looks a good deal more like a mosque than the real National Mosque nearby! Fast trains go from here to Butterworth at 7.30 a.m. and 3 p.m. (six to seven hours), and to Singapore at 7.30 a.m. and 2.30 p.m. (seven hours). The second-class air-conditioned fare to either destination is MS$28.

Notes: the early train to Singapore is cooler, quicker and better. The later train gets you there around 9.45 p.m. which is too late to look out a hotel, especially when you have up to an hour of border formalities to go through. Exit from Malaysia is simply a matter of an offical boarding the train and stamping your passport. This happens at Johore Bahru. It pays to arrive at Singapore station reasonably well dressed. If you turn up in your Koh Samui T-shirt, drawstring pants and flip-flops, expect to spend a lot longer in answering questions and waiting around before clearing immigration than anyone else!

Road
Most long-distance buses and taxis run from the Pudu Raya terminus on Jln Pudu. Air-conditioned buses leave at 9 a.m. and 1 p.m. for Singapore (MS$17), at 8 a.m., 10 a.m. and 12 noon for Butterworth (MS$15.50), at 8.30 a.m. for Cameron Highlands (MS$10, four and a half hours) and every hour or so for Malacca (MS$6, two hours). If there is a group of you, it is worth taking a taxi to Malacca (MS$15 per person), to Singapore (MS$32) or to Butterworth (MS$30). Taxis leave from the bus-station, but if you ring ahead (tel: 01-2322779) they will pick you up from your hotel. Buses for east coast destinations like Kuantan (MS$10.90), Kuala Trengganu (MS$20) and Kota Bahru (MS$25) leave from the Putra terminus near Putra World Trade Centre.

Notes: left luggage facilities are offered from 7 a.m. to 10 p.m. at the Pudu Raya terminus and the rail station (platform 4) at a charge of MS$1 per bag per day.

TOURIST SERVICES
The main TDC tourist office, presently located on the twenty-sixth floor of the Putra World Trade Centre, Jln Tun Ismail (tel: 03-2935188), is moving in early 1990 to Tuanku Abdul Rahman Hall, a beautiful old colonial house behind the Merlin Hotel in Jln Sultan Ismail. Opening hours are 8 a.m. to 4.15 p.m. weekdays, 8 a.m. to 12.45 p.m. Saturday. Staff are very helpful and handout magazines like *Kuala Lumpur This Month* and *Selamat Datang to Malaysia* are full of up-to-date information. TDC also have booths at 3 Jln Sultan Hishamuddin, opposite the railway station, and in the arrival hall of Subang Airport.

The main GPO is in Jln Sultan Hishamuddin, open 8 a.m. to 5 p.m. Monday to Saturday. The Putra World Trade Centre has a small post office on level 2. Banks close early: at 3 p.m. on weekdays and at 11.30 a.m. on Saturday. After that, use moneychangers. Overseas calls can be made round-the-clock at Kaunter Telegraf STM, Wisma Jothi, Jln Gereja and at the airport's Kedai Telekom. The Times bookshop in the Yaohan store of the Mall, opposite the Pan Pacific Hotel, has a vast selection of 'local interest' books about Malaysia and Indonesia – quite a few are by Chinese Malay writers, with interesting political comment!

KL has several foreign missions, including Australia, 6 Jln Yap Kwan Sweng (tel: 03-2423122); Singapore, 209 Jln Tun Razak (tel: 03-2616277); Thailand, 206 Jln Ampang (tel: 03-2488222); UK, 13th floor, Wisma Damansara, Jln Semantan (tel: 03-2541533); USA, 376 Jln Tun Razak (tel: 03-2489011).

GETTING AROUND

Getting around KL is not that easy. There is too much traffic, too few pedestrian crossings and a one-way system which always seems to be going the wrong way (I travelled 3 km by taxi to get to a hotel in the next street!). There are two local bus systems in KL, fare 20 *sen*, but there is no decent bus map so they are difficult to use. The faster minibuses post their destinations and charge 50 *sen* anywhere along their route. They are very useful for long hauls like Batu Caves and the Batik Factory. Taxis are metered and are a cheap, convenient way of getting around town. They charge 70 *sen* for the first kilometre, 30 *sen* for each subsequent 0.6 km. If you do not want air-conditioning (20 per cent surcharge), you have to inform the driver before setting off. The one place taxis *don't* use the meter is the railway station, where you have to haggle really hard for a sensible fare! Car rental costs around MS$100/120 per day and can be arranged from Avis (tel: 03-2417144), Budget (tel: 03-2611122) or Hertz (tel: 03-2433433).

SIGHTS

Sightseeing in KL is low priority as the city has few sights, and none of them are memorable. You can cover all points of interest on a short two to three hour organised tour by private car (MS$22) from Tina Travel, 197 Jln Ampang-Ulu Kelang, tel: 03-4578877, or by coach (MS$15) from the tourist office. If you are short on time, it is sufficient to see the museum and Masjid Jame by taxi.

Most tours start at **Masjid Jame** in Jln Perak, at the junction of the two rivers which gave Kuala Lumpur its name. Built in 1907, this is the oldest mosque in the city, a beautifully balanced piece of work in red brick and white Italian marble. Visiting hours are 9 a.m. to 12.45 p.m. and 2.30 to 4.15 p.m. Saturday to Thursday, 8 to 10.30 a.m. and 2.45 to 4.15 p.m. on Friday. Men must wear long trousers, or hire a sarong, to enter. For the best photography, revisit the mosque around sunset. The nearby **Sultan Abdul Samad Buildings**, formerly the Federal Secretariat, are also worth a snap. Built between 1894 and 1897, this is a striking example of Moorish architecture, featuring a 43-m-high clock tower. Heading south of Jame Masjid, you may catch a glimpse of the **Selangor Club**, the late nineteenth-century social centre which looks onto the cricket fields, before plunging into **Chinatown**, with its colourful street life and crowded night market. **Chan See Shu Yuen Temple**, the decorative Chinese temple at the end of Jln Petaling, was built in 1906. Nearby on Jln Bandar is **Sri Mahamariammon**, an ornate Hindu temple constructed in 1873. A short drive east is the 60-hectare

Lake Gardens, the city's main lung, with its **National Monument** (a huge militaristic montage in bronze, depicting the triumph of Malay virtues over Communism) and a beautiful park area dotted with scarlet hibiscus (Malaysia's national flower) and futuristic sculptures. If you want to take a boat out on the lake (MS$2 per hour), get a No. 10 minibus back there later on from the Toshiba terminal on Jln Sultan Mohamed. At the southern end of Lake Gardens is the **National Museum** (Muzium Negara), with good displays of textiles, coins, costumes and ceramics. It is open 9 a.m. to 6 p.m. daily, admission free.

Out-of-town attractions include the not-to-be-missed **Batu Caves**, 12 km north of KL (No. ll minibus, 60 *sen*, from Jln Pudu or Jln Semarang). This massive 400 million-year-old limestone outcrop is a living shrine for Malaysia's 1.4 million Hindus. At the end of 272 steps are vast caverns housing Hindu deities and temples. Thousands of pilgrims come here every February for the important Thaipusam festival. The Indian restaurant closest to the caves does good vegetarian snacks. The **National Zoo & Aquarium**, 13 km east of KL (No. 17 or 23 minibus from city centre) has sea-lion, elephant and orang-utan shows and is open 9 a.m. to 5 p.m., admission MS$3. Best times to visit are early morning or late afternoon, when the animals are liveliest. Back in town, while waiting for a train perhaps, you could see the **National Art Gallery** in the ex-Hotel Majestic opposite the railway station. It is open from 10 a.m. to 6 p.m. daily, admission free.

ENTERTAINMENT

For details of current entertainments, get a *Calendar of Events* from the tourist office and a *Malay Mail* newspaper. There are exhibitions and cultural events daily at the **Central Market** between the GPO and Chinatown (full programme from the tourist office) and good traditional dance shows on the second floor of **Putra World Trade Centre** every Tuesday and Friday, from 8 p.m. to 9 p.m., admission free. The **Yazmin Restaurant**, 6 Jln Kia Peng, puts on an excellent Malaysian dinner-dance show from 8.30 p.m. nightly. It costs MS$28.90 with dinner, MS$14.70 show only, and is very popular so ring ahead (tel: 03-2415655) to avoid disappointment.

KL's top nightspot is the **Sapphire** disco at Yow Chuan Plaza, close to Ampang Park. It has a big dance-floor, good sounds and an 'overseas educated' DJ. The MS$20 cover charge includes one free drink. The **Tin Mine** disco at the Hilton Hotel is also well patronised. For early evening relaxation, go to the **City Palace** next to Hotel Malaya. This place

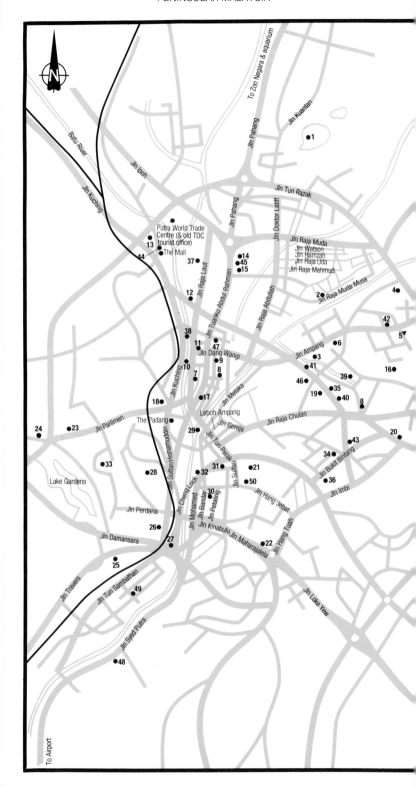

KUALA LUMPUR

Key:
1 Lake
2 Sunday Market
3 Tuanku Abdul Rahman Hall & new TDC tourist office
4 Ampang Shopping Complex
5 To zoo
6 Le Coq d'Or restaurant
7 Coliseum Cinema
8 Foodstalls
9 Campbell shopping complex
10 Export Trade Centre
11 Pertama shopping complex
12 National Library
13 Bus Terminal
14 International Hotel
15 Market
16 Race Course
17 Rex Hotel
18 Bank Negara
19 MAS office
20 Karyaneka Handicraft Centre
21 Pudu Raya Bus Station
22 Merdeka Stadium
23 National Monument
24 Parliament House
25 National Museum
26 National Art Gallery
27 Railway Station
28 National Mosque
29 Masjid Jame
30 Sri Mahamariaman Temple
31 Chinatown
32 Central Market
33 Orchid Garden
34 Apollo Hotel
35 Equatorial Hotel
36 Federal Hotel
37 Grand Central Hotel
38 Holiday Inn City Centre Hotel
39 Holiday Inn on the Park
40 Kuala Lumpur Hilton Hotel
41 Merlin Hotel
42 Ming Court Hotel
43 Oriental Hotel
44 Pan Pacific Hotel
45 South-East Asia Hotel
46 Shangri-La Hotel
47 Shiraz Hotel
48 Wisma Belia
49 YMCA
50 YWCA

has a happy hour between 4 and 8 p.m. and, of all things, poker machines and snooker tables!

SHOPPING
The best buys are local handicraft items like batik-dyed cloth and *songket* weaving, combining silk with silver and gold thread. **Batik Malaysia**, on Jln Tun Perak, holds a Wisma Kraftangan (Handicraft Exhibition) every Monday and Tuesday from 6 p.m. and **Karyaneka Handicraft Centre**, on Jln Raja Chulan, has a permanent 'village' of 14 traditional houses selling the full range of Malaysian produce, basketware, embroidery, ceramics, silver jewellery, etc., from 9 a.m. to 7 p.m. daily. Malaysian pewterware consists of 97 per cent Straits refined tin and has a very distinctive sheen – check **Selangor Pewter**, 4 Jln Usahawan 6, Setapak for demonstrations and sales.

Like Singapore, KL has any number of air-conditioned shopping complexes and supermarkets, open daily from 10 a.m. to 10 p.m. Try the **Ampang Park** shopping centre in Jln Ampang, near the Ming Court Hotel. It has a vast selection of clothes and goods at very reasonable prices. Another must for the enterprising shopper is the Sunday market (actually held on Saturdays) at Kampung Bahru, off Jln Chow Kit. This is the place to browse (and bargain) for hand-woven mats, batik and wood carvings. Down in Chinatown, the Night Market in Jln Petaling sells high-quality pirate music cassettes and the usual range of fake Guccis and Rolexes, Pierre Cardins and Lacostes. The Nepalese and Burmese traders form an exotic part of this lively market with their ivory bracelets, fragile beaded necklaces, semi-precious stones, antique tea caddies and snuff boxes, wooden masks and smiling Buddhas. Out at Selayang, a 30-minute drive from KL, you can see the complete range of batik products being made at **Khadani Batik Factory**. If you visit at a quiet time, you can often buy batik prints at cost.

ACCOMMODATION
You can get up to 50 per cent discounts off tariffs of most major KL hotels, either by booking through a travel agent in London or by phoning the hotel direct from Subang airport and asking for their 'confidential' tariff. Students seeking a good-quality hotel can buy vouchers at MSL Travel, lst Floor, South East Asia Hotel (tel: 03-2989722) and get put up at very reasonable rates, e.g. a double room at the plush **Equatorial Hotel** (tel: 03-612022), Jln Sultan Ismail, for only MS$90 (normal tariff MS$150). Other good first-class hotels include **Shangri-La Hotel**, ll Jln Sultan Ismail (tel: 03-2322388, singles/doubles from MS$200/MS$250), **Kuala Lumpur Hilton**, Jln

Sultan Ismail (tel: 03-2422122, from MS$155/MS$175) and **Pan Pacific** KL, Jln Chow Kit Baru (tel: 03-4426555, from MS$190/MS$210). All rates are subject to 10 per cent service charge and 5 per cent government tax.

Hotel Grand Central (tel: 03-4413011) in Jln Putra/Raja Laut is a classy mid-bracket hotel, with nice rooms (air-conditioning, colour TV) from MS$46 and a good Muslim-Malay restaurant downstairs. The newly renovated **South East Asia Hotel** (tel: 03-2926977) at 69 Jln Haji Hussain is very well located, close to many shops and the big Chowket food market. It has 24-hour room service, a cheap downstairs restaurant and air-conditioned rooms at MS$90 single, MS$105 double. If you speak to MSL Travel on the first floor (open from 9 a.m. to 5 p.m. weekdays, 9 a.m. to l p.m. Saturdays) you may well get a discount. The **Merlin** (tel: 03-2480033) on Jln Sultan Ismail is a very personal, comfortable old hotel with a pool, two restaurants, a health club, a small business centre and well-priced rooms from MS$75 net.

There is a batch of good cheap hotels along Jln Tuangku Abdul Rahman, north of the city centre. At 132-134, the popular **Rex** (tel: 03-2983895) has large clean rooms at MS$15.80 single, MS$18.90 double, with free soap/towels and big beds. Manager Leong is very informative and the downstairs bar-restaurant serves cheap snacks and cold beer. At 142-146, the **Kowloon** is a friendly, lively Muslim hotel with air-conditioned rooms (bathroom attached) at MS$27 single, MS$30.80 double. It is a bit musty round the edges, but otherwise fine. A few doors along, the old-style **Coliseum** and the ramshackle **Tivoli** have clean, adequate rooms around MS$17 single, MS$19 double. The Coliseum has a wonderfully antique restaurant offering great steaks and grills.

If in KL and travelling on a shoestring, it is well worth picking up a youth hostel card at MSL Travel for cut-price tours and accommodation. MSL has a list of youth hostels right through Malaysia giving 20 per cent discounts to card holders. At **Wisma Belia** (tel: 03-2744833), 40 Jln Syed Putra, for example, students pay just MS$7 for a dormitory bed and MS$30 for a comfy air-conditioned room. This place is a bit out of the centre, but bus 52 gets you there. Far more central is the brand-new **KL City Hostel** at Jln K G Atap, with fan cooled dormitory-style accommodation at MS$10 per person. Also well located is the Brickfields **YMCA** (tel: 03-2741439) at 95 Jln Padang Belia. Dormitory beds are MS$10 and rooms range from MS$18 (fan single, common shower) to MS$50 (air-conditioned twin, private bath and TV). Facilities include restaurant, launderette, barber, games and travel service.

FOOD

KL has excellent food (Chinese, Malay, Indian and European) sold from street stalls and by top class hotels. The open-air night bazaar in Chinatown's Petaling St is a great place for cheap evening snacks. Choose your dishes from the numerous stalls and watch your food being prepared. The famous item here is roast duck, but do not miss *satay* (skewered meat cubes barbecued over a charcoal fire) and iced '*kacang*' (shaved ice served with sweetcorn, nuts, jelly, milk and syrup, popularly known as 'ABC'). The Saturday night market in Jln Raja Muda, Kampung Baru, and the Chowket market behind the South East Asia Hotel, are two good places to sample Malay specialities such as *nasi ayam* (chicken rice) and *nasi lemak* (rice cooked with coconut milk). Other popular night markets include the stalls at the crossroads of Jln Bukit Bintang and Jln Sultan Ismail and the huge open-air complex along Jln Benteng near the Lang River. Also check out the large food stall area behind the Hilton Hotel and the wide variety of stalls inside the Mall shopping complex. A busy little breakfast place with cheap, satisfying Indian-Malaysian snacks is **Welcome to Malaysia** in Jln Tengah, opposite The Weld. Here you can enjoy a cup of strong south Indian coffee and a tasty *dal roti* for the princely sum of MS$l!

If you are feeling nostalgic for Western food, go to 'high tea' at the **Shangri-La Hotel**. For just MS$ll.50 net, you get a real 'smorgasbord' of pasta, salad, fruit, cakes, sandwiches, other hot dishes, plus all the coffee and tea you can drink. Service is excellent and the atmosphere refined. 'Wear something nice,' suggested one diner, 'You'll feel a bum otherwise!' Check the local press for special deals on buffet lunches and dinners at the big hotels – the **Merlin**, for example, does a very nice lunch at MS$15 (plus taxes) between 12.30 and 2.30 p.m.

KL has several shopping centres, each of which has a supermarket (good places to pick up a cheap beer in an expensive city) and a **McDonald's** or **Pizza Hut** (do not knock them – many hardened backpackers find their way here, renewing their acquaintance with Western fast food!). **The Weld**, on Jln P Ramlee, off Jln Sultan Ismail, has just about everything, – a McDonald's, a Pizza Hut, a delicatessen, a supermarket, a multi-cuisine food corner, a bakery and an ice-cream parlour. It is an economical spot to eat (and shop).

Recommended Chinese restaurants (mid-priced) include the **Marco Polo** (tel: 03-2425595), lst Floor, Wisma Lim Foo Yong, Jln Raja Chulan and the **Dynasty Garden** (tel: 03-2430678), Mezzanine Floor, Yow Chuan Plaza. Merlin Hotel's **Golden Dragon** restaurant is well known for its Hong Kong *dim sums*, served between 8 a.m. and 2.30 p.m. only. If you have a taste for Indian food, go to **Bangles** (tel: 03-2983780) at 60A Jln Tuanku Abdul Rahman, or **Devi Annapoorna** (tel: 03-2556443) at 94 Lorong Maarof. Malay cooking is best sampled at **Yazmin** restaurant (cf. Entertainment) or at **Restoran Terapung Nelayan Titiwangsa** at Lake Titiwangsa Park, off Jln Kuantan. Finally, for European appetites, there is **The Ship** (tel: 03-2418805) at 40/l Jln Sultan Ismail. This is a typically 'British' grill house with a good selection of steaks, poultry dishes, cakes and desserts.

MALACCA

Malacca is the up-and-coming tourist destination along the west coast. It is finally coming into its own as *the* historical centre of Malaysia, having far more to offer the culture-vulture than Penang (which is now overcrowded and over-priced) and KL (which has no history at all). Malacca is full of history, and it is all within easy walking distance. The old Malay houses, the tombstones of warriors such as Hang Tuah, the ragged Portuguese fortress, the big bright red 'Stadthuys' and the impressive British-built monuments will take you back to the days when Malacca was wooed by nations in both East and West.

The oldest city in Malaysia and once the capital, Malacca (or Melaka, as the Malays spell it) began life as a small fishing village founded in 1403 by Parameswara, a Sumatran prince whose territory had been Temasek (Singapore) but who had fled from an invading force with his piratical followers. Within the short span of 100 years, Malacca had become the greatest centre of sea commerce east of India – traders from as far west as Arabia and as far east as China congregated on its shores to exchange goods, leaving a little of their heritage behind with each trip. The port's lucrative spice trade attracted European interest; it was conquered by the Portuguese in 15ll and came under Dutch rule in 1641, before being seized by the British in the late 1700s. When the Dutch moved out, the Chinese moved in. They did so because Malacca was *the* port of the south-west coast, the logical place to export their gold, silk, tea, opium and tobacco. Their community married into the local one, creating a unique society of their own which, in the nineteenth century, reached notable heights. The 'Nyonya' ladies and the 'Baba' men of Peranakan (Chinese-Malay) families enjoyed great prosperity and an elaborate, sophisticated lifestyle. In the late nineteenth century Malacca, Penang and Singapore (the Straits Settlements) became a Crown Colony under the British. It was during these days and into the first decades of the twentieth century that much of today's Malacca was built.

Although its former pomp and grandeur is gone, Malacca is now the kind of place people go to for a day or two and end up staying four or five. It is a very nice traditional low-paced town and there is a great deal to see and do. Not that its sleepy backwater charm can last for much longer, however. Presently poised on the brink of modernisation, Malacca is at an interesting stage of development. The whole coastline is changing as newly reclaimed land is prepared for factories, houses and tourist hotels. The town itself, designated an 'historical city' on 15 April 1989, is receiving a complete facelift, designed to make it the showpiece of the 1990 Visit Malaysia Year. The whole city centre is being sealed off from traffic, leaving tourists free to visit the sights without the inconvenience of dodging cars and rickshaws. The idea is to turn Malacca into a 'Little Lisbon' of relaxing promenades and calm riverside vistas. The big question is, will all this 'beautification' destroy the city's antique character or not? If you have been to Singapore, you'll know the answer.

ARRIVAL/DEPARTURE
Air
There is no railway to Malacca, but you can fly there from KL or Johore Bahru. Aquarius Travel (tel: 06-224847), 52 Madonna Building, Jln Laksemana, sells a cheap flight from Malacca to Pekan Baru in Sumatra.

Road
The main bus station is in Kilang Rd, a cheap MS$2 rickshaw ride from the town centre. When leaving Malacca, take a public bus No. 17 (30 *sen*) from outside the tourist office to Kilang Rd for hourly buses to Singapore (MS$8.50 to MS$ll), Kuala Lumpur (MS$4.85 to MS$6.25), Butterworth (MS$10.70 to MS$21), Kuala Trengganu and Kuantan. The Singapore/KL buses can be heavily subscribed, so book well ahead. Taxis to all the above destinations leave from the local bus/taxi stand off Jln Hang Tuah, just across the river.

TOURIST SERVICES
The tourist office (tel: 06-236538) on Jln Kota is open from 9 a.m. to 5 p.m. every

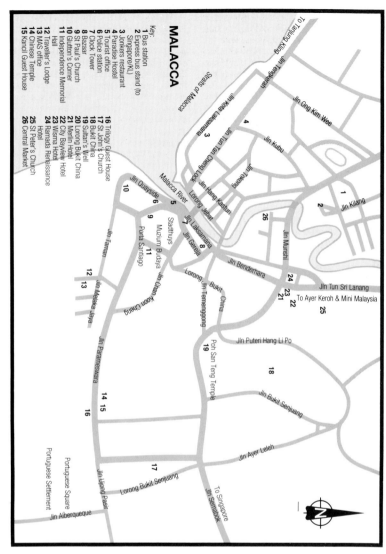

MALACCA

Key:
1 Bus station
2 Express bus stand (to Singapore/KL)
3 Jonkers restaurant
4 Paradise Hostel
5 Tourist office
6 Police station
7 Clock Tower
8 Bazaar
9 St Paul's Church
10 Glutton's Corner
11 Independence Memorial Hall
12 Traveller's Lodge
13 MAS office
14 Chinese Temple
15 Kancil Guest House
16 Trilogy Guest House
17 St John's Church
18 Bukit China
19 Sultan's Well
20 Lorong Bukit China
21 Merlin Hotel
22 City Bayview Hotel
23 Wisma Hotel
24 Ramada Renaissance Hotel
25 St Peter's Church
26 Central Market

day of the year. The GPO on Jln Laksemana is open from 8 a.m. to 6 p.m. Monday to Saturday. Banks are open from 10 a.m. to 3 p.m. weekdays, 9.30 a.m. to 11.30 a.m. Saturday. There are two good bookshops on Jln Laksemana.

SIGHTS

Trishaws meet travellers off the KL and Singapore buses, offering cheap, relaxed tours of the city for around MS$12/15 per hour. The larger hotels and travel agents like Aquarius can arrange sightseeing tours at around MS$18 with qualified guides. However, Malacca is such a small town that you can walk right round it in a day, or hire bicycles (MS$4 per day) from two shops on Jln Parameswara.

A good place to start your tour is the tourist office, which looks onto a typical-ly Dutch square with salmon-coloured churches, administrative buildings and a clock tower. Here you will find the **Stadthuys** or State House, reputedly the oldest Dutch building in the Far East. Built between 1641 and 1660 to house the residence of the Dutch Governor, it features beautiful louvred windows with wrought-iron hinges, thick masonry walls, and heavy hardwood doors and arches. Also of interest is the adjoining **Christ Church**, a Protestant church built in 1753. Its ceiling beams were cut from a single tree and have no joints at all. The hand-made pews are originals dating over 200 years. Note the old Dutch tombstones set into the floor and the many ancient plaques on the walls.

Heading up Jln Istana and taking the first turning left, you will find a few mementos of Portuguese rule. Alfonso d'Alberqerque arrived in 15ll and seized the settlement from the Melaka Sultan, creating one of many Portuguese trading posts on the route to the Orient and also a base from which to convert Asians to Christianity. In the same year, he began building **A Famosa**, the stone fort that now rings **St Paul's Hill**. This fort fell to the Dutch in 1641 and was almost totally destroyed by the British in 1708. All that remains today is the imposing gateway of **Porta De Santiago** or the Gateway of Saint James, which Stamford Raffles intervened to save. A short walk up the hill brings you to **St Paul's Church**, originally built by the Portuguese in 1571. Apart from being part of a once-mighty bastion, this church also gained fame as the temporary home of St Francis Xavier's body – one of his several posthumous stopovers on the way to Goa in India, his final resting place. Among the ruins are a collection of Dutch tombstones, also the wire-grilled open grave where Xaviar was once interred.

The country's only model of a palace of the Malay sultans during the Sultanate era is to be found in Malacca. Albeit a replica, it was designed to comply as closely as possible with the original as described in the *Malay Annals*. Built by the State Government in 1985, the wooden **Sultan's Palace**, just up from Porta de Santiago, now houses the State's cultural museum or **Muzium Budiya**. This museum is open from 9 a.m. to 6 p.m. (except Monday), entrance is MS$1 and it has good displays of costumes, shadow puppets, musical instruments, Peranakan porcelain and 'prayer time devices'. The set piece on the first floor – mannequins made up to look like the famous Malay princes, their consorts, court officials and warriors such as Hang Tuah and Hang Jebat – provides glimpses of life during the pre-Dutch Sultanate. The nearby **Independence Memorial**, formerly the Malacca Club, is a beautiful old Dutch colonial building housing a permanent exhibition tracing the events leading up to Malaysian Independence following the Second World War. Admission is free.

The inevitable inter-marriages between local Malays and the Portuguese during the sixteenth and seventeenth centuries gave birth to a generation of Malayan Portuguese who still live in a little hamlet known as the **Portuguese Settlement**, 3 km east of the town. What sets this community apart from their brethren in Portugal and Macau is that they still speak an archaic Portuguese dialect known as 'Cristoa'. This dialect is almost obsolete in Portugal and is mainly found in the country's old literature. The people live mainly from fishing and the Lisbon-style square is famous for its seafood restaurants. A 1-km walk away is **St John's Fort**, with beautifully preserved Dutch cannon and sweeping views.

Ask your trishaw peddlar to take you on to **Bukit China** (Chinese Hill) north east of Malacca. The hill was a gift from Sultan Mansur Shah (1458-77) to his bride, Princess Hung Li Po, and her entourage of 500 ladies-in-waiting. Here is located the largest Chinese cemetery outside China, 65 hectares in area, with a number of graves dating back to Ming times. At the foot of the hill is the **Sam Po Kong Temple**, built in 1795 to commemorate Cheng Ho, the famous Chinese admiral who paved the way for Mansur Shah's marriage to the Chinese emperor's daughter. The legend attached to the **King's Well** in the temple grounds is that whoever drinks from it will one day return to Malacca. Today, however, the well is full of goldfish and tourists can only drink boiled water from the small adjoining 'Princess Well'.

Heading back towards the river, drop in on **St Peter's Church**. This is the oldest known Catholic church in Malaysia, built by the Dutch in 1710. Its lime-green façade is an interesting mix of Eastern and Western architectural styles and one of its bells was cast in Goa in 1608. There are some noteworthy stained-glass decorations and old tombstones within, also a casket in a side-chapel containing a life-sized Christ after the Resurrection. By way of contrast, visit **Cheng Hoon Teng Temple** on Jln Tokong. Founded in 1646, this is the oldest Chinese temple in Malaysia, with a richly decorated roof, a beautifully lacquered interior and tall ceremonial masts towering over the surrounding houses. Inside, a stone inscription commemorates the important visit of Cheng Ho to Malacca.

Back in town, there is an opportunity to see old Malacca by riverboat. The old port, where it all began 600 years ago, is behind the tourist office. So are a number of old Dutch trading houses, looking onto the river from the bottom of Jln Tun Tan or 'Dutch Street'. Each of these merchant's houses, with their red-tiled roofs and white plaster exteriors, is about 30 m long, and not one of them has a window. This was a deliberate device to evade the window tax of the seventeenth century. Sailing boats still drift up the river here, bringing cargoes of charcoal, rattan and wood for barter and trade. They take away sugar, milk powder and other commodities to Indonesia. If you take a riverboat trip from the tourist office (MS$5 for 45 minutes, MS$10 for one and a half hours), you can see the quaint bridges and houses along the river which have given this sector the name 'Little Venice of Malacca', as well as many areas of historical interest like Stadthuys, the Central Market and the original old Malay *kampong* or village.

In the central area of town, around the pastel shop houses of Jln Hang Jebat, bulging with antiques, and Jln Hang Kasturi, full of small retail businesses, you will come across homes and shops built by the Chinese at the turn of the century. Pay a visit to the Chinese temples and see a fortune-teller who will advise you on all matters from love to business. From the narrow alleys of Chinatown, you can walk over to nearby Jln Tun Tan Cheng Lock, where the houses of the Baba and Nyonya are located. One such house (actually three houses joined together) is the privately run **Baba Nyonya Heritage** museum, one of the best places in Malaysia to learn about the traditions and lifestyle of the Straits-born Chinese, whose fine tastes in wedding costumes, food and silverware exceeded those of the Chinese or the Malay. The museum displays some of the finest Baba and Nyonya furniture, household wares, clothes and art. It is open from 10 a.m. to 12.30 p.m., 2 to 4.30 p.m. daily and the hefty MS$7 entrance fee (includes conducted tour) is probably worth it. For the same price, however, you can enjoy a 'free' meal at nearby **Jonker's Restaurant**, the only authentic Nyonya house where you can sit down, enjoy good food and take in a world gone by.

ENTERTAINMENT

The central city sights (A Famosa, St Paul's Church, Independence Memorial and the Sultan's Palace) are now the subject of a nightly **Sound & Light Show**, with English commentary at 8 p.m. The **Portuguese Settlement** down Jln Alberquerque has a lively cultural show every Saturday and Sunday from 7 to 10 p.m. There's a MS$2 charge and you can enjoy a good dinner here too. If you fancy a swim, you can use the pool at the Ramada Hotel for MS$10 per day. The Ayer Keroh Country Club has a magnificent 18-hole golf course. It costs MS$60 (non-member green fees) for four hours' play and you should ring ahead (tel: 06-324351) to fix a game if you wish to play here.

SHOPPING

Malacca is a good hunting ground for antiques. All along Jln Kota Laksamana, better known as 'Antique Street', the shops are crammed with brass bedsteads, porcelain pieces, mother-of-pearl furniture, curios, handicrafts and other priceless items from the past. **Sykt Abdul Fatimah, Malaccan Junk Shop** and **Klassic** are three shops worth visiting even if you do not want to buy – they inform you about the period. Take note that for exporting antiques less than 100 years old you must obtain a licence from the Director-General of the National Museum.

ACCOMMODATION

The travellers' choice at the top end is the plush **Ramada Renaissance** (tel: 06-248888), an international-class hotel with luxuriously furnished rooms (MS$120 single, MS$140 double) and a multitude of services. Discounts are very possible if you buy from a travel agent. The high-rise **Merlin Melaka** (tel: 06-240777) on Jln Munshi is the tallest building in town, providing a panoramic view of the historic city and the islands along the Straits. Rooms are good value from MS$75 and facilities include a pool, a bowling alley, a squash centre, a supermarket and a shopping centre. The similarly priced **City Bayview** (tel: 06-239888) on Jln Benderhara is Malacca's newest luxury option, providing all mod cons and amenities.

The moderately priced **Majestic Hotel** (tel: 06-222455) at 188 Jln Bunga Raya has quite a bit of character and is pleasantly located near the river. Rooms start at MS$15 with fan or MS$30 with air-conditioning and attached bathroom. A popular fallback is **Wisma Hotel** (tel: 06-228012) at 114A Jln Munshi, with rooms from MS$22 to MS$48.

As Malacca's popularity grows, cheap hostels and guest houses are springing up all over the place. The well-equipped **Paradise Hostel** at 4 Jln Tengkera has dormitory beds at MS$5, fan cooled rooms from MS$10 to MS$15, free tea and coffee, use of fridge, darts, snooker, cooking facilities and a fine noticeboard, full of useful tips and information. South of the river is **Kancil Guest House** at 177 Jln Parameswara, an old Chinese house with a large front porch and a garden to sit out in round the back. It is a new place, trying hard, with dormitory beds at MS$4, rooms from MS$7 to MS$12, a roof for drying clothes, up-to-date information, bicycle rental and friendly staff. Across the road at No. 218a, **Trilogy Hostel** is an established favourite, with dormitory beds at MS$5, rooms from MS$8 to MS$14, free tea and coffee, travel tips, use of fridge, newspapers, security lockers, games, book exchange and cheap bike rental. If you are not met at the express bus terminal, take town bus No. 17 (30 *sen*) or an Aziz bus and get off at the Chinese temple crossing on Jln Parameswara. Anyone who likes their food should stay at **Hotel Nan Tai**, 36 Jln Laksamana. This is a nice clean little guest house, sandwiched between two of the best restaurants in town, with rooms at MS$5 single, MS$10 double. Owner Roy cooks great Portuguese food, arranges local sightseeing and offers boating/fishing trips (MS$50 per person) to nearby islands. He can even book you into the government rest house, newly erected on the islands, for MS$20 per night. If a man with a handlebar moustache, a cowboy hat and an Apollo physique approaches you at the bus-station, he is selling rooms for **Cowboy Lem's**, an offbeat little place on the reclaimed land near the football field. His rooms are MS$6 to MS$12 and he will take you home and show you photos of when he was a weightlifter. If he has enough people, he will take you out in a ten-person minibus (MS$20 per person) to the rubber plantations and a good local waterfall. **Yashica**, off Jln Tengkara (on the way to the beach), is brand new, quiet and relaxing, with clean MS$10 rooms. It is a bit difficult to get to, but has far more atmosphere than the Paradise or the Kancil as it is on the water and in the middle of a *kampong*. **Travellers Lodge**, 214b/215b Taman Malacca Riya, is another out-of-the-way goodie. It has bright comfy rooms at MS$9 single, MS$11 double and a pleasant lounge, with balcony, overlooking the Straits of Malacca. To get there from the main bus-station, catch town bus No. 17 towards Bandar Hilar and U Pasir. If you need to stay near the bus-station, try **New Livo Hotel** at 332 Kilang Rd, with clean rooms at MS$20, bathroom attached.

FOOD

The food in Malacca is probably the best in Malaysia. Every weekend, crowds of Singaporeans and Malaysians from other states drive over just to dine on sumptuous Nyonya fare, Portuguese cuisine at the Portuguese Settlement, or to indulge in a culinary marathon at the rows of eating-stalls at the famous **Glutton's Corner** along Jln Taman in Bandar Hilar. The **Restoran De Lisbon** is one of four seafood restaurants ranged around the small square in the Portuguese settlement. Here you can enjoy a delicious range of seafood cooked Portuguese-style with lots of sugar, spice and chillies thrown in. Ignore the cockroaches plastering the walls, and tuck into speciality dishes like 'curry devil' (very hot, with chicken), crispy fried cuttle-fish, baked fish, sambal prawns and sweet-sour crabs. It is a good idea, since getting home can be difficult, to travel up by rickshaw and ask it to wait while you eat. Calling out a taxi is expensive and it is a long walk back!

Nyonya food, a subtle blend of Chinese and Malay cooking, is best sampled at **Jonker's** (tel: 06-235578), a brand-new restaurant at 17 Jln Hang Jebat. With its art deco furnishings, wrought-iron spiral staircase and taped salon music, this beautiful old Nyonya house is like a mini-Raffles! Prices are cheap (MS$12 for a three-course meal) and the menu makes a refreshing change for anyone looking for home-style cooking. There is chilli con carne, spaghetti bolognese, beef and burgundy pie and a sumptuous range of cakes and ice-creams. A lot of backpackers come here, enjoying their first decent Western meal in six months. Equally, there are gourmets eager to try Nyonya favourites like beef *rindang* (beef in dried coconut curry), fish in assam sauce, chicken and vegetable curries and sweet pineapple tarts.

A good breakfast place is **Kim Swee Huat** at 38 Jln Laksamana, serving Chinese fast food, nyonya and baba snacks, fresh juices, and beer at reasonable prices. A couple of doors along, **Mitchell Raaji Nivas** is a wonderful Indian restaurant with popular banana-leaf meals, fish curries, fruit *murtabaks*, Sri Lankan pancakes, shakes, lassis and juices. The special birianis on Monday and Thursday nights are exceptional! Two other good Indian restaurants are **Laxmi Vilas** and **Sri Krishna Bhavan**, next door to each other on Jln Benderhara. Here you get even better south Indian food than in Madras – as-much-as-you-can-eat banana-leaf *thalis* for less than £1!

For a bit of class, try a buffet lunch (MS$12 plus taxes) at the **City Bayview** hotel, or an evening meal at the Merlin's **Golden Dragon Restaurant**, well known for its Chinese cuisine. **McDonald's, Kentucky Fried Chicken** and the big supermarkets are a long 3-km walk north of town, along Jln Gajah Barang. This is the old part of the city and few foreigners go there.

TIOMAN

Tioman must be the gem of the South China Sea. A paradise of pristine white-sand beaches, spectacular flora and fauna and colourful coral, this island was immortalised as the mythical Bali H'ai in the movie *South Pacific*. Some 38 km long and 19 km wide, it is the largest and the most accessible of the 60 or so islands lying off Malaysia's east coast. Tioman, according to legend, was a tragic dragon princess who turned herself into stone after being disappointed in love. The tail of the dragon is at Salang, while its two horns are formed by the twin peaks at the south of the island, where Bali H'ai mountain is. The island itself is made up of towering volcanic peaks clothed in thick impenetrable jungle and trees of immense height. There are good coral reefs for skin-diving and snorkelling and the crystal-clear waters are safe for swimming, although, as at any tropical island, it is not wise to step on any sea-urchins or fire coral. Tioman is thinly populated – with only ten or so fishing villages – but the locals are a friendly lot, given to

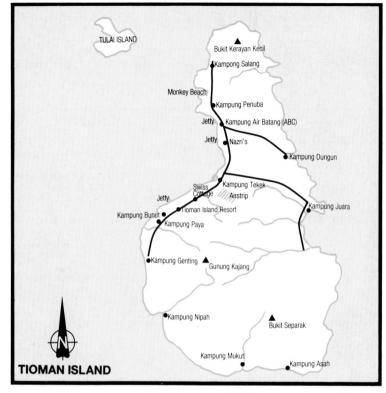

TIOMAN ISLAND

painting foreigners' nails on the beach in the traditional marriage style.

Accommodation is rather primitive and falls into three general categories: A-frame huts (MS$3/4), two to three person long houses (MS$25/30) and four-person hillside chalets (MS$30). The long houses and the chalets usually have attached bathrooms, but few places yet have electricity, so bring a flashlight. Tioman Island Resort, the single luxury hotel, is located on the north-western shore of the island, below Tekek.

Although little developed for tourism, Tioman is already popular with back-packers as a relaxing pit-stop between Singapore and Kuantan. The island is most pleasant from January to May, i.e. after the monsoons of October to December and before the high-season crowds of June to August.

ARRIVAL/DEPARTURE
Air
Pelangi Air flies daily to Tioman from Kuala Lumpur and Singapore. During the rains, when boat crossings are rough, flying makes sense unless you are a totally intrepid adventurer.

Road/Sea
Tioman is three to four hours by boat (MS$15), two hours by hovercraft/cata-maran (MS$25) and one hour by hydro-foil (MS$35) from the small fishing village of **Mersing** on the coastal road. Since the last boat goes around 5 p.m. and since Mersing is four to five hours by bus from Singapore, KL or Kuantan, an early start is required if you want to make Tioman the same day. On arrival in Mersing, you have a ten-minute walk from **Malaysia Restaurant** (cheap eats, bus ticketing service to Kuantan/ Singapore) down to the ferry jetty. Here several travel offices sell boat trips over to Tioman. Unless you stay overnight in Mersing, or can afford to charter a boat out to Salang or Juara (around MS$120, seats eight) you'll probably have to get a late boat out to Nazri's jetty above Tekek, a miserable prospect, since the chalets there are often full. Far better to spend your first night at friendly **Omar Backpackers Dorm** (MS$5 dormitory) in Mersing, on the way down to the jetty. Omar and Helene, the helpful co-owners, run a nice clean place and offer advice on how to go to **Sibu Island** a quiet, unspoilt alternative to Tioman, with cheap accommodation, white-sand beaches, great snorkelling and interesting walks. In the morning, you can go over to Tioman on a comfortable early boat. Afternoon boats often hit rough seas and take longer. If you need a room in Mersing, try **Hotel Embassy** at Jln Ismail 2 (tel: 07-791301; MS$21 fan,

The clock tower in Penang

MS$32 air-conditioning) or **Mandarin Hotel**, opposite the bus station (MS$12 fan, MS$20/25 air-conditioning). Returning from Tioman, it is easy to pick up share-taxis to Singapore from Mersing pier.

GETTING AROUND THE ISLAND

Most of Tioman's 'resorts' have their own beach and each beach is connected by a sea-bus service. The sea-bus runs every hour or so from 8.30 a.m. to 5.30 p.m. between Tioman Island Resort, Tekek (Airport), ABC (Air Bintang Cottages), Penuba beach and Salang. Fares one-way range from MS$l to MS$5. The island's only road runs from the telecom tower 1 km south of Tioman Island Resort up to the airstrip at Tekek, about 2 km north.

TEKEK

Whether you are dropped at Tekek jetty, or Nazri's jetty just above it, start walking – both these places are dirty, overcrowded and unfriendly. A 20-minute stroll north brings you to ABC beach, where the food and bungalows (MS$4) are much better. A lot of travellers end up here – communal eating, no theft, good diving and snorkelling. Walking south, the accommodation gets more expensive but you get more for your money – a real bedroom with a bathroom, etc. **Swiss Cottage** is 20 minutes' trudge south of Tekek wharf. It is a popular place, run by Capt Mustapha, with good food, useful facilities and chalets from MS$20 to MS$40. Just below it is the high-class **Tioman Island Resort** (tel: 09-445445), offering comfortable rooms and chalets from MS$80 to MS$800. It may be touristy and overpriced, but if you want Western comforts, this is the place to come. Three-star facilities include pool, 9-hole golf course, scuba-diving, tennis courts, bar-restaurant (the only place I found on Tioman to get a cold beer) and a monkey specially trained to pluck coconuts. The hotel looks onto a tiny coral island, ideal for snorkelling.

There is a small post office at Tekek and a money-changing service at Tioman Island Resort. **Zaha's** information service, at the Tekek pier, sells boat tickets to Mersing and Salang, also excursions to the waterfall near **Mukut** (south of the island) where *South Pacific* was filmed and to nearby **Tulai Island**. Round-trips of the island cost MS$25 per hour.

SALANG

A 40-minute seabus ride from Tekek (MS$2), Salang is the up-and-coming beach. It has a pretty coral island, abundant marine life and much better diving than Tioman Island Resort, which doesn't run many courses. **Ben's Diving**

Centre is a reliable outfit, offering five-day open-water courses at just US$200. **Zaif's Place** is a good place to stay, with a small clean beach, informative staff, volleyball, hammocks, cheap accommodation from MS$6 (A-frame huts) to MS$18 (hillside chalets) and all the traditional travellers' fare: banana pancakes, chips, *nasi goreng* and shakes. Decent fallbacks are **Bidin's** (MS$6 to 35) and **Salang Indah** (MS$5 to 20). **Monkey Bay** is a very beautiful spot, well worth the rather punishing 45-minute walk over the hills from Salang beach. Zaif can suggest other local hikes.

Salang has early-morning boats direct to Mersing (slow, MS$20). Soon, there will be fast boats too.

PENUBA

Penuba beach, between Salang and ABC, opened up in May 1989. It is another good snorkelling spot, with A-frame huts at MS$5 per person and a camping site.

JUARA

An enjoyable two- to three-hour trek down a jungle path (via a pretty waterfall, good for swimming) takes you across the island from Tekek to Kampung Juara. This is the quietest, least accessible beach, with long stretches of squeaky-clean sand and outstanding coral. The only problems with Juara are rough seas (especially from November to February) and sandflies (bring tiger balm and repellent). **Rainbow Huts** on the far end of the beach are highly recommended. Mohammed is a great host. He owns rights to all the turtle eggs on the island and knows all the best snorkelling and turtle spots. His food is excellent (worth the long wait for it), and his two-person bungalows are a snip at MS$3 a night. If he is full, stay at **Ali Awang's Chalets** and eat at **Turtle Cafe**.

Note: take some small change, beer and fruit juice to Juara as there is none available on this side of the island. There is a direct boat to Juara from Mersing, but only in the morning. This service is erratic and most people end up walking there from Tekek.

KUANTAN

Kuantan is just a town, with nothing much to do or see. 'The only reason for staying in Kuantan', observed one traveller, 'is if you fall asleep on the bus, miss Cherating and end up there by mistake!' A good cheap hotel, right out of the bus station, is **Ming Heng Hotel** on Jln Mahkota. It costs MS$12.60 per night and was recommended by someone who adds 'The guy who runs it has a face like a burnt wellie – see if you can make him smile!' An alternative is **Hotel New Embassy** on Jln Besar, with clean adequate rooms from MS$12.50 to MS$18. In the same street, **Samudra Riverview Hotel** (tel: 09-522688) charges MS$70 to MS$120 for a taste of luxury, while **Suraya Hotel** (tel: 09-524266) has cheaper air-conditioned rooms for MS$45/52. Kuantan has a **Kentucky Fried Chicken**, some decent food markets and a lot of hawker stalls near the bus-station – this is where most travellers eat.

If you do get stuck in Kuantan for any reason, walk down to the jetty and get a boat across the river (30c) to the small fishing village of Tanjung Lumpur. There is no tourism here and the people are so friendly! A good way of spending a morning is just strolling around, observing a fast-vanishing traditional way of life. Something else to do is the trek to Pancing Caves, 28 km out of Kuantan. Take a green bus to Sungai Lembing, get off at Pancing and walk 4 km through oil, palm and rubber-tree plantations to the caves. A guide will take you through the caves for MS$3 (this includes the MS$1 charge to see the 9-m-long Reclining Buddha) and will afterwards direct you to the nearby waterfall. If you do not want to walk, local lads will run you out there on motorbikes.

Kuantan's rather tacky beach resort, 5 km out of town, is Teluk Chempedak. Two world-class hotels are located here: **Hyatt Kuantan** (tel: 09-525211, rooms from MS$130), and **Merlin Inn Resort** (tel: 09-522388; singles from MS$90, doubles from MS$110). A choice budget option is **Asrama Bendahara**, across the road from the beach. It has cool rooms, with clean bathrooms and big verandahs, for MS$8, also tasty food, friendly people and windsurfing lessons. Manager Mike Foo is a charming host and Chico, the DJ, plays music and sings until midnight. After that, you can rock on at the Hyatt disco till 1 a.m.!

ARRIVAL/DEPARTURE

MAS fly to Kuantan from KL (MS$61) and Singapore (SS$120). Air-conditioned buses run regularly beween Kuantan and Johore Bahru (MS$15, seven hours), Singapore (MS$16, six to seven hours), KL (MS$10.90, four and a half hours), Malacca (MS$13, five to six hours), K Trengganu (MS$8, three to four hours) and Kota Bahru (MS$15.80, six to seven hours). Non-air-conditioned buses are slightly cheaper. Taxis are MS$25 per person from KL, MS$30 from Kota Bahru, MS$20 from Mersing and MS$30 from Johore Bahru.

TAMAN NEGARA

Peninsular Malaysia's national park is 4,300 sq km of virgin tropical rain forest housing a myriad species of flora and fauna. It extends over three states, but only the section in Pahang state is accessible to tourists. From Kuala Tahan, the park headquarters, you can make jungle treks out to hides and salt licks to watch the wildlife. Further afield, you can take boat trips up the river, or climb 2190-m-high Gunung Tahan. The park is most pleasant between March and September. It closes from mid-November to mid-December and is generally a poor bet in the rainy season. The most convenient jumping-off point to Taman Negara is probably Kuantan, especially if you are drifting northwards up the east coast of Malaysia.

ARRIVAL/DEPARTURE

Accessibility to Taman Negara has improved and Pelangi Air now flies to Kuala Tembeling from Kuala Lumpur every Tuesday, Thursday and Sunday (MS$160 return). Even better, restrictions on the park are lifting, although it is still a good idea to make prior booking in Kuala Lumpur at the Dept. of Wildlife & National Parks, 10 Km Jln Cheras (tel: 03-9052872), even though this is no longer strictly necessary. Making your own arrangements, you pay: MS$22 for bus-fares (MS$7 KL to Temerloh, MS$2 Temerloh to Jurantut, MS$2 Jerantut to Kuala Tembeling; same deal coming back), MS$1 for the entry permit and MS$5 camera fee (both issued at Kuala Tembeling) and MS$30 for the return boat journey from Kuala Tembeling to the park HQ at Kuala Tahan (three-hour trip). A guide is not essential but you can share the costs of one (MS$30 per day) without breaking the bank. The park hostel in Kuala Tahan is cheap, with dormitory-style rooms at MS$10 and two-person chalets at MS$40, but should be pre-booked in busy months like April and August. Alternatively, hire tents (M$2.50) or put up at the rest house in Jerantut (rooms at MS$30 fan, MS$40 air-conditioned). The general conclusion is that you can do Taman Negara on your own for around half the price of a MS$500 three to four day organised tour out of Kuala Lumpur. Extra costs might include MS$10 for a fishing permit and MS$20 for a direct taxi from KL to Kuala Tembeling. You should allow MS$25 a day for food. Don't bother with the hostel restaurants at Kuala Tahan unless you really like Westernised Malay food. Dine in a romantic exotic setting on the cheaper floating 'restoran' across the river – if the staff see you on the jetty waving to come over, they will send a longboat to fetch you!

The easiest approach to the park is from Kuantan – three hours by bus to Kuala Tembeling, changing at Jurantot. From Kuala Trengganu catch a bus down to Kuala Berang, then a taxi to Kenyir Dam, then a boat into the park – expensive! Most people coming in from Thailand approach Taman Negara from Kota Bahra – taking a train straight through the jungle to Jerantut. The train leaves Wakaf Baru (bus 19 or 27 from Kota Bahru) at 11 a.m. and arrives at Jerantut at 8.30 p.m. An overnight stay in Jerantut is required. From here, it is a 30-minute taxi ride to Kuala Tembeling, for the 9 a.m. or 2 p.m. boat to Kuala Tahan. If you go by bus (dep. 8.30 p.m. and 10 p.m. from Kota Bahru), you reach Kuala Tembeling in good time to buy your permit and catch the 9 a.m. boat into the park.

THINGS TO DO

Alhough there are many hides and salt licks at which to observe animals, do not expect heaps of wildlife. This is a jungle, not a zoo. It is worth trying, though, as with luck and determination tigers, tapirs, snakes, civet cats and hornbills can be seen. If you want to preserve the experience, a tape-recorder is better than a camera. Here are some useful tips from travellers:

We sat up in hides most nights and saw lots of animals by torchlight. The set-up here is wonderfully flexible. You can either go and do it all yourself, wandering off with a tent and camping out in the hides by the lake (MS$5 per night), or you can join an organised tour.

We took food supplies and water-purification tablets and went on a glorious four-day trek from park headquarters up to the north and back. We saw lots of barking deer and sambhar deer. At night, we even saw tapir. Torches and tents can be hired, but you have to bring your own binoculars.

There are all sorts of caves in the park. Look out for the Bat Cave, it's a potholer's dream, with thousands of bats, snakes and toads. A real Indiana Jones experience!

Watch out for leeches, especially after heavy rain. They're tiny and do not hurt, but they sneak into your socks when you are not looking. Be careful they do not climb up your legs and into your underwear. Soap, onions and repellent work wonders – apply generously to shoes, socks and ankles.

If mountain-hiking is your thing, Gunung Tahan is really nice. It takes five days to get up there and three to four days to return. You *have* to hire

a guide. They cost MS$400 for the first week, MS$50 per day thereafter, but it is worth it – the trail can be hard to find otherwise. If you go with a group, you can share the costs. Bring waffle-soled shoes that aren't pretty, but practical. Plan your food supply carefully; a lot of hikers fail to make the peak because of insufficient food. If you are doing the full ten-day trip, bring about 7-9 kg apiece and dump some food as you go along to save on weight – your guide will show you how. A sleeping bag is a *must* at the top of the mountain. It gets really cold up there, especially at night.

CHERATING

This is another place where people come for a night or two and end up spending a week. Cherating has a wide palm-fringed bay with calm clear waters and a long white-sand beach, virtually deserted. Set back from the beach are a number of *kampong*-style guest houses. Each of these sits within a small enclosure, offering cheap bungalow accommodation, local food etc. It is a far more livable option than nearby Kuantan (45 km south) and has far more to offer too.

The lure of Cherating is the opportunity to spend some time in a typical Malay *kampong* or village. Ironically, there is no *kampong* here any more as the original fishing village was swept away by the advances of the sea and the government has relocated all the ex-villagers at 'new' Cherating, 5 km down the road. Today, the only accommodations actually run by locals are the three originals: Maklong The, Maklong De and Hussein's. All the rest are managed by people from other parts of Malaysia. The name Cherating comes from the Malay word *ranting* meaning branch. This harks back to the time, only 50 years ago, when the river was full of crocodiles which attacked even a stray branch falling into it. There are no crocs left today: they got in the way of villagers collecting mangrove in the swamp and were promptly exterminated.

ARRIVAL/DEPARTURE

Coming up the east coast from Mersing, get off the bus at Kuantan (four to five hours, MS$10.25) and ask around in the bus-terminal for an onward bus to Kampong Cherating (MS$2.20, 45-60 minutes). If you are coming from the north, look for a Mini Motel sign on the left.

You cannot go direct to anywhere from Cherating by bus. If heading north, you have to change at Kemaman, the next village up (12 km, 80c, half-hourly service) for Marang (MS$5.25, two and half hours; hourly departures, on the half-hour – [except 12.30 p.m.] – from

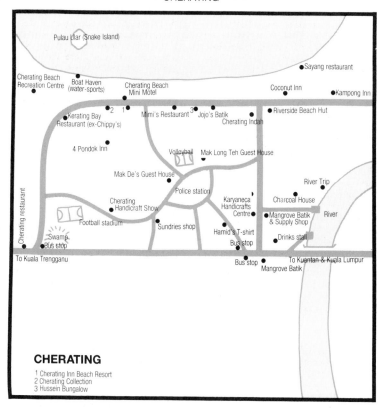

CHERATING

1 Cherating Inn Beach Resort
2 Cherating Collection
3 Hussein Bungalow

8.30 a.m. to 5.30 p.m.) and Kuala Trengganu. If going south, you have to change buses at Kuantan. There is an interesting Orchid Farm ll km out of Cherating, on the way to Kemaman.

THINGS TO DO
Cherating's one supply shop, **Mangrove Mini-Mart**, is just off the main road and has excellent information. This should be your first port of call off the bus from Kuantan or K Trengganu. Friendly Nasir caters to all travellers' needs, offering free maps/information, toilet paper, mosquito repellent, ice-cream, cold drinks, book exchange, bicycle rental, etc. He is even planning day-trips by van (MS$15 per person) to **Lake Chini**, a two and a half hour drive away. Once there, you will be able to whizz around the lake all day long by speedboat. For now, however, the big thing to do in Cherating is river trips. Most of the guest houses can arrange river trips (MS$6 to 8 per person), but Mini-Mart and Riverside do the best ones. There is a winding river behind the village and they take you down all sorts of pretty little waterways where you can spot monkeys, snakes, huge iguanas, etc. Mini Mart hires out fishing rods to go fishing in the river; Cherating Inn gives free nets to go prawn-fishing in the swamp opposite

Mini's. Cherating Beach Recreation Centre offers water-skiing (MS$60/hour) and windsurfing (MS$10/hour) and a couple of places along the beach advertise boat trips out to nearby Snake Island. The beach itself is not so good for swimming. It is very often low tide and you have to walk *miles* even to get up to your kneecaps in water! If, however, you climb 2 km over the headland from the Cherating Beach Recreation Hotel (or walk over the rocks at low tide) you will come to a series of lovely little bays with better beaches and swimming. Beyond these is the big **Club Med** (tel: 09-591131) hotel, with expensive rooms from MS$165, excellent water-sports, nightly cultural shows and a good beach where you can watch the turtles laying their eggs at night (May to October only).

Note: you can change money (US dollars cash only) with Lan at the batik shop next to Mini-Mart.

SHOPPING
The two souvenirs most travellers come away with are a hand-printed batik T-shirt from **Cherating Collection**, next to Chippy's restaurant, and a filigree silver brooch from **Jojo**'s, next to Hussein's. The brooches are especially good buys as not much silver is made in

Malaysia. The **Handicraft Centre** opposite Mini-Mart produces lots of cheap little souvenirs – wall-hangings, rugs, bags, purses, even mosquito-swatters. Next to Mini-Mart, you can see demonstrations of batik. Over the road at **Mangrove Batik**, a man called Jay teaches it. With his help, you can batik your own T-shirt, shorts or sheet sleeping-bag.

ACCOMMODATION/FOOD

Mak Long Teh's and **Mak De's House** are close to the main road, ten minutes' walk from the beach. They are the only two guest houses which do an all-in price of MS$10 per person, including breakfast and dinner. What they offer are delightful self-contained bungalows on stilts, with a clean double bed, a mosquito net, a useful clothes rack and a cosy verandah to sit out on. But the food is the thing – a fantastic variety of local Malay dishes and lots of it, eaten around communal dining tables. It was Mak Long Teh who opened the first guest house here 15 years ago. She is a sweet lady who, even after all this time, still does not speak a word of English!

If you need to be near the beach, try **Riverside**, **Coconut Inn** or **Hussain's**. Chalet prices range from MS$5 single/MS$8 double up to around MS$25 if you want a bathroom. **Cherating Beach Recreation Centre** and **Cherating Mini-Motel** are a bit more upmarket than anywhere else. They have the best situations, right on the beach and some of their rooms (MS$20/30) have fans and attached bathrooms. They don't, however, include food with the price. You pay for that separately and it can work out expensive! All the guest houses have restaurants, but many travellers eat out at **Chippy's**, which has good sounds and cheap food, or at **Mini's**, where you can get a real Malaysian breakfast of *nasi lemak* (rice with roasted peanuts, slivers of dried fish and chicken in a hot spicy sauce) or Western-style 'eggy bread'. **Lianee Cafe**, next to Hussein's, has a licensed bar and live music in the evenings. Last time I was there, it was showing traditional Malay dances and 'breakwater revivals'!

RANTAU ABANG

The 32-km stretch of beach at Rantau Abang, 43 km south of Marang, is the prime nesting site of the famous giant leatherback turtles, who travel thousands of miles across the oceans to lay their eggs here between May and September. This is one of only two areas in the world (the other is Surinam) considered significant in the propagation of the species. The beach at Rantau Abang is also said to be the best place in the world to observe these magnificent creatures as they toil ashore after their long arduous journey to deposit 50 to 140 eggs in holes dug in the moonlit sand.

More than anything else, it was the turtles of Rantau Abang that started bringing tourists to the east coast in the first place. However, tourism has not done these poor animals any favours – many eggs get stolen or broken and few turtles make it up the beach before being stood upon for a photo. Such disturbances during nesting drive many turtles away and they never return. Compared to 10,671 leatherback turtles that came ashore in the 1950s, the landings have now declined to less than 600 per year. Each turtle is thought to be laying fewer eggs and the nesting season is getting shorter and shorter. The government now collects many of the eggs laid and hatches them at a nearby farm under a 24-hour guard!

ACCOMMODATION/FOOD

Rantau Abang Visitors' Centre, just north of the village, shows videos of the turtles and answers any questions you may have about them. It also has family-size cottages (sleeping four) from MS$90, a bar-restaurant, a marine museum and a handicraft display. Nearby **Awang's** has better food and cosier huts at MS$10 double. From here, it's only a five-minute walk to the hatchery to see the baby turtles. **Dahimah's**, 1 km south of the visitors' centre, offers clean chalets with bathrooms at MS$10, longhouse rooms with showers at MS$6 per person, a nice quiet beach and good food. Manager Abdul provides weekly beach BBQs, free windsurfing lessons and boat trips to nearby Tinggol Island for snorkelling and fishing. **Marantau Inn**, 2 km further south, has comfy two-person chalets (with fan/bath) from MS$38 and a restaurant. Some 8 km south of the visitors' centre, is the luxury **Tanjong Jawa Beach Hotel**, with rooms around MS$100, a restaurant and water-sports.

ARRIVAL/DEPARTURE

Rantau Abang is a popular stop between Cherating and Marang. Most buses go through the village and there is a bus stop right by the visitors' centre.

MARANG

Marang is an idyllic fishing village, just 17 km south of K Trengganu. Travellers like it for its relaxed atmosphere, long stretch of beach, friendly local people and tranquil sunsets. The sea is safe for swimming (except from November to February) and there is good fishing in the river. Many people spend a week here, snorkelling off Kapas Island, freshwater swimming at Sakayu Falls and viewing

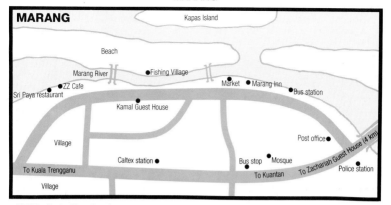

MARANG

Kapas Island

Beach

Marang River

Fishing Village

ZZ Cafe

Sri Paya restaurant

Kamal Guest House

Market • Marang Inn

Bus station

Village

Post office •

To Zachariah Guest House (4 km)

Caltex station •

Bus stop • Mosque

To Kuala Trengganu

To Kuantan

To Zachariah Guest House

Police station

Village

wildlife (including lions) on river trips.

Marang became an overnight sensation in late 1988, when a rich gold mine was discovered 6 km up the road at Rusila. Within three months, the area had a full-scale gold rush on its hands. In February 1989, deciding that the mine was too accessible to the public, the government ruled that nobody could pan for gold without taking a MS$30 'lesson' first!

THINGS TO DO

The town is interesting. It has several good shops for supplies, a busy morning market on Saturday and Monday, a night market on Sundays and a small post office open daily (except Fridays) from 8 a.m. to 4 p.m. There is nowhere to change money, but you can make phone calls from Marang Inn.

During the turtle season (May to August) you can watch small green turtles coming up the beach at night. Marang is a far better venue for turtle-spotting than Rantau Abang, which has become rather commercialised of late. To see the big leatherbacks, take a MS$15 boat-trip from one of the guest houses to nearby **Kapas Island**. This island is renowned for its clear emerald waters and fantastic coral, perfect for boating, fishing and snorkelling. Turtles can be seen on, and paddling around, Kapas between March and September. You can also view large, inquisitive iguana, some of them 1.5 m long, emerging from the jungle and climbing the coconut palms to be cooled off by sea breezes. **Pulao Kapas Resort** on the island is owned by a very pleasant and helpful Malay called Ali, who has an office in Marang village (tel: 632989). Accommodation ranges from MS$10 to MS$28, depending on whether you take a hut or bungalow, single or double. The food is excellent and helpings are huge. To avoid day-trippers (who turn up in the afternoons), walk through the jungle to quieter beaches on the other side of the island. Sunsets can be spectacular here!

If you intend to go, get to Kapas quickly; a big luxury hotel is scheduled for construction in 1990.

Kamal Guest House offers good boat trips up the Marang River (you see a lot of wildlife: monkeys, otters, water-snakes, lizards, iguanas, etc.) to visit two local villages to experience the traditional way of life. Kamal also lays on trips to Sekayu Waterfall (MS$10-12 per person), best seen between March and September.

ACCOMMODATION/FOOD

Kamal's Guest Houe is near the beach, about eight minutes' walk from the town or from the main road. It is a very homely place, with good information, friendly staff, use of kitchen, free tea and coffee, BBQs on the beach, etc. Dormitory beds are MS$4 and rooms cost MS$10 or MS$12. The better rooms are chalet-style, with fans and big double beds. **Marang Guest House**, just up the hill behind Kamal's, has a smart MS$5 dormitory and clean double-bedded rooms (with bath/shower) at MS$15, but Kamal's is definitely more in touch with travellers and their needs. **Marang Inn** is located right on the jetty in the heart of town. It is noisy and glitzy, but the fan-cooled dormitory beds (MS$4), the large double rooms (MS$5 single, MS$10 double) and the downstairs restaurant are always packed. The success of this place is attributable to a young Chinese-Malay, Alex, who provides bicycles, guitars, indoor games, book exchange, laundry service and free bananas.

If you are fed up with eating Western food with other travellers, walk past Kamal's to the adjoining **ZZ Cafe** and **Sri Paya Restaurant**. Both places have TVs, are packed out with locals and stay open till late. ZZ does the better food, but (because it is fresh) you have to wait longer for it. Try the *roti chanai* for breakfast!

ARRIVAL/DEPARTURE

If coming from Kuantan, Cherating or

Kemaman, get off the bus at the big Caltex station past Marang bridge (for Kamal's guest house) or at the police station just before the bridge (for Marang Inn). From Kuala Trengganu, stop the bus as soon as you see a Caltex station and Marang District Office. Leaving Marang, it is 80c by bus or MS$l by share-taxi to Kuala Trengannu. There are no direct buses to Cherating/Kuantan – you have to change at Kemaman.

KUALA TRENGGANU

This town is best seen as a day-trip from nearby Marang. The large **Central Market**, hailed as the best market on the east coast, is rather disappointing. Recent renovations have robbed it of a lot of atmosphere. All it has got now are not particularly good Western goods at not terribly good prices. Nevertheless, there is fine photography to be done on Saturday mornings and the covered market has some decent batik shops in the upstairs section. Apart from the market, the other big thing to see is **Sutera Semai** silk and batik factory at Chendering, 8 km south west of K Trengannu. You can book your bus ticket there (60c) from the Pelancongan Nini stand at the bus-station. Open from 8 a.m. to 4 p.m. daily (closed Thursday p.m. and all day Friday), this is the only silk factory in Malaysia and has a good workshop layout. The nearby museum is worth seeing too. It has a marvellous collection of *kris* knives.

Batu Buruk, 15 minutes by bus (40c) from the main bus-station, is a beautiful white-sand beach with calm clear waters and gentle rolling surf. It is the venue of the annual Trengganu Beach Festival, which takes place from 22 to 29 July and which features kite-flying, top-spinning, boat racing and many other traditional arts. There are culture shows every Thursday, Friday, Saturday and Sunday at the new stage area in front of the food centre on the beach. Performances start at 3.30 p.m. and 9 p.m. and admission is free.

Because taxis are not metered in Kuala Trengganu, you have to negotiate a rate for sightseeing (around MS$60 per day) in advance. Trishaws hire out for short journeys only – they go nowhere for less than MS$2.

TOURIST SERVICES

The TDC tourist office (tel: 09-621433), ground floor, Wisma MCIS, Jln Sultan Zainal Abidin, is open 8 a.m. to 12.45 p.m., 2 to 4 p.m. daily (until 12.45 p.m. Thursday, closed Friday). It's well worth a visit if you are planning a tour of east coast Malaysia. Staff are very helpful and there is a wealth of printed information. Useful handouts are entitled *East Coast*

Malaysia and *Destination Trengganu*.

The post office, near the market jetty, is open 7 a.m. to 5 p.m. (closed Friday). Hong Kong Bank, near the bus station, changes money and travellers' cheques.

Note: don't drop cigarette butts at the bus-station, unless you want a MS$30 fine. Malaysia's new anti-smoking campaign is rigorously enforced in Kuala Trengganu!

ARRIVAL/DEPARTURE
Air
MAS offers daily flights from Singapore (MS$210), Penang (MS$80) and KL (MS$80). Kuala Trengganu's airport is 18 km from town, around MS$12-15 by taxi.

Road
The taxi stand is near the jetty at the end of Jln Sultan Ismail. The bus stand is in Jln Masjid Abidin, just off Jln Sultan Ismail. Air-conditioned buses cost MS$7 to Kota Bahru (three hours), MS$8 to Kuantan (three and a half hours), MS$20 to KL (six hours), MS$20 to Malacca (seven hours), MS$23 to Johore Bahru (seven to eight hours) and MS$25 to Singapore (eight hours). There is one non-air-conditioned bus daily to Butterworth (dep. 9 a.m., MS$22, eight hours), one bus a day to Kemaman (dep. 7.30 a.m., MS$5.25) and frequent buses to Marang (MS$l) and Rantau Abang (MS$3). Share-taxis are MS$12 to Kota Bahru, MS$15 to Kuantan, MS$20 to KL and MS$24/25 to Johore Bahru/Singapore.

Note: if you are only in Kuala Trengganu for the day, you can leave your bags at the bus-station (50c per piece) while you go sightseeing.

ACCOMMODATION/FOOD
Awi's Yellow House is a rustic waterside guest house located on Pulao Duyong Besar (Big Mermaid Island) in the Trengganu river. Here you can watch the island's famous boat-builders at work, experience the peaceful Malay lifestyle, or just lie on the sun-deck and watch the fishing boats go by. Awi can arrange good charter trips up the river by boat and sailing voyages on a Malay schooner. Dormitory-style rooms are good value at MS$5 per person, including free tea and coffee and a modest breakfast. To get to Awi's place, go down to the boat jetty by the taxi-stand and ask to go to *rumah Awi* (ten-minute crossing, 40c). On the island, turn left and walk near the shore for five minutes. (Note: the house isn't yellow any more!)

To stay at the beach, get a bus to Batu Burok and ask to be put off at the second roundabout from town. A short walk takes you to **New Ibi's Guest House** at

Chinese signs in Leboh Chulia

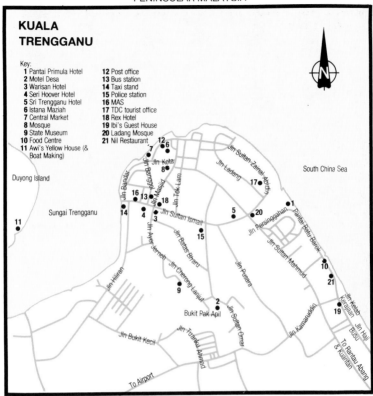

KUALA TRENGGANU

Key:
1 Pantai Primula Hotel
2 Motel Desa
3 Warisan Hotel
4 Seri Hoover Hotel
5 Sri Trengganu Hotel
6 Istana Maziah
7 Central Market
8 Mosque
9 State Museum
10 Food Centre
11 Awi's Yellow House (& Boat Making)
12 Post office
13 Bus station
14 Taxi stand
15 Police station
16 MAS
17 TDC tourist office
18 Rex Hotel
19 Ibi's Guest House
20 Ladang Mosque
21 Nil Restaurant

Duyong Island

South China Sea

Jln Sultan Zainal Abidin

Jln Ladang

Jln Kota

Jln Banggu

Jln Bandar

Jln Masjid

Jln Tok Lam

Jln Persinggahan

Pantai Batu Barok

Sungai Trengganu

Jln Sultan Ismail

Jln Ayer Jerneh

Jln Banas Bharu

Jln Cherong Lanjut

Jln Sultan Mahmud

Jln Hiliran

Bukit Pak Apil

Jln Pesera

Jln Sultan Omar

Jln Kamaruddin

Jln Kelab Kerajaan

Jln Haji Kerajaan Busu

To Bantau Abang & Kuantan

Jln Bukit Kecil

Jln Tuanku Ahmad

To Airport

898 Jln Kelab Kerajaan (tel: 634210). This is a quiet breezy place, a bit ramshackle, with a MS$4 dormitory, rooms at MS$10 and a pleasant beach-front location. Ibi, the friendly owner, can arrange for trips to Kapas Island and local handicrafts villages.

In town, travellers favour the **Rex** and **Evergreen** hotels, both opposite the bus-station with rooms for MS$15/20. The Chinese restaurant at the Rex is not bad and the **Family** restaurant, up the road from the Evergreen, does European and Malaysian food at low prices. The food centre along Batu Burok seafront is a row of seafood stalls (plus a couple of seafood restaurants) selling cheap and tasty snacks. There are more open-air eating stalls (Malay and Chinese) at Kampong Tiong, located just off the central market, between Jln Bandar and Jln Bangor. For Western fare, try a burger at **Wimpy** or **A & W** (both near the bus-station) or a steak/grill at the **Pantai Primula Hotel** (tel: 09-622100) on Jln Persinggahan. This is the top hotel in town, with water-sports, disco, designer pool and well-appointed rooms from MS$140 to MS$160. Two good mid-range hotels, both very central, are **Hotel Seri Hoover** (tel: 09-24655, MS$20 to MS$65) at 49 Jln Paya Bunga, and **Sri Trengganu Hotel** (tel: 09-634622) at 120 A-B Jln Sultan Ismail.

KOTA BAHRU

Kota Bahru, the capital of Kelantan state, is just a few kilometres from the Thai border and makes a good introduction to Malay town and market life. Here, traditional pastimes such as top-spinning, drumming, dancing and sha-dow-puppet shows can be observed. Here also you can rest up after Thailand before plunging into Malaysia, or vice versa. Kota Bahru is now the main transit town for Thai visas, having replaced Penang. It is much closer to the Thai border than Penang and is far less expensive and crowded.

ARRIVAL/DEPARTURE
Air
Kota Bahru's airport is 18 km from town. MAS lays on a free bus shuttle service. Otherwise, it is MS$5 per person by share-taxi, or MS$l by minibus. You can buy MS$66 onward flights to Penang or Kuala Lumpur from MAS (tel: 51455) at Kompleks Yakin, Jln Gajah Mati.

Rail
The railway station is across the river at Wakaf Baru, a 50-*sen* bus ride (Nos 19 or 27) from town. There is an 11 a.m. train daily to Jurantut for Taman Negara national park (cf. p 98). If you are coming north from the park, get off the

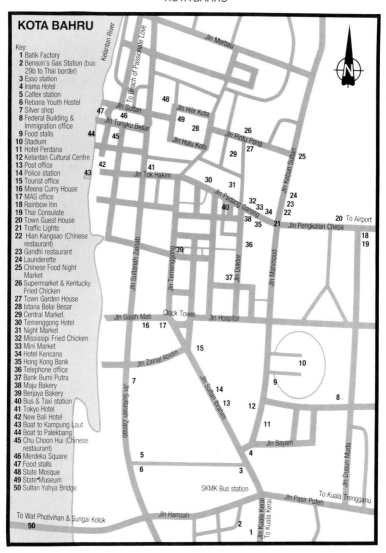

KOTA BAHRU

Key:
1 Batik Factory
2 Benson's Gas Station (bus 29b to Thai border)
3 Esso station
4 Irama Hotel
5 Caltex station
6 Rebana Youth Hostel
7 Silver shop
8 Federal Building & Immigration office
9 Food stalls
10 Stadium
11 Hotel Perdana
12 Kelantan Cultural Centre
13 Post office
14 Police station
15 Tourist office
16 Meena Curry House
17 MAS office
18 Rainbow Inn
19 Thai Consulate
20 Town Guest House
21 Traffic Lights
22 Hian Kangsao (Chinese restaurant)
23 Gandhi restaurant
24 Launderette
25 Chinese Food Night Market
26 Supermarket & Kentucky Fried Chicken
27 Town Garden House
28 Istana Belai Besar
29 Central Market
30 Temenggong Hotel
31 Night Market
32 Mississipi Fried Chicken
33 Mini Market
34 Hotel Kencana
35 Hong Kong Bank
36 Telephone office
37 Bank Bumi Putra
38 Maju Bakery
39 Berjaya Bakery
40 Bus & Taxi station
41 Tokyo Hotel
42 New Bali Hotel
43 Boat to Kampung Laut
44 Boat to Palekbang
45 Chu Choon Hui (Chinese restaurant)
46 Merdeka Square
47 Food stalls
48 State Mosque
49 State Museum
50 Sultan Yahya Bridge

train at Pasir Mas (the station before Wakaf Baru) and take a taxi or bus into Kota Baru (saves an hour of train travel). Or continue straight on from Pasir Mas to Rantau Panjang at the Thai border.

Road

Air-conditioned express buses to Penang (MS$28, seven hours), Kuala Lumpur (MS$25), Johore Bahru (MS$30), Singapore (MS$30) and Kuantan (MS$18) leave from the main SKMK bus-station, south of town on Jln Hamzah. You can book tickets from the local bus-station, next to the taxi-stand in the centre of town. Going to Singapore, it's best to get a taxi to Johore Bahru (MS$55), then a bus from there to Singapore. Some other taxi fares are MS$12 to Kuala Trengganu, MS$25 to Kuantan, MS$30 to

Penang and MS$35 to Kuala Lumpur.

For Thailand, take a 29b bus (MS$2) or share-taxi (MS$3.50) to Rantau Panjang, the border town. The trip takes one hour and you should get off, if coming by bus, as soon as you see the Immigration Post. Through Malay immigration, it is a five-minute walk across the bridge to Thai immigration at Sungai Kolok. Then hop on a motorbike/rickshaw (MS$l) to either the bus or rail station. Put your watch *back* one hour for Thai time and see if you have arrived in time for the 10.05 a.m., 10.50 a.m., 11.05 a.m. or 1.35 p.m. trains to Hat Yai. Fares to Hat Yai are 42B third class, 55B second class and it is a four and a half hour ride. The 10.05 a.m. and 10.55 a.m. trains carry on to Bangkok (220B third class, 420B second class) and go via Surat Thani, for

Koh Samui. There is no direct bus to Hat Yai from Sungai Kolok, but the 12.30 p.m. express bus goes to Songkhla (100B), where you change onto another bus for the short half-hour ride into Hat Yai (13B). This bus leaves from the local bus-stand near An-An Hotel, next to the cinema theatre, 2 km from the Thai immigration point in Sungai Kolok. It continues on to Surat Thani (200B, arriving 9 p.m.), Hua Hin (342B, arriving 3 a.m.) and Bangkok (416B, arriving 6 a.m.).

Note: you can change money (even small Malaysian currency) into Thai *baht* when you buy your train ticket at Sungai Kolok, but at a poor rate.

TOURIST SERVICES
The tourist office (tel: 09-785534) is on Jln Sultan Ibrahim, below the clock tower. It is open from 8.30 a.m. to 12.45 p.m., 2 to 4.30 p.m. Saturday to Wednesday (until 1.15 p.m. Thursday) and is quite good – the officers sometimes take tourists on private tours in the afternoon. As elsewhere in Malaysia, however, you have to go to the budget lodges (notably Town Guest House and Town Garden House) for correct up-to-date information.

The GPO on Jln Sultan Ibrahim is open from 8 a.m. to 5 p.m. daily, except Friday. Overseas calls can be made from the Telegraph Office in Jln Docktor, or from the Town Guest House. A good place to change money is Hong Kong Bank, opposite the mini-market in Jln Padang Garong.

The immigration office on Jln Bayam (third floor, Federal Building) is open from 10 a.m. to 3 p.m. (closed Thursday p.m. and all day Friday). Apply here for a two-month extension to your original two-month Malaysian tourist visa. A second two-month extension costs MS$10, but after that you must go out to Thailand and come back in again. The maximum stay in Malaysia is six months.

The Thai Consulate on Jln Pengkalan Chepa is open from 9 a.m. to 12.30 p.m., 2.30 to 4.30 p.m. Sunday to Thursday. You have to leave your passport (and three photos) overnight when applying for a visa. The cost is MS$20 for one month, MS$30 for two months (same prices if you are extending an old visa). If you are only going to be in Thailand for 15 days or less, you don't need to visit the embassy. A 15-day transit visa will simply be stamped into your passport at the Thai border. If you overstay your welcome in Thailand, expect a 100B per day fine on leaving the country!

SIGHTS
There is a great deal to see and do in Kota Bahru area. The town itself is small, friendly and relaxing – a pleasure to walk around or to tour by bicycle. Several guest houses hire out bikes at MS$3 per day. Trishaws are clued into tourist money – they charge MS$2 just to go down the street.

The 'new castle', after which Kota Bahru is named, is now the **State Museum** (Muzium Kelantan) inside the central market. It was built along with the town just over a century ago and little remains of the original structure as most of it was destroyed in the floods of 1936. The museum is open from 10.30 a.m. to 5.45 p.m. daily (except Wednesday) and houses the Sultan's family collection of costumes, weapons, ornaments, musical instruments and circumcision carriages. A modest, but fascinating display.

The **Beach of Passionate Love**, 10 km north of Kota Bahru, gets its exotic name from a Thai prince who liked bringing local lovelies here for seaside frolics. You can stay over at **Long House Beach Motel** (bungalows from MS$20 to 40, dormitory beds for MS$7) but don't go on a Friday when the beach is crowded with honeymooners. Along the road to the beach, you can see cottage industries like batik printing, batik painting, *songket* weaving, kite-making, etc. They are concentrated near Kampong Penambang, Kampong Kijang and 1 km before the beach. To get there, take bus No. 10 or 28 from the bus-stand opposite the Hong Kong Bank at Jln Padang Garong. If, however, you intend going to the beach, take bus No. 10 only.

Sabak Beach is 13 km from Kota Bahru, near the airport. This is where the Japanese landed in the Second World War, just one and half hours before they bombed Pearl Harbor. Sabak has a picturesque fishing village and long, wide beaches lined with casuarina trees. To get there, take bus 8a or 9 from the bus-stop along from Town Guest House (opposite Milton Hotel). At Sabak, follow the stream after the bridge to the village. Arrive between 2 and 3 p.m. to see colourful fishing boats and villagers young and old pulling them in. Anour, at Town Guest House, puts up travellers in a charming little beach house (four rooms, self-catering) in the village.

From Kota Bahru, you can make a number of interesting river trips. To visit the traditional village of **Dabong**, take bus No. 5 (yellow express, MS$3.20, 85 minutes) to Kuala Krai, 64 km south of Kota Bahru. At Kuala Krai, walk past the post office and police station to the jetty and hop on a public boat (departures from 11 a.m. to noon, MS$4.50) for the scenic one and a half hour trip upriver through the rubber plantations. Look out for monkeys, monitor lizards, kingfishers, wild boar and sometimes deer drinking near the bank. To see the

Fish Cave and Kampung Jelawan water-fall, you will need to stay at the government rest house in Dabong (chalet-style rooms at M$15, tel: 740725 for reservation, or contact Town Guest House). If you prefer to return to Kota Bahru the same day, go straight to Dabong railway station. Usually, there are trains back to Kuala Krai at 1.30 p.m. and 4 p.m. The 4 p.m. train arrives in Kuala Krai around 7 p.m., when there are only taxis back to Kota Bahru (buses stop at 6 p.m.). A shorter boat trip goes to **Palekbang**, a sleepy railway town just across the Kelantan river. Further downstream is **Kampong Laut**, an interesting village with batik crafts. Both boat trips start from the jetties near the raft-houses and both provide fascinating insights into riverbank life. From Palekbang, you can take bus 19a (red label) back to Kota Bahru, or you can get off at Wakaf Baru and wait for bus 19 (Tumpat) or 27 (Pengkalan Kubur) to take you to Chabang Empat. Off the bus here, turn left and walk 4 km (or charter a taxi, 50 *sen* per person, from Chabang Empat junction) to see the largest reclining Buddha in South-East Asia (41 m long, 11 m high) at **Wat Jambu** in Kampong Jambu. Founded in the seventeenth century by a group of Siamese (Thai) settlers, the temple features seven 'auspicious places of worship' and contains a large number of decorative hand-sculpted statues. Bus No. 29 goes direct from Kota Bahru to Kampong Jambu. Once there, a well-signposted turning indicates the way to Wat Jambu. For a small donation, you can stay overnight at the temple, but bring a sleeping bag if you want comfort!

Finally, there are the beautiful and totally unspoilt **Perhentian Islands** – twin islands in the South China Sea about 20 km away from Kuala Besut. The smaller of the two, Perhentian Kecil, is not being developed for tourism. It accommodates a fishing village of 75 families and is being promoted as 'a model example of a typical Malay fishing community and how it lives'. Perhentian Besar, the larger island, has clean beaches, lush tropical jungle and fantastic marine life. Fishing and snorkelling are superb and inland treks provide fine opportunities to watch giant iguanas, flying squirrels, sea-eagles and gibbons. To go there from Kota Bahru, catch bus No. 3 to Pasir Putih, then another bus to Kuala Besut. Get off at the market before the bus-terminal and walk to the jetty behind it for boats over to the island. If you arrive in Besut before noon (leave Kota Bahru by 8 a.m. at the latest), you have a good chance of getting a boat-ride from the islanders, who come to Besut to do their shopping. The correct fare is M$10 per person so don't let the boatmen from the mainland, who usually take visitors to the island,

charge you any more! The crossing takes around two hours, and the boatman will drop you off at your chalet on Perhentian Besar. I recommend **Rosli's chalets** – clean twin-bedded rooms at M$10 and four-bedded chalets at M$10 too! Rosli also has a small boat, which he uses to buy in supplies from Kecil island for his guests. If he is full, try the chalets next door. The more expensive government chalets cost M$15 to M$35 and you have to make prior reservation at the Kampung Raja district office (tel: 976326), just across the bridge from the bus terminal in Kuala Besut. **Perhentian Island Resort** (tel: 01-333810) is Besar's one big hotel, with deluxe chalets from M$40 to M$60, dormitory-style accommodation from M$20 and a M$5 campsite. During the high season months (February to October), it is wise to book ahead. There is a coffee shop next to the government chalets on Besar, but all the supply shops are in Kecil, so, unless you are staying with Rosli, bring your own food, toilet paper, drinking water, etc. Snorkelling is great off the chalets on Besar, but bring your own equipment. Rosli can advise on local jungle treks, and can arrange boats for fishing.

Notes: with any luck, Anour at Town Guest House will soon be offering a one and half hour direct boat service from Kota Bahru to Perhentian Besar – a real timesaver! If you want to go to Perhentian from Kuala Trengganu, take an express bus to Jertih (hourly service, M$4.60), then a M$10 share-taxi for the final 15 km to Kuala Besut. Another option is a bus from Kuala Trengganu to Bandar Permaisuri, then a second bus up to Besut. If you miss the last boat to Perhentian, the government rest house in Besut village has double rooms for M$15.

ENTERTAINMENTS

Kota Bahru is the acknowledged centre of Malay culture. Every Monday, Wednesday and Saturday (February to October), you can see traditional Kelantan-style entertainments like *gasing* top-spinning, *wau* kite-flying, *rebana* drumming, *Mak Yong* dancing and *silat* self-defence, from 3.30 p.m. to 5.30 p.m. at **Gelanggang Seni** opposite Hotel Perdana on Jln Mahmood. *Wayang kulit* (shadow puppet plays) are shown every Wednesday from 9 p.m. to midnight. All performances are free.

You can also see kite-flying on the way to the Beach of Passionate Love. Get off the bus 6 km out of Kota Bahru and visit **Ismail** the kite-maker. He shows how *wau bulan* (moon kites) are made and puts on special demonstrations (M$5) every Thursday. There is no official kite-flying season, but it normally takes place from March to June when the winds are high. During the week-long International Kite Festival, enthusiasts come from all over Asia to fly their kites at Kota Bahru! The all-round best time to see top-spinning and, indeed, all traditional Kelantan arts, is the King's 'birthday party' from 30 March to 1 April.

For a nominal fee, you can play tennis and squash at the Perdana Hotel, but their pool (the only one in town) is for house guests only.

SHOPPING
The best buys in Kota Bahru are batik, *songket* weaving and silvercraft. Go to the third floor of the bazaar next to the central market for batik, bamboo items, clothes and shoes. Try the silversmiths along Jln Sultana Zainab for Kelantan-style jewellery. Look out batik and *songket* pieces (woven with gold thread) at the handicraft factories on the road out to the Beach of Passionate Love.

ACCOMMODATION
Avoid the new crop of guest houses around the bus-station. They promise a lot of things (TV, restaurant, information, etc.) which they don't actually have. Instead, walk 800 m from the local bus station to the **Town Guest House** at 4959-B, 1st and 2nd floor, Jln Pengkalan Chepa, where Anuar and Leang are going all out to provide a complete service for travellers: clean rooms with spring mattresses at MS$8 single, MS$10 double; carpeted dormitory with fan at MS$4 a bed; rooftop restaurant with breakfast snacks and evening BBQs; safety deposit lockers and luggage store; excellent noticeboard and guest comments book; laundry service, use of fridge, book exchange, etc., etc. For my money, it is the best budget lodge in Malaysia! **Town Garden House** at 2921 Jln Pintu Pong ranks a very close second. This is a large bamboo house, attractively renovated in kampong style, with free safety deposit, bicycle rental, TV lounge and otters in the garden. Dormitory beds are MS$4 and double rooms cost MS$10 or MS$15. The garden cafe is a very relaxing spot, with cheap food (lots of variety) and good music. Mr Lee and his part-time 'staff' of European travellers are both helpful and informative.

Rainbow Inn, next to the Thai Consulate at 4423a Jln Pengkalan Chepa, is a 15-minute walk from the local bus-station (or get bus No. 4 or 9 towards the airport). It has dormitory beds at MS$4, double rooms at MS$10, cooking facilities, bicycle rental and a beautiful garden. **Rebana Hostel**, opposite 1218a Hadapan Istana Kota Lama in Sultanah Zainab Rd, is a lovely traditional house with cosy rooms at MS$6/9 and a MS$4 dormitory. The tropical garden has deckchairs, swingseats, umbrellas and a colourful assortment of exotic birds. Other facilities include music bar, mini-library, video/TV centre, mini-zoo, postal service, free tea and coffee and bicycles for sightseeing. There is even a 'blah blah' room for late-night chatterboxes! Mr Pok Jak, the owner, is a congenial host.

Two decent mid-range hotels are **New Tokyo Hotel** near the Chartered Bank on Jln Tok Hakim and **New Bali Hotel** at the river-end of Jln Tok Hakim, near the raft houses. Both provide clean double rooms with fan and bathroom at MS$30/35 – air-conditioning is a little extra. **Murni Hotel** (tel: 09-782399), on Jln Dato Pati, is a very comfortable place, with singles/doubles from MS$52/MS$58. **Hotel Perdana** (tel: 09-785000) in Jln Mahmood is Kota Bahru's only first class hotel. It has a good pool, luxury rooms from MS$80 and several facilities.

FOOD
The night market opposite the local bus station is a really good one offering marvellous Thai/Malaysian snacks (*murtabak, satay,* seafood, barbecued chicken, *tom yam,* etc.) at low prices. It is very photogenic too, so bring your camera! Nearby is the central market area, where you can see Kelantanese women selling local fruits, dried fish, Malay cakes and all kinds of handicrafts. The Chinese food night market runs all the way up Jln Kebon Sultan to the junction of Jln Merbal. The big food plaza near Merdeka Square and the State Mosque serves many east-coast delicacies like *ayam percik, nasi dagang* and *nasi ramas.*

Two excellent Indian restaurants are **Meena Curry House** at 3377 Jln Gajah Mati and **Gandhi** at the bottom of Jln Kebon Sultan. Both offer cheap and delicious banana-leaf curries – MS$2 vegetarian, MS$3 fish/chicken. If you want a sit-down Chinese meal, try **Chu Choon Hui** in the old Chinese settlement or **Hian Kang Lao** next to Gandhi's. **Town Guest House** is where to go for Western-style breakfasts of brown bread, muesli, pancakes, fruit salad, banana yogurt shakes and real Nescafé! **Town Garden House** has a very popular bar-restaurant, recommended for curries, cold beers and evening BBQs. Across the road is **Kentucky Fried Chicken** and a handy air-conditioned supermarket. **Satu Bakery** at Jln Temenggong is probably the best of Kota Bahru's many fine bakeries, with a delicious range of cakes and patisseries.

Singapore

You cannot come to South-East Asia without seeing Singapore. It is convenient, good value, comfortable and mystical, a remarkable combination in itself. The principal attraction of this glittering tropical island is as a stopover on the way to Australasia, although it is also a popular watering-hole between Malaysia and Indonesia. The city itself reminds a lot of Australians of Sydney – it is clean and ultra-safe, with futuristic high-rise buildings and a preponderance of green open spaces. The cost of living is expensive compared to Thailand or Malaysia, but you can still get by on S$15 a day – S$6 on accommodation, S$2 for a bowl of *laksa* or noodles for lunch, a *roti prata* for 40 cents during the day and an occasional beer or two in the evening.

Singapore doesn't really cater for backpackers (they don't spend enough money!) but they turn up here anyway with a long list of things to do in one week: renewing passports, changing money, processing visas (very quick), making telephone calls home (very cheap), arranging for cash transfers, getting vaccinations and booster jabs, shopping for hi-fi speakers, watches and Walkmans, sampling the amazing food and perhaps even cramming in a windsurfing course! Some are here to take connecting flights onward or home (lots of cheap air-fares available), while others entrust their excess luggage and belongings to dormitory operators for safekeeping, before taking off on short excursions to Asian countries.

There is a ceaseless drive towards excellence in Singapore. The tourist attractions, few as they now are, are constantly being upgraded and moved around to make each new visit to the city a fresh and completely new experience. The only problem is that half the sights are now closed for renovation! Singapore is trying to sell itself as the Gateway to Asia, as well as to South-East Asia. It is admirably placed for flights to China, Hong Kong, Thailand and Indonesia.

LAND AND HISTORY

Singapore consists of a main island (connected to the tip of the Malay peninsula by a causeway) and 57 smaller islets with a combined area of only 617 sq km. Originally known as Temasek ('Sea Town'), a trading centre of Sumatra's Srivajaya empire, it was later renamed Singa Pura (Sanskrit for 'Lion City') after a Sumatran prince stopped by in the twelfth century and saw an animal he mistook for a lion – it was probably only a native tiger. After the destruction of Singa Pura sometime in the fifteenth century, this once-mighty city was reclaimed by the jungle. The modern history of Singapore began in 1819, when Sir Stamford Raffles selected the island as a trading base for the British East India Company. The settlement rapidly developed as an international free port and a crossroads for travellers in South-East Asia, although it was only in recent times that this tiny city-state made its influence felt around the world.

British rule saw the introduction of rubber trees, following their propagation in the Singapore Botanic Gardens, and a boom in tin was created by the American canning industry which brought another era of economic prosperity. The heyday of British colonialism ended in 1942, when the Japanese invaded, but a second golden age began on 3 June 1959, when the colony emerged as a self-governing state with Lee Kuan Yew as its first (and to date only) Prime Minister. On 9 August 1965, after two years as part of the Malaysian Federation, it became an independent republic. Today, just 25 years on, Singapore has been hailed as the economic marvel of the century. A great manufacturing as well as trading and financial centre, it has the second highest per capita income in Asia after Japan and is the world's second busiest port after Europort in Rotterdam. Although trade, banking and manufacturing are the main earners, the new big money-spinner is tourism – in 1989 alone, over four million tourists visited Singapore.

A vibrant city, bubbling with energy, with well-designed buildings, plazas, promenades and parks – this is the vision the Government has for Singapore. It wants Singapore to be one of the world's leading cities, perhaps the first developed city in the equatorial belt, by the end of the century. Critics have often lamented the disappearance of old buildings and areas in the big rush to modernise and maximise land usage on this land-scarce island. This, they claim, has left Singapore without a soul. 'No character, clinical and boring,' bewailed one traveller, 'Everything Asian has been hidden away off the road, in the backstreets and that loses a lot of atmosphere. They've really overdone it. Not long ago, they knocked down Bugis St, the old transvestite hangout, because it just didn't fit the image. Then they were knocking down Chinatown and to such an extent that, by the time they realised that tourists were actually coming to *see* Chinatown, it was nearly all gone!'

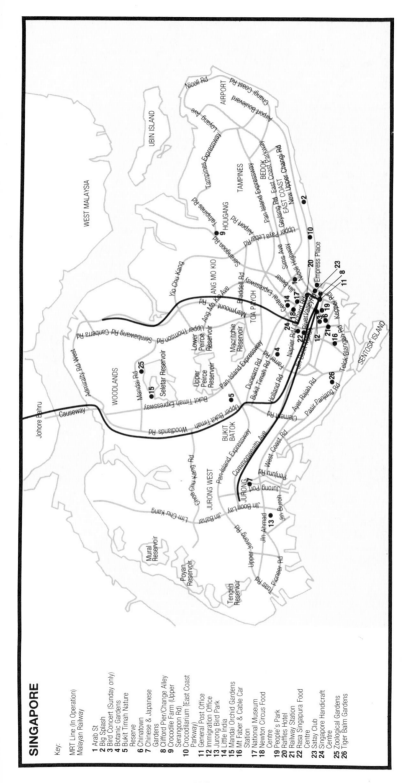

SINGAPORE

Key:

MRT Line (In Operation)
Malayan Railway

1 Arab St
2 Big Splash
3 Bird Concert (Sunday only)
4 Botanic Gardens
5 Bukit Timah Nature
  Reserve
6 Chinatown
7 Chinese & Japanese
  Gardens
8 Clifford Pier/Change Alley
9 Crocodile Farm (Upper
  Serangoon Rd)
10 Crocodilarium (East Coast
  Parkway)
11 General Post Office
12 Immigration Office
13 Jurong Bird Park
14 Little India
15 Mandai Orchid Gardens
16 Mt Faber & Cable Car
  Station
17 National Museum
18 Newton Circus Food
  Centre
19 People's Park
20 Raffles Hotel
21 Railway Station
22 Rasa Singapura Food
  Centre
23 Satay Club
24 Singapore Handicraft
  Centre
25 Zoological Gardens
26 Tiger Balm Gardens

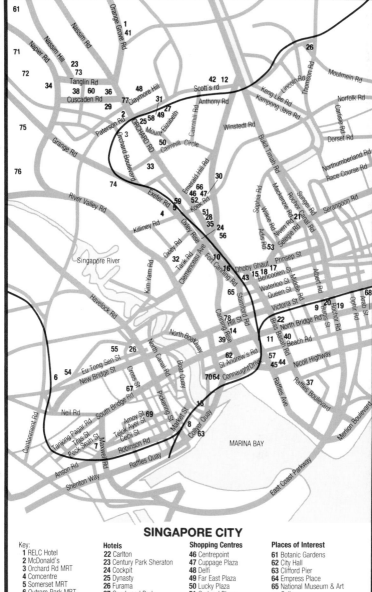

SINGAPORE CITY

Key:
1 RELC Hotel
2 McDonald's
3 Orchard Rd MRT
4 Comcentre
5 Somerset MRT
6 Outram Park MRT
7 Tanjong Pagar MRT
8 Raffles Place MRT
9 Bugis MRT
10 Dhoby Ghaut MRT
11 Tourist Office
12 Newton MRT
13 GPO (Fullerton Rd)
14 Telephone House
15 Tiong Hoa Hotel
16 YMCA & McDonalds
17 Airmaster Travel
18 Bencoolen Hotel
19 JB Bus
20 Airport Bus Arrival Point
21 Sim's Rest House

Hotels
22 Carlton
23 Century Park Sheraton
24 Cockpit
25 Dynasty
26 Furama
27 Goodwood Park
28 Grand Central
29 Hilton
30 Holiday Inn Park View
31 Hyatt Regency
32 Imperial
33 Mandarin
34 Marco Polo
35 Meridien
36 Ming Court
37 Pan Pacific
38 Pavilion Inter-Continental
39 Peninsula
40 Raffles
41 Shangri-La
42 Sheraton Towers
43 Strand
44 Westin Plaza
45 Westin Stamford

Shopping Centres
46 Centrepoint
47 Cuppage Plaza
48 Delfi
49 Far East Plaza
50 Lucky Plaza
51 Orchard Plaza
52 Orchard Point
53 Peace Centre
54 Pearls Centre
55 People's Park Complex
56 Plaza Singapura/Yaohan
57 Raffles City
58 Scotts
59 Specialist's Centre
60 Tanglin Shopping Centre

Places of Interest
61 Botanic Gardens
62 City Hall
63 Clifford Pier
64 Empress Place
65 National Museum & Art Gallery
66 Peranakan Place
67 Sri Mariamman Temple
68 Sultan Mosque
69 Thian Hock Keng Temple
70 Victoria Concert Hall & Theatre

Foreign Missions
71 Australia
72 Britain
73 Burma
74 India
75 Indonesia
76 Malaysia
77 Thailand
78 USA

This wholesale destruction of the past began back in the 1970s, and it is very hard to reverse. In 1983, however, when tourism went into a steep downturn, the bulldozers suddenly ground to a halt. The Government realised that the city's most popular and enduring attraction, its ethnic diversity, was vanishing fast. The colourful potpourri of cultures, religions, races and festivals, Chinese, Malay, Indian and European, which attracted tourists was being replaced by an antiseptic, featureless façade of high-rise flats, expensive hotels and wall-to-wall shopping arcades. Out of this realisation grew a tourist development project plan aimed at holding on to the charm of old Singapore and preserving something of its original culture. To date, the Government has put aside S$1 billion towards conservation, preservation, creating new places of attraction and upgrading existing ones. The perfectionism of the Singaporeans is quite astounding and all conservation programmes are being executed to the highest standards, although whether tourists will respond to these efforts is open to doubt. As someone 'in the know' confided:

Really, tourists are their own worst enemy coming here. Because while they *say* they don't want to see just skyscrapers and shopping complexes, in reality they get caught up in the glitter and shopping of Orchard Rd. They come here, do a day's shopping, take a quick organised island tour and then they leave. They don't tend to stick around. Sure, shopping is one of our biggest attractions, but there are several things to do off the beaten track if you're prepared to be adventurous. It's so important to delve below the surface, to understand the 'soul' of the place. The soul of Singapore is, despite its European veneer, essentially Asian. It's quite unique, the multi-racial society that exists here. Singapore has had the benefit of taking the best out of the Western world, while wisely holding on to its Asian values and culture. But that's what the tourist has to discover for himself.

PEOPLE AND SOCIETY

As a people, Singaporeans are shy in character, almost inhibited. The island has undergone quite an intense transition in a short space of time and the Westernisation of society has produced an obvious conflict in individuals as well – between their Asian soul and their Western way of life. They are very welcoming to foreigners and they put a lot of emphasis on appearances. Even more so than the Thais, they dress to impress. Going out on the streets in Singapore,

you will soon notice that it is unlike anywhere else in South-East Asia. The customary costume of the beachcombing backpacker (singlets, shorts and flip-flops) looks a little bit silly here. Singaporeans are among the best-dressed people in the world. Walking down Orchard Rd is like watching a fashion parade! You will not actually be snubbed for wearing hippie garb, but you will not get far if you try walking into a smart hotel or restaurant. A friend of mine was thrown out of a high-class disco for wearing a pair of trainers. The fact that they were a brand-new pair of Stan Smith trainers, purchased only that morning, was irrelevant. If you want to go up to, say, the 70th floor restaurant of the Westin Plaza, you must wear a decent shirt, long trousers, socks and shoes – in short, you have to look the part.

Singapore society is very conservative and ultra-clean. It imposes fines of up to S$50 for jaywalking, S$500 for smoking on a bus, S$1000 for littering and S$300 for 'not flushing the toilet after use'. On the plus side, such tight social control has done away with the Chinese gangs, the opium trade and poor slum housing. It has also produced a well-planned city virtually free of rubbish and graffiti. The person who has made such a difference to the place is Lee Kwan Yew, who has given Singapore a zealous thrust towards progress and has produced a people of total commitment. When they take something on, they take it on with a vengeance! Of the almost three million population, some 70 per cent are Chinese, 15 per cent Malay, 7 per cent Indian and the remaining 8 per cent a mix of Arabs, Armenians, Ceylonese, British and other Westerners.

The big discussion of the moment is whether the different ethnic communities should be kept apart or come together in a 'melting pot'. Whatever decision is made, English will be retained as the main working language and the main medium of instruction in the schools. Other languages in common usage, like Chinese, Malay and Tamil, are expected to survive.

CLIMATE

Just 136 km north of the equator, Singapore has a warm, tropical climate all year round. Temperatures average 81-84°F (27-29°C) during the day and 77-81°F (25-27°C) at night. Rain is always likely (especially from November to January), so keep an umbrella handy. Although humidity is high, you can always cool off in an air-conditioned restaurant, coffee shop or shopping plaza. The city is very safe both night and day, with little risk of robbery or physical attack and you are much safer here than you would be in many large Western cities.

IMMIGRATION AND HEALTH

The 2 week stay permit issued on arrival can be extended at the immigration office at South Bridge Centre, South Bridge Rd. Cheap immunisations are given at the vaccination centre (tel: 222 7711) at 5th floor, 1226 Outram Rd. The no. 123 bus will take you right there from Orchard Rd.

TIME

Singapore time is eight hours ahead of London, two hours ahead of Sydney and 12 hours behind New York. Malaysia has the same time as Singapore, but Indonesia is one hour behind.

ELECTRICITY

Electrical voltage in Singapore is normally 220-240 volts and 50 cycles, but most hotels have 110-volt outlets for guests using Western appliances such as shavers and hair-driers.

ARRIVAL/DEPARTURE

Air

Singapore's Changi International Airport is one of the largest and most efficient in the world. It is only a few minutes from the downtown area of the city, on the eastern tip of the island. It has a great duty-free section and free domestic phone call booths. It also has a McDonald's, a Svenson's ice-cream parlour and (on basement 1 level) an excellent hawker food centre. Between 7 and 10 p.m. daily, you can watch free 'Singapore Experience' audio-visual shows in the transit lounge. Twice a day (2.30 and 4.30 pm) there is even a free tour of the city for transit passengers!

Arriving by air, you can clear all airport formalities (immigration, customs, etc.) in less than 20 minutes. From Changi airport, the No. 95 bus runs right down to Orchard Rd-Scotts Rd for 80c – not bad for a 16-km journey! For the cheap hotels, catch a No. 390 bus to Bencoolen St. This bus returns to the airport from Sungai Rd or from the Peace Centre in Selegie Rd. Taxis to or from the airport are S$10-12, plus S$1 for each backpack/bag. After midnight, they charge double.

Singapore is a major international flight centre, connected by air to most major cities worldwide. Check the introductory 'Getting There' section for more details. Malaysian Airline System (MAS) offers cheap daily flights between Singapore and Kuala Lumpur (S$130), Penang (S$150) and Langkawi (S$180). These fares include the S$5 airport tax to Malaysia. Airmaster Travel Club (tel: 3383942) and Why Not Homestay sell discounted air tickets from Singapore to Jakarta (S$160), Bangkok (S$170), Bali (S$450), Bombay (S$430), New York (S$1150), Darwin (S$340), Sydney (S$630) and anywhere in Europe (S$660). Other cheap flight specialists are concentrated round the peak shopping centres like Lucky Plaza (opposite Mandarin Hotel) or People's Park.

Note: airport tax is S$5 to Malaysia, S$12 to other countries.

Sea

Going to Indonesia by sea can work out half the price of a direct flight. There are daily boats from Singapore to Batam, the Indonesian entry point, or via Batam to Tanjung Pinang. Tanjung Pinang is the main town in the Riau Archipelago, the group of Indonesian islands south of Singapore. Boats leave from Finger Pier, Bukit Timah Rd (bus 131/250 from Sungai Rd). Tickets are sold by Pelni (tel: 2206185) at Hong Deng Building in Robertson Rd. From Tanjung Pinang, you can pick up a Merpati flight to Jakarta for 104,000rps, or a flight to Pekan Baru for Sumatra. Every two weeks on a Friday, a ship leaves Tanjung Pinang for Medan (27,600rps economy, sold by the Pelni office behind TP bus-station). Since the Jakarta boat only leaves when full, you may be stuck in Tanjung Pinang for two or three days. If so, stay at Bong's Guest House, Lorong Bintan 2 (2600rps dormitory, breakfast included) or Jonny's next door. Going the other way, there are three boats daily from Tanjung Pinang to Singapore, leaving 9.30 a.m., 12.30 p.m. and 3.30 p.m. (three and a half hours, 30,000rps), also a few slow boats (five hours, S$20) and a speedboat service. All boat tickets are sold at Osaka shop, Jln Merdeko, Tanjung Pinang.

Rail

Singapore's railway station is in Keppel Rd, some 5 km south of the city centre. Arriving by rail, there is a handy bookshop in the station, where you can change money (including Malaysian bills and coins) and pick up a free island map and *This Week in Singapore* magazine. There are three express trains out of Singapore daily: two to Kuala Lumpur (seven to eight hours) leaving at 7.45 a.m. and 3 p.m. and one to Butterworth, via KL (13 hours) leaving at 7 p.m. Fares are S$28 to KL and S$50 to Butterworth. Daily train services to Johore Bahru depart at 8.30 a.m., 3.20 p.m., 8.30 p.m. and 10 p.m. Trains return to Singapore from Johore Bahru at 5.15 a.m., 6 a.m., 12.34 p.m., 1.23 p.m., 5.05 p.m., 7.32 p.m. and 8.40 p.m. The one-way fare is S$1 third class, S$1.60 second class and the journey takes 30 minutes. Purchase your tickets an hour ahead of departure and (if coming in from Johore Bahru) allow an extra half-hour to clear customs and immigration.

Road

A good central place to buy bus tickets to Malaysia is Masmara Tours (tel: 7326555) at 05-53 Far East Plaza, 14 Scotts Road. It is far more convenient than the main bus-station at Lavender St, 4 km north of the city centre, which services all buses to Malaysia. Masmara sells seats on daily buses to Butterworth (S$30, 14 hours), Kuala Lumpur (S$18 air-conditioned, seven to eight hours), Kuantan (S$16 air-conditioned, seven to eight hours), Malacca (S$ll air-conditioned, five hours), Mersing (S$ll air-conditioned, three to four hours) and Penang (S$31, 14 hours). To get to Johore Bahru, which has fleets of buses and taxis going all over peninsular Malaysia, hop on bus No. 170 from Queen St or Bukit Timah Rd (80c) or take the direct bus there from Bansan St terminus (S$l.50). Malaysia Taxi Service (tel: 298 3831) at 290 Jln Besar has taxis to Johore Bahru (S$5 per person; S$20 for a full car) and to other points in Malaysia.

TOURIST SERVICES
Information

Singapore has an excellent tourist information centre (tel: 3300431/2) on the ground floor of Raffles City Tower, 250 North Bridge St. It is open from 8.30 a.m. to 5 p.m. weekdays, 8.30 a.m. to l p.m. on Saturdays. The regularly updated *Official Guide Book* is the best handout, along with the American Express city map. The small hotel booking desk at the airport also has maps and information.

The Malaysian Tourist Board is on the ground floor (unit 3) of Ocean Building, near Raffles Place. The Indonesian tourist office is on the twelfth floor of the same building.

Post and Telephone

The imposing GPO (and poste restante) on Fullerton Rd is open from 8.30 a.m. to 5 p.m. weekdays, 8.30 a.m. to l p.m. on Saturday. Most other post offices (e.g. at the Peace Centre in Selegie Rd, at the airport and at Orchard Point) keep the same hours, but the Killiney Rd post office is open 8 a.m. to 9 p.m. every day, including Sundays and holidays. Most hotels provide postal services at the reception desk.

One of the great things about Singapore is the telephone system. If you want to reserve a restaurant table or contact an airline, your hotel can generally find the number and put you through in seconds. There are none of the usual Asian problems – no wrong numbers, engaged signals or blank silences at the other end of the telephone. Overseas calls, telex and telefax are quicker and cheaper in Singapore than anywhere else in South-East Asia. If you call the UK from the Comcentre (open 24 hours) in Killiney Rd, charges are only S$2.86 per minute (noon to 9 p.m.), S$2.53 per minute (9 p.m. to midnight) and S$2.20 per minute (midnight to noon). Across the road, while waiting for friends to phone home perhaps, you can enjoy a delicious Peranakan-style breakfast (toasted bread with *kaya* egg-jam and butter, or half-boiled eggs with pepper and soya sauce) at the little coffee shop at 67 Killiney Rd. Other places open 24 hours for international calls are the GPO at Fullerton Rd and the Telecom Building (tel: 2686633) opposite Phoenix Hotel on Exeter Rd. Or you can use Telephone House in Hill St, open from 8.30 a.m. to 9 p.m. daily. IDD calls can be made direct from the luxury of your hotel bedroom, but you pay 25 per cent extra.

Money

The Singapore dollar (S$) divides into 100 cents. Bills come in 1000, 500, 100, 50, 20, 10, 5 and 1 dollar denominations; coins in S$l and 50, 20, 10, 5 and 1-cent denominations. The current rate of exchange is S$3.30 to the £ and S$l.88 to the US$.

There are many banks along Orchard Rd (and elsewhere), open from 10 a.m. to 3 p.m. weekdays, 9.30 a.m. to ll.30 a.m. on Saturdays. Some moneychangers (e.g. Golden Homes Moneychanger, 01-26 Orchard Point) offer a better rate for cash than banks do and they are open for longer hours, seven days a week. There is a 24-hour money changing desk at the airport. For credit card withdrawals, go to the business district at Collyer's Quay, try the Bank of America or Barclays International and allow time for clearance.

Books and Film

Singapore's best two bookshops, with a wide selection of fiction, non-fiction and travel books in English, are MPH on Stanford Rd (near the National Library) and Times Bookshop in Orchard Rd's Specialist Centre. Most bookshops sell the *Straits Times* and the *New Paper* – Singapore's morning and afternoon English-language newspapers – and the useful S$2.50 bus-map. Standard Photo, 2-44 Orchard Plaza and Good Eastman Supplies, 1-34 Orchard Point, offer a quick, cheap film processing service. If your camera needs repair, try Goh Kin Camera Service Centre, 02-37 Orchard Plaza, but give him plenty of time.

Airline Offices

Singapore is a good place to confirm flight tickets. All the airline offices are

The old and new buildings of Singapore

Chinatown in Singapore

very central and they can all be easily contacted by phone. Here are a few addresses:

Aeroflot
Meridien Shopping Centre, 100 Orchard Rd (tel: 234 5252)

Air India
UIC Building, 5 Shenton Way (tel: 225 9411)

Air New Zealand
Ocean Building, 10 Collyer Quay (tel: 535 8266)

ALIA (Royal Jordanian)
Beach Centre, 15 Beach Rd (tel: 338 8188)

Bangladesh Biman
Fidvi Building, 97 Market St (tel: 535 2155)

British Airways
Paragon Plaza, 290 Orchard Rd (tel: 253 5922)

Cathay Pacific
Ocean Building, 10 Collyer Quay (tel: 533 1333)

China Airlines
Orchard Towers, 400 Orchard Rd (tel: 737 2211)

Garuda
Goldhill Square, 101 Thomson Rd (tel: 250 2888)

Japan Air Lines
Hong Leong Building, 16 Raffles Quay (tel: 221 0522)

KLM
Mandarin Hotel, 333 Orchard Rd (tel: 737 7622)

Lufthansa
Tanglin Shopping Centre, 19 Tanglin Rd (tel: 737 9222)

MAS
Singapore Shopping Centre, 190 Clemenceau Ave. (tel: 336 6777)

Pakistan International
Ming Court Hotel, 1 Tanglin Rd (tel: 737 3233)

Philippine Airlines
Parklane Shopping Mall, 35 Selegie Rd (tel: 336 1611)

Qantas
Mandarin Hotel, 333 Orchard Rd (tel: 737 3744)

Royal Nepal Airlines
SIA Building, 77 Robinson Rd (tel: 225 7575)

Singapore Airlines
77 Robinson Rd (tel: 223 8888); Mandarin Hotel, Orchard Rd (tel: 229 7293/4); Raffles City, North Bridge Rd (tel: 229 7128/9)

Thai International
Keck Seng Towers, 133 Cecil St (tel: 224 9977)

United Airlines
Hong Leong Building, 16 Raffles Quay (tel: 220 0711)

CONSULATES AND EMBASSIES
Most foreign embassies are closed on Saturdays and some are open only in the morning. Phone ahead to check office hours before visiting.

Australia
25 Napier Rd (tel: 737 9311)

Burma
15 St Martin Drive (tel: 235 8704)

Canada
IBM Towers, 80 Anson Rd (tel: 225 6363)

Denmark
Goldhill Square, 101 Thomson Rd (tel: 250 3383)

Finland
Goldhill Square, 101 Thomson Rd (tel: 254 4042)

France
5 Gallop Rd (tel: 466 4866)

India
31 Grange Rd (tel: 737 6809)

Indonesia
7 Chatsworth Rd (tel: 737 7422)

Italy
Goldhill Rd, 101 Thomson Rd (tel: 250 6022)

Japan
16 Nassim Rd (tel: 235 8855)

Malaysia
310 Jervois Rd (tel: 235 0111)

Netherlands
Liat Towers, 541 Orchard Rd (tel: 737 1155)

New Zealand
13 Nassim Rd (tel: 235 9966)

Pakistan
20a Nassim Rd (tel: 737 6988)

Philippines
20 Nassim Rd (tel: 737 3977)

Sri Lanka
Goldhill Plaza, 51 Newton Rd (tel: 254 4595)

Sweden
PUB Building, lll Somerset Rd (tel: 734 2771)

Thailand
370 Orchard Rd (tel: 737 2644)

UK
Tanglin Rd (tel: 473 9333)

USA
30 Hill St (tel: 338 0251)

West Germany
Far East Shopping Centre, 545 Orchard Rd (tel: 737 1355)

GETTING AROUND

Getting around Singapore is not too difficult. English is the main spoken language, so it is easy to pick up directions. The island divides up roughly into the city (south), the airport (east), Jurong industrial centre (west) and the causeway to Malaysia (north). The city itself has Orchard Rd-Bras Basah Rd running through the centre, Chinatown to the south and Little India/Arab St/ Bugis St to the north. Walking round town is no problem, but watch out for open storm-drains and take care at pedestrian crossings. You could be fined for crossing on a red flashing light – wait for the green.

Bus

Singapore has a good bus service. Buses are either red and white, or orange and yellow and they go all over the island. Fares range between 40 and 80 cents and you must have the exact change since none is given. Though buses post their destinations, there are over 200 routes in the city and you may need to buy the SBS Bus Guide – 70c at any bookshop. If you intend doing a lot of bus travel, it may be worth buying a one-day (S$5) or three-day (S$12) 'Singapore Explorer'

bus pass, available at most hotels and travel agents. Although cheap, bus travel can be slow and hot, especially if you get stuck in traffic jams!

MRT

The brand-new Mass Rapid Transit System (MTR) is a model of safety and cleanliness. It comprises 42 underground stations running north-south from Yishun down to Marina Bay (via Orchard Rd) and east-west from Pasir Ris to Boon Lay. The two central stations are City Hall (for Old Raffles Hotel) and Raffles Place. Trains run every few minutes from around 6 a.m. to midnight and they glide from one spotlessly clean station to the next on a strict timetable. The system is due for completion in 1990 but is already the quickest, most convenient method of local transport. Fares range from 50c to S$1.20 and you will need some small change for the vending machines.

Taxis

Taxis run on meters and are very cheap, especially if there is a group of you. The flag-down fare is S$1.80 (S$1.60 for the first 1.5 km plus 20c for air-conditioning) and you can cross town for less than S$4. There is a 50 per cent surcharge on the metered fare between 12 midnight and 6 a.m., a S$3 surcharge from (but not to) Changi airport and a S$1 addition for any luggage placed in the boot. A final hidden surcharge is the S$2 you pay for travelling in the central business district between 7.30 a.m. and 10.15 a.m., Mondays to Saturdays.

Other

Most hotels can arrange car hire – either limousine with driver, or self-drive. Trishaws are horrendously expensive. Because there are so few left, people only ride in them for the novelty value. The standard rate from an Orchard Rd hotel to the quayside is S$32!

SIGHTS

A few years ago, Singapore's main attractions were plate-glass skyscrapers, fast-food restaurants and basement bargains. Where was the mystical East so lavishly portrayed in the tour guides? It was not so much that the ethnic areas had been swamped by new modern buildings, but that they had become run down and forgotten. Since 1987, however, the Government has made every effort to preserve and promote them. All Singapore's major sights – Raffles Hotel, Chinatown, the Chinese Gardens and the National Museum – are getting a complete facelift, designed to boost tourism and most of them will not open again until 1991/2. They are even going to reopen Bugis St, resiting it (after recreating it) bang opposite the old Bugis St. Whether the transvestites will be allowed to drift back there is 'a very touchy question', said a tourist officer, 'We're just going to let nature take its course!'

Organised sightseeing tours, sold by most hotels and travel agents, are a little expensive at S$16 to 30 per half-day. But Singapore is a big island and trying to see everything by bus could be time-consuming and by taxi rather more expensive. A typical city tour costs S$22, lasts three and a half hours, and is a quick, convenient way of taking in the major sights. If you don't like organised coach tours, hire a private guide (S$60 for three hours) from the Registered Tourist Guides Association (tel: 338 3441) and a car (S$70/80 for three hours) from Avis/Hertz. Two reliable tour agents are MRJ and Tour East. All major hotels sell their tours.

To get a true picture of Singapore, you really have to explore all aspects of its multi-cultural heritage: Chinatown, Little India, Arab St, Holland Village, the Malay quarter of Geylang Serai and the British area round Raffles/Empress Place. If you are short on time, however, give priority to big attractions like Raffles Hotel, Chinatown, Jurong Bird Park and the zoo.

BRITISH HERITAGE

The obvious evening treat is a Singapore Sling, a delicious concoction of gin, Cointreau and fruit juices, at the Long Bar of **Raffles Hotel**. What you want is *old* Raffles Hotel (entrance off Beach Rd), not the new Raffles City shopping complex. Though the hotel itself is currently closed for renovation, you can still have dinner in the Palm Court, with the ceiling fans spinning briskly under the green-striped awning, the caged birds trilling into the evening, the piano playing softly and it is 1930 once more. A Japanese invasion is unthinkable. Somerset Maugham will soon come shuffling in between the travellers' palms in the garden. Founded as a tiffin house by a Captain Dare, built as a hotel by the Sarkie brothers in 1886, used as a watering hole by the rich and famous for over 100 years, Raffles is quite possibly better-known than Singapore itself. Kipling mentioned it as *the* place to eat in Singapore. Conrad and Maugham featured it in their novels. Noel Coward's autographed photographs still adorn the suite which bears his name in the writers' complex. Take a leisurely stroll around the shady courtyards and the long, cool verandahs. Enjoy a pot of tea on the manicured lawns. Settle into a high-backed cane armchair in the Garden Bar and imagine yourself in colonial times sipping a sundowner. Above all, dress respectably – or you won't be allowed in!

Raffles is a short walk from City Hall MRT station. Walking south down Connaught Drive (via the Cricket Club), visit **Empress Place** on the banks of the Singapore River. This 125-year-old block of neo-classical government buildings, once an East India Company court house, was recently restored at a cost of S$18 million and was reopened in April 1989 as the showpiece museum of Singapore. It has a spectacular rotating exhibition upstairs (it changes every year), shops and tourist information on the ground floor and outdoor dining at a plaza overlooking the river. Admission is S$6 adults, S$3 children and it is open from 10 a.m. to 10 p.m. daily.

Empress Place has a lot in common with London's South Bank. Surrounded by reminders of British rule – elegant churches, beautiful parks and gracious colonial buildings – it has a charming old pedestrian suspension bridge to the rear and the Victoria Theatre (used by the Singapore Symphony Orchestra) right next door. Nearby are **Parliament House**, a magnificent two-storey mansion built in 1827, the **High Court** with its fine Italian murals and high vaulted archways and columns and **City Hall**, where the Japanese formally surrendered to Mountbatten on 12 September 1945. Walk down to **Clifford Pier** for good views over the bustling harbour and hire a boat to go on the river – the whole of the Singapore River has been cleared up, at enormous cost, to attract more tourists.

CHINATOWN

If you have not been to China or to Penang, then Chinatown is definitely worth a visit. It is one of the few places in the city with some charm and character still clinging to it and some of the renovated buildings are very colourful. Start your streetwalk at **Thian Hock Keng**, the Temple of Heavenly Happiness, on Telok Ayer St. This interesting temple was completed in 1842 by Hokkien immigrants wishing to give thanks to Ma Chu P'oh, the Queen of Heaven, for a safe passage across the South China Sea. Originally, the sea came right up to the entrance steps, although reclamation of land has now left it high and dry. Architecturally, the temple is a mixture of Eastern and Western styles – with cast-iron railings from Glasgow and decorative tiles from Holland. From the courtyard within, you can take the quintessential 'contrast shot' of Singapore – traditional pagoda roofs framed against an unearthly backdrop of high-rise build-

A Chinese pork butcher in Singapore

ings. The temple is best visited after ll a.m., when all the tour buses have gone.

Walk on to Club St, which still has some *kongsis* (Chinese clan houses) and clubs. At Nos ll and 19, you can see a couple of deity carvers at work. No. 35 is a typical example of Cantonese architecture, with a high stately façade, pagoda-style roof and squarish windows surmounted by auspicious Chinese words. At the end of Club St, turn right into Ann Siang Hill. There is a small shop here at No. 3 which makes the colourful lion and dragon heads for Chinese processions. Outside, letter-writers ply their (dying) trade on the pavement. At the bottom of the hill, turn right to find Eu Yan Sang at 267/273 South Bridge St. This is one of the city's most famous Chinese medicine halls. It has all sorts of intriguing remedies from pearl powder (good for ladies' complexions) to *bezoar* of monkeys (extracted from cancerous growths in monkeys' stomachs and used for 'curing phlegms of the throat'). Good buys here are ginseng and natural pearls. See all the traditional Chinese herbs being prepared at the back of the shop.

Stroll up South Bridge St, past all the pavement astrologers, goldsmiths and pawnshops, to **Sri Mariammon Temple**. This small, colourful temple with its decorative *gopuram* (entrance tower) and South Indian ceiling murals was built in 1843 by Raffles's Indian clerk, Nariana Pilay. It is dedicated to Sri Mariammon, a manifestation of Shiva's wife Parvati. A little way back along South Bridge St, turn into Temple St. Here are all the porcelain wholesalers, selling cheap Chinese bowls, plates, vases and teapots. At No. 22 you will find a paper effigy shop, which makes paper houses, cars and even videos for relatives of the dead to burn at the temple – it's the Chinese way of sending presents to their ancestors!

In Trengganu St, running off Temple St, you can see how the renovation of Chinese houses, due for completion in 1995, is proceeding. In the 1970s, at the height of the Government's clean-up campaign, Chinatown's 'wet market' was taken off the streets and relocated at the new Chinatown Complex, a grim concrete building at the junction of Sago and Trengannu Streets. Recently, however, the illegal hawkers have been slowly but surely drifting back onto the streets again, and the Government is turning a blind eye, because this is what tourists want to see. Apart from the basement wet market, the Chinatown Complex has bargain-price bags, shoes and clothes on the ground floor and a great food centre, with hundreds of cheap Malay, Chinese and Indian dishes – on the second floor.

The junction of Tanjong Pagar and Neil Roads, at the bottom of South Bridge Rd, is a whole block of newly renovated shop houses, all colourfully done-up, but retaining the original façades. The white building on the corner of the junction was once the old rickshaw station. At 22 Tanjong Pagar Rd you will find a traditional Chinese tea shop, offering a variety of refreshing herbal teas and health snacks. It is an ideal place to sit down and relax before catching your bus back home.

LITTLE INDIA

The area around Serangoon Rd has become familiar to tourists as 'Little India' or the 'street of temples'. Here you are instantly in Delhi or Calcutta. The aroma of spices hangs languorously in the air. Small wizened men in *dhotis* peer from the dark interiors of narrow shops where rolls of silk in scores of hues are stacked to the ceiling. Crimson blotches of betel juice stain the ground. In the sidewalk food shops, the rhythmic hands of *pratha*-makers spin lumps of dough into tissue-thin pancakes in a hypnotic display of skill.

Little India is best visited in the evening. Enjoy a banana-leaf meal at one of the curry restaurants in Race Course Rd, then walk up to **Sri Srinivasa Perumal Temple** on Serangoon Rd. This temple has a 20-m-high *gopuram*, prettily illuminated at night, with intricate sculptures depicting five manifestations of Vishnu. Turn up at 9 p.m. sharp to see the deity being 'put to bed' – very atmospheric! A short way back down Serangoon Rd, you can turn into Desker Rd, one of the seediest red-light districts outside Bombay. It's safe enough and (this being Singapore) fairly clinical. Look out for novelty buys like 'Mighty, Loving and Happy Tablets – good for gentlemen whose nerves are not strong. They increase the happiness and are quite convenient.' The transvestites hang out in Queen St, below Desker St. Don't go alone, men – take a female escort!

GEYLANG SERAI

Once you have seen the Chinese in Chinatown and the Indians in Little India, it is time to see the Malays of Singapore at Geylang Serai. Just 30 minutes from Orchid Rd (bus 14, 16) or Bras Basah Rd (bus 13, 17), Geylang Serai began as a nineteenth-century Malay *kampong* or village and is today most notable for its morning wet market. A wet market is literally wet – you wade through puddles of water which have dripped off all the fish and vegetables. Messy, but authentic. Shop here for beautiful fabrics, sarongs and batik dresses, all very cheap. If coming by bus, ask to be put off at the Malaysian Handicraft

Centre on Sims Avenue. From the wet market, stroll down Changi Rd and into Joo Chiat Rd. On the corner of these two roads is **Bun Wah Lung**, offering the best *rojak* (squid and potatoes in a gravy dip) and south Indian coffee in Singapore. There are lots of pre-war Chinese shop-fronts in Joo Chiat Rd, selling herbal medicines, making spring rolls (No. 95), or fashioning traditional window frames (No. 99). On the corner of Joo Chiat Road and Joo Chiat Place is **Poh Chee Tong** shop, famous for its herbal tea. Further down Joo Chiat Place is colourful **Joo Chiat Kwan Win** (Goddess of Mercy) Temple, built in 1919.

Past this is East Coast Road, a fascinating enclave of original Baba culture. The 'Babas' or Peranakans were Straits-born Chinese who adopted many Malay customs and developed their own unique culture. Their fathers were usually Chinese traders who came to Singapore to seek their fortunes and married local Malay women. In Koon Seng Rd, off Tembeling Rd, the original Baba terrace houses have been imaginatively restored. They are excellent examples of what is known as Singapore 'eclectic' architecture, where classical European features such as Roman Doric or Corinthian columns and French louvred windows were combined with *pintu pagar* (fence doors), brightly coloured decorative tiles and quaintly ornate plasterwork. Since the Government earmarked this area for preservation, Koon Seng Rd has become a street of rainbow colours, just like the many-layered Peranakan cake made at 126 Tembeling Rd. To find out more about 'Baba' culture and history, visit Peter Wee at **Katong Antique House**, 208 East Coast Rd. He is one of only a handful of 100 per cent pure-blood Peranakans left in Singapore and his shop is a fascinating museum of Baba-Nyonya antiques and crafts. A few doors down at No. 204, try Peranakan *kaya* or egg-jam at **CMC Coffee House**, then walk down to **Jong Heng Bakery** at No. 126 to see the old-fashioned way of making bread in brick ovens. For lunch, drop into **Makmur** at Lerong 108, a 24-hour Peranakan restaurant famous for its Malay-style *roti changi* and coffee. If you want to stay in this area, **Song Hua Boarding House** (tel: 3449055) at 246 Tembeling Rd has clean, quiet and comfortable air-conditioned rooms (with bath) at S$40.

A rather more touristy display of renovated Peranakan houses can be found at **Peranakan Place**, on the corner of Emerald Hill and Orchard Rd. There is a small museum here, open from ll a.m. to 8 p.m. daily and a half-hourly guided tour costs S$4. Peranakan Place is a short walk from Somerset MRT station.

HOLLAND VILLAGE

The high-class residential area of Holland Village, 15 minutes by bus (No. 7) from Orchard Rd, is where Singapore's smallest minority group, the European ex-pats, live. This area has an atmosphere all of its own, very low-key cosmopolitan, with Dutch pastry shops, Islamic mosques, Chinese seafood restaurants, French patisseries and British wine-bars – it's a real hotchpotch! Shopping is a lot cheaper here than in the city centre, especially for antiques and furniture. Visit **Meng Antique** at Lorong Liput 25 for top-quality restored Peranakan furniture, and the shops along Jln Mambong, round the back of Jln Lorong Liput, for Chinese ceramics, lacquerware, porcelain and bamboo/cane furniture. **Holland Road Shopping Centre** has a great supermarket, cheap fabrics, Peranakan arts and crafts, Chinese embroideries, fashion clothes, etc., all at half Orchard Rd prices. For lunch, try traditional Peranakan cuisine at **Oley Sayang**, Lorong Liput 25B, or Western-style fare at **Milano Pizza** or **Palms Wine Bar** at Holland Rd/Holland Ave. junction.

ARAB STREET

This is the Muslim quarter, a short walk from Victoria St (bus 13 from Orchard Rd). Follow the *bilal's* recorded wail to the gold-domed **Sultan Mosque** at noon on a Friday to discover the cool green-carpeted interior, thick with the forms of male Muslims at prayer (women may not enter). In adjacent Arab St the goldsmiths will fashion jewellery to order and wickerwork from all over Asia spills from shops across the pavements. Go shopping for batik goods, carpets, clothes and semi-precious stones, and try a *murtabah* pancake or a *biriani* at the Indian restaurants along North Bridge Rd.

FLORA AND FAUNA

This is a great day out, recommended by many travellers. Start with the excellent **Zoological Gardens** at 80 Mandai Lake Rd (bus No. 17l from Royal Holiday Inn at Scotts Rd). Open daily from 8.30 a.m. to 6 p.m. (admission S$5), this is one of the best zoos in Asia, with over 1,500 animals in near natural conditions – as far as possible, moats are used instead of bars. You can have breakfast with the orang-utans at 9 a.m. and see snake, sea-lion and elephant shows at 3.30 p.m. From the zoo, stroll 1 km down the road to **Mandai Orchid Gardens** – 4 hectares of high-class orchids, including the Bandar Miss Jaochim, Singapore's national flower – open from 9 a.m. to 5 p.m. daily, admission S$l. All the white orchids in Buckingham Palace come from here!

Wildlife enthusiasts should go straight from the zoo to **Jurong Bird Park** at Jln

Ahmad Ibrahim (S$12 by taxi, 80c by bus). This has over 3,000 birds (more than 350 species) in 20 hectares of landscaped parkland. In one section, there is the world's largest walk-in aviary, where exotic birds of every description fly free. In another, some 2,500 crocodiles and other reptiles roam around within huge glass-sided aquariums. Jurong is open from 9 a.m. to 6 p.m. daily (admission S$5 for the bird park, S$4.50 for 'Crocodile Paradise'); the bird-shows and croc-wrestling shows take place in the early morning and late afternoon. Finish off at the nearby **Japanese Gardens**, off Yuan Ching Rd, Jurong. These are 15 hectares of tranquil lakes, tiny islands and shady arbours, connected to the adjoining **Chinese Gardens** by a pretty ornamental bridge. Return to Orchard Rd by MTR train or by bus.

Note: an offbeat breakfast venue is the **Bird-Singing Concert** at the junction of Sengpoh and Tiong Bahru roads. This delightful event takes place every morning between 8 a.m. and 11 a.m. (best on Sundays) and features rows of caged songbirds 'training their voices' while locals and tourists look on over a breakfast of rice dumplings, rice-flour rolls and strong black coffee. It is a constant round of activity, as owners hop up and down, looking out the more experienced birds and moving their own younger birds next to them, to improve their voices, pick up new tunes and sometimes to compete. A good songbird can fetch up to S$300 but it must eat at least two grasshoppers or two cockroaches every day, or it won't sing well!

BOAT TRIPS

Singapore has a total of 57 islands, only a few of them tourist-worthy. The most developed island is **Sentosa**, which, despite its monorail, beach, wax museum and swimming lagoon, is gimmicky and dull. The best thing about it is the cable-car ride across from the World Trade Centre (S$4.50 return). There is also a great 'high-up' photo opportunity from the top of Mt Faber. If you don't like heights, take a ferry to Sentosa from Jardine Steps at the WTC (one-price ticket S$7 includes everything on the island, including the monorail). Budget travellers rate the cheap S$5 harbour cruise from WTC to **Kusu Island** and **St John's Island**. It stops at both places for 15 minutes each (just enough time for a quick swim) and gets you back after two hours. It is definitely the best deal by boat – all other cruises are S$20 or more! If, however, you want to see what a typical Malay fishing village looks like, hire a bum-boat from WTC or Clifford Pier (S$25 per hour) to **Pulao Sekeng**.

Many older Singaporeans drop in here at weekends to remind themselves of their childhood days, when Malay *kampongs* like this covered the mainland. 'Many young Singaporeans come here to see what a chicken looks like,' quipped my guide, 'because the only chicken they know is a Kentucky Fried drumstick!'

To get to the World Trade Centre, take yellow bus No. 5 from Royal Holiday Inn on Scott's Rd (50c) or SBS bus No. 143 from Orchard Rd. By taxi, it costs around S$5.

ENTERTAINMENT

The Instant Asia show at Raffles Hotel (11.45 a.m. daily, S$5) is 45 minutes of condensed Chinese/Malay snippets – strictly for those short on time. The Cockpit Hotel has similar shows at 11.45 a.m. (S$5) and at 7 p.m. (S$30 with dinner).

Sports take low priority in Singapore, but **The Big Splash** on the East Coast Parkway has a giant waterslide and a flow swimming pool. Entrance is S$3 and it is open from 10 a.m. to 6 p.m. daily. If you want to play golf, you can drop in at most of the golf clubs as a non-member and get a game. Green fees are around S$50 on weekdays and the most accessible course for tourists is Sentosa Golf Club (tel: 472 2722) on Sentosa Island.

Nightlife is mostly based in the clubs and discos of the top class hotels. Look in the *New Straits Times* for films, cabaret performances, etc. and in the free tourist magazines for up-to-date news on jazz clubs, discos, pubs and lounges. Many nightspots have stiff entry charges (S$12 to 20), but if you are prepared to be a bar-fly, you can save a lot of money touring the many bars and clubs of Orchard Rd and Orchard Point, hopping from one 'happy hour' (half-price drinks) to the next.

Brannigan's, next to the Hyatt Regency, is a basement club with good live evening jazz and a happy hour from 4 to 7.30 p.m. **Top Ten** at Orchard Towers has bands, descending overhead lights, AIDS-warning posters and penguin-suited waiters and waitresses. Both places apply cover charges at weekends. **Saxophone** at 23 Cuppage Terrace has live jazz from 9 to 2 a.m. and a happy hour from 6 to 9 p.m. **Chinoiserie** at the Hyatt Regency is *the* Singapore disco, popular with both the local and foreign crowd – entrance is S$18 on weekdays, S$28 on Friday/Saturday. In Holland Village, pubs like **Palm's Wine Bar** and **Bob's Tavern** enjoy the spill-over crowd from the many restaurants and cafes in the area.

SHOPPING

Be warned, many of the goods sold here can be bought cheaper in Hong Kong and even (if you know the right market) in London. Don't be carried away by Singapore's reputation for cheap goods and remember to bargain hard for everything. Most of the shopowners are Chinese, and they have the psychology of selling you something you are not sure you want down to a fine art. Don't buy *anything* until you have been round a few places and compared prices. Be especially on your guard against being sold old models of cameras. Unless you know what the new model looks like, you can quite easily be fobbed off with old stock! Cassette players, CD players, watches, calculators, contact lenses, spectacles, trainers, freshwater pearls, perfumes, golf clubs, squash/badminton/tennis rackets and scuba-diving gear are all much cheaper here than in the UK or Australia – if you are good at bargaining! Quite often you will get a better deal in a supermarket than in a high-street shop. Another tip is to buy big. Small items like Walkmans don't represent much of a saving, but the big deals are absolutely breathtaking – particularly the large hi-fi stack systems, which cost the same in Singapore dollars as they would in British pounds! Department stores generally have fixed prices, but you can haggle most goods in shops down by 50 per cent (or less) of the label price. Be careful with cameras and Walkmans, they often try to sell you the camera-case and the headphones separately! The walk-away technique in bargaining works very well in Singapore shops – with skill, you can get a Minolta AF Tele-Super 38.80 mm lens camera down to £130 (less than half London prices) and a Sony Sports Walkman with solar alarm clock for only £35 (about £100 in the UK). Always insist on an international guarantee for expensive items.

Like Hong Kong, Singapore has numerous high-street shops and multistorey air-conditioned shopping complexes. They are open from around 10 a.m. to about 10 p.m. daily and prices on the same goods vary a lot, so look around. The 'million dollar mile' of Singapore (the glittering five-lane mall of Orchard Rd) is where *not* to shop generally. It has a wealth of choice, but very high prices. The only outstanding buy I found here were bootleg cassette tapes and compact discs, not as cheap as Bangkok or Bali perhaps, but an amazing selection! If you must spend money in Orchard Rd area, look for fashion clothes at **Metro** and **Isetan** complexes, arts and crafts at **Singapore Handicraft Centre**, Chinese silks and leather shoes at **Orchard Plaza**, and all kinds of goods (toys, fashion, stationery, household, electrical) at **Yaohan** in Plaza Singapura. Perfumes and clothes are generally cheapest at the sales, particularly the warehouse-type sales round the back of

Orchard Point. Freshwater pearls are sold in the basement of **Centrepoint**, next to the supermarket. The supermarket itself is very useful, especially if you have a fridge in your hotel room and want to lay in a few cheap beers or a bottle of wine. **Lucky Plaza** is where to go for sporting goods, optical wear and copy watches. The fake watches sold in Singapore are better quality than those sold in Bangkok or Bali. The nicest ones come from Japan and cost around S$60/70 with leather strap, around S$100/120 with steel strap. Buy Japanese-made brand names like Gucci, Corum and Rolex and pass over 'gold' watches (which flake) in favour of 'silver' (which don't). If you are feeling lazy, shop for watches, hi-fi and electrical ware at JT'S, 901 72-74 Orchard Plaza – Annie and Jenny are nice people to do business with and you can examine all their goods at leisure with no pressure to buy. Their prices are hard to better, too. The only place I know that is consistently as cheap is **Shaw Towers**, down by Raffles, which has a good variety of shops and all sorts of clothing bargains. If you want materials made up into shirts or dresses, try the tailor at the back of Grand Central Hotel (ground floor) or **Hamco**, 901-ll Delfi Orchard plaza. Two things *cheaper* at the airport than in town are perfumes and alcohol.

ACCOMMODATION

When the tourist boom of the mid 1980s exploded, Singapore found itself with too many big hotels and not enough people to put in them. The international standard hotels were forced to cut their rates and they now represent superb value for money. Enquiring at the Student Travel office in Ming Court Hotel, or even at the airport desk, can turn up some amazing discounts – sometimes 40/50 per cent less than the listed tariffs. Good first-class hotels include the **Mandarin Singapore** at 333 Orchard Rd (tel: 7374411; S$180 single, S$205 double), the **Shangri-La Singapore** at 22 Orange Grove Rd (tel: 7373644; S$190 single, S$215 double), the **Hyatt Regency** at 100 Orchard Rd (tel: 7338855; S$160 single/double), the **Westin Plaza** at 2 Stamford Rd (tel: 3388585; S$190 single, S$220 double); and the **Marco Polo Singapore** in Tanglin Rd (tel: 4747141; S$160 single/double). Until the new-look **Raffles Hotel** reopens sometime in 1991, the place to stay in old-colonial style is **Goodwood Park Hotel** at 22 Scotts Rd (tel: 7377411; S$190 to 220). Two less expensive options are **Hotel Grand Central** at 22 Orchard/Cavenagh Rd (tel: 7379944; S$68 single, S$78 double) and **Carlton Hotel** at 76 Bras Basah Rd (tel: 3388333, S$90 single, S$95 double). All rates quoted above are subject to 10 per cent government tax and 3 per cent service tax.

The best mid-range deals are **Relc** at 30 Orange Grove Rd (tel: 7379044; single/double from S$55 with breakfast) and **Metropolitan YMCA** at 60 Stevens Rd (tel: 737755; singles from S$30, doubles from S$38). Both places have a pool and spacious air-conditioned rooms with private bath, colour TV and IDD telephone. The new YMCA at l Orchard Rd (tel: 3373444) has great facilities (pool, squash courts, overseas phone, etc.) but the air-conditioned rooms (S$50 single, S$60 double) are small. Fourth, I would say is the **Strand Hotel** at 25 Bencoolen St (tel: 3381866; air-conditioned rooms with phone, TV, bath at S$65 single/double) but it has no pool. Fifth, for people who want some privacy and a modicum of comfort, there is the YWCA at 6 Canning Rd (tel: 3361212; singles/doubles from S$30/45, dorm-style accommodation at S$13), but men take note, you can't stay unless accompanied by a woman! Lastly, in the east coast area, try **Seaview Hotel** at 26 Amber Close (tel: 3452222). It is near Peter Wee's Peranakan shop, with a pool, good facilities and air-conditioned rooms at S$62.15 net.

Bencoolen St has long been the backpackers' stretch. The pre-war shophouses here conceal a multitude of 'crash pads' and budget hotels for the traveller on a shoestring budget. The crash pads are mildly illegal and don't advertise, but if you carry a backpack and walk up Bencoolen St, you will soon be approached by people offering rooms. Most places are pretty grim (S$5 for a bed in a stuffy six to eight person dormitory) but the three rooms of double-decker bunks at **Airmaster Travel Club**, 36B Princep St (parallel to Bencoolen St) are always full by night-time. Its third floor location means fresh air and good views and the noticeboard, TV, fridge, washing machine and slide-shows are all popular features. One of the newer crash pads, also highly rated, is **Why Not Homestay** on the sixth floor of Selegie Centre (Rainbow Building) at 189 Selegie Rd. This is a well-run, homely establishment with a wide range of accommodation – dormitory beds at S$5/6, twin-bedded rooms at S$18 and double-bedded rooms with private bath/shower at S$30. Added attractions are security lockers, laundry service and free breakfast, tea and coffee. Managers Richard and Katy are extremely helpful. If full, they send people up to **Mama's Apartments** on the eighth floor, or next door to **Stanley's Place**. In McKenzie Rd, off Selegie Rd, two well-established favourites are **Sim's Rest House** at 114a (S$4 dormitory, S$16/27 rooms, fridge, TV, good information) and **Backpackers** at 15a (airy S$4 dormitory, free tea and

coffee, security lockers, etc.). Friendly **Sandy's Place** at 355 Balestier Rd, Goodwill Mansion, fourth floor, is reached by bus 145 from the railway station. It has a S$5 dormitory, fan rooms at S$10/18 single/double and air-conditioned rooms (with bath/TV) at S$25/30. Coffee and tea are free and there is lots of information.

The attraction of Bencoolen St area is its central location, close to Orchard Rd and the shopping centres. If a crash pad will not do and you want a room, you will often be directed to small Chinese hotels like **Kian Hua** on Bencoolen St and **Sun-Sun Hotel** on the corner of Bencoolen St and Middle Rd. Room rates here are around S$18 fan, S$27 air-conditioned. **Tiong Hoa Hotel** at 2-4-6 Princep St is recommended: 'free toilet paper, iced water and advice on Singapore's extensive public transport system!'. Rooms cost S$25 fan, S$30 air-conditioned. If you are looking to stay in Chinatown itself, try the popular **Chinatown Guest House** at 325-D, fifth Floor, New Bridge Rd, opposite the Pearls Centre. It has a S$7 dormitory, clean double rooms at S$20, lots of information/free maps, and you can cook your own food. Nearby **Southern Hotel**, 37 New Bridge Rd (next to Majestic Theatre) has more comfortable rooms at S$20/30. If you want class, there is **Furama Singapore Hotel** (tel: 5333888; deluxe rooms at S$91 single, S$104 double) at 10 Eu Tong Sen St, right on the edge of Chinatown.

FOOD

Singapore doesn't really have a cuisine of its own – whatever you can find in Malaysia, you can find here. What it does have, however, is an astounding amount of choice, everything from Straits Chinese Peranakan cooking to Indonesian to Japanese, all the way to Orange Julius! Most of the top class hotels have European (usually Swiss or French) cooks in their restaurants, which often specialise in certain styles. **Hotel Asia**, **Ambassador** and **Ming Court** have good Cantonese restaurants. The **Marco Polo** specialises in French food. **Pine Court** in the Mandarin Hotel and **Jade Room** in the Orchard Hotel, serve Peking food. Several big hotels advertise buffet lunches/dinners at an abbreviated rate (S$12-15) to get the business trade. The lunches are much better value than the dinners. **Pool Park Hotel** is famous for its Malay lunches and the **Taman Ramada** for its Thai lunches. All the rest have promotional periods, changing all the time, so check in the *Straits Times* or at the tourist office.

Singapore has been aptly named the food capital of Asia. While **McDonald's** at the Penang Rd YMVA is a regular stake-out for the cautious traveller, those blessed with strong stomachs can try spicy *nasi padang*, *nasi biryani*, *laksa* or *satay* at the various hawker centres. At the open-air **Newton Circus** food centre, it is possible to dine al fresco under the moon on the offerings of some 100 stalls, a memorable gastronomic pick n' mix. Imagine oyster omelette with spring onions, Chinese parsley, garlic and chilli sauce, followed by *satay* pork with sweet peanut sauce, cucumber, rice cake and fried Indian noodles, the whole washed down by the frothing juice of freshly crushed sugar cane. **Picnic** in Scotts Rd is another popular food-centre, much used by Singaporeans as a lunch-time or after-work rendezvous. This is an assortment of booths selling Thai, Chinese, Malay and European dishes, ranged round a central sit-out eating area and the prices are cheap.

All the big food centres have at least one stall doing a duck dish, and a dish of duck-noodles is only S$2.50. **Satay Club** on Queen Elizabeth Walk, off Connaught Rd, has stall upon stall of delicious Malay food: *soto ayam* (spiced chicken soup), *tahu goreng* (deep-fried beancurd in peanut sauce) and charcoal-grilled *satay* at 30c a stick. On the edge of **Cuppage Plaza** you will find two or three little cafes which have spilled out into the plaza, along with lots of umbrellas and foodstalls. This is about the cheapest place to buy beer in the area, although **Golden Beer Garden** in Orchard Plaza has happy hours for drinks from 3 to 7 p.m. and from 12.30 a.m. to 2.30 a.m. It also offers a good-value S$3.90 American breakfast from 8 to ll a.m. Right opposite, in Orchard Point, there are similar breakfast deals at **Milano Pizza** and **Orchard Point Coffee House**.

Several restaurants have cheap lunch offers, mainly because so many people are now eating for S$2 at the hawker centres! At Centrepoint, just off Food St, you'll find **Satay Anika** (weekday set lunch for S$5.50), **Noodle Garden** (Chinese), **Parkway** (Thai), a Penang Nyonya restaurant, an international coffee house and a patisserie – all well patronised. In the same complex is **Burger King** and another **McDonald's**. Orchard Plaza has a chintzy but nice Indian restaurant – the **Maharajah** – on the second floor and a good Chinese restaurant on the fifth floor.

Little India has a host of inexpensive Indian restaurants and coffee houses. The **Apollo** at 56-58 Racecourse Rd (tel: 2938682) is famous for its banana-leaf meals (S$2 vegetarian, S$3 non-vegetarian) and its curried fish-heads. If full, try **Muthu's Curry Restaurant** at No. 76-78, or **Nur Jehan** (north Indian tikkas and tandoories) at No. 66. Both **Bombay Coffee House** at Broadway

Hotel, Serangoon Rd and **New Woodlands** in New Dixon St do good set breakfasts/lunches at S$3.50/S$4.50. Back in town, you can enjoy top-quality Indian fare at the pricey **Maharani** at Far East Plaza, 5th floor, Scotts Rd.

For Chinese food, go to **Happy Realm** vegetarian restaurant in Pearls Centre, Chinatown. It is mid-priced and excellent. **Peking Mayflower**, near British Airways at Orchard/Scotts Roads junction, does marvellous *dim sum* and Cantonese food. **Imperial Herbal Restaurant**, 3rd Floor, Metropole Hotel, 41 Seah St, off Beach Rd (tel: 3370491) has a wide variety of Chinese herbal dishes – and the weirdest menu in Asia. If you are male and are feeling adventurous, try the 'Whip', an aphrodisiac soup made from bull's or deer's penis. Seafood enthusiasts should make their way to **Red House** at the **UDMC Seafood Centre**, East Coast Parkway (S$7 by taxi from Orchard Rd). Here you can enjoy two dozen drunken prawns, chilli crabs and various other items for less than S$20 a head. Peranakan cuisine, a mix of Chinese and Malay cooking, is best sampled at **Keday Kop Peranakan**, Peranakan Place, 180 Orchard Rd (tel: 7326966) or at **Oley Sayang** in Holland Village.

Other specialist restaurants include **Salero Bagindo** (Indonesian) at 903-239 Marina Square, **Kampachi** (Japanese) at Hotel Equatorial, **Her Restaurant** (Thai) in Serangoon Plaza, Serangoon Rd, **Korean Restaurant** (Korean) at 5th level, Specialists Centre, **Elizabethan Grill** (English) at Raffles Hotel, **Movenpick** (Swiss) at Bl-01 Scotts Rd, **Eden Cafe** (Chinese/European) at 252 Orchard Rd and **TGIF** (Western bar-restaurant-disco) at 04-44/50 Far East Plaza.

If you are on a budget and can hold out without eating till mid-afternoon, save yourself for 'the highest tea in Asia' at the 70th floor **Compass Rose** restaurant, Westin Stamford Hotel, opposite Raffles. This has a sumptuous spread of pastries, sandwiches, desserts and petits fours (plus a selection of Indian and Chinese teas) from 3 p.m. to 5.30 p.m. daily – all you can eat for S$15 (plus taxes) and breathtaking views.

Cold Store Supermarket, behind McDonald's in the basement of Centrepoint, has everything you would find in Safeways back home in Britain: wine, cheese, cold meats, tinned beer, biscuits, etc. The **Yaohan** in Plaza Singapura is just the same, plus a few more Japanese items and food delicacies.

Note: many eateries close suprisingly early, around 9.30 p.m. Check if dining late and watch out for ++ on the menus. This means 10 per cent service charge and 3 per cent extra tax.

Java

Java is quite a relief after the Westernised cities of Thailand, Malaysia and Singapore. Here, you have arrived in real Asia. The Javanese are a happy, smiley people. They are open, they will come up and talk to you and they want to know what is going on. Even if they don't speak English (and this is common), they will still want to make friends. Learning some *bahasa* Indonesian (the national tongue) goes a long way here, but pointing and sign language is okay too. Opinions on Java vary. Some travellers complain of hassles, rip-offs, tiresome bargaining and travel frustrations; many more rave about the *gamelan* music, the amazing scenery, the colourful costumes, the frenetic markets and the vegetarian food. There is something for everyone in Java, from ornate palaces and bustling cities to active volcanoes and ancient temples. A little way off the beaten track, there are a couple of beaches and national parks too!

THE LAND
The thing that strikes you, on your first bus or train trip through Java, is the landscape – the countryside is beautifully cultivated and so alive with people! Long and narrow and the political centre of Indonesia, Java is the most heavily populated land-mass in the world. It is a relatively small island (129,625 sq km) occupying only 8 per cent of the Indonesia land area, but it has something like 65 per cent of the nation's population on it! What you see in Java is rice, rice and more rice – and in between it, anything else they can get their hands on: ducks, eggs, frogs, fish, tapioca, chillies, some beans and (up on the volcanoes) cabbages, potatoes and carrots. There are a remarkable amount of food production. With 100 million mouths to feed, this is hardly surprising. Java is a very rich country – especially in oil, vegetables, rice, spices, tobacco, coffee, cocoa and all the tropical vegetables. The Javanese are tremendously hard workers, mainly on the land. The Dutch knew that when they chose Java as their 'big farm' in Indonesia. Outside of Jakarta, all you see is masses of fields, dotted here and there with farmers' houses. There are still a lot of people on the land, but more and more are moving into the cities. Jakarta, for example, is one of the fastest-growing cities in the world.

Java is the principal 'spice island' of the Indonesian archipelago and divides into three provinces: west Java, where you can visit the famous Bogor Botanical Gardens and the royal palaces of Cirebon; central Java, which contains Borobodur and the Prambanan temple complex, as well as the *kratons* of Solo and Yogyakarta; east Java, home of the famous Mt Bromo volcano and several hill stations. The real Javanese are found in the centre and in the east, while the Sundanese occupy the western region, from Pangandaran up to Jakarta. These two major ethnic groups have very different language, customs and cuisine. The Sundanese kitchen, for example, is far more *pedas* (hot) than that of Yogya and it uses a lot of palm-sugar in its cooking, so it is sweeter too. Historically, the Sundanese kingdom originated from Ciamis and pre-dated even the Javanese kingdom of Mataram.

Thankfully, Java has such a huge population and (as yet) so few tourists that, outside of Jakarta and Yogya, it is relatively hassle-free. The bulk of travellers visit Yogya and do Bromo and Bali, and that's it. This leaves the rest of Java to adventurous types who invariably find the Javanese at their best, uncorrupted by tourism and all that goes with it.

CLIMATE
Java's rainy season is roughly November to March, but it is not very clearly defined – heavy tropical showers are interspersed with brilliant sunshine. Otherwise, it is hot and humid except in mountain areas. Humidity ranges from 60 to 95 per cent. In the coastal areas, temperatures range from 75-95°F (23-33°C). Inland, temperatures range from 68°F (36° C) at night to 86°F (46°C) during the day. Because of the humidity, the night air often feels chilly.

HISTORY
The history of Java is more or less the history of religion in Indonesia as a whole. First came the powerful Buddhist kingdom of Srivijaya, which, in the seventh century, expanded beyond Sumatra and the Malay peninsula and which produced the spectacular Borobodur Buddhist sanctuary in central Java. Then it was the turn of early Hindu states like Mataram, Pajajaran, Kediri and Singosari, which rose and fell between the eighth and twelfth centuries. Trade and the arts flourished and the focus of power slowly shifted from central to east Java. The thirteenth century saw the rise of the Majapahit, the last (and the greatest) Java-based Hindu empire, which united the whole of Indonesia and parts of the Malay peninsula and which ruled for two centuries.

JAVA

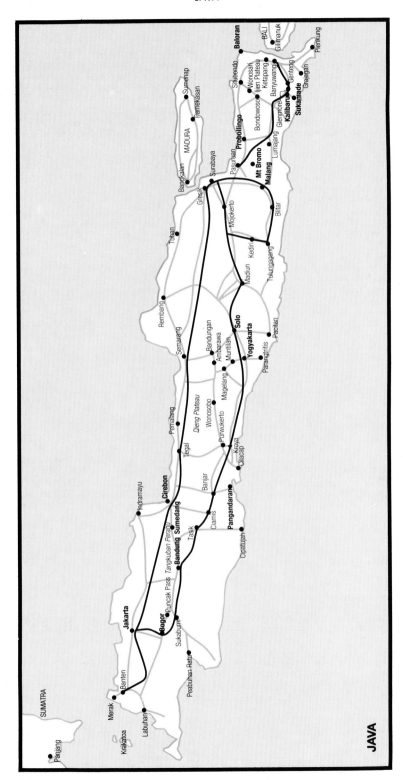

The arrival of Islam in the fifteenth century drove the Majapahits to Bali, while Java split into a number of small Muslim sultanates, none of them strong enough to withstand the European incursions which followed. The Christian Portuguese were soon ousted by the Dutch, who, by the mid-eighteenth century, had extended their control over the whole of Java. Resistance to Dutch rule, centred in Yogyakarta (the traditional seat of Mataram power), flared up in 1825 – when the Javanese Prince Diponegoro launched a five-year revolt, and culminated on 17 August 1945 when, after 350 years as a Dutch colony, the Indonesians made their declaration of independence. This was after three years of rule by the Japanese, who had seized the archipelago during the Second World War. In December 1949, after four more years of bloodshed, the Dutch gave up their attempts to repossess their old territories and were persuaded (by the UN and the USA) to grant Indonesia her freedom.

Forty years on, Indonesia is still a young state (like India) trying to find the ability to govern itself. It has not had independence long enough to know what to do with it. In 1955, there were 169 political parties contesting only 257 seats! It was to stop this sort of chaos that Sukarno, elected President of the new state in 1949, declared, in 1956, his policy of 'Guided Democracy' which gave him a more or less free rein to run the country. The result was internal strife and economic ruin. A coup was inevitable and when President Suharto took power in 1965, he ousted Sukarno by borrowing a 'very magic' death mask from the priests in Bali. This mask was taken from Gajah Mada, the powerful fourteenth-century prime minister of the Majapahit kingdom. Suharto was allowed to keep the mask for just 100 days, in which time he displaced Sukarno (who only had a magic sword to play with) and rocketed himself to power. Suharto has been a very good unifier (his philosophy is 'unity in diversity') and he has successfully pushed *bahasa* as the common language of Indonesia, as well as drilling the *pancasila*, a kind of state philosophy defining Indonesia's view on politics, morals, etc., into the whole population.

Suharto has also made sure that Indonesia is not too reliant on oil. They are exporting textiles at a phenomenal rate now and have wonderful raw materials like coal and iron. Tourism is likely to be the new big earner, especially after the Visit Indonesia year in 1991. At present, though, the infrastructure is weak – Java and Sumatra have a long way to go before they reach the standards set by Bali. Tourism has obviously provided a good income for Indonesia. They are promoting it everywhere and are working hard at finding things of interest for the tourist to see and do. Just as obviously, the impact of tourism is not all good news – a day of being hassled by *becak* drivers in Yogya or by massage ladies on Bali's Kuta Beach is enough to show you that. However, it is bringing much-needed money to the people and at least they now have a market for their produce – and a good reason for reviving dying arts and crafts. Indonesia has a very strong culture, which is certain to be exploited and diluted by tourism in time, but you have still only got to go one block behind the main roads, even in Jakarta and Yogya, to find society unchanged.

Note: the legacy of the Dutch can be seen everywhere in Java, in the bakeries and patisseries, in the art deco houses and buildings, in the cuisine (e.g. *rijstafel* or rice-table), in the legal system (still based on the old Dutch model) and in the language (lots of Dutch words have crept into the Indonesian vocabulary). The Javanese in particular did very well out of the Dutch, despite being treated like second-class citizens and many of them wish the Dutch were still here today!

PEOPLE AND RELIGION

The Javanese are a short, small-boned, neat people with dark skin and a wavy shock of black hair. The men seem to be incessantly chain-smoking and the women permanently toting around babies. Both sexes smile a lot and are very welcoming to foreigners. Even in Jakarta, it is rare to come across a Javanese not prepared to help you, even if it is, in the case of so-called 'students' or 'guides', at a price! On a bus, they will always move up to make room for you and they will sit on your lap if they have to. Touching doesn't mean anything to them – as in so many other ways, they are not very strict Muslims.

Religion in Java is hard to pinpoint really. There are very few Buddhists and Hindus, but there are still bits of everything slopping around in the old Muslim basket. Some 80 per cent of the population are nominally Muslim, but when Islam came the Javanese only took from it what they wanted, i.e. what fitted in with their society. Consequently, it is a much softer brand of Islam than in, say, the Middle East. Women get a pretty good deal in this 'loose' Muslim society. They have equal rights and women's emancipation is celebrated on a special day!

The Javanese are very proud of their history, culture and nationality, which all take precedence over religion. In Yogya, for instance, there was much dissension about the choice of the new sultan when the old one died in late 1988. The eldest son was the obvious choice, but he had been to Mecca! Not only was this a precedent (no previous sultan had been), but it showed him to be a hard-line Muslim and the people were not sure they trusted a 'religious fanatic'. The question was, was he a good *Javanese*?

VISAS

A free 60-day stay is granted to most nationalities (including UK, USA, EC, Australia) on arrival, provided your passport is valid for six months from the date of entry and provided you have proof of onward passage from Indonesia (either an air ticket or a letter from a travel agent). If, for any reason you cannot fulfil these conditions, you can pick up a four-week (£5) or fiive-week (£12) 'social visa' before entry from the Indonesian Embassy, 38 Grosvenor Sq, London WIX 9AD (tel: 01-499 7661), open 10.30 a.m. to 12 noon and 2.30 to 4 p.m. Monday to Friday. Visas can also be obtained en route in Singapore or Penang.

If you need more than two months in Java/Sumatra/Bali and don't want to waste time and money going in and out of Indonesia to get re-entry visas, you have two main options. First, you can apply to the Indonesian embassy for a 'social visa' (cf. above). This gives an initial stay of only four to five weeks, but the immigration office in Jakarta or Yogyakarta will extend it for two to three months, and probably again, for the same period, giving a total stay of up to six months. Second, if you want to study here and can make a good enough case in writing, you can apply for a one-year 'study visa'. The only problem is, you have to order it (again from your nearest Indonesian embassy) at least a year ahead! Whatever you do, *don't* tell them you are going out to study batik, which potentially takes away the living of the local people in Indonesia, or your application will automatically be turned down. You are safe with *gamelan*, dance, massage, acupuncture, etc., but in all cases you must have a sponsor (a reputable resident living in Indonesia) who can support your application in writing. What many people do nowadays, is go to Indonesia on a normal two-month visa, look out a *gamelan* teacher prepared to be their sponsor, nip out to the Indonesian Embassy in Singapore armed with their sponsorship letter and return with maybe a three-month extension stamped on their old visa. Another good idea is to travel through Sumatra on one visa, exit to Singapore for a well-earned rest and then continue on to Java and Bali for a further 60 days.

Note: visitors without visas may enter and leave Indonesia only through certain air and seaports like Jakarta, Bali, Medan, Padang, Batam and Pekanbaru.

DOMESTIC TRANSPORT
Air

Most major towns in Java are connected to Jakarta by air. The two big domestic airlines are Garuda and Merpati. Merpati has smaller planes but the fares are around 10 per cent cheaper, as are other airlines like Bouraq, Mandala and Sempati. If, however, you are going to be doing a lot of air travel, you can visit five to 35 destinations in Indonesia on a Garuda 'Air Pass' from only US$300 to 500 and that includes any of Indonesia's gateway cities, like Jakarta, Medan and Denpasar.

Notes: during the peak tourist months of June, July and August, it is essential to confirm air tickets at least one day in advance. Airport tax is now 9900rps for international flights and between 2000 and 2650rps for domestic flights. You often pay it in with the price of your ticket.

Rail

Trains run from end to end of Java, from Merak in the west (where you can catch the ferry to Sumatra) to Ketapang in the east (for the ferry to Bali). Train travel is more popular in Java than bus, probably because it is safer. The Javanese themselves travel a lot by train, but they don't book. There is no booking on third class, which is usually what they can afford. Trains in Java only occasionally have a single carriage for first class – more often than not, there are one or two second class carriages and the rest are third. With third class, you just turn up at the station an hour before departure and buy your ticket at the desk. If you are travelling second class in Java, it's worth booking a seat – it is a long, hot, uncomfortable journey when you stand the whole way! Having a seat booking is one thing, but finding the right carriage is a real problem. They don't seem to mark carriages – often, your only hope of tracking down your seat is first to track down the ticket collector, who is somewhere (could be anywhere) on the train. Once found, he will allocate you your seat.

Most trains tend to run late, but usually only by a few minutes. Some of them, especially the ones running out of Jakarta, have a good food service and attendants in the cars who walk up and down, asking what you want to eat and drink; you can buy seat cushions on some of these trains too. You cannot always buy a train timetable though as they are not readily available; check at Gambir station, Jakarta. The busy tourist routes are Jakarta-Yogya and Bandung-Yogya and these trains have just a couple of second-class carriages which are always full. You should book ahead, immediately you arrive in Jakarta if you can. The alternative to all this hassle is to make your first hop out of Jakarta a short one – to Cirebon, Bandung or Bogor. If you are leaving Jakarta in the afternoon, this is about as far as you can get if you want a comfortable journey.

Note: there is only one train out of Jakarta with a sleeper facility, and that's the one to Yogya. It is incredibly busy and you will be lucky to get a berth. To be certain, you will have to send a message into Gambir rail station two weeks ahead!

Bus

Buses run all over Java and they are often quicker, cheaper and more regular than trains, although nothing like as safe or as comfortable. They tend to make lengthy stops for tea and snacks, and then try to make up the time by hurtling down the roads like creatures possessed. Indonesian buses are piloted by kamikaze drivers who drive like lunatics at times. A beep on their horn is like a space zap – it clears everybody out of the way, as far as the driver is concerned, and gives him a clear road for the next two minutes. They are particularly fond of overtaking at high speeds on hairpin bends – it's heartstopping stuff, but you don't get bored.

Any night bus in Java is well worth avoiding. Most accidents happen in the dark, as do most thefts. The lone traveller is especially at risk on night buses as he will often fall asleep and wake to find his camera and valuables gone. Day buses are fine, but hot. They are not as uncomfortable or as hazardous as Indian buses, but I always try to get a back-left seat. If you bus is going to have an accident, it is either going to be on the right side (from something coming the other way) or on the front left (from your bus hitting a tree on your side of the road). The best thing about sitting at the back, of course, is that you cannot see what's going on up front, and what you can't see doesn't worry you! Luggage travels on the roof. Make sure yours is securely tied on . Better still, chain it to the roof rack.

There are nearly always one or two bus-boys aboard. They man the front door and the back door. They drag people in from the road and kick people out without stopping. They know where all the passengers are going and 60-year-old ladies with three sacks and a big basket just get pushed off. They don't seem to mind being 'helped off'; it's all great fun. There are plenty of food-stops too, but you don't need to leave your seat, because people are always getting on to sell drinks and snacks. One of the funniest things I have ever seen was while travelling on a local bus in east Java. We pulled into a tiny village and some 30 sellers boarded the bus. They all had their little trays of refreshments (very reminiscent of the old-fashioned usherette in the cinema) and every tray sold *exactly* the same stuff: a couple of cigarettes, a few tubes of sweets, some little bags of peanuts and an assortment of fruit and drinks. And they went up and down the bus, one after another, asking every passenger in turn whether they wanted something. The funny thing was that by the time they all got off, I was the only person on the bus who wasn't eating. They talked everybody into buying something.

The Indonesians *cannot* resist food, and they get travel-sick because they eat all the time! Put local people on a bus (Javanese and Sumatrans especially) and within ten minutes of setting off they all fall asleep. Then they wake up and they either smoke or they eat. As soon as they feel they have done enough of both, they go back to sleep. After a few hours of this, your eyes are red-raw and there are tears rolling down your cheeks because of the smoke in the bus.

Here there is little distinction between an air-conditioned and a non-air-conditioned bus, because on air-conditioned buses they open all the windows and everybody smokes! All Indonesians seem to smoke and if you get 70 people on a bus, it is odds on that 55 of them will be smoking strong *kretek* (clove) cigarettes. Trains are a little better, but in general, if you are a non-smoker, you are going to suffer on any form of transport!

Sea

The state shipping line is Pelni and there are fairly regular boats (every week or two) between Java and Singapore/Sumatra. Check the arrival/departure sections of Jakarta, Padang, Medan and Singapore for more details. Pelni ships are quite modern and luxurious and travel on them is cheap if slow.

LOCAL TRANSPORT

The most common forms of local transport are *oplet* or *colt* minibuses, *bemo* pick-up trucks, *becak* bicycle rickshaws, *bajaj* motorised three-wheelers (Jakarta only) and *dokar* horse carts. Many towns have taxis and in Yogya you can hire bicycles or motorbikes to go touring.

ENTERTAINMENT/SHOPPING

Yogyakarta and Surakarta (Solo) are the best places to hear *gamelan* music, to watch classical dance and to buy batik paintings and sarongs. Cirebon has something of a reputation for batik too – very unusual designs at low costs. Bandung is another cultural centre, famous for its *wayang goleg* wooden puppets and Sundanese dances. Like Bali, the dance dramas of Java are highly stylised in movement and costume and their themes are derived from Hindu mythology, usually fragments from the Ramayana and Mahabaratha Hindu epics. If you cannot wait till Bali, silver and woodcarvings are good buys in Yogya, as are *gamelan* music cassettes.

ACCOMMODATION

Jakarta has the high-class hotels and they are twice as expensive as anywhere else in Java. In certain places along your route (notably Mt Bromo and Cirebon) quality accommodation is simply not available. You will make have to make do with old-colonial Dutch hotels (charming, but often rundown) or settle for cheap *losmen*, which are the commonest form of travellers' accommodation in this neck of the woods. *Losmen* are pretty basic – often just a room with a bed and a small table – but at around £1/2 a night they are cheap enough and tea and coffee are usually thrown in for free. You can forget about hot water, but there are *mandis* (big water tanks with dippers) to wash in and sometimes a shower. Toilets may be just a hole in the floor, but some *losmen* are now providing Western-style loos with (cracked) seats and even toilet paper! Java is far less geared to tourists than Bali, but a lot of mid-range accommodation is coming up now, making it easier for travellers who have come for a holiday and not just for a survival trip. Moderately priced guest houses/hotels start at around £3/4 per night per couple. It is worth paying the extra, even if only to escape the bugs and mosquitoes!

FOOD

In major cities like Jakarta and Bandung, there are international restaurants offering European, American, Japanese, Chinese and other cuisines. In Javanese restaurants, the emphasis is on rice and spicy hot mixtures of vegetables, chicken, seafood and various meats. Street stalls, food stalls (*warung*) and *rumah makan* (eating houses) sell local dishes such as *sate*, skewered grilled meat/fish in a flavoured sauce, *gado gado*, a cold vegetable salad smothered in a rich peanut sauce and *nasi campur*, a mixture of rice, vegetables, peanuts, coconut, meat, fish or egg, all with a thick sauce or hot soup (*soto*). Every area of Java has its own *nasi* (rice) dish, but *nasi goreng* (fried rice, with an egg on top) you'll find everywhere and, *mie goreng* (fried noodles) also. Everything is incredibly cheap, but watch out for those little red and green peppers – they set your mouth

on fire! The cheaper you eat, the better the quality of food seems to be. Indonesians have a very well-balanced diet – rice and chopped nuts make up a complete protein, the same as meat or fish would.

Indonesians drink sugary tea and black coffee with everything. Very good coffee is grown in Java ('Java Jive'); it is just that they make it badly! They grind it down into a powder and pour on boiling water as if it was instant coffee. Then you've got to wait for it all to settle before you can drink it. However, if you have a percolator back home, it is worth buying coffee powder loose in Java, at only £1 per kilo for the cheaper grades! Tea is usually given free with your meal. It is light, not strong and without milk. If you want Lipton's (the popular brand in Indonesia), you can buy it in a supermarket.

MONEY

The currency of Indonesia is the *rupiah* (rps), which is divided into 100 sen. Bills come in 100, 500, 1000, 5000 and 10,000 *rupiah* denominations. At the time of writing, there are approximately 2800rps to the £ and 1800rps to the US$.

TIME

Java, like Sumatra, is seven hours ahead of GMT, so bear this in mind when making phone calls home!

ELECTRICITY

Electrical current is generally 220 volts and 50 cycles, with two-pronged plugs. Some provincial hotels have 110-volt appliances.

LANGUAGE

You can get by without Indonesian in Bali, where everybody speaks English, but you will need some *bahasa* for Java. Most Javanese know just three questions in English: what's your name? where are you coming from? and where you go? After that, they burst into Indonesian.

In contrast to Thai, the Indonesian *bahasa* language is very easy to learn. It has a virtual lack of tenses (*akan* before a word puts it in the future tense, *sudan* places it in the present and *sudah* puts it in the past), plurals are achieved by saying the singular twice (there is a wonderful restaurant in Kuta, Bali, which is called Chitty 2 Bang 2 – Chitty-Chitty Bang-Bang to you!) and there are no masculine or feminine terms. It is a very economical, concise language in which one word often takes in a whole phrase or sentence. Thus, *jalan* means street, or to go, or let's go. *Jalan-jalan* means fast. It's like building blocks, adding little bits to turn adjectives into verbs and verbs into nouns. With a small addition, *makan* (eat) becomes *makanan* (food) becomes *rumah makanan* (eating house, or restaurant). There are some complications. For example, there are about a dozen different ways of saying 'you' in Indonesian. There is *saudara* which is formal, *kamu* which is informal, *bapak* if you are speaking to someone old enough to be your father, *abang* (elder brother) if it is someone slightly older than you, *mas* (brother) if he is the same sort of age and *dik* (younger brother) if he is slightly *younger* than you. And you don't say 'do you go?' but 'do *brother* go?' With women, you start all over again, from *ibu* (old lady) down.

Tips

In *bahasa*, Indonesians often drop first words (*bagi* rather than *selamat bagi*) and sometimes first letters too (*ibu* often becomes just *bu*). The letter 'c' is pronounced as 'ch'(*kecil* is said *keCHil*) and as a rule the second to last syllable of a word is stressed (e.g. *baHAsa*, *laGI*).

The best short Indonesian phrasebook (the one most relevant to travellers' needs) is the APA one by John Barker, on sale in many Javanese bookshops. You hear some strange stories in Java, a country much renowned for its magic and mysticism. A *becak* driver in Yogya told me: 'If you want to do a crash course in Javanese, if you want to learn the language real quick, go to Solo. The water there is very magic and it loosens the tongue. A girl came to me complaining that she'd been living in Jakarta for two months and she couldn't speak Javanese so well. "But of course!" I told her, "The water in Jakarta is so *dirty*!" '

Civilities

good morning	*selamat pagi*
good day	*selamat siang*
good afternoon	*selamat sore*
good night	*selamat malam*
goodbye (if you're staying)	*selamat jalan*
goodbye (if you're leaving)	*selamat tinggal*
how are you?	*apa kabar?*
I'm fine	*kabar baik*
please	*silikan*
thank you	*terima kasih*
you're welcome	*kembali/sama-sama*
excuse me/sorry	*ma'af*
what is your name?	*siapa nama mu?*
my name is John	*nama saya* John
how old are you?	*berapa umur mu?*
I am 30 yrs old	*tigapuluh tua*
I don't understand	*saya tidak mengerti*

Simple Words

yes	*ya*
no	*tidak*
good	*bagus*
very good	*bagus s'kali*
bad	*tidak baik*
big	*besar*
small	*kecil*
hot (temp)	*panas*
hot (food)	*pedas*
cold	*dingin*
fast	*cepat*
slow	*lambat*
beautiful (thing)	*indah*
beautiful (lady)	*cantik*

Money

money	*uwang*
how much?	*barapa harga?*
too much	*terlalu mahal*
no deal	*tak bisa*
come down	*turun*
cheap	*murah*
right price	*harga biasa*
I don't want it	*tidak mal*

Food

rice	*nasi*
steamed rice	*nasi putih*
fried rice	*nasi goreng*
noodles	*mie*
potatoes	*kentang*
chips	*kentang goreng*
sausage	*sosis*
chicken	*ayam*
fish	*ikan*
meat	*daging*
lamb	*domba*
beef	*sapi*
pork	*babi*
soup (Indonesian style)	*soto*
vegetables	*sayur*
fruit	*buah*
water	*air*
drink	*minum*
black tea, bitter	*teh tawar*
black tea, sweet	*teh manis*
milk tea	*teh susu*
black coffee, bitter	*kopi pahit*
milk coffee	*kopi susu*
no sugar	*tidak gula*
just a little	*sedikit*
please bring a menu	*beri saya se daftar*
may we have the bill?	*coba berikan rekening saya?*
delicious	*enak!*

Numbers

0	*nol*
1	*satu*
2	*dua*
3	*tiga*
4	*empat*
5	*lima*
6	*enam*
7	*tujuh*
8	*delapan*
9	*sembilan*

10	*sepuluh*
11	*sebelas*
12	*duabelas*
13	*tigabelas*
20	*duapuluh*
21	*duapuluh satu*
30	*tigapuluh*
42	*empatpuluh dua*
100	*seratus*
1000	*seribu*
10,000	*sepuluh ribu*
100,000	*seratus ribu*

Time

minute	*minit*
hour	*jam*
week	*minggu*
month	*bulan*
year	*tahun*
today	*hari ini*
tommorrow	*besok*
yesterday	*kemarin*
how many hours?	*berapa jam?*
what time is it?	*jam berapa?*
two o' clock	*jam dua*
Monday	*Hari Senen*
Tuesday	*Hari Selasa*
Wednesday	*Hari Rabu*
Thursday	*Hari Kamis*
Friday	*Hari Jumat*
Saturday	*Hari Sabtu*
Sunday	*Hari Minggu*

Travel

ticket	*karcis*
bus	*bis*
train	*kerata-api*
ship	*kapal*
plane	*kapal terbang*
where is the bus/ rail station?	*dimana stasiun bis/kereta api?*
I want to go to…	*saya mau ke…*
what time does the night bus leave?	*jam berapa bis malam berangkat?*

Miscellaneous

I want	*saya minta*
bank	*bank*
street	*jalan*
post office	*Kantor Pos*
immigration	*immigrasi*
room	*kamar*
toilet	*kamar kecil*
one night	*satu malam*
two persons	*dua orang*
sleep	*tidur*
here	*ini*
stop	*berhenti*
again	*lagi*
one more	*satu lagi*
maybe	*barangkali*
with	*sangat*
without	*tanpa*
what	*apa*
when	*kapan*
who	*siapa*
where	*dimana*

JAKARTA

The capital of Indonesia and the main gateway to the country, Jakarta is located on the northern coast of west Java. A busy cosmopolitan city of seven million people, it sprawls over an area of some 600 sq km and is very built-up, very hot and humid. Average temperatures are 81°F (27°C) during the day and 77°F (25°C) at night, slightly lower during the December-January rainy season.

Despite the government sales talk ('Jakarta is more than a transit city'), most people stay only long enough to recover from jet-lag and to book onward travel, and then they get out. Second-time visitors don't stay in Jakarta at all – they go straight from the airport to Gambir station (for Cirebon/Yogya-karta) or to Cililitan bus-station (for Bogor/Bandung). For the average traveller, Jakarta must be one of the least likeable cities in the world. It's hot, sticky, dirty, polluted, annoying and generally mind-numbing. There is a lot of theft, lots of mosquitoes and not a lot to see. People might tell you there is enough to do for a day or two, but there is really nothing (apart from the harbour and a couple of museums) that you could see better and cheaper somewhere else. Rather like Kuala Lumpur, they have ripped out what was mainly the old town and have put an ugly heap of new buildings in its place. The only thing they have left unchanged is all the surrounding poverty. In short, Jakarta is pretty horrid, but most South-East Asia travellers have to come here sometime to make a connection.

HISTORY

The first Europeans to discover Jakarta, then known as Sunda Kelapa, were early-sixteenth-century Portuguese traders on their way to the Spice Islands of Maluku. Realising the port could be of great strategic importance, they quickly signed a treaty with the Hindu Raja of Pajajaran and built a small trading post. This was overrun on 22 June 1527 by the Muslim prince of Cirebon, Fatahillah, who renamed the settlement Jayakarta or 'City of Victory'. The Dutch East India Company captured the town in 1619, changed its name again (to Batavia) and made it their centre of trade in the East Indies. The British briefly occupied Batavia during the Napoleonic Wars (Stamford Raffles based himself here from 1811-16) but after that it returned to the Dutch. Shortly after the outbreak of the Second World War, the occupying Japanese army renamed the city Jakarta (in an attempt to win the sympathy of the Indonesians) and the name was retained when Indonesia gained its independence in 1945. With such a varied backround, it is small wonder that Jakarta today is such a mixture of different cultures. Muslim mosques, Portuguese churches, Dutch residences, British clock-towers and modern high-rise blocks often stand side-by-side, while the city's inhabitants represent a real melting-pot of the many and diverse peoples living on the 13,677 or so islands of the archipelago.

ORIENTATION

The recent changes in Jakarta have taken place amid growing alarm from residents who remember the 'good old days' before independence. As one of them commented:

> Jakarta is trying to become a big international city. The price to pay is pollution. If you stand on the cross-bridges in the city centre at noon it's terrible! Some gas stations are starting now to sell liquid gas instead of gasolene, which is a step forward, but there's still so much traffic. We Jakartans have a little joke which goes: 'If it's five minutes to walk, it's an hour on the bus and an hour and a half on the telephone!' When the Dutch left, we had a population in Indonesia of around 60 million. President Sukarno said 'You are a big nation and a big nation must think big!' So, much to the disappointment of Sumatra and the other outlying islands, he started developing Jakarta and Java first. In Jakarta, he wanted a showpiece and, being an engineer, he planned the whole thing himself. Whether he succeeded or not, you can judge for yourself!

Current government initiatives are aimed at (a) the development of Ancol, on the northern coast, as a tourist recreational area ('Dreamland', opened in 1975, is a vast complex with an oceanarium, swimming pool, nightclubs, amusements, art markets, etc.); and (b) the preservation of Old Batavia, the area leading up to Glodok (also in the north), as a tourist heritage area with museums and exhibitions reflecting the glory of early Jakarta. The trouble is, most tourists, especially at budget level, stay in the south of the city, and transport up to these new attractions is slow, troublesome and fraught with risk as the northern-bound buses are rife with pickpockets and slash-thieves. The city is not all doom and gloom, however, here is a little chuckle from the *New Straits Times*:

CONDOM FESTIVAL TO BE HELD IN JAKARTA

JAKARTA, Fri. – A condom festival will be held here over the weekend to encourage wider condom usage among Jakarta men to curb population growth ...The Chairman of the FPA (Family Planning Association) said the public had so far given 'encouraging response' to the festival which would consist of talks and distribution of condoms.

He said prizes would be given to winners at the festival but declined to give details on how they would be selected.

Jakarta is very different to anywhere else in Indonesia – it is more electric and much more progressive. Go anywhere else in the country (even Yogya) and the pace just slows right down. Because Jakarta has such a lack of aesthetic and cultural beauty you must look to the people, who are the best and the worst thing about Jakarta. 'It's very exciting', observed one traveller, because you feel you're living in a revolution! I mean, it's like Victorian England all over again, because there is so much happening, so much developing. Talking to the students here, they're making comments about parents, sex, marriage, etc. which young Indonesians anywhere else wouldn't *dare* say! So much is on the move in Jakarta and if you get in underneath the surface you'll find such a wealth and diversity of different peoples. . .'

He's right, of course. Jakarta is essentially a huge extended village, made up of scores of smaller villages or *kampongs*, each with its own individual character. Take the *kampong* areas of north Jakarta, for instance. If you walk around there at night, you will feel very unsafe. I went through there and someone tried to remove my trousers on the bus – he said he liked them, he wanted them and he tried to pull them off! A lot of people up here are on drugs and the atmosphere is very unsavoury, but you can go to other *kampongs* (try Gelora, further south) and feel the most welcome person on earth!

The staggering thing about the city is the contrasts. Very often, you find the desperately poor and the affluent rich living right next door to each other. If you really want to see Jakarta, take a trip down to the railway line below Slipi flyover. There is a *kampong* here, along both sides of the track and very dramatic it is too – a heaving slum of penniless destitutes framed against a glittering backdrop of high-rise hotels and business blocks. You can just stand here and watch the poverty moving up the line and into the wealth of the city. If you want one photo that sums up Jakarta, this is the one.

ARRIVAL/DEPARTURE

Air

The new Soekarno-Hatta International Airport is 23 km west of the city, a long 40-50-minute drive from central Jakarta. The airport has adjoining terminals for international and domestic flights, also a

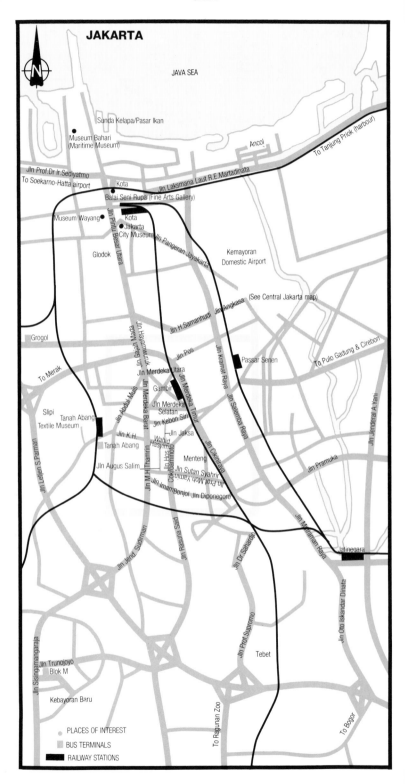

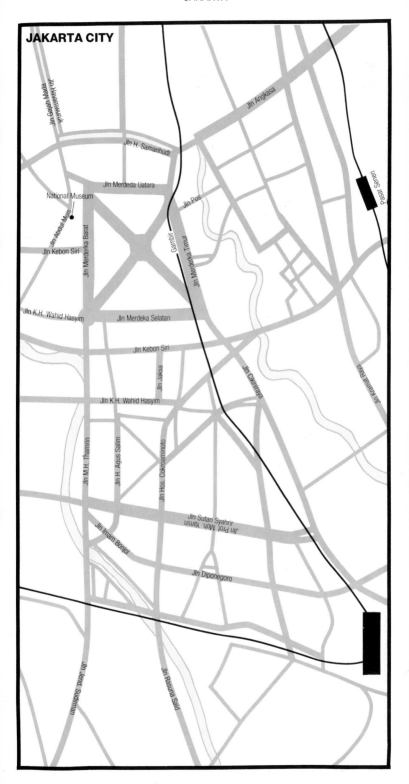

bank, a post office, an information counter and a hairdresser! Outside, it is a five-minute walk to the bus-stop, where you can catch an air-conditioned Damri bus to Gambir station, Blok M, Kemayoran or Rw Mangun. Buses leave every half-hour or so, from around 5 a.m. to 9 p.m. at night and the fare is 2000rps. By air-conditioned taxi (rates posted at the airport rank), you will pay 9000-14,000rps to the various city-centre hotels. Avoid touts selling uncomfortable, overpriced trips on private buses. From Gambir station, it is a 20-minute walk to Jln Jaksa (for budget accommodation) or 600rps by *bajai*. From Jln Jaksa back to the airport, walk into Jln Kebon Sirih, cross the road and take a P15 minibus (200rps) or a 500rps *bajai* to Gambir station. Damri buses return to the airport from Gambir every half-hour from 3 a.m. to 10 p.m. Other ways to get to the airport are (a) share-taxis (15,000 for one to four persons), sold by Jln Jaksa *losmen*; and (b) minibuses (around 5000rps per person) operated by the larger hotels.

Garuda airlines have offices at BDN Bldg, Jln Thamrin (tel: 334425), Hotel Borobudur, Jln Lapangan Banteng (tel: 359901), Wisma Dharmala Sakti, Jln Jend. Sudirman 32 (tel: 588707) and Hotel Indonesia, Jln Thamrin (tel: 325288). Other domestic airlines, often 10-20 per cent cheaper, are Merpati at Jln Angkasa 2 (tel: 417404), Mandala at Jln Veteran I/34 (tel: 368107) and Bouraq at Jln Angkasa 13 (tel: 655194). Merpati offer flights to Denpasar (for Bali) at 104,200rps, to Padang (for Sumatra) at 115,000rps, to Yogyakarta at 60,100rps, etc. If you have time, it is worth shopping around for discounts – a number of travel agents in the Pasar Baru area offer them. One or two, like Raptim Travel on Jln Cut Meutia (tel: 335326), are particularly helpful. They even give you a free airport transfer on any Merpati flight out of Jakarta!

Several international airlines have offices in the big hotels, for example, Cathay Pacific, Swissair and Philippine Airlines at Hotel Borobudur, Jln Lapangan Banteng; KLM and Malaysian Airlines System (MAS) at Hotel Indonesia, Jln Thamrin. Others are listed in the monthly *Guide to Jakarta*, issued by the tourist office. Travel agents like P T Amanda, Jln K H Wahid Hasyim (tel: 334967) (just round the corner from Jln Jaksa) offer discounts on flights. Some typical one-way fares from Jakarta are Sydney (US$370), London (US$430), Bombay (US$400), Los Angeles (US$650), Bangkok (US$180) and Kuala Lumpur (US$100).

Notes: if flying into Jakarta from Singapore, remember to put your watch *back* one hour. If flying out of Jakarta, have your *airport tax* handy – 9000rps on international, 2500-4000rps on domestic flights.

Rail

Gambir station has a central location next to Merdeka Square, and services most Javanese cities. There are half-hourly trains to Bogor until 8 p.m. (one and a half to two hours, 500rps), at least four trains a day to Bandung (three and a half hours 8000rps second-class, 6000rps third-class), two fast trains to Yogya at 6 a.m. and 6 p.m. (ten to twelve hours, 11,000rps second class) and two to three trains daily to Cirebon (three and a half hours).

Notes: watch your belongings on Gambir station which is a favourite haunt of pickpockets and snatch-thieves – they can be disarmingly well dressed and polite. Be at the station a good hour before your train arrives, to buy your ticket, especially if you want to catch the (heavily subscribed) early train to Yogya.

Road

Jakarta has three main bus-stations: Cililitan, to the south (*P3, P11, or P13 buses from Jln Thamrin), which services Bogor (40 minutes, 800rps) and Bandung (four hours, 2500rps non-air-conditioned, 3750rps air-conditioned); Pulo Gadung, to the east (*buses 50 or 509 from Jln Thamrin), which departs for Cirebon (four hours, 4000rps air-conditioned) and Yogya (14 hours, 10,000rps non-air-conditioned, 12,000rps air-conditioned); and Kalideres, to the north west (buses 92 or 93 from Jln Thamrin), which has buses for Sumatra. All services are very regular, often every 20 minutes or so and boarding the right bus is no problem – you are often dragged on!

Notes: Norbek Hostel in Jln Jaksa sells seats on air-conditioned buses to Bali (32,000rps, 26 hours) and to Probollingo (27,000rps, 17 hours); also share-taxis to Bandung (8000rps per person, four hours).

Sea

Tanjung Priok, Jakarta's harbour, is 20 km north east of the city centre – about an hour by bus (P14 from Jln Kebon Sirih, near Jln Jaksa, 350rps), a little less by taxi (12,000-15,000rps from Jln Jaksa). From Tanjung Priok you can take comfortable, if slow, Pelni boats to Padang, for Sumatra (33 to 36 hours) and to Tanjung Pinang, for Singapore (42 to 48 hours). Pelni is the state shipping line and their head office is at Jln Pintu Air 1 (tel: 358398), near the Tanjung Priok bus-station. It's open 8 a.m. to 3 p.m.

weekdays, Saturday until ll a.m. and you should book tickets at least three days ahead, to be sure of a seat. There is a second Pelni office, perhaps more convenient, at Jln Angkasa 18 (tel: 416262).

The Pelni boat **Kerinci** leaves for Padang every second Friday. Fares are 75,000rps for a first-class air-conditioned cabin (sleeps three to four people, includes three good meals and hot water showers), 37,000/30,800rps for a third- or fourth-class cabin (same deal, but no bathroom) and 28,600rps for deck class (flat hard beds in a large open dormitory, poor security and atrocious food). This boat is, by Indonesian standards, a luxury liner. All classes can use the swimming pool and the disco and the scenery is fantastic – look out for Krakatoa volcano!

There are no direct boats to Singapore, but Pelni sails for the town of Tanjung Pinang, on Bintan Island, every second Wednesday. Fares are 106,000rps first class, 77,000rps second class, 43,000rps third class. There is no deck class. From Bintan, take a longboat (around 2000rps) over to the neighbouring island of Batam, cross Batam by taxi (share the 10,000rps fare with others), clear Indonesian customs, then take a ferry-boat (regular service, 2000rps) to Singapore. By this route, it takes just six hours from Tanjung Pinang to Singapore. It is complicated but far cheaper than a Jakarta-Singapore Garuda flight (130,000rps inclusive of airport tax). Young travellers can get a student Garuda ticket from Jakarta to Batam (the island where you clear customs, before sailing to Singapore) for only 85,000rps. To get this ticket, you have to apply to any major Garuda office in Indonesia, *not* to their agents!

Notes: at Tanjung Priok harbour, all Pelni ships leave from Pelubuhan (dock) No. l. On Bintan Island, it's around one hour by bus from the harbour to Tanjung Pinang town.

TOURIST SERVICES
The main Visitors Information Centre (tel: 364093) is in the Jakarta Theatre Building (ground floor), opposite Sarinah Department Store at Jln Thamrin 9. Like all government offices, it is open 8 a.m. to 4 p.m. Monday to Thursday, until 2.30 p.m. Friday, until 12.30 p.m. Saturday. Staff are informative and handouts (including free map and *Guide to Jakarta*) are useful. This office, like the VIC desk at the airport, deals with Jakarta only. If you want information on the rest of Indonesia, it is a long tedious drive east to the Directorate General of Tourism's office (tel: 359001) at Jln Kramat Raya 81.

The main GPO and poste restante is on Jln Pos (north east of Merdeka square) and is open 8 a.m. to 4 p.m. weekdays, until l p.m. on Saturdays. To go there from Sarinah Dept Store, catch bus 10, ll, 12, or pay 1500rps by *bajai*.

The International Telephone Office, next to VIC in Jakarta Theatre Bldg, is open 24 hours for overseas calls – three minutes to the UK costs 28,600rps (£10) and connections are normally good. Most banks handle foreign currency and are open from 8 a.m. to 2 p.m. or 3 p.m. Money-changers stay open till the evening and give good rates if you shop around. American Express (tel: 587401) is in the Arthaloka Bldg on Jln Jen Sudirman. The Immigration Office (tel: 34981l, 349812) is on Jln Teuku Umar, Menteng l, open from 8 a.m. to 2 p.m. Monday to Thursday, until 12 noon Friday, until 2 p.m. Saturday. Be there early to get processed quickly and be on your way.

Foreign embassies on Jln Thamrin include UK at No. 75 (tel: 330904); West Germany at No. 1 (tel: 324908); Japan at No. 24 (tel: 324308); France at No. 20 (tel: 332807); Australia at No. 15 (tel: 323109). Others are USA, Jln Medan Merdeka Selatan 5 (tel: 360360); India, Jln Rasuna Said 51, Kuningan (tel: 518152); Malaysia, Jln Imam Bonjol 17 (tel: 332864); Netherlands, Jln Rasuna Said Kav. S-3 (tel: 511515); New Zealand, Jln Diponegoro 41 (tel: 330680); Singapore, Jln Rasuna Said Block X-4 Kav. No. 2 (tel: 5201489); Thailand, Jln Imam Bonjol 74 (tel: 349180).

TRANSPORT AROUND TOWN
Bus
Public buses are cheap (200rps anywhere), but hot and overcrowded. They attract pickpockets and slash-thieves and should be avoided. Far safer are the blue **Patas** express buses (flat fare 350rps), which have a 'P' before the number. They have less people (no standing passengers allowed) and stop where you want.

Notes: many noticeboards in Jln Jaksa now carry warnings like this one: 'Theft on buses is becoming rife. The main problems are public buses Nos 70 and 700 and Pata buses 1 and ll, when going to Kota or back. In fact, any buses which go to the harbour or to Gambir station are bad! Pickpockets work in a team and specialise in bag-slashing and money-belts. If you have a camera, keep it in your knapsack and tie the strap to the backstrap on your bag. It saved mine. All I lost was some cash and my knife.' The message is clear – carry the absolute minimum (money, belongings, etc.) and *don't* travel alone.

Taxis/Hired Cars

Jakarta has three types of taxi: the old yellow ones, which are owned by private sharks and which should be avoided at all costs (they overcharge, are not insured and give you no comeback in the event of a crash); the new yellow ones, which are a lot more standardised and have insurance; and the blue company taxis, which are best. All the new taxis will go on the meter (flagfall, for the first km, is 500rps non-air-conditioned, 600rps air-conditioned; each subsequent km is 250 or 300rps), while the older ones prefer to 'negotiate' a price instead. Taxis are expensive, but a whole lot safer (and quicker) than buses. Their meters, curiously, are set not on the basis of distance, but on speed. 'That's why we drive so fast, you see!', said my driver, 'Because if we drive fast, the counter goes quicker!'

Reliable car rental firms include Avis, 25 Jln Diponegoro (tel: 331974), Hertz, Chase Plaza Podium, 7th Floor, Jln Jen Sudirman Kav. 21 (tel: 5782240) and Blue Bird, 107 Jln H.O.S. Cokroaminoto (tel: 325607). Licensed taxis from Blue Bird cost ll,000rps for the first two hours (only 4,500rps per hour after 2 p.m.) or 50,000rps if chartered for a whole day.

Bajai/Becak

Bajai (motorised three-wheelers) are easy to use and fairly cheap. They charge around 500rps for short hops, 1500rps for longer hauls. *Becak* (bicycle rickshaws) cost even less, but you will have a job finding them. Two or three years ago, they began dumping *becaks* in the sea. Today, they are prohibited from the city centre and only operate up in Kota and in the quieter suburban areas. Even *bajai* are not allowed on the main highways.

SIGHTS

Sightseeing in Jakarta is nobody's idea of a good time. The city is uncomfortably hot, hopelessly congested and its few decent sights are so far out of the centre that most people don't bother and just take the first bus or train out to 'real' Indonesia. The sheer difficulty of getting round this vast teeming city of seven million souls is enough to stultify even the most adventurous of travellers. There is no easy way to see the sights. All I can suggest is a quick half-day tour from a reliable travel agent like Smailing at 2b-2c Jln Hayam Wuru (tel: 258171), followed by a leisurely sights round-up on public transport or by taxi. There is actually very little in Jakarta that cannot be seen more enjoyably somewhere else, so why hang around? Whatever you do, avoid travelling in the rush hour (2 p.m. to 7 p.m.) – it's murder!

The city runs roughly north to south, with the old Dutch settlement up near the sea at Kota and the old Chinatown of Batavia below it in Glodok. Jln Thamrin, down south, is for most travellers the 'city centre'. This is the vicinity of Jln Jaksa, Sarinah Dept Store, the tourist office, the luxury hotels and scores of pubs, restaurants and discos. It is also near the city's unofficial landmark: the **National Monument** in Merdeka Square. This huge phallic column, dubbed 'Sukarno's last erection' by locals, is an amazingly tacky monument with kitsch dioramas describing the course of Indonesian history, a water-slide with hundreds of kids climbing over it and swarms more people trying to jam into the lift to the top. 'Leave Jakarta fast', wrote one traveller, 'but see the Monument first – it's quite laughable and will perk you up if you're feeling a bit sour. You can take a photo of it, then go to the top and take another photo down from it.' Admission is 1500rps and it is open from 8.30 a.m. to 2.30 p.m. Tuesday to Thursday, Friday until ll.30 a.m., Saturday until l.30 p.m.

For an interesting day-trip, take a Pl or Pll bus (or, safer, a taxi) up to Glodok, otherwise known as Kota. It takes 45 minutes to one hour from the city centre to the old Dutch harbour of **Sunda Kelapa**. Entrance to the harbour is 100rps and a rowing boat round the docks to see the tall-masted Bugis sailing schooners ('... spectacular, quite the best thing to go and see, even if you do have to say hello to hundreds of sailors!') is around 3000rps per hour. If you arrive early in the morning, drop into the nearby **Pasar Ikan** (fish market) for the fish auction. Then walk across to the **Maritime Museum** to see its collection of nautical paraphernalia. Open every morning (except Sunday), there is a 200rps charge for admission. Three more museums in old Jakarta, all grouped round Fatahillah Square (near Kota railway station) are **Jakarta History Museum** (archaeological exhibits, antique furniture, Dutch colonial heritage items, etc.), **Wayang Museum** (5,000 puppets from all over the world) and the **Fine Arts Gallery** (good collection of modern Indonesian paintings). Like most of Jakarta's 29 museums, these three are open every morning (except Monday) and admission is 200rps. To see *wayang kulit* or *wayang goleg* puppet shows at the Wayang Museum, turn up on a Sunday morning between 10 a.m. and noon.

If you are still in a museum-mood, finish off at the **Textile Museum**, Jln K S Tubun, near Tanah Abang rail station (batiks, weaving and costumes from all over Indonesia), and the **National Museum**, Jln Medan Merdeka Barat 12 (biggest museum in the country, with worth-while archaeological and cultural displays). These two are relatively close to Jln Thamrin and Jln Jaksa. The National Museum has free guided tours in English on Tuesday, Wednesday and Thursday from 9 a.m. to 10 a.m. Also *gamelan* performances on Sundays, from 9.30 a.m. to 10.30 a.m.

For day two, you could visit **Taman Mini-Indonesia**, an imaginative attempt to pack the whole of Indonesia into 100 metres of parkland. Located south of Halim airport (Pll bus to Cililitan, then a T55 minibus to the park entrance), it is open 9 a.m. to 4 p.m. daily and admission is 300rps. Taman Mini features 27 traditional houses (one for each of the Indonesian provinces), a fine bird park (with walk-in aviary), an orchid display, a museum (**Museum Indonesia**), handicrafts, cable-car rides, etc. It also has cultural performances on Sunday mornings. Use any remaining time to visit **Ragunan Zoo**, also located in the deep south. Open from 8 a.m. to 6 p.m. daily, entrance 500rps, this has Komodo lizards, tapirs, Java tigers, lots of birds and an antique market. You can get to the zoo direct from Sarinah on bus P19, but avoid busy Sundays.

To escape the city altogether, get a bus/taxi up to Ancol pier (on the northern coast) and take a cool, relaxing boat-trip out to **Pulau Bidadari**, one of the 'Thousand Islands' dotted about in the Bay of Jakarta. Boats leave 10 a.m., return at 3 p.m. and the fare is 6000rps return. If you want to stay over, Bidadari has a few four-person bungalows for rent.

ENTERTAINMENT

Traditional entertainments include Balinese Theatre at Indonesian Bazaar complex, Jakarta Hilton Hotel (7 to 8 p.m. except Monday), *wayang kulit* and *wayang goleg* (leather/wooden puppet shows) at Wayang Museum (cf. Sights), *wayang orang* (human puppet shows) at Bharata Theatre, Jln Kalilio, Jakarta Pusak (8.15 p.m. to midnight except Monday and Thursday), Javanese dinner-dance shows at Pondok Garminah, Jln Taman Kebon Sirih 2-6 (7 to 9 p.m. every Wednesday and Sunday; 15,000rps with dinner, 8000rps without), dance performances at Taman-Mini Indonesia (cf. Sights) and all kinds of cultural events at TIM Jakarta Cultural Centre, 73 Jln Cikini Raya (programme listed in daily *Jakarta Post*). The big Jakarta Fair takes place in Merdeka Square from early June to mid-July.

Dreamland, up at Ancol, is a vast recreational and leisure complex with dolphin displays, bowling, theatre, an art market, a wave-making swimming pool (charge 1000rps), a 'Disneyland' and a disco. It is open from 9 a.m. to midnight daily and admission is 600rps. To get there, take bus Pl or Pll to Kota, then a minibus M14. The day *not* to visit Dreamland is Sunday, when it's packed with Indonesians making whoopee!

Most of the bigger hotels have discos, but they are pricey and plastic. Try **Tanamur** disco (much used by Westerners) at Jln Tanah Abang Timur 14. Or **Ebony** disco (classier, more expensive) at Kuningan Plaza Bldg, Jln Rasuna Said. Before hitting the town, enjoy a few beers at the **George & Dragon Pub**, down Jln Telukbetung, off Jln Thamrin, or at the more sedate **Green Pub** opposite Sarinah. Green Pub has happy-hour (half-price) drinks from 4 to 6 p.m. and most evenings there is 'live entertainment'. When I went, this was four Javanese cowboys in gingham shirts and Levis singing 'Blowin' in the Wind' against a painted John Ford location backdrop and going 'Yee-Ha!' at the end of every chorus. Riveting stuff.

Full details of current cultural entertainments are listed in the *Permanent Exhibitions and Regular Performances* leaflet handed out by the tourist office.

SHOPPING

In general, shopping in Jakarta is not a good idea. Singapore-style shopping complexes are springing up all over the city, but although they stock handicrafts from all over Indonesia, prices are often much lower at the point of origin. As a friend complained: 'An ebony-wood statue I bought for 60,000rps in Ubud turned up in Jakarta, the exact same one, priced at 300,000rps! And the quality in Bali was much better!' **Sarinah Department Store**, at the corner of Jln Thamrin and Jln Wahid Hasyim, is very central. It is open 9 a.m. to 9 p.m. and (like most big shopping centres) all goods are fixed price. Sarinah has a useful post office (just inside the entrance), a supermarket (in the basement), a money changer and a good range of batik, leather, *gamelan* instruments, *wayang kulit* puppets, ceramics and fashion shoes. Shop for crafts at the **Indonesian Bazaar** at Taman Jakarta Hilton (open from 10 a.m. to 6 p.m.), for antiques along Jln Surabaya, for paintings and carvings at **Pasar Seni Art Market** in Ancol Dreamland complex (open round the clock), for books and magazines at **Gunung Agung**, Jln Kwitang, near Pasar Senen and for cheap tapes (and beer!) at the **Golden Truly** supermarket opposite Sarinah. If you want to do all your shopping in one place, go to **Blok M** in Kebayoran Baru suburb, south of the city centre. This sells just about everything – clothes, shoes, perfumes, handicrafts, copy goods, etc. – at low prices, so why go anywhere else? Blok M is a particularly good place to pick up last-minute purchases before flying home as air-conditioned Damri buses connect it straight to the airport!

Finally, here is a useful tip from a 'real traveller': 'You can get fake Rolexes in Chinatown, which is round Gajah Mada and Glodok Plaza. Really fantastic food (mainly seafood) here in the *warungs*! Hang out at these a while and you'll always get watch salesmen coming up. You can get a pretty nice (flashy) copy watch for around 10,000rps (£3). Quality isn't that brilliant, but they're cheap!'

ACCOMMODATION

Jakarta's international-class hotels are all quite central and represent good value for money. Prices may seem high (especially when you add 15.5 per cent taxes), but stiff competition means cheap weekend rates, and if you book through a travel agent (like Raptim, 8 Jln Cut Mutiah, tel 337704; or Mitra, Royal Oriental Bldg, Jln Thamrin 51, tel 332032) you can often get 10/20 per cent discounts. Most of the better hotels have nightclubs, shopping arcades, multi-cuisine restaurants, swimming pools, sports facilities, etc. Good bets are **Hotel Borobudur Intercontinental**, Jln Lapangan Banteng Selatan (tel: 370108, singles/doubles from US$110/120); **Hotel Indonesia**, Jln Thamrin (tel: 320008, US$90/100); **Jakarta Hilton**, Jln Jend Gatot Subroto (tel: 583051, US$120/135); and, in the same road, **Kartika Chandra** (tel: 511008, US$70/77).

Recommended mid-range hotels (places to go if you want air-conditioning and a few home comforts) are **Sabang Metropolitan Hotel**, Jln Agus Salim 1 (tel: 354031, rooms from US$25, pool, restaurant), **Marco Polo Hotel**, Jln T.Cik Ditiro 19 (tel: 325409, rooms at US$18, pool, nightclub), **Karya Two** on Jln Sultan Syahourir ('It's round the corner from the Marco Polo and cheaper. Looks a bit like a brothel, but it is okay inside and has lots of atmosphere!') and **Grand Menteng Hotel**, 21 Jln Matraman Raya (tel: 8580893, single/double rooms at US$27/32, fitness centre, bar/disco and coffee shop). Nowadays, the tourist office is sending anyone looking for something better than Jln Jaksa to **Yannie International Guest House** (tel: 320012) at 35 Jln Raden Saleh Raya. This is a comfortable, centrally located place costing US$20 single, US$25 double and offering free airport-city transfers.

Budget accommodation is concentrated in and around Jln Jaksa, a small street running between Jln Kebon Sirih and Jln K H Wahid Hasyim. Just ten minutes' walk from Jln Thamrin (Jakarta's 'Fifth Avenue'), it's very central. Jln Jaksa has any number of cheap *losmen*, most of them basic and overcrowded (arrive early to get a decent room), but they are clean and friendly enough and you get to meet a lot of other travellers.

Some places offer a travel service (bus/train/plane bookings, share-taxis to the airport, etc.), while others post noticeboards full of handy tips for new arrivals. Still worth a mention (just) is **Wisma Delima** at No.5. It is the oldest lodge in Jaksa and the stuffiest, but at 2250rps for a dormitory bed (2000rps with a YH card) and 5000rps for a double room, who's complaining? Good information here and chummy staff, but it's noisy, dirty and none too safe, so watch your belongings.

Norbek Hostel at No. 14 has rooms from 6000rps (fan) to 9000rps (air-conditioned). It is popular, but there are too many 'boys' hanging around. **Jaksa 17 Hostel** has nicer people and clean, if basic, rooms with fan at 4000rps single, 5000rps double. **Bloemsteen** and **Kreshna** hostels, both down Gang l, are quieter and more comfortable, with fan-cooled rooms at 8-9000rps. **Borneo Hotel**, also off Jln Jaksa, has a 2000rps dormitory and rooms from 6000rps to 10,000rps. **Djody Hotel** at Jaksa 35 (tel: 346600) is excellent value – far and away the best place on the street. Very clean and secure, it has rooms from US$4.50 (small singles, no fan) up to US$15 (large doubles, with air-conditioning and private bath). Amenities include safe deposit, laundry service, shop and bar-restaurant. The associated **Djody Hostel** at No. 27 is a good second string – fan-cooled dormitory with comfy beds at 3500rps, well-priced rooms at 8000rps (one double bed) or 10,000rps (twin-bedded) and spotless showers/toilets. **Kebon Sirih House Homestay** at Jln Kebon Sirih Barat GG l, No. 10 (around the corner from Jaksa) is a brand-new place with double rooms at 5500rp. It is clean, quiet and friendly.

FOOD

Eating out is expensive in Jakarta, especially if you are homesick for European food. This said, a lot of the bigger hotels offer value-for-money buffets. 'Particularly good food at the Hilton Pizzeria', suggested a friend, 'and the best live band (Filipino) I've heard in Jakarta. They play every evening and cover Western songs extremely well. I ate as much pizza as I could and had a couple of beers and paid only 20,000rps – very cheap for a 5-star restaurant. The ambience is really nice too – you're on a little island in the middle of a lake and it's so peaceful!' The tourist office's *Guide to Jakarta* carries a full listing of hotel speciality restaurants.

Regular restaurants offer a wide range of cuisine. You can go Japanese at **Hanamasa Yakiniku**, 166 Jln Mahakam I (tel: 715852); Chinese at **Cahaya Kota**, Jln Wahid Hasyim 9 (tel: 353015); Korean at **Korea Garden**, Jln Teluk Betung

33 (tel: 322544); Indonesian at **Natrabu**, Jln Agus Salim 29a (tel: 335668); Thai at **D'jit Pochana**, Forestry Building, Jln Gatot Subroto; French at **Le Bistro**, Jln Wahid Hasyim 75 (tel: 364277); Italian at **Pizza Hut**, Jakarta Theatre Bldg, Jln Thamrin (tel: 352064); Mexican at **Green Pub**, also Jakarta Theatre Bldg (tel: 359332); Indian at **Omar Khayyam**, Jln Antara (tel: 356719); British (steaks and grills) at **La Bodega**, Jln Terogong Raya, Cilandak (tel: 767798). All these places are pricey, but good. For something different, try **Paregu**, near Blok M bus-terminal at Jln Sunan Kalijaga 64. Here you can enjoy seven courses of yummy Vietnamese dishes (very palatable, not spicy) for under £10 a head, inclusive of cocktails. The waiter service is unbeliev-able!

For cheap eats in Jln Jaksa, go to **Nick's Corner Cafe** at no.16 (standard travellers' fare) or to **Kahyani** opposite (great Indian curries). However, food in Jaksa is generally poor value – walk ten minutes in any direction and you will find something better. **Satay House Senayan**, on the corner of Jln Jaksa and Jln Kebon Sirih, is a typical example – well-priced *satay*, steaks and seafood, served in relaxed air-conditioned surroundings. Five minutes' stroll along Jln Kebon Sirih (left at bottom of Jaksa) brings you to **Puja Sera**, a large international food-hall with an amazing range of cuisines, every-thing from Yogya *gudeg* and Japanese *tempe* to American hot-dogs and Califor-nian patty-meat! Since everything is so cheap (most dishes are around 2000rps), it is the ideal place to experiment before you launch into Indonesia proper. A short walk along Jln Wahid Hasyim (right at the top of Jaksa) brings you to **El Pollo Loco** (Southern Fried Chicken) and, right outside it, a whole host of cheap and delicious Madura-style *satay* stalls. Past this, between Hotel Indonesia and Kartika Plaza on Jln Thamrin, **Vic's Viking Restaurant** does an 80-dish smor-gasbord (European, Chinese and In-donesian) at 7000rps for as much as you can eat. There are several Padang and Chinese restaurants on Jln Haji Agus Salim, behind Sarinah, but be warned, Padang food is notoriously hot! If you haven't had it before, try the non-spicy Westernised version at **Salero Bagindo** on Jln Menteng.

CIREBON

Out of Jakarta, the obvious choice of destination is Yogyakarta, the cultural centre of Java. If you are heading that way, you have a choice of route. The traditional tourist track, favoured by most overland tours, is south via Bogor/ Bandung. The quieter, more enjoyable option is along the northern coast to

Cirebon, dropping down to Yogya from Bandungan. Few people take this route as yet, which is a good enough reason for trying it!

Cirebon is a small, relaxing seaport, offering a wealth of culture and history. It is particularly worth visiting for its high-quality batik and its historical monuments. Apart from Solo and Yogya, this is one of only three Javanese cities which still have *kratons* (palaces) retained as the private properties of sultans.

Situated on the border of west and central Java, the ancient sultanate of Cirebon is a fascinating potpourri of Sundanese, Javanese, Chinese, Islamic and European influences. Its courts once rivalled those of central Java in opulence and splendour, its museums contain mar-vellous treasures and relics from a turbu-lent past and its artisan villages maintain the highly distinctive traditions of callig-raphic painting on glass, *wayang* puppet-ry, mask dancing and Java's most unique batik textiles.

Seat of an ancient Islamic kingdom (founded by Cakrabumi around 1378), Cirebon's rule once extended as far as Banten on the north-west coast of Java. The most revered of its rulers was Sunan Gunung Jati (Sultan of Teak Mountain), one of the nine *wali* or evangelists who disseminated Islam in Java. He reigned from 1479 to 1568 and his marriage to Ong Tien, a Chinese princess of the Ming dynasty, has become the subject of many folk tales. The Chinese influence evident in Cirebon art and crafts today is attri-buted to her court. In the late seven-teenth century, now under the control of the Dutch East Indies Company, the sultanate split into principalities and formed three separate royal houses. The Dutch valued Cirebon's harbour, using it to create a monopoly in cotton and opium imports. They also valued its tobacco, which explains the presence of the (British-American) tobacco factory in town today, together with such presti-gious residences as the old-world Grand Hotel, built in 1903. Still an important north-coast port, Cirebon is famous for its seafood and is often referred to as the 'City of Shrimps'.

ARRIVAL/DEPARTURE
From Jakarta, 256 km east, you can fly Merpati/Garuda to Cirebon, or take the popular Cirebon Express train (dep. Gambir 3.50 p.m., arr. 7.30 p.m.). From Bandung, 125 km south east, Cirebon is two and a half hours by car, four hours by bus. At Cirebon railway station, you can hire porters to take your bags to your hotel for 1000rps.

From Cirebon, buses to Jakarta (five to six hours), Yogya (six hours) and Bandung (four hours) leave from the

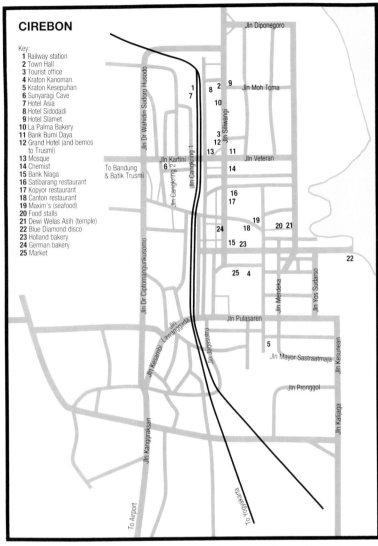

CIREBON

Key:
1 Railway station
2 Town Hall
3 Tourist office
4 Kraton Kanoman
5 Kraton Kesepuhan
6 Sunyaragi Cave
7 Hotel Asia
8 Hotel Sidodadi
9 Hotel Slamet
10 La Palma Bakery
11 Bank Bumi Daya
12 Grand Hotel (and bemos to Trusmi)
13 Mosque
14 Chemist
15 Bank Niaga
16 Satibarang restaurant
17 Kopyor restaurant
18 Canton restaurant
19 Maxim's (seafood)
20 Food stalls
21 Dewi Welas Asih (temple)
22 Blue Diamond disco
23 Holland bakery
24 German bakery
25 Market

stasiun bis, 5 km south west of town (minibuses G7 or G9 go there). If you can get a train to Jakarta (three to four hours) or to Yogya (five and a half hours), it's quicker.

TOURIST SERVICES

The tourist office (Dinas Pariwisata) is at Jln Siliwangi 88, just along from the Hotel Grand. Bank Bumi Daya, on the same road, changes foreign currency. The telephone office is on Jln Pagongan and the main post office is on Jln Yos Sudarso, near the harbour.

SIGHTS

Cirebon's few sights are nothing special, but they are enough to keep you occupied for a few hours. The town has character and, because there are so few

tourists about, the people are happy to see you. *Becaks* are very cheap, only 750rps from, say, the railway station to the harbour (2 km). The drivers put the price up for tourists, but they soon drop it back down if they think you are not going to take them on. They don't speak much English, but they know the few sights well. If you give them a written list of what you want to see, they will take you on a pleasant three-hour tour for around 3000rps.

The two best-known *kratons* (Kasepuhan and Kanoman) are worth a look. They are surrounded by thick high walls, studded with tiles and porcelain from Holland and China. More of these are found inlaid on interior walls, together with Delft tiles which cover stairs and frame colourfully painted and carved windows. Although both *kratons* were built around 1678, when the sultanate split, the larger Kesapuhan *kraton* (where the older prince had his court) is an extension of the original fifteenth-century Pakungwati *kraton*, the old palace of Sunan Gunung Jati. The smaller Kanoman *kraton* was erected for the younger prince and his descendants still live in part of the building.

Take a *becak* ride down to **Kanoman Kraton** and look around the atmospheric market place outside. Then visit the small *kraton* museum, full of dusty court treasures and get the caretaker to open up the garage inside the compound. This houses the famous Paksi Nagalima sacred royal cart, carved in the shape of a mythical animal – part *garuda*-bird, part sea-serpent and part elephant – which symbolised the sultan's power over air, sea and land. Fantastic in design, the carriage was once pulled by pure white oxen at traditional ceremonies. Next to it is a second (smaller) carriage which was used by the queen. Other exhibits include Dutch cannon, weaponry, jewellery and antique sewing machines. It is customary to give the caretaker a small tip.

Move on to **Kesapuhan Kraton**, where you have to sign a book, pay for entry (500rps) and tip the guide who shows you round (200/300rps). Like the other *kraton*, it's open from 7 a.m. to 5 p.m. daily and is best visited in the afternoon, when all the domestic tourists have come and gone. Before you go through the main gate of the *kraton* (which is executed in European style), note the Sitinggil split gate with its walls embedded with Chinese ceramics and bowls, a very unusual combination. The most prominent feature of this *kraton* are the two mythical stone lions flanking the peak-style portico. These are the 'white tigers of Pajajaran' and signify the crest of the Cirebon kingdom. Inside the palace, European lamps dangle from the ceiling, while the walls are decorated with Dutch plates and tiles. The small museum has some interesting exhibits, including a large wicker cage for babies and an amazing set of ball-and-spike suicide instruments for army officers. A small garage houses the Singa Barong cart, a beautiful gilded coach in the shape of a giant lion-bird or *singha*. Don't leave Kesapuhan without buying a 500rps 'brochure' – it is hilarious!

Across the square from the Kesapuhan palace is **Masjid Agung** or Grand Mosque. Built around 1500, it is a very early example of Javanese 'peak' architecture and is made entirely of wood. A short *becak* ride south brings you to **Vihara Dewi Welas Asih**, Cirebon's oldest Chinese temple. Open from 9 a.m. to 4 p.m. daily, it is notable for its beautiful screens, gory wall-murals depicting life in Hell and famous anchor (allegedly from an ancient Chinese ship) which attracts many pilgrims. The best time to visit is early evening, just after dark, when you may be let in to savour the eerie, smoky atmosphere produced by hundreds of burning incense sticks, oil lamps and candles. If the front gate is closed, try the side gate up the lane on the left.

No photography is allowed down at the **Port**, but it is still worth a quick walk round to see old wooden Bugis schooners being loaded and unloaded by hand.

ENTERTAINMENT

A big effort to promote culture in Cirebon is its new open-air theatre at Sunyaragi, the old pleasure-garden of the sultans, located 4 km west of the city. Here fairly regular performances of *Nyi Mas Gandasari* are staged, a dance drama based on a Javanese folk tale about a beautiful young maiden (Nyi Mas Gandasari) who challenged all her suitors to combat and who, armed with supernatural weapons (including a hairpin), overcame them all. The performance is participated in by some 200 dancers accompanied by two *gamelan* orchestras. Contact the tourist office for timings.

Nightlife is thin in Cirebon, but the **Blue Diamond Disco** down by the port is fun in a group. It has wall videos, a modern sound system and a 'waltz hour' for locals! It is open from 8 p.m. to 2 a.m. nightly and the 5000rps admission includes one free drink.

SHOPPING

The thing to buy in Cirebon is batik, which is characterised by Chinese-influenced motifs like *wadas* and *megamendung*, or 'rocks and clouds'. The centre of the batik cottage industry is the village of **Trusmi**, 14 km west of Cirebon. You can catch a blue minibus there (150rps, 30 minutes) from the crossroads below Sidodadi Hotel. Arrive early in the morning to see women at work in the various batik co-operatives, then go shopping at **H. Masina** and **Madmil** in the high road. Prices are not that cheap but some really specialised stuff is sold here, and it is so much better than the more fêted batik of Yogya! Ordinary two-piece sarongs go for around 10,000rps, but the top-quality sets, the result of ten months' work, sell for £80, mainly to rich Jakartans. Madmil has some particularly nice 150 x 90 cm 'blue cloud' pieces, suitable either as tablecloths or wall-hangings, at around £25.

ACCOMMODATION

Being off the beaten track, Cirebon has few places to stay. The pre-war **Grand**

International Hotel (tel: 2288) is the 'luxury' option, well located on Jln Siliwangi (ten minutes' walk from the railway station or the town centre) but seriously in need of renovation. The gardens and restaurant are nice, but the standard air-conditioned rooms (15,000-rps, plus 21 per cent taxes) are dark and tacky. The larger, brighter, deluxe rooms (30,000rps ++) have hot water, colour TV, fridge, vast bathrooms, etc., and are a far better bet. All rooms have a 'guest discipline list' which states: 'Every hotel guest must not do something who law invade, such as gambling, intoxicating and have sexual intercourse. Transgression for these certainties become guest risk!'

The mid-priced **Sidodadi Hotel** (tel: 2305), Jln Siliwangi 74, is five minutes' walk from the railway station and has clean double rooms (with fan and bath) from 17,000rps to 35,000rps, breakfast included. There are several cheaper places along Jln Siliwangi, including **Hotel Asia** (tel: 2182) at Jln Kalibaru Selatan 15, with nice rooms from 8000rps and a friendly English-speaking manager.

FOOD

Try *nasi lengko* (rice, *tempe*, *tahu*, beansprouts, cucumber and fried onions) at the small **Warung Tegul** outside Hotel Sidodadi or from the street-carts outside Hotel Asia. There are several fine seafood restaurants along Jln Bahagia, but **Maxim's** at No. 45-47 is the only one with a menu written in English. **La Palma** bakery on Jln Siliwangi is a good place to pick up buns and cakes before boarding the train to Jakarta or Bandungan.

BANDUNGAN

One wonders why this quiet, scenic hill resort attracts so few travellers. There are thousands of them down in Yogya, which is only a four-hour bus ride away! Don't let stories of crowds at weekends put you off. Bandungan does get a lot of Javanese trying to escape the humid heat of the north coast, but the last time I went up there all I saw were four busloads of local tourists from Semarang and none of them stayed overnight, which is odd, since there are stacks of good hotels up here and hardly anyone staying in them!

Easily accessible from either Cirebon or Yogyakarta, Bandungan has a beautiful location on the lower slopes of Mt Ungaran, about 900 m above sea level. It is a cool relaxing spot with often fantastic views of the surrounding volcanoes and of Lake Rawapening, the largest lake in central Java. Despite a tendency towards rain (early morning is the best time of day for walks and volcano-spotting),

Bandungan is the perfect alternative to Mt Bromo. It has far fewer crowds (except during the June to August high season) and there is lots more to see and do.

ARRIVAL/DEPARTURE

From Cirebon, catch the 11.45 a.m. train to Semarang (five hours), then a taxi up to Bandungan (one and a half hours). If you cannot afford the taxi, get a minibus from Semarang to Ambarawa. From Yogya, you need a bus to Ambarawa (900rps, two and a half hours), then a horse and cart to Ambarawa colt station, finally a colt (250rps, 30 minutes) to Bandungan.

Note: there is an interesting little steam engine museum at Ambarawa, definitely worth a look.

SIGHTS

There are two things worth doing in Bandungan and they both involve getting up early. On one morning, set your alarm for 3 a.m., equip yourself with warm clothing and a torch and set off for **Gedong Songo**, 7 km out of town, to see sunrise over the volcanoes. Gedong Songo means 'nine temples' and refers to the group of small eighth-century Shivaite Hindu shrines (only five of them still in good shape) dotted around the southern slopes of Mt Ungaran, in what must be one of the most beautiful temple locations in central Java. It is a bracing two-hour walk from town to the top of the hill, where you will find one of the temples, popularly known as the Gedong Songo Monument, within a small fenced enclosure. From here, you can see the sun coming up over Mts Merbabu and Merapi (straight ahead) and Mts Sumbing and Sundoro (off to the right). If you are around at the full moon, you can also see the phenomenon of the moon setting and the sun rising at the same time. There is lots of birdlife to be seen from the top of the hill (look out for buzzards, woodpeckers, shrikes, doves, even kingfishers) and walking down gives you a good chance to get acquainted with Javanese fruits and vegetables – corn, tobacco and tapioca grow up here, bananas, coconuts and cloves too, but the main produce is cabbages and roses. This is tremendously productive terrain, very well cultivated and terraced the whole way down. They take their gardening very seriously, do the Javanese, and are out there on the volcano slopes working their vegetables at 5 a.m. in the morning!

To approach Gedong Songo, walk 3 km out of town along the main road, turn right at the junction (well signposted) and take the steep hill road 3 km up to the archaeological park. Inside the park, go past the little entrance booth (200rps charge, but there will be no one around to collect the money this early!) and up to the first monument. Go left here, then walk round the hill and follow the snaky path ascending to the 'viewpoint' temple. Sometimes, if you are lucky, you can hitch a lift part of the way up. If you are not a sunrise walker and just want to go to the top and look around, there is a colt service from town to the junction from 6 a.m. and a motorcycle taxi service from the junction to the village near the top from 7 a.m. However, the later you leave it, the more chance there is that it is going to cloud up, the volcanoes will disappear and you will get no view. People with time and initiative do the thing properly. They stroll up to the junction on day one and arrange for a motorbike to pick them up from their hotel at 4.30 a.m. the next morning. This way, they can go up the mountain without effort, see the sunrise, and hop on the bike to come back down again, and it doesn't cost them more than £1! People with initiative and no time cut out Gedong Songo altogether. They do the 'poor man's' sunrise walk up to Amanda Cottages (another good viewpoint) and are back in bed within the hour.

Put aside a second morning (and defer another breakfast) to see Bandungan's colourful market. Between the hours of 4 a.m. and 7.30 a.m., the main road between the town and Rawa Pening Hotel is a constant bustle of activity, as local farmers try to wholesale huge baskets of cabbages, beans, onions and other garden produce, and get them into Semarang for sale. It is quite a spectacle and if you are not down there by 8 a.m., you will have missed it. The morning market runs all the way round the village square and inside it too. Fruit and vegetables are the main produce, but also visit the small car park above the square, which is where they sell the flowers. Novelty buys in the market include what must be the cheapest pair of flip-flops in the world, at only 23 pence!

ACCOMMODATION

It is hard to find hotels which are not cheap and clean. However. be prepared for *huge* price increases at Christmas and the Chinese New Year. Sometimes, because this is mainly a weekend resort, you can bargain discounts on rooms during the week.

Rawa Pening Hotel (tel: Ambarawa 134), 10 minutes' walk from town, has nice bungalows for two to five people, with separate rooms, lounge, bathroom, etc., at 10,000rps per person. Tea, coffee and breakfast are included, as is use of the pool and tennis courts. This hotel is Bandungan's best, with lovely gardens and (on a clear day) marvellous views. **Amanda Cottages**, 15 minutes' walk up the hill above Rawa Pening, has smarter rooms at around 30,000rps and superior views, but the (noisy, smelly) chicken farm behind it is a big deterrent! Far better value is **Kusuma Madya Inn** (tel: Ambarawa 136) on the main road leading into town. This is a friendly place with tropical gardens, tennis courts overlooking the volcanoes, a restaurant-bar and a good range of rooms from 18,500rps (large double bed, TV, phone, toilet/*mandi*) up to 23,000rps (the biggest beds I have seen in South-East Asia – 2.5 m square!).

You will find the cheaper *losmen* at the bottom of the market street, turning left. The best bet is **Kalinyamat Guest House** (tel: Semarang 23640), a typical garden-style *losmen* with quiet, clean rooms around 8/10,000rps and a little cafe. The Javanese owners speak no English, but they really look after their guests.

FOOD

Tio Ciu New Orient, just up from the market place, is a reliable Chinese restaurant with good seafood. Next-door **Slamet** does a filling meal of *satay* for less than £1. Just across from the market place, the **Shinto** offers *nasi rames*, *nasi soto* and *nasi gudeg* at 600-800rps a dish. At these prices, you cannot really go wrong!

BOGOR

Bogor is one of the wettest places in Indonesia, but most people prefer to stay there rather than Jakarta. This city gets rain virtually every day, even in the dry season, and the surrounding hills cool it off beautifully. Bogor has long been famous for its botanical gardens, zoological museum and mountain resort of Puncak, 30 km to the south. Whether you are on your way to Yogya, or just waiting for a plane out of Jakarta, this is the perfect place to escape Java's humidity and heat.

Bogor's situation in the more exposed uplands – 290 m above sea level, only 60 km south of Jakarta – made it an obvious choice of official residence for the Dutch governors-general from 1870 to 1942. It was first discovered in 1745 by Baron Gustaaf van Imhoff, who built a small rest-house here named 'Buitenzorg' or 'free from worries'. At that time, Bogor was a small peaceful village in the middle of a tropical forest, a world away from the heat, noise and mosquitoes of Jakarta. Over the years, as it became a popular weekend retreat for the Dutch elite, the baron's modest mansion was repeatedly restored and enlarged until (in 1850) it became what it is today – the impressive **Bogor Palace**, built in the nineteenth-century European style to reflect the glory of colonial rule. Most of

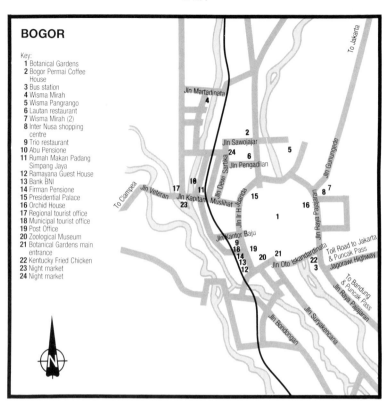

BOGOR

Key:
1 Botanical Gardens
2 Bogor Permai Coffee House
3 Bus station
4 Wisma Mirah
5 Wisma Pangrango
6 Lautan restaurant
7 Wisma Mirah (2)
8 Inter Nusa shopping centre
9 Trio restaurant
10 Abu Pensione
11 Rumah Makan Padang Simpang Jaya
12 Ramayana Guest House
13 Bank BNI
14 Firman Pensione
15 Presidential Palace
16 Orchid House
17 Regional tourist office
18 Municipal tourist office
19 Post Office
20 Zoological Museum
21 Botanical Gardens main entrance
22 Kentucky Fried Chicken
23 Night market
24 Night market

the palace's Dutch treasures were looted by the Japanese during the Second World War, but a fine collection of Indonesian paintings and sculptures (mainly erotic) still remains. Getting to see them is difficult as the palace is usually closed to the public. The Municipal Tourist Office can arrange special visits, but the hefty guide fee (20,000rps) makes it advisable to go in a group.

ARRIVAL/DEPARTURE
Many people make Bogor their first base in Java. They fly into Jakarta, get an airport taxi up to Cililitan bus-station, hop on an express bus to Bogor (frequent departures, 600rps) and arrive just 40 minutes later. The other option is a quick but uncomfortable train trip (one hour, 500rps) from Gambir station.

Regular express buses return to Jakarta from Bogor's 'terminal bis'. On arrival at Cililitan station (total chaos) walk out onto the street and start shouting '*Sarinah!*' or '*Jalan Jaksa!*' at passing buses. One of them will eventually take you into the city centre for 350rps.

There are frequent buses from Bogor to Bandung (1500rps, three hours) and a few private buses (dep. 2 p.m. daily) to Yogya from the large bus garage in Jln Sukasari.

Note: watch out for 'tourist guides' at Bogor railway station. They get 20 per cent commission on any hotel/restaurant they take you to. They also sometimes steal money and they offer 'volcano tours' for 25,000rps which you can do on your own for 2000rps!

TOURIST SERVICES
The Municipal Tourist Office (tel: 21350), Jln Ir H Juanda 46, is manned by helpful, informative Mr Bustami. A few doors along, at No. 9, the PPA office gives information on (and grants permits for) all Indonesia's wildlife reserves. The smaller District Tourist Office at Jln Veteran 23 is handy if you are staying at Abu's Pensione. Like the main office, it is open from 7 a.m. to 2 p.m. except Sundays.

The post office is located at Jln Ir H Juanda 3 and the immigration office (tel: 22870) at Jln Jenderal A Yani. Change money at Bank BNI near the Municipal Tourist Office.

TRANSPORT AROUND TOWN
Bogor has *becaks*, but they are reluctant to go anywhere for less than 1000rps. Use the little green minibuses instead – they go most places for 100rps and if you ask a local person they will put you on the right one.

SIGHTS

You cannot miss the Botanical Gardens or '*Kebon Raya*' They are right in the middle of town and the town has risen up around them. They cover a vast area of 110 hectares and are planted with 15,000 species of tropical plants from all over the world – from Africa, Asia, Australia and Latin America, as well as from Indonesia. Though originally laid out by Sir Stamford Raffles, it was the Dutch who, in 1817, began assembling the collection. They wanted to develop tropical agriculture and they were particularly interested in developing oil palms, since oil was a principal export. The original oil palm, from which all oil palms in South-East Asia in the commercial market were developed, was planted in the 1840s and is still alive in the gardens. Today, the botanical gardens in Bogor are the best in Asia, with an amazing selection of trees (400 species of palm tree alone), 3,000 hybrids of orchid in a glass house (including the famous Black Orchid from Kalimantan) and a beautifully landscaped park of lawns, paths, pools and ponds. The most famous plant in the collection is the gigantic 'corpse flower' from the forests of Sumatra. It grows to a height of 2.5 m and its pale yellow bloom emits the sickly-sweet odour of death.

The Botanical Gardens are open from 8 a.m. to 5 p.m. daily and there is an admission charge of 1000rps (only 500rps on Sundays). If you need a guide, ask around for 'Mr Antique'. He hangs out at the main entrance (opposite the Municipal Tourist Office) and he is happy if you give him 5000rps for his services. He is as 'old as the trees', speaks Dutch, Japanese and English, and what he doesn't know about the gardens isn't worth knowing!

Other plants not successfully grown in Bogor were moved to nearby **Cibodas**, above the Puncak Pass, which has cooler air. This branch of the botanical gardens has over 5,000 species of flora from the temperate zones around the world and it is huge – the layout is even bigger than the one in Bogor! To visit, take a colt or any Bandung bus to Cibodas (two and a half hours), then a 150rps minibus from the main road up to the top of the hill (4 km). Here you will find Cibodas village and, at the end of the main street (just 150 m from the botanical gardens), Pak Kliwoan's *losmen*, with rooms from 3000 to 5000rps.

Puncak Pass itself makes a good daytrip. Get a bus out there from Bogor's 'bis terminal' (500rps, 30 minutes). Go on a weekday (weekends are packed) and arrive early in the morning for stunning views from Mt Gede summit. Walk 200 m down for lunch at the (good) restaurant, then ask the fruit-sellers for directions to nearby **Telaga Warna** (Water-Colour Lake). The water here reflects the red, yellow and green hues of the surrounding trees – very pretty on a sunny day. Back on the main path and a little further down, visit Gunung Mas Tea Factory. This is the largest tea plantation in the Bogor area, famous for its black tea. If you arrive before 1 p.m. (when it closes) you can arrange a short tour. To stay overnight in the tea plantations (very cool and relaxing) take a room (8000rps) or a dormitory bed (2500rps) at **Kopo Hostel** in the village of **Cisarua** below Puncak. From Bogor, the hostel is 45 minutes by bus or colt – ask to be put off at the '**pompa bensin Cisarua**'. From Cisarua, you can continue by minibus (150rps) to the **Safari Park of Indonesia** at Cibeureum village. This large 55-hectare park has a wide assortment of animals from Indonesia and abroad. The 2000rps admission includes a worth-while guided tour by bus.

Bogor's local volcano is **Gunung Salak Indah** ('Mountain of the Beautiful Snake-Fruit'). It is the personal discovery of Abu at Abu Pensione and he is very proud of it! To get there, take a bus to Cibotak (300rps), then a *bemo* to Pasar Jumat (500rps), then walk for two hours, through beautiful countryside, to Locapurna village. Stay overnight at Haji's *losmen* (very basic rooms at 3000rps, with awful toilet, but all meals included!) and set out for the volcano at 7 a.m. next morning. Climb for one and a half hours on the good hill road, then two hours or so up a difficult jungle path (take strong shoes and warm clothing) to the top. On the walk back, there may be a *bemo* waiting at Locapurna, otherwise it is a long one and half hour walk back down to Pasar Jumat. Arrive here before 5 p.m. (last *bemo* back to Cibotak) or stay another night at Haji's. It is a hard trip, especially in two days, but apparently worth it. Don't, however, visit the volcano when it is raining as you won't see anything!

Though many of Bogor's attractions are out of town, the interesting **Zoological Museum** (right at the entrance to the botanical gardens) is not. Founded in 1894, this is home to a whole host of lifelike stuffed animals, insects, reptiles, birds and fish from all over Indonesia. Key exhibits include a male rhino weighing in at 2,280 kg and the 27-m-long skeleton of a blue whale. The museum is open daily from 8 a.m. to 2 p.m. (except Friday, when it closes at 11 a.m.) and admission is 200rps. If you want to make a day of it, take a *bemo* (300rps) from opposite the museum to **Ciapus**, then a second *bemo* (400rps) up to **Curug Lehar** or 'high waterfall', which is five minutes' walk off the main road. Enjoy an invigorating swim below the falls, savour the lovely surroundings and then stroll back to Ciapus, a pretty one and a half hour walk, with friendly people all along the way. It is much more comfortable than the bumpy *bemo* ride down!

ARTS AND CRAFTS

Bogor is famous for its *wayang goleg* or wooden puppets, although the only place you can see a puppet show, or any traditional entertainments for that matter, is **Genggong Village** (tel: 021-870875), 25 km out of town on the way to Jakarta. If you cannot afford to stay overnight (and at 40,000rps a room, that's probable), just turn up for the nightly cultural show (puppets, *gamelan* and dancing) and perhaps a meal. Minibuses go there for 400rps from Bogor bus station.

To see **Bengkel Gong**, the one and only *gamelan* factory in west Java still working in bronze, take a *bemo* from Ramayana cinema to **Ciampea** village, 15 km north east of Bogor. Here, wide 10-kg discs of bronze are pounded, flattened and turned up at the edges to make big gongs – it is a fascinating process to watch! Most other *gamelan* factories, like **Sukarna's Gong Workshop** at Jln Pancasan 17 (near Bogor town centre) have now switched to copper and brass because bronze is so expensive.

SHOPPING

Gamelan instruments and *wayang goleg* wooden puppets are sold across the road from Bengkel Gong in Ciampea. Prices are very reasonable. Bamboo handicrafts are the speciality at **Nusa Penida Souvenir Shop** in Jln Ir H Juanda, while **Kenari Indah** at Jln Bondongan Blok 30 (in Lolongok area) is well known for its silver jewellery, wooden puppets and *wayang topeng* masks. For all general buys, go to **Inter-Nusa** supermarket (Bogor's biggest) at the northern entrance to the Botanical Gardens.

ACCOMMODATION

Bogor's close proximity to Jakarta means overpriced hotels and a shortage of rooms, especially at weekends. Best value are private guest houses like **Wisma Pangrango** (tel: 28670) at Jln Mandalawangi 10 (fan rooms from 17,500rps, air-conditioned from 35,000rps, nice pool and restaurant) and **New Mirah Hotel** (tel: 28044) at Jln Mandalawangi 3 (rooms from 25,000rps fan, 34,000rps air-conditioned, many facilities). Both these places are quiet and comfortable, ideal for couples and families. Regular travellers prefer **Wisma Ramayana Pensione**, Jln Ir H Juanda 54, for its good information, friendly staff and bright, well-furnished rooms at 9000-12,500rps. The garden courtyard is a bonus and the

mandis are so big that many people mistake them for a bath!

Pick of the cheap *losmen* is **Abu Pensione** (tel: 22893), 100 m from the rail station at Jln Mayur Oking 7. Rates are a little high (dormitory beds at 3000rps, rooms from 8000rps single, 10,000rps double) but Abu and his family really make you feel at home. Information is first-rate (the guest-comments book is well worth reading if you are heading into Java) and the food is phenomenal. Abu himself is a real character, full of ideas on how to make the most of your stay in Bogor and always turning up with free fried bananas, ice-cream, tea and coffee, etc. Many reckon this the best *losmen* in west Java and I agree. If full, try **Firman Pensione** (tel: 23246), 100 m from the Botanical Gardens at Jln Paledang 28. This is another friendly family-run place with simple rooms (5000rps for one person, 7000rps for two, breakfast included) and clean toilets/*mandis*. Owner Wardah is very proud of her big double beds, 'good for honeymoon', she suggests, 'like jogging!'. If she's asleep when you arrive, observe her sign: 'Please knuck the door as hard as possible until I can wake up'. This place is well spoken of.

FOOD

For cheap local-style snacks like *talas Bogor* (black radishes, steamed with coconut or fried with brown sugar) take a No. 2 bus from the town centre down to the night market in Sukasari. In the same market is **Tan Ek Tjoan** Chinese restaurant, good for seafood. Two other night markets, both more central, are located on Jln Veteran and Dewi Sartika.

Sit-down Sundanese food (cheaper and less hot than *padang* cooking) is best tried at **Asinan Segar** on Jln Veteran. Ask for *asinan*, a potpourri of fruit, vegetables and peanuts in a hot peanut sauce. **Kedai 89**, opposite Firman Pensione, also has Sundanese cuisine at low prices. The speciality here, *nasi rames*, means rice with anything you want and you can have as much as you want of it for 750rps! **Restoran Dua Saati**, just up from Abu Pensione, is a popular open-air restaurant with 333 dishes on the menu. The *sate ayam* is delicious. **Trio** restaurant, just below the bus-station (and next to **Kentucky Fried Chicken**) does good *padang* food, while **Bogor Permai Coffee Shop** on Jln Sudirman is an all-in-one bakery, supermarket and multi-cuisine restaurant which merits a visit.

BANDUNG

Some say Bandung is the Paris of Java. Well, it does have stately, tree-lined boulevards and elegant art deco homes.

Active Mount Bromo

A village group, Java

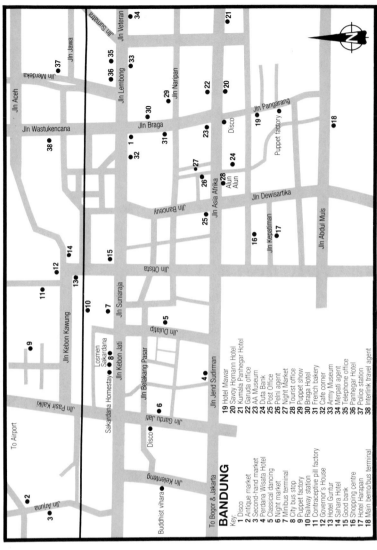

BANDUNG

Key:
1 Disco
2 Antique market
3 Second-hand market
4 Perdana Wisata Hotel
5 Classical dancing
6 Night market
7 Minibus terminal
8 City bus stop
9 Puppet factory
10 Railway station
11 Contraceptive pill factory
12 Governor's House
13 Hotel Guntur
14 Sahara Hotel
15 Good bank
16 Shopping centre
17 Hotel Harapan
18 Main bemo/bus terminal
19 Hotel Mawar
20 Savoy Homann Hotel
21 Kumala Panhegar Hotel
22 Garuda office
23 AA Museum
24 Duta Bank
25 Post Office
26 Pelni agent
27 Night Market
28 Tourist office
29 Puppet show
30 Braga Hotel
31 French bakery
32 Cafe corner
33 Army Museum
34 Merpati agent
35 Telephone office
36 Panhegar Hotel
37 Police station
38 Interlink travel agent

Moreover, at 700 m above sea level, the climate is pleasant. However, Bandung has about as much in common with Paris as Jakarta has with, say, Rome. To make anything of Bandung, you have to get out into the country. Still, it's a pleasant getaway from Jakarta and many people stop off here on their way to or from Yogya.

Bandung is a centre of culture and education, as well as a popular leisure-holiday spot for west Javans. On the surface of things, it is a noisy, smelly and polluted city. Beneath that, however, it remains typically Javanese. The people here go out of their way to help you and when you go off the main roads, you will quickly forget your first impressions. Stroll around the Pasar in the morning, the Alun-Alun in the evening and the Asie-Africa A Venue in the afternoon. Look at the old colonial buildings there, and let your mind float back to a time gone by.

HISTORY
The capital of west Java and the third largest city in Indonesia, Bandung is set in a high valley surrounded by volcanic peaks. Like Bogor, its cool mountain air and close situation to Jakarta (180 km SE) endeared it to the Dutch, who named it the 'Paris of the East'. Bandung was *the* place to go in pre-war Dutch days – it was the number one tourist destination in all Indonesia. People came here for the mountains, the volcanoes, the lakes and the cool climate. They also came for the shopping. Jalan Braga was the 'Fifth Avenue' of South-East Asia –

it had branches of all the best boutiques in Europe. This was where you found the latest Paris fashions or bought a brand-new Packard car. This was where you had your hair styled, your tailor-made suit made up, and your expensive 'haute cuisine' meal at the Braga Permai restaurant. The Dutch had a lot of money when they developed this place and during the 1920s and 1930s, which was, of course, the high-water mark of European colonialism around the world, they did a lot of building, particularly in Bandung, which they built from scratch. They discovered its coffee-growing potential in the late eighteenth century and literally chopped a brand-new city out of the jungle. In the year 1900, there were 28,000 people in Bandung. In 1945, when the Japanese invaded, there were still only 250,000. By 1989, that figure was almost 2 million, making this one of the fastest-growing cities in the history of the world!

Bandung lost much of its colonial atmosphere after the fire of March 1946, when a lot of its beautiful Dutch architecture disappeared behind horrid modern façades. In 1955, the city played host to the first (and so far only) Asia-Africa Conference. In the 1960s, it began concentrating on education, spawning some 50 universities, colleges, academies and research centres. Today, it is a city of young people, full of students wanting to practise English on you. A bit tiring after a while, but fun, and you can do your bit for international relations!

ARRIVAL/DEPARTURE
Air
Garuda, Merpati and Bouraq have regular daily flights between Bandung and Jakarta. Bouraq flies once a day between Bandung and Yogya. At Bandung airport, do not pay 5000rps for a taxi into town (4 km). Instead, walk 300 m to the main road, turn right and get a public bus for 150rps.

Rail
There are several trains daily from Bandung to Jakarta (8000rps first class, 6000rps second class; three hours) and three trains a day to Yogya (dep.5.25 a.m., 7.40 a.m. and 5.30 p.m.; 5000rps second class, 3800rps third class; six hours).

Road
Buses to Bogor (1500rps, four hours) and Jakarta (1900rps non-air-conditioned, 2750-3600rps air-conditioned, five hours) leave every few minutes from Bandung's Kebon Kalapa bus-station, a short 1.5 km *bemo* ride from Alun Alun Square. Buses to Yogya (6000-9000rps air-conditioned, 12 hours) and to Cirebon (1900rps, four hours) go from Cicaheum

station, a much longer *bemo*/bus trip to the east of town. Quick, convenient minibuses run out daily to Cirebon (2500rps) and to Pangandaran (5000rps, six hours) from Rusty's Sakardana *losmen*.

TOURIST SERVICES
The tourist office, on the corner of the Alun Alun, is open from 8 a.m. to 8 p.m. Monday-Thursday, until ll a.m. Friday, until 2 p.m. Saturday. Staff speak little English, so go armed with precise questions and limitless patience. Still better, go to Rusty Muchfree at the new Sakardana Homestay. He is a walking guide-book!

The Pelni agent (open from 8 a.m. to 2 p.m., closed Sunday) and the post office are both close to the tourist office. Jaya Arta Bank in Jln Otista gives a good rate of exchange, especially if you mention Rusty. The best travel agent (open from 8 a.m. to 4 p.m. weekdays, Saturday until ll a.m.) is Interlink (tel: 50614) at Jln Wastukencana 5, just above the railway crossing. This place can confirm most flights within 30 minutes, far quicker than the official Garuda or Merpati offices!

TRANSPORT AROUND TOWN
Fortunately, most points of in-town interest are within walking distance – if, that is, you don't mind hazardous pavements and murderous traffic. The *becak* drivers here are the most lethargic in Java. They heavily overcharge or they don't go at all. Minibuses (called Hondas) are the best way of getting round. They charge a standard 150rps, have their destinations posted and you can wave them down anywhere. Taxis are metered and cost around 1000rps per kilometre, but they are worth using at night!

SIGHTS
To be quite honest, there are none. The only thing worth putting yourself out for (just) is the **Geological Museum**, which had a friend of mine almost weeping with enthusiasm. 'I'm a museum fanatic,' he confessed, 'but I have never seen a museum anywhere in the world that has a finer collection of anthropological fossils, skulls and human remains. They have either original human skulls – like Java Man, Solo Man or Heidelberg Man – or exact-model latex casts. I've never seen anything like it! They've got a special room just on volcanology, a room on just earthquakes and a room on all different kinds of oil sludge. For an intellectual charge, the Geological Museum is really very special!' My friend went into similar raptures about **Gedung Sate** across the road from the museum. 'Aaah!', he moaned, 'It's comparable to

Borobodur and Prambanan in terms of being the best example of architecture from any age or style in Indonesia! In fact, it is *the* premier example of Indo-European architecture in Indonesia! You're a fool not to see it!' Well, maybe I was, but according to other travellers I didn't miss much. Make your own mind up and get a green-and-yellow *oplet* No. 13 (bound for Sadang-Serang) from outside Rusty's Sakardana *losmen*. Ask to be put off at Diponegoro St and walk 150 m up the hill to the museum on No. 57. It is open 9 a.m. to 2 p.m. Monday to Thursday, Friday until 11 a.m., Saturday until 1 p.m.

Bandung's main attraction is **Tangkuban Perahu** volcano, 29 km north of town. Its name means 'upturned boat' and refers to the legend of Sangkuriang, a Sundanese prince who fell in love with his own mother. She challenged him to build a lake and a canoe for their honeymoon in a single night, but then had second thoughts and brought the sun up early, causing him to kick his nearly completed *perahu* over in a fit of pique. In historic times, this volcano erupted in 1829, 1846, 1887, 1910, 1926 and 1929. It is still active and has approximately ten craters. To visit, take a Subang minibus from the minibus terminal (1000rps) and ask for *kawah* (volcano). Get off at the park entrance, pay your 400rps admission and walk 4 km along the main road to the top. Alternatively, turn right at the *warung* about 1 km after the entry post and take the (punishing) 2 km short-cut through the jungle to Kawah Domas crater. Enjoy a soak in the hot springs on the way up and aim to be at the summit before noon, before it clouds over. Then walk back to the park entrance, go to **Lembang** by minibus (500rps), change to another minibus (350rps) for **Maribaya**, enjoy a scenic two-hour stroll through a river gorge to **Dago Tea House**, stop here for snacks at sunset, and get a Honda minibus back to town. To go to the tea house direct, take a Dago minibus (150rps) from Bandung's minibus terminal.

For something special, visit the village of **Sumedang**. It is one and a half hours from Cicaheum minibus station and has one of the best small museums in all South-East Asia. Sumedang was the seat of the last Sundanese kingdom in west Java – it picked up where Bogor left off. When the powerful Pajajaran kingdom (Java's last great Hindu dynasty) was crushed by the Muslim sultans in 1578, a small band of people from Bogor (then known as Pakawan) ran off with the crown jewels and offered them to the Raja of Sumedang. He then became the spokesman of Sundanese power. Today, in the new museum here, they have the original crown and all the jewellery, together with nine old *gamelan* sets, eighteenth-century costumes, ancient manuscripts and the best collection of weaponry of any museum in Indonesia. It is all housed in four buildings in the old *kraton* of Sumedang on the outskirts of the village and although it is only open to the public on a Sunday, they will open up any day for foreign tourists and will show you around. The really valuable stuff (including the crown jewels and the fabulous *kris* knives) is, however, locked up. To see that, you have to write a letter (giving a week's notice) to the Museum Conservator, R. M. Abdullah Kartadibarata, at Jln Pangeran Geusan Ulun No 28, Sumedang.

ENTERTAINMENT

Bandung is the cultural centre of west Java. Some of the traditional performances regularly shown in the city include **Wayang Goleg** (wooden puppet show) every Saturday night at Yayasan Pusat Kebudayaan, Jln Naripan 7; **People's Play** every Friday night at Rumentang Siang building, Jln Baranangsiang; **Bamboo/Angklung Music** most afternoons at Pak Ujo's Bamboo Workshop, Jln Padasuka; **Ram Fighting** every other Sunday (8 a.m. to 1 p.m.) at Ledeng or Ranca Buni hill towns; **Jaipong Dance** every Wednesday night at Hotel Panhegar, Jln Merdeka 2; **Classical Dancing** every Sunday from 10 a.m. to 1 p.m. at Sekar Pakuan, Dulatip 60; and **Panca Silat** (Sudanese self-defence) every Monday and Thursday night just down the road from Sakardana Homestay. The knowledgeable Rusty Muchfree gives full details on all the above shows and is himself an accomplished magician. Every second Saturday, he entertains travellers with special demonstrations of Sundanese *debus* magic. The dark bloodstains on the floor of his roof show where his friend's head has been 'separated' from his body and connected up again!

If you want to dance, there's **Studio 81** in Hotel Preanger, Jln Preanger (described by one girl as 'the best disco in the southern hemisphere') and **Marabu Club**, just up from Cafe Corner (Wednesday is 'Romantic Night', Saturday is 'Lovely Night' and Sunday is 'Pretty Sunday'). For something completely different, there is Sundanese *gamelan* disco at **Langen Setra**, Jln Otista 541.

SHOPPING

Good buys in Bandung are wooden puppets, leather, textiles and clothes. You can buy new *wayang goleg* puppets from the **Cupu Manik Puppet Factory** on Gang Haji Umar (off Kebon Kawung), although if you want authentic old ones, with double-faces and wings, Sakardana Homestay has a fair selection. Rusty

Terraces of the Dieng Plateau

Tea plantations near Bandung

brings them in from Cipancing village, 50 km out of Bandung. Ask him to take you to the **Bamboo Instrument Factory** at nearby Madurasa. With his help, you can get a beautiful bamboo lounge set (two chairs and table) for only 135,000rps. If you go on your own, you'll be charged double!

Bandung's second-hand market (**Pasar Jatayu**) on Arjuna St is open every day from 8 a.m. to 3 p.m. It is good if you need a backpack, tent or walking boots as there is lots of army surplus stuff here. The antiques market (**Pasar Jatayu**) is behind the motorbike parts shop across the road. Have a look around, but don't waste your money on clever fakes.

ACCOMMODATION

The recently restored **Savoy Homann Hotel** (tel: 58091) at Jln Asia-Afrika 112 is an art deco masterpiece. The rooms, which start at US$31 + 21 per cent taxes, look like sets from old Cary Grant movies and the restaurant is designed just like an ocean liner, with curved chrome railings and so on! A decent alternative is **Hotel Panghegar** (tel: 57584) at Jln Merdeka 2, with rooms up to US$50, pool, air-conditioning, disco, etc. It is well located near the shopping centres and is famous for its excellent service.

Recommended hotels in the mid-range include **Hotel Guntur** at Jln Otista 20 (tel: 50763), air-conditioned rooms from 20,000rps), **Hotel Harapan** at Jln Kapatihan 14-16 (tel: 51212, rooms from ll,000rps) and **Hotel Sahara** (tel: 51684, doubles from 7500rps). All three places are clean, centrally located and good value.

With *losmen,* you basically have a choice between **Sakardana Homestay** and **Losmen Sakardana**. They are both within 50 m of each other on Jln Kebonjati (Nos 34 and 50/7B) and they are run by opposing factions of the same family. The 'old' Losmen Sakardana is rather cheaper but the rooms are small and cramped. The 'new' Sakardana Homestay is definitely nicer. You get space, no crush for the bathrooms and a restaurant to boot. Manager Rusty is a positive treasure-house of information, eager to help anyone get the best out of their stay in Indonesia. His rooms are 5000rps single, 7000rps double and the dormitory is 3000rps. If he is full, take clean quiet rooms (5500rps single, 6000rps double) at **Hotel Mawar**, Jln Pangaran 14.

FOOD

The night market is opposite the tourist office, off Asia-Africa. It caters mainly for rich domestic tourists and the food is pretty expensive by Indonesian standards (e.g. *gado-gado* at 1500rps a dish), but

most travellers are happy with a cheap and tasty *martabak* pancake – either *martabak manis* (sweet, with cheese and peanuts) or *martabak telor* (salty, with egg and vegetables). A good sit-down place in the market is a *rumah makan* called **Bapakan Siliwangi**.

The best Sundanese food in Bandung can be found at **Ponyo Restaurant**, Jln Malabar 60. Every third restaurant in west Java is called *ponyo* (delicious), but this one really *is* delicious! Be warned, Sundanese cuisine is not to everyone's taste! It is in the goat-gut range of things – lots of organ meats, bat tongues, etc. If you are not into internal medicine, stick to the fish dishes which happen to be very good. Or try the Sundanese *rijstafel* at **Sakardana Losmen**. It is steamed fish, rice, coconut milk, vegetable soup, *tempe*, egg and prawn crackers – good value at 3500rps per head, but you must order a day in advance. **Top Restaurant**, the seafood restaurant famous for its frogs' legs in butter sauce and chicken steak in tomato, has recently moved to beyond the hospital – ask Rusty for the new location.

Western food is good at **Tizi's**, high above the city on Jln Hegarmanah 14. The spot is said to be managed by the wife of a former Indonesian ambassador to Germany and offers several German specialities. You can eat well here for 15,000rps in a spacious garden setting. For an even bigger splurge, go to the **Braga Permai** on Jln Braga. It is Bandung's equivalent to Raffles in Singapore, with top-notch European/Chinese cuisine and a fantastic range of cakes and ice-creams. **Cafe Corner**, at the top of Suniraja, has a cheap Western menu of steak and fries, spaghetti bolognese, pizzas, etc. The English-speaking manager is friendly and informative.

PANGANDARAN

You do not often come across a beach in Java that is safe for swimming, so make the most of Pangandaran. Situated on a peninsula bounded by the Indian Ocean, this small fishing village cum coastal resort is a surfing spot, a beach and a game park in one, the perfect place to rest up and relax between Bandung and Yogya. Pangandaran literally means 'nomads who move from place to place like migratory birds', but there's nobody going anywhere now that tourism has arrived. The past couple of years have seen a sudden surge in popularity and new restaurants, *losmen* and homestays have sprung up all over the place. Crowds of domestic tourists roll in at weekends, but during the week Pangandaran is still a quiet little backpackers' centre and very cheap.

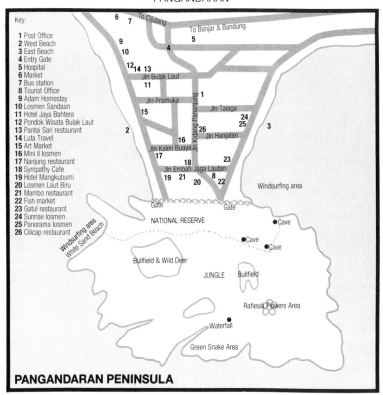

Key:

1 Post Office
2 West Beach
3 East Beach
4 Entry Gate
5 Hospital
6 Market
7 Bus station
8 Tourist Office
9 Adam Homestay
10 Losmen Sandaan
11 Hotel Jaya Bahtera
12 Pondok Wisata Bulak Laut
13 Pantai Sari restaurant
14 Luta Travel
15 Art Market
16 Mini II losmen
17 Nanjung restaurant
18 Sympathy Cafe
19 Hotel Mangkubumi
20 Losmen Laut Biru
21 Mambo restaurant
22 Fish market
23 Gatul restaurant
24 Sunrise losmen
25 Panorama losmen
26 Cilicap restaurant

To Cijulang
To Banjar & Bandung
Jln Bulak Laut
Jln Pramuka
Jln Kidang Pananjung
Jln Talaga
Jln Hanjatan
Jln Kalen Buaya
Jln Embah Jaga Lautan
Windsurfing area
Gate
NATIONAL RESERVE
Cave
Cave
Cave
Windsurfing area
White Sand Beach
Bullfield & Wild Deer
JUNGLE
Bullfield
Raflesia Flowers Area
Waterfall
Green Snake Area

PANGANDARAN PENINSULA

ARRIVAL/DEPARTURE

Pangandaran is 223 km east of Bandung, about two hours by bus (l100rps) from the town of Banjar (63 km north) where the Ekspres Siang train from Bandung (five to six hours) and Yogya (seven hours) stops. There are also buses from Bandung and Yogya to Banjar. The 4848 taxi company runs direct minibuses between Bandung and Pangandaran for 6000rps and Metro Guest House in Yogya offers an express minibus service (four and a half hours) which connects with the last of four daily ferries (7 a.m., 8 a.m., 12 noon and l p.m.) from Cilicap to Kalipucang. This option is the most pleasant: a fascinating three and a half to four and a half hour (800rps) trip down the backwaters, offering excellent photography. Off the ferry at Kalipucang, walk for five minutes down the road to the bus-station for the final 17-km bus-ride (30 minutes, 200rps) into Pangandaran. Be prepared, a screaming mob of demented *becak* drivers board the bus at Pangandaran, each of them determined to drag your bag into their vehicle. The reason for their enthusiasm is simple, they get big commissions from the *losmen*. Hang on to your bag and don't lose your cool! The correct *becak* fare into town from the bus-stop (2 km) is 300rps and it is an extra 300rps to enter the beach area.

Leaving Pangandaran is simpler. For Bandung, either get a *bemo* out to Banjar for the 5 p.m. express train (arr. 9 p.m.), or go direct to Bandung by express minibus from Luta Travel (dep. 6 a,m., arr. 12 noon, 6000rps). For Yogya, go via Cilicap on a Luta minibus (dep. 6 a.m., arr. 4/5 p.m., 10,500rps) or take a *bemo*/boat to Cilicap, then a horse cart (30 minutes, 800rps) to the new Cilicap bus-station for a bus to Yogya (six hours, 2000rps).

Note: Bandung buses go via the town of Ciamis, just past Banjar, from where you can go by bus to Cirebon.

TOURIST SERVICES

Luta Travel Agency, Jln Sumardi 672 (tel: 65) has much better information than the (useless) tourist office. Run by a helpful Dutch lady (Willy) and her Javanese husband, it offers jungle trips, fishing trips, bicycle/motorbike rental, car hire, surfing, windsurfing, horse-riding, jungle treks and express mini-buses to Java and Sumatra. It doesn't confirm air tickets though, you will have to do that in Yogya or Bandung. Changing money is also a problem because there are no banks as yet and the only place which changes cash/travellers' cheques is the Cilicap Restaurant. If you are short on reading material, the small library at Adam's Homestay (near Luta) has second-hand books for sale.

SIGHTS

All Pangandaran's sights are natural. There are beaches on either side of the town and because the town is at the narrowest point of the peninsula they are only 300 m apart. The west beach overlooks a wide bay sheltered by a coral reef and is good for swimming and sunsets. The east beach, where the fish market is, is unsafe for swimming but good for surfing – hire windsurfers and surfboards from Mambo restaurant. The best beach is Pasir Putih (White Beach), located on the western side of the National Park, just 15 minutes' walk from town or 3000rps by *prahu*. It has lovely white sand and calm sea, just right for swimming, sunbathing and snorkelling. You can hire *prahus* to go out on fishing trips (around 30,000rps for up to five people) or to snorkel out at the coral reefs (around 5000rps per person), but you must bargain hard! Luta Travel do a one-day boat trip to nearby 'Paradise' island. It costs 17,500rps per head, includes a BBQ and drinks, and runs two or three times a week in the dry season only. This island has a small rain forest, a virgin white-sand beach, lots of colourful birds and schools of dolphin leaping offshore.

The National Park occupies the whole peninsula south of the fishing village. It is a large 530-hectare area of hardwood forest and dense jungle with much interesting wildlife (black monkeys, giant fruitbats, hornbills, buffalo, lizards, scorpions and snakes). Look out for rare rafflesia (giant cabbage-sized flowers named after Sir Stamford Raffles) which produce blooms of up to 1 m in diameter. Entrance to the reserve is 300rps, plus an extra 50rps for 'insurance' – worth it, in view of the number of broken legs reported! The 4000rps 'jungle treks' sold by *losmen* are a bit of a cheat. There are two old guides who know the forest back to front, but whether you get them is pot luck. The local mafia have organised things so that there is a different guide on every day, so you only have a two in seven chance of getting one who knows anything! Bring a compass, however, and you will not need a guide – a 10-km beach path leads all the way round the peninsula and you can walk it easily at low tide. A good guide can show you the waterfall where you can swim, although when I was there (in the dry season) it looked like someone throwing *mandi*-dippers of water over a cliff!

There are several worth-while day-trips in and around Pangandaran which has very pretty surroundings. Contact Luta Travel for directions to local beauty spots like Batu Hiu (Shark Rock), Parigi and Batu Karas, all accessible by bicycle, motorbike or minibus.

ACCOMMODATION

Pangandaran has accommodation to suit every pocket – finding somewhere to stay is only a problem at weekends and during the July/August marriage season. Most *losmen*, however, will not put you up unless you stay at least two nights. This is because they have had to pay the *becak* man who brought you a hefty 2500rps commission!

The older *losmen* are at the end of the main road, in town. **Mini II**, run by a French/Indonesian couple, is much recommended, with very clean rooms at 3500-7000rps a double, and great fish BBQs on the beach at night. Standards at **Laut Biru** have dropped since it got in the guidebooks, but it is still good value at 4000rps single, 7500rps double and the breakfasts are superb. **Sunrise**, on the east beach just above the fish market, has lovely sea-views and superior bungalows at 10,000rps with breakfast. It is wonderfully quiet, apart from noisy fishermen in the morning. In the reserve itself, there is a four-room house that puts up travellers. They ask 10,000rps for what amounts to a flat (own living room and bedroom, shared bathroom) and a short stroll takes you down to a private beach with fantastic sunset views. You just turn up there to book it.

The new *losmen* area is up on the west beach, near Luta Travel. **Bamboo House** has a quiet location and charges 5000rps with breakfast; **Sandaan** is new and smart and offers 'deluxe' rooms for 7500rps with breakfast/dinner; **Arpoloka** is for couples and asks 7000rps for cosy rooms with big double beds. For something better, try **Pangandaran Beach Hotel** at the bottom of the west beach (12,500rps and up) or **Hotel Bumi Nusantara** on the east beach, with bungalows from 25,000 to 60,000rps.

FOOD

Fish is the dish, but watch the price. Seafood should be less than 1000rps per kg, but I've seen people pay 8000rps for 500rps worth of shrimps! Watch the locals carefully, and be prepared to pay a bit more than they do. Try the fish and crabs at **Gatul's Seafood Shop** on the east beach. It doesn't look much on the outside, but the food is terrific. For really traditional Indonesian fare, try the little **Warung Jambu** just above the fish market. Everything is served fresh and the *nasi rames* (rice with anything you like) is superb. Travellers' fare like chips, banana pancakes and fruit salad can be found at **Sympathy Cafe** and **Restaurant Cilicap**, both on the main road, while **Nanjung** restaurant on the west beach has just about everything – *mie goreng*, *sate*, lobster, shark, etc. – prepared by the best cook in town.

YOGYAKARTA

It is easy to spend a lot of time in Yogyakarta. This is the artistic and cultural centre of Java, the equivalent of Chiang-Mai in Thailand or Ubud in Bali, and there is much to see and do. Travellers flock here in their hundreds daily, to shop for crafts, to watch cultural entertainments and to take courses in dance, *gamelan* and batik. One of the biggest villages in the world, Yogyakarta (usually shortened to Yogya, and pronounced Jog-ja) has long been a focus of higher learning. Some 15 per cent of the city's half-million population are students, many of them engaged in studies of performing arts. Recent tourist popularity has led to a revival in dying art forms like *wayang kulit* (shadow-puppet plays) but also to a lot of Western-style development and building, depriving certain areas of their old character. Most of the city's charm and interest is now off the main drag. Yogya, be warned, is one of the few places in South-East Asia where beggars are evident and hassle from over-zealous *becak* drivers inevitable. If you have rushed here straight from Jakarta or Bromo and find the place too squalid or the pace too hectic, do not be shy about moving quickly on to Solo or Kaliurang for some peace and quiet.

HISTORY

Located at the foot of the active volcano Merapi, the fertile plain of Yogyakarta was, in the sixteenth and seventeenth centuries, the seat of the second Mataram empire, which had seized power from the Hindu-Buddhist Majapahits in 1487. Artistically, the period was marked by a process of Islamisation which left its mark on writing and textile decoration. The ongoing influences which form the basis of the performing arts found in Yogya today originate, however, from the seventh-century kingdom of Srivijaya in Sumatra.

The city came into being in 1755, when the Dutch capitalised on power struggles within the Mataram kingdom and split it into two separate sultanates: Yogyakarta and Surakarta (Solo). Yogya gained its first sultan, Hamango Kubowono I (1755-72), a new *kraton* or palace (1757) and, not long after, a reputation for stubborn resistance to foreign rule. The ensuing 200 years were mainly ones of peace, in which artistic and cultural pursuits flourished. In 1812, however, the British, under Stamford Raffles, stormed and looted the *kraton* and between 1825 and 1830 Prince Diponegoro led a fierce five-year guerilla war against the Dutch.

He was eventually tricked into captivity and exiled to Sulawesi. In December 1948, shortly after Yogya became capital of the new Republic of Indonesia, the Dutch bombed the city and captured several Republican leaders. A year later, under pressure from the US Senate, they were forced to recognise the new Republic officially and Yogya became one of Indonesia's three Special Districts (the other two being Jakarta and Aceh in north Sumatra) with full self-government through its sultan governor. The neighbouring sultanate of Solo, on the other hand, found itself instantly dissolved for its part in helping the Dutch.

ARRIVAL/DEPARTURE
Air

Many people like to fly from Yogya direct to Bali. You miss Mt Bromo, but this is a bit of a tourist-trap nowadays and in the rainy season it is nothing special. The benefit of flying is that you arrive in Denpasar in no time at all, awake and refreshed. The cost of the Garuda flight is just over 60,000rps (a little less on Merpati) and you should book a week ahead. The same goes for flights from Jakarta, which are similarly priced and just as busy.

Yogya's airport is 7 km from town – around 5000rps by taxi (up to four persons) or 250rps by public bus from the main road 200 m past the gate.

Rail

Yogya's train station is centrally located, just off Jln Mangkubumi. From here, there are regular trains to Jakarta (the Bima AC is best: dep. 9.35 p.m., arr. 7.03 a.m.; 17,000rps first class or 20,000rps for a private cabin sleeper), three trains daily to Bandung (quickest is the Mutiara Express: dep. 11.37 p.m., arr. 8 a.m., fare 9000rps second class) and one train a day to Banjar (dep. 8.10 a.m., arr. 12.30 p.m., 2400rps third class) for Pangandaran. If you want to go to Bromo, the K A Argo Puro leaves Yogya at 6.35 a.m. daily (3800rps third class) and arrives at Probollingo at 4.30 p.m.. Minibuses run from outside Probollingo railway station up to Ngadasiri, for Bromo, until 5.30 p.m. at a cost of 750rps per person. Yogya to Bali by train is a long, tiring 20-hour journey via Surabaya, and is not recommended!

Road

You may need the Umbulharjo bus station (5 km out of town near Kota Gede) for short-hop buses out to Kaliurang and Borobodur. For longer hauls, shop around the numerous ticket agencies lining Jln Sosrowijayan. They sell seats on express buses (often leaving from outside their office at night) to Bandung (8500rps, or 10,000rps with

YOGYAKARTA

Key:
1 Sosrowijayan
2 Zoo
3 Immigration office
4 Railway station
5 Seno Batik
6 Hanoman Forest restaurant
7 Indoor market (fruit & veg)
8 Academy of Dance (ASTI)
9 Merpati office
10 Bank Niaga
11 Gudeg restaurant
12 Buses to Borobudur
13 Telephone exchange
14 Bank Bumi Daya
15 Garuda office
16 Arjuna Plaza Hotel
17 Garuda Hotel
18 Hotel Aziatic
19 Hotel Kartika
20 Buses to Bali
21 Hotel Indonesia
22 Legian restaurant
23 TIC Tourist Office
24 TIS Tourist Office
25 Mutiara Hotel
26 Money changer
27 Prambanan Guest House
28 Hotel Puri
29 Big Market
30 Happy Restaurant
31 Nitour office
32 Bank BNI
33 Post Office
34 Taxi stand
35 Batik Research Centre (BPKB)
36 Nirwana Guest House
37 Bus station
38 People's Park (THR)
39 Dalem Pujokusuman
40 Sultan's Palace (Kraton)
41 Bird Market & Water Castle
42 Agastya (shadow puppets)
43 Surya Kencana (batik clothes factory)
44 Airlangga Guest House

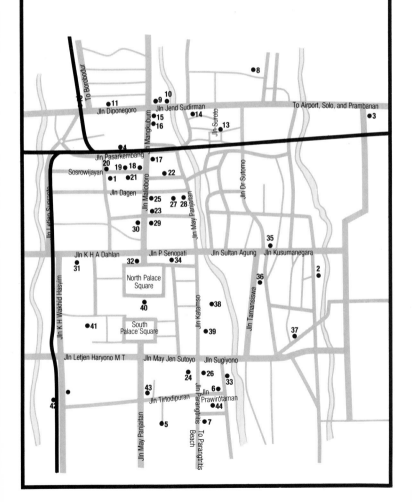

air-conditioning, 13 hours), Malang (8500rps or 11,000rps, ten hours), Probollingo for Bromo (12,000rps, ten hours), Bogor (9000rps, 15 hours), Jakarta (8000rps, with air-conditioning 11,000rps, 14 hours) and to Denpasar (13,000rps or 17,500rps, 15 hours). Three early buses (dep. 6 a.m., 7 a.m. and 8 a.m., 2100rps) go daily to Cilicap, for Pangandaran, from Jln Sosrowijayan. From Cilicap, there are at least two ferries a day (dep. 12 noon and 1 p.m.), to Kalipucang. The two and a half hour boat trip costs 1200rps. Minibuses from Kalipucang cost 750rps and reach Pangandaran one and a half hours later. For convenience, get the quick express bus to Cilicap (dep. 7.30 a.m. daily, 4500rps) from Metro Guest House, Prawirotaman. It connects beautifully with the last boat out to Pangandaran. To get to Solo, either wave down a colt in Jln Mataram (750rps, two and half hours) or splash out on a scheduled *bemo* from Jln Diponegoro (1500rps, two hours). If you miss one of these and have to wait an hour, there is an excellent pastry/coffee shop on the north side of Diponegoro. It has bread in the window and advertises steaks. It is an excellent place to while away time. The scheduled *bemos* go quickly, do not stop for more passengers and drop you at the door of your accommodation in Solo.

TOURIST SERVICES

The main TIC (tourist information centre) at Jln Malioboro 16 (tel: 2543) is open from 8 a.m. to 8.30 p.m. Monday to Saturday. Come here for up-to-date information on transport and a full listing of cultural entertainments. The small TIS (tourist information service) at Jln Parangtritis 42 (tel: 5512) changes money, books flights, sells a decent city sightseeing tour (25,000rps for two persons, 2500rps for each extra person) and offers air-conditioned buses to Jakarta, Bali and Padang.

The main GPO is located at the junction of Jln Senopati and Jln Jen A Yani. If you are staying in Prawirotaman, you can use the small Kantor Pos (open from 8 a.m. to 1 p.m. only) on Jln Sisingara Angaraja. The Immigration office (open 7.30 a.m. to 1.30 p.m. Monday to Thursday, 7.30 a.m. to 11 a.m. Friday, 9 a.m. to 12.30 p.m. Saturday) is on Jln Adisucipto, 8 km out of town on the way to the airport. The telephone office is north of town at Jln Laksda Yos Sudarso 9, off Jln Suroto, and two banks offering good exchange rates are Bank Niaga and Bank Bumi Daya on Jln Sudirman. Airline offices are all central: Garuda at Jln Mangkubumi 56 (tel: 4400), Merpati at Jln Sudirman 9-11 (tel: 4272) and Bouraq at Jln Mataram 60 (tel: 86664).

TRANSPORT AROUND TOWN

Yogya has one inherent problem and that is the *becak* drivers. They are a lot more aggressive and a lot more persistent than anywhere else in Java. This is purely because Yogya is a shopping centre. There are lines of *becaks* outside the hotels and up and down the main streets, but none of them want to drive you anywhere unless there is some business involved. They are not rich people (average earnings around £12 per month), they are all into commissions and all they want to do is take you shopping. You may not like them, but you must come to terms with them, because every time you go out the door they will give you a hard time. And you do need them to get around – Yogya is too big and hot to walk around, *bemos* (standard charge 100rps) are hard to work out and hotel taxis are expensive. Rented bicycles (1500/2000rps per day) are okay, but many get stolen and cycling can be hot work. *Becak* drivers often speak good English and they can be good town guides, so you might as well find yourself a nice one who will help you as well as himself. Let him take you to the shops, even if you do not buy anything. He gets a little bit of 'appearance' money for getting you in the door, he gives you a pleasant ride round town, he teaches you a few words of Indonesian, he lets you out to take a few photos, he shows you a bit of Yogya. You can tour round with him all day and it will not cost you more than £4. When you get to a shop, just tap him on the shoulder and say, 'Look, I do not mind you getting a bit of commission, but if it is anything ridiculous like 40 per cent, I'm simply not buying!' You cannot cut him out completely. After all, you are paying a middleman, whether you know it or not, whenever you buy a pair of shoes from a shop in London, so why not here? However, before you board your *becak*, you *must* make it clear whether you are going shopping or sightseeing. If you do not mind seeing some shops, you can get an hour's ride for 500rps. If you do not want to see any shops, you must say so and the fare will automatically double or triple. If you do just want to take a ride, it is much better to stop a *becak* on the street. The ones who sit outside hotels are usually the people who want business.

SIGHTS

The sights of Yogya are nothing special. The Bird Market, the Water Castle, the *Kraton* are okay, but do not expect wonders. The real attractions of the city are the friendly people, the good shopping, the big indoor market, the small outdoor market, and, of course, the music and dance.

Hire yourself a *becak* for the morning

and take a ride down to the **Sultan's Palace** (*Kraton*). Built in 1756, one year after Hamengku Buwono I became the first Sultan of Yogya, this vast complex of courtyards, halls and pavilions – virtually a city within a city – gives little hint of its glorious past. 'I should mention', wrote Raffles in an 1812 report, 'that the Kraton was a regular fortified position about three miles in circumference, surrounded by a wide and deep ditch, with a wall forty-five feet high...'. Drawbridges further protected the *Kraton's* five massive arched gates in typical European fashion. Today, the moat is long gone. The 4-m thick, 3-m high walls are partly hidden behind crowded neighbourhoods. The gates, massive and still imposing, stand like memorial arches over roads buzzing with traffic. A series of open courtyards display *gamelan* instruments, portraits of former sultans and various gifts from Europe, but the *Kraton* lost most of its treasures when the British looted it in 1812 and took away an estimated US$7 million worth of goods. Instead of pomp and splendour, the *Kraton* now offers peace and tranquillity. Though spruced up for the recent coronation of the new sultan (Hamengku Buwono X) in March 1989, it remains a simple, straightforward example of classical Javanese architecture, its ornate carvings and heavily gilded beams testifying to its royal origin. When you get here, let the obligatory guide (500rps) take you round. He will make it come alive. He will also probably show you round the backstreets, where small cottage industries beaver away making batik and jewellery for the royal family. Some 20,000 people live within the palace complex, while the Sultan himself resides in a rather modest building just east of the pavilion, painted ivory-yellow, called the 'Gedong Kuning'. The *Kraton* is open only from 8.30 a.m. to 12 noon and there is usually a rehearsal of *gamelan* music (as performed by the court musicians) in one of the pavilions in the inner courtyards from 10.30 a.m. to noon on Mondays and Wednesdays. You can also see classical dancing here on Sundays from 10.30 a.m. to noon.

Behind the *Kraton* is **Taman Sari** or the Water Castle. Built in 1758 by Hamengku Buwono I as a beautifully landscaped pleasure garden, it is now a ruined complex of canals and pools, damaged beyond repair by war and earthquake. The actual Water Castle is an enclosed bathing pool used by the ladies of the harem. From the pavilion above, the sultan used to make his selection for the night. Hire a local guide for a small tip. He will show you the underground mosque, then the underground tunnel (now blocked up) which ran 23 km all the way to Parangritis

beach. In the old days, when the sultan wanted to recruit 'new talent', he sent his army down the tunnel to shanghai local lovelies from the beach! The small lanes of the Water Castle area are good for a wander. There are several small batik shops round here, including **Batik Asli**, which has a songbird trained to sing the Indonesian national anthem!

Songbirds are big business in Yogya. At **Pasar Burung** (Bird Market), located right next to the Water Castle, competition winners can command prices of up to 10 million *rupiah*! Most birds are imported from Thailand, just as fighting cocks are brought in from Bangkok. The Bird Market itself is a seedy world of caged birds, dogs, cats and monkeys.

OUT OF YOGYA

There are several places around Yogya worth a day-trip or even an overnight stay. Don't bother with organised tours sold by hotels or travel agents; you can save time, trouble and money by doing it yourself.

Borobodur is one of South-East Asia's most famous temples, standing majestic on a hillock at Magelang, 42 km north west of Yogya. Its name probably derives from the Sanskrit words *vihara Buddha uhr'*, or the 'Buddhist monastery on the hill'. Constructed in the eighth century by the Cailendra dynasty, it is believed to have taken 10,000 workers ten years to build and is today the largest Buddhist shrine in existence. It is also the biggest jigsaw in the world. Left for 1,000 years to fall into decline, it was rediscovered as a pile of rubble in 1814, while Raffles was governor of Java. The Americans, through UNESCO, put a lot of money into Borobodur and, because of poor drainage on the original site, rebuilt it completely around a new drainage system. That is how they know there are two million pieces in it – it was the ultimate jigsaw puzzle, costing several millions of dollars to reassemble.

Borobodur is not spectacular in terms of any great height, size or span. It is low and compact. Built entirely of grey andesite stone, it rises nine terraces – seven rectangular bases, each smaller than the one below it, with two circular tiers on top surrounding the 40-m high Great Stupa. There are approximately 2 km of walking round the terraces, which have 1460 carved friezes on them, depicting various aspects of the Buddha and his life. Though Borobodur is not a monument you stand back and rave over, it has stood the test of time very well. Interestingly, if you stand at the base of it, you cannot see the top. Certain theologians have speculated that Borobodur was built as a symbol of life – i.e. when you start off in life, you cannot see what's at the end. At first, your path is laid out

Becak drivers

The Borobodur temple, near Yogyakarta

for you by parents, teachers, etc., so the first few terraces have high walls containing lots of information (instructive bas reliefs). But then, as you get older, your horizons broaden out and so the walls drop a bit. Finally, as you reach your prime, life (hopefully) becomes easier and less complicated and the terraces suddenly give way to a round and the walls disappear altogether. The idea is that, by the time you reach old age, there is nothing left to restrict your happiness. It is a really nice story.

Borobodur is one and a half hours' drive from Yogya – first by bus from Umbulharjo terminal to Muntilan (450rps), then another on to Borobodur (250rps). Watch out for pickpockets on the buses. On arrival, pay your 2000rps admission fee and pick up a copy of Dr Soediman's *Glimpses of Borobodur* (also 2000rps) from the ticket desk. There are a few cheap *losmen* nearby if you need to stay overnight, although I do not know why you would.

Prambanan, 17 km out of Yogya on the Solo road, is also worth a visit. As impressive as Borobodur, in intricacy if not in size – this large Hindu temple complex is dedicated to Shiva and dates to around the ninth century AD. Built in the traditional style of Hindu architecture, it is your big chance (if you haven't been to India) of seeing a little bit of India without the Indians! The main Shiva shrine, flanked by two others to Vishnu and Brahma, is 50 m high and contains statues to Shiva, his consort Durga and his elephant-headed son Ganesh. It has fine carvings both inside and out and the parapets are adorned with bas reliefs depicting the Ramayana epic. Restoration on the 16 temples in the central courtyard, and on the 224 shrines in the outlying compound, will shortly make Prambanan the most beautiful Hindu temple in Indonesia. It is already the biggest.

To get there, hop on any Solo bus or colt from Yogya. Or go by bicycle. Like Borobodur, Prambanan is open from 6 a.m. to 6 p.m. and is best visited (for quiet and photos) in the early morning or early evening. Admission is 100rps and you can hire guides at the entrance for 1000rps. See the 'entertainment' section for details of full moon dance shows at Prambanan – unmissable!

Kaliurang, 25 km north of Yogya, is the cool mountain resort on the southern slope of Mt Merapi where people go to climb the volcano (which erupts every five years or so) or simply to escape Yogya's heat and noise. It is a very relaxing spot, with pleasant walks, clean fresh air, waterfalls and a swimming pool. Some crowds arrive at the weekend, but during the week you have the place more or less to yourself. The

only problem with Kaliurang is that it is the difficult side of Merapi to walk up. If you want to see sunrise from the summit (worth it for the spectacular views) you have got a pretty horrendous six-hour hike up there in the dark. Most travellers stay with helpful Christian at **Vogel's** *losmen*. He gives instructions for climbing every night, wakes you up at 11.30 p.m., gives you a lunch-packet, loans you a lamp and even offers a guide (although you do not really need one). All you need are warm clothes to climb in (Merapi gets cold at night) and decent walking shoes. Vogel's has great information, clean rooms (3500rps per person) and good cheap food. Once you have climbed Merapi, ask Christian to direct you to the small village five hours' walk from Kaliurang where traditional dance shows are held three times a week. It is not touristy and you can stay there overnight. At dawn, the road leading down to Yogya from Kaliurang is full of great markets. It is worth losing some sleep to see them!

The common approach to Kaliurang is by colt (regular departures, 700rps) from Jln Mataram in Yogya. There are also four buses a day (300rps) from Umbulharjo bus-station.

ENTERTAINMENT

Classical dance and *gamelan* music can be seen to good advantage at the *Kraton* (cf. page 162), but nothing compares with the **Ramayana Ballet** at Prambanan. This takes place on full moon nights between May and October and features nearly 100 dancers and musicians performing on a huge open-air stage, the spot-lit temple providing the perfect backdrop. Performances run over four consecutive nights each month and each night tells a different part of the Ramayana tale. Most guest houses/travel agents sell tickets (7000rps), which include transport there and back. For an additional 5500rps, you can also take dinner there. During the rainy season, the Ramayana Ballet is performed every Thursday evening at the new closed theatre. **Dalem Pujokusuman** in Jln Katamso also offers Ramayana dance (Monday, Wednesday and Friday nights, 4000rps) as well as non-costumed dance instruction at 4 p.m. daily.

Until about 20 years ago, *wayang kulit* or shadow-puppet plays used to be the main form of entertainment at Javanese weddings, an incentive for the party of relatives and friends to stay the night and help with the preparations. Then TV and videos came along and nobody watched shadow-puppets any more. **Agastya Art Institute** at Jln Gedongkiwo MJ III/237 was formed in an attempt to revive what was a dying art. Here, young musicians train under the old and the tradition is handed down unbroken. It has been a very successful experiment, greatly helped by the tourist trade. Agastya has daily shows (except Saturday) from 3 p.m. to 5 p.m. and a minimum donation of US$1 is charged. You may never see a professional performance here, because they are always training people, but it is informal enough for you to wander round taking photos and you need not feel obliged to sit through the whole thing – about half an hour is enough for most punters! The *dalang* (story-teller) is the main man. He works the puppets and leads the orchestra. In a traditional setting, he ad libs the script according to local circumstances, occasionally ribbing the villagers or sometimes paying compliments to the family. Here, he is lucky if he can hold the band together – musicians quite often stop for a chat, or wander off, or pass along the cigarettes. It is really that informal! If you want to see something more polished, the Arjuna Plaza hotel has proper *wayang kulit* shows from 7 to 9 p.m. every Tuesday – 2000rps well spent. *Wayang goleg* (wooden puppet) plays take place at Nitour Inc, Jln KHA Dahlan 71, from 11 a.m. to 1 p.m. except Sunday.

There is great *gamelan* music from noon to 1 p.m. and from 5 to 7 p.m. daily in the lobby of the Garuda Hotel, just up from the TIC tourist office. Savour it over a slice of lemon cheesecake and a cup of real coffee – at 4600rps it is a worth-while extravagance! The Podo Moro music shop next door has a wide selection of *gamelan* cassettes and the tourist office can suggest some good titles. If you want to learn *gamelan*, ask around. One reliable teacher is Toto – ask for him at the museum facing the north square. He teaches one of the *gamelan* orchestras from the Sultan's palace, and is very happy to give people instruction.

The best disco by all accounts, is the **Rainbow**, attached to Mutiara Hotel in Malioboro St. It is very central (so there is no problem getting home late at night) and it is close to several restaurants. The 4000rps admission fee includes one free drink and the 8-9 p.m. happy hour at the hotel bar is ideal for a pre-boogie beer.

SHOPPING

Yogya is the batik centre of Java and there are literally hundreds of shops, studios, galleries and factories selling batik materials and paintings. Unlike Solo, where most batik fabrics are press-printed by machine, in Yogya they are mainly hand-made. Expect, therefore, to pay a little extra. Batik is an age-old process of dyeing cloth painted in patterns with the aid of molten wax. It was first invented by the Persians and Egyptians and was introduced to Indonesia around the thirteenth century by early traders. The Javanese took the art to their heart and in the case of Yogyakarta brought it to perfection. Traditionally, the design is drawn on paper, then traced onto the cloth using a copper funnel (*chanting*) filled with hot wax. It is a very skilled process. The wax has got to be the correct temperature and it has to be drawn onto the cloth with quick, definite strokes. If the wax gets too hot, it will run everywhere. If it is too cold, it sits on top of the fabric and doesn't penetrate the dye. The areas of the cloth on which colour is not required are covered with wax, while the rest is left free to be dyed a new colour. A batik is built up like an oil-painting, with a series of wax-and-dye colour introductions. They start with a light colour like yellow and the stronger ones are added at the end. At each stage, the wax is boiled out or scraped back, ready for the next colour application. The final design sometimes takes a month or more to achieve. A batik is generally priced by (a) the number of colours in it, and (b) the time it takes to make it. A high-grade batik (and I do not think you are likely to see many of these in Yogya any more – is waxed on *both* sides. In this case, the design is equally clear front and back.

You get two different kinds of picture batik in Yogya – one where the artist does it himself (he does the waxing, he paints the design, he actually applies some of the colour by hand as well) and one where the artist's work is mass-produced (the cloth is laid over the paper-pattern of his original piece and an exact copy pencilled onto it). Most batiks sold in shops, especially the ones with traditional Ramayana designs, are copies. The only guaranteed originals nowadays are modernistic abstracts produced by younger artists. You know their work is original because abstracts are extremely difficult to copy. The main thing is, do not buy the first day. So many people do and find, to their chagrin, that what they were assured was an original piece is, in fact, an assembly-line copy. As with anything, the surest guide to quality is the human eye. Take your time with looking at batik – does it look like a free drawing or does it look like a tracing? If it has been traced, it will quickly appear static. An original picture, by contrast, has got interest. You never get bored with it, because it says something different each time you look at it. You can always tell when a batik painting has been done by a top artist – it has a definite rhythm and flow, and contains a lot of information. The word batik comes from *banyak tik-tik*, which means a mass of descriptive dots. A good batik should therefore have a lot of *tik-tiks* in it. It is worth noting that most copies are outlined in white. This is because copiers often draw everything in white before adding the layers of colour. A good artist, however, doesn't do his first drawing in white, he uses a combination of colours to start with, in order to create a variety of tones. Like Manet, he can create the illusion of one colour at a distance – say, mauve – which, up-close, is a mixture of violet and blue.

Yogya is now mainly making batiks for money, not art. If you go direct to an artist, his price will be high. This is because he can sell an original to an art-shop and pick up lots of commissions by signing numerous copies of it. At present, the five artists of high repute are Amriyaha and Parasinta (modern-school), Affandi (realistic), Astuti (sur-realist) and Saptohudoyo (decorative). These guys produce mainly large canvases from 100,000rps up to two million *rupiah*, depending on the amount of work involved. There are also a number of up-and-coming young artists whose work is considerably cheaper. Their paintings, if you hunt around, probably represent the best investment. The **Something Different** gallery at Lotus Cafe in Prawirotaman is a good place to start. Friendly Marsha is full of useful tips and information. With regard to batik material, do not buy in the market. Go to the stores on Malioboro St that are full of Indonesians, not foreigners. There is high-quality stuff here, at fixed prices. Alternatively, visit the **Batik Research Centre** at Jln Kusumanegara 2, about 3 km east of town. This is where new material designs are tried out and you can find sarongs of a very unusual style, Chinese-influenced, with red and blue. The research centre also offers a very thorough three-month course in batik. Several places offer shorter batik courses – the three- and five-day 'intensive' course run by Dr Hadyir at the main entrance to the Water Castle and the one-day course offered by Tulus Warsito at Jln Titodipuran 19a, are both good value at US$4 per day. All materials are provided and you take out what you make.

Note: once you have bought your batik, look after it. Like any artwork, it will fade if left in direct sunlight. Also, because it contains chemical dyes, expect it to run if not washed carefully – use warm water, at the very most.

Silver is a pretty good buy. Here, you have basically a basic choice between traditional Yogya styles and more modern Bali designs – the former have 88 per cent silver content and the latter 92.5 per cent. All silver is stamped, so it is easy to check which is which! To see a traditional silver-works, using original tools and techniques to hand-craft royal jewellery and ornaments, visit **Sri Moeljo's Siiver** at Jln Menteri Supeno. For fashion jewellery, try **Yasir Silver** at Jln Tirodi-puran 2, Prawirotaman. Most of his stuff comes from the village of Kotagede, 6 km out of Yogya. To go there yourself, catch an orange city bus 1 or 4 (150rps, 30 minutes) from the TIC tourist office.

The Main Market in Malioboro St (open till 4 p.m.) is a vast covered labyrinth of shops and stalls selling second-hand sarongs, shirts, beachwear, etc. at low prices, provided you bargain hard and pay only half of what you are first asked! Take a torch to check for defects, since it is dark inside. Malioboro St has any number of pavement sellers vending children's clothes (amazingly cheap), leather bags and sunglasses. There are also many little boutiques with jackets/skirts from 25 to 35,000rps, tops around 20,000rps and T-shirts for 7500rps. Prima Mini-Market on Malioboro is the cheapest place in Yogya to buy beer and spirits. This is where all the local hotels come to stock up their bars!

ACCOMMODATION

There is no problem finding somewhere nice to stay in Yogya. This town is full of cheap and cheerful accommodation. Ask around, new places are appearing all the time.

Hotel Garuda (tel: 86353) at Jln Malioboro 60 is *the* hotel in the centre of town. Modern and elegant, with a pool, a restaurant-bar, many facilities and rooms from US$46 single, US$55 double (plus 15.5 per cent taxes), it is an all-round good deal. The nearby **Mutiara Hotel** (tel: 4531) at Jln Malioboro 18 is similarly priced and equally popular. For a stylish stay out of town, try **Sahid Garden Hotel** (tel: 3697) at Jln Babarsari, 7 km down the road to Prambanan. Rooms here start at US$45 single, US$55 double (plus taxes) and there is a pool, a restaurant-bar and 4-star facilities.

Down south in Jln Prawirotaman, there is a different brand of traveller. Most of the guest houses here have a bit of a garden, some have a pool and the atmosphere is friendly and cosy, rather like a big family! Several places offer three classes of accommodation: cheap rooms with shared *mandi*, fan room with own bath and air-conditioned room with own bath. Breakfast is usually included in the price of rooms. Three guest houses of special note are **Airlangga** at Nos. 6-8 (tel: 3344, rooms from 20,000rps fan, 26,000rps air-conditioning), **Borobudur** at No. 5 (tel: 3977, fan doubles at 12,500rps, three-person family rooms at 15,000rps) and **Metro** at Prawirotaman MG 7/71 (tel: 5004, rooms from 7500 fan to 23,000rps air-conditioning). There are many others.

The Prambanan temple, near Yogyakarta

Budget travellers tend to stay in and around Jln Sosrowijayan, below the railway station. This area is more central, with a whole batch of inexpensive *losmen* to choose from. Backpacker favourites along Sosrowijayan include **Hotel Asiatic** (2500rps per person), **Hotel Kartika** (5000rps doubles, 7500rps triples), **Dewi Homestay** at Nos 66-68 (3000rps single, 5000rps double) and **Jaya** down Gang 2 ('It is quiet and much water.' 2500rps one person, 3000rps for two). **Hotel Puri**, off Jln Malioboro at Sosrokusuman 22, is still good value at 3500rps double, or 4500/5000rps with fan. All the above places handle bus/train reservations and offer sightseeing tours.

FOOD

The speciality in Yogya is *nasi gudeg*, rice with young jackfruit cooked in coconut milk. It is served in Indonesian restaurants all over town. The *gudeg* of **Bu Citro's** on Jln Adisucipto, just outside the airport, is particularly famous. For cheap local snacks like *nasi padang*, *nasi rames*, *martabak* (Arabian pancakes) and *sate*, check out the *warungs* along Jln Pasar Kembang – **Mama's** in particular – and (after 9 p.m.) the street-stalls on Jln Malioboro.

In Jln Prawirotaman, two pleasant garden restaurants, **Hanoman Forest** and **Palm House**, offer nightly puppet shows/ *gamelan* along with mid-priced European/Chinese/Indonesian food. In the same road, **Lotus Cafe** has a special vegetarian menu (try the *gudeg ayam*) and mellow *gamelan* sounds. Like **Tante Lise**, on the corner of Jln Prawirotaman and Jln Parangritis, it is an ideal spot for a late-night beer. Tante Lise displays a 'personal recommendation' from the National Guard of Saudi Arabia and is apparently the only place in Indonesia where you can get half a chicken. 'It is very hard to explain to people in Indonesia that you want half a chicken,' said a friend of mine, 'so I told the lady at Tante Lise "One chicken – and cut it in half!" and she understood. It cost 2400rps and tasted fantastic. The next day, I went back and ordered another half a chicken and she said "So sorry – I'm *sold out*!"

Popular eating-places along Jln Malioboro are **Shinta's** (great iced drinks and snacks), **Colombo's** (big menu, Chinese/Indian fare) and **Helen's** (travellers' fast-food). The **Legian** at Jln Perwakilan 9 is a relaxing rooftop restaurant with first-rate Western/ Indonesian cuisine and an attached snooker hall – shoot some pool while waiting for your meal! Round the corner in Sosrowijayan, **Hotel Asiatic** does 'scrummy banana pancakes', while **Superman II** and **Anna's** (both down Gang 2) are typical ethnic travellers' haunts with chips, shakes, pancakes, fruit salad and popcorn. Who could ask for anything more?

SOLO (SALA or SURAKARTA)

It is very strange how Yogya has caught all the tourist trade, and Solo, just 64 km down the road, has not. I say strange, because most Westerners, myself included, agree that Solo is just as good a town as Yogya. An instantly likeable place of broad, airy streets and relaxed people, the traffic never approaches Yogya levels and the air is fresh and cool. Travellers like Solo for three reasons: – it is very cheap, there are no mosquitoes and you do not get hassled for business. If this weren't enough, it has everything that Yogya has – antiques and batik, *gamelan* and dance, museums and palaces, markets and crafts – only without the crowds and the hard sell. The obvious stop on the overland trail between Yogya and Malang/Bromo, Solo has an atmosphere all of its own, very relaxed, very 'Indonesian', and many people much prefer it to anywhere else in Java.

HISTORY

Solo's transformation from forest village to seat of the Mataram kingdom took place in 1745, when Pakubuwono II abandoned his previous capital of Kartosuro (12 km west) and moved into his newly completed *kraton* here. After his death in 1755, the dynasty split in three: his uncle became the first Sultan of Yogyakarta, his son became *susuhunan* of the main (Surakarta) *kraton* in Solo and his son's dissident cousin became Mangkunegoro I of a small, separate court within Solo's domain. By 1866, this city had two rival *kratons*, along with an unsavoury reputation for endorsing Dutch rule. Solo's support of the Dutch during the Diponegoro revolt of 1825-30 was considered the supreme act of betrayal by most Javanese and as soon as Indonesia became a republic in 1950, the sultan was stripped of all his authority.

ARRIVAL/DEPARTURE

Air

Garuda flies twice a day to Solo from Jakarta and Denpasar. From the airport to town (10 km) is around 7000rps by taxi.

Rail

There are daily trains to Yogya (one hour), Malang (eight hours), Bandung (ten hours), Probollingo (12 hours), Jakarta (12-14 hours) and Bali (two days). Solo's railway station is north of town on Jln Balapan. If arriving here, it

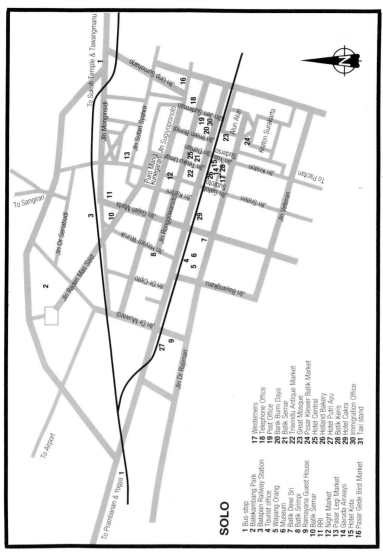

SOLO

1 Bus-stop
2 Balekambang Park
3 Balapan Railway Station
4 Tourist office
5 Wayang Orang
6 Museum
7 Batik Dewi Sri
8 Batik Srimpi
9 Ramayana Guest House
10 Batik Semar
11 RRI
12 Night Market
13 Pasar Legi Market
14 Garuda Airways
15 Hotel Kota
16 Pasar Gede Bird Market
17 Westerners
18 Telephone Office
19 Post Office
20 Bank Bumi Daya
21 Batik Semar
22 Triwindu Antique Market
23 Great Mosque
24 Pasar Klewer Batik Market
25 Hotel Central
26 Holland Bakery
27 Hotel Putri Ayu
28 Batik Keris
29 Hotel Cakra
30 Immigration Office
31 Taxi stand

is 700rps by *becak* (or 5000rps by taxi) to the hotel area off Jln Slamet Riyadi.

Road

You can reserve air-conditioned express bus seats for Bali (14 hours, 19,000rps), Bandung (10,000rps), Jakarta (ll,000-rps), Malang (9000rps), Bogor (12,500rps) and Probollingo, at Westerners *losmen* or at the main bus-station, 3 km from the town centre. Fast non-stop minibuses leave for Yogya (two hours, 1500rps) every half-hour from the Elteha office, Jln Hongowonso 90. They are quicker than regular buses or colts and drop you right at the door of your hotel/*losmen*. For Prambanan temple, hop on any Jakarta-bound bus from the bus-station (500rps, two hours). If you want to go to Borobodur, take a bus to

Magelang (1500rps), then another to Borobodur (700rps, 40 minutes).

TOURIST SERVICES

The small tourist office (tel: 6508) at Jln Slamet Riyadi 235 is open from 7 a.m. to 5 p.m., closed Sundays. The staff are very helpful – they even plan your day's sightseeing for you – but their information can be confused. Good handouts though and bus/rail timings are posted on the board.

The GPO is located at Jln Sudirman 7c, behind the police station. It is open from 8 a.m. to 8 p.m., closed Sundays. Across the road is the telephone office, open 24 hours for overseas calls. Change money at Bank Bumi Daya on Jln Slamet Riyadi, or Bank Negara Indonesia 1946 at Jln Jen Sudirman 19, both open from 8 a.m. to 2 p.m. weekdays, until 12 noon Saturdays. Flights can be confirmed at the main Garuda office at Kusuma Sahid Prince Hotel.

TRANSPORT AROUND TOWN

Probably your best way of discovering Solo is to hire a *becak* for the day. It is far cheaper than taking lots of short hops. Like Yogya, Solo has an excess of unemployed *becak* riders. Unlike Yogya, none of them bother you for business. A convenient double-decker bus service (150rps) runs west to east along Jln Slamet Riyadi and Westerners *losmen* hires out bicycles for 1000rps per day. Most people, however, are content to walk. Solo is that kind of city.

SIGHTS

Do all your touring in the morning as everything closes around noon. Visit the batik/antique markets in the afternoon and finish off with a culture show in the evening. Allow three days to see everything at leisure.

The **Radya Pustaka Museum** on Jln Slamet Riyadi is a good place to start. Admission is 100rps and it is open from 8 a.m. to 1 p.m. Sunday, Tuesday, Wednesday, Thursday, 8 a.m. to 10.30 a.m. Friday, 8 a.m. to ll.30 a.m. Saturday, closed Monday. Here are gathered together a fascinating (albeit dusty) collection of *gamelan* sets, *wayang topeng* masks, dance costumes, leather/wooden puppets and folk artefacts, together with Dutch chandeliers, old mechanical clocks and 'very magic' *kris* knives. Out of the museum, if you are visiting on Sunday morning or any evening, you can pop next door to Wayang Orang for culture, or to the adjoining tourist office for information.

Tickets for **Surakarta Kraton** (open from 8.30 a.m. to 1 p.m., except Friday) are sold at Hayuningrat Tours at the north-east corner of the *kraton*. Admission is 600rps, camera fee is 1000rps and good English-speaking guides cost around 2000rps per hour. Some 60 per cent of the original *kraton* burned down in 1985 and the new version, although an exact reconstruction of the old, requires a guide to inject it with life. The destruction of the *kraton* was a catastrophe. The official reason for the fire was an electrical fault, but the people saw it as divine retribution both for the licentiousness of the present sultan and for centuries of past collaboration with the Dutch. In atonement, they consecrated the new *kraton* – which today they regard simply as a monument, devoid of any spiritual power – by burying the heads of a buffalo, a tiger, a snake, a deer, a monkey, a fish and a bird in the grounds. The sultan has promised to mend his ways and everybody is praying hard that the spirits will return to the *kraton* and reinvest it with the power which made it, for 200 years between 1745 and 1945, the spiritual centre of Java. The *kraton* itself covers an area of 54 hectares. Dotted around the reconstructed sections – the *pendopo* (king's audience hall), the dining hall, the library and heirloom room – are Dutch cannon, a Hindu watchtower, a Muslim minaret and statues of Persian pirates. The excellent museum contains over 1,000 years of history, including eighth-century Hindu/Buddhist bronzes and ancient Chinese porcelain. Look out for the three eighteenth-century Dutch-built royal carriages – the oldest one, Kyai Grudo, was presented by the Dutch to Pakubuwono II when he moved the capital here from Kartosuro in 1745. Elsewhere, there are weapons and costumes, masks and murals, demonic mastheads (once attached to eighteenth-century royal barges) and vast rice-cookers capable of making 40 kg worth of *nasi goreng* !

The smaller *kraton*, **Puro Mang-kunegaran** (open 9 a.m. to 1 p.m. Monday to Saturday, closes on Friday at 11.30 a.m.), also has English-speaking guides (included with the 500rps admission fee) and, of course, it is more authentic than the main *kraton*, not having been burnt down. Founded in 1757 by the renegade Prince Raden Mas Said, it is now Solo's main attaction. The *pendopo* is a vast dance-stage of Italian marble measuring 38 x 35 m. Each of its eight ceiling panels is painted a different colour – to protect the dancers and musicians against sleepiness (yellow), disease (blue), anger (black), evil (red), frustration (green), fear (orange), lust (white) and bad thoughts (purple). Above the *pendopo* is an outside verandah called the *pringgitan*, where royals still receive guests and view *wayang kulit* puppet plays from behind a screen. Beyond this is the *dhalem* or main ceremony hall, used only for weddings, coronations and funerals. Inside the *dhalem* is a fascinating museum of royal memorabilia, including a pure gold chastity-belt worn by the sultan. It was supposed to keep him out of trouble when he went on long expeditions. It is in four fragments now, suggesting that he failed.

Candi Sukuh, 40 km east of Solo, makes a good side-trip. This fourteenth-century Hindu temple, built on the western slope of the extinct volcano Lawu, is fascinating both for its erotic carvings and for its stepped pyramidal shape, reminiscent of ancient Maya. Candi Sukuh gets many people's vote as 'the holiest place in central Java', whatever that means. Certainly, the drive out there is beautiful, through the hills and rice paddies. Get a bus from Solo bus-station to Karangpandan via Tawang-mangu (300rps, one hour), then a colt (500rps, 30 minutes) up to Sukuh temple. Skip the walk to nearby Tawangmangu waterfall, described by one disappointed visitor as 'a tall stream of rubbish-filled, polluted water'.

ENTERTAINMENT

The Wayang Orang theatre in Surya entertainment complex, Jln Slamet Riyadi, offers shadow-puppet plays every evening (except Sunday) from 8.30 p.m. to ll p.m. and on Sunday mornings from 10 a.m. to l p.m. Admission is 350rps, plus 100rps entrance to the park. Costumes, make-up and acting are all first-rate – better than anything I've seen in Yogya. So is *wayang orang* at RRI, opposite the railway station. It takes place every third Tuesday and Saturday of the month, from 8 p.m. to midnight, at the home of Pak Anom Suroto.

Gamelan and dance practice sessions can be seen at Kraton Surakarta (Moro-koto Hall) every Sunday from 10 a.m. to noon, at Mangkunegaran Palace every Wednesday from 10 a.m. to noon and at ASKI music academy, Pageleran Alun Utara, daily (except Friday and Sunday) from 9 a.m. to 5 p.m.. *Gamelan* at the Kusuma Sahid Prince Hotel (4.30 to 6.30 p.m. daily) is a wonderfully slow and soporific reciting of the Ramayana – the best set in town apparently. This hotel also has a cool pool, which non-residents can use for 2000rps per day.

SHOPPING

Shopping in Solo is a far more relaxed experience than in Yogya. You can stay here a week and not one person will try to sell you anything. Since there is (as yet) no commission system for *becak* drivers, it is easy to bargain low prices on batik and antiques, which are the two best buys. Solo's batiks are deeper in colour than Yogya's – dark-brown to black, rather than yellow to light-brown – and their designs are more classic. The main batik market is **Pasar Klewer** (open 8 a.m. to 4 p.m.) on Jln Secoyudan. There is a lot of choice here, but mainly rolls of material and sarongs, not many paintings. With clever bargaining, you can get striking *lurik* shirts for 4000-6000rps and eye-catching sarongs for 5000 to 10,000rps. Quality can be very good, but colours do fade after a few months on a lot of items. Be very careful what you buy – check the reverse of the batik items and make sure that the pattern is standard and not cracked or blurred. Batik means 'same both sides' and it should look like it! In general, you are probably better off going to reputable factories like **Batik Srimpi** (hand-printed batik) and **Batik Semar** (press-printed batik) where you can see the process in the workshops and know you are buying quality. There is not much room for bargaining here, or at modern batik shops like **Batik Keris**, Jln Sudarso 37, but stunning sarongs in silk are still a snip at between 16,000 and 30,000rps and certain items, like quilted, hand-painted silk pillows (15,000rps apiece at Semar), you simply cannot find in the market.

The antique market of **Pasar Triwindu** is located down a side-alley off Jln Diponegoro 29, a short stroll from Kra-ton Mangkunegaran. The main 'anti-ques' on sale are bits of old cars, but if you poke around you will soon find a small section devoted to the real McCoy – old coins, cabinets, pottery, paintings, ex-turtles, Buddhas, shadow puppets and musical instruments. Bargain very hard. Several shops along Jln Slamet Riyadi, like **Toko Parto Art** at No. 103, sell Dutch-period memorabilia at reasonable prices. A lot of this stuff, particularly the furniture, is so cleverly faked that you will need written verification (saying they are *not* antique) in order to clear customs!

Novelty buys in Solo include children's clothes (two baby jumpsuits for less than £2 in the batik market) and sunglasses. Everyone in town wears sunglasses and the area fronting the main *kraton* is a mass of stalls selling nothing but sunglas-ses. Very strange!

ACCOMMODATION

Compared to Yogya, accommodation is very cheap. Solo's classiest establish-ment, the 4-star **Kusuma Sahid Prince Hotel** (tel: 6356), Jln Sugiyopranoto 20, is fantastic value at just US$38 single, US$45 double for standard rooms and US$55 for superior bungalows or suites. This is a traditional building, with a big pool, a *gamelan* hall and beautiful gar-dens. Originally a royal palace, it was completely rebuilt and renovated in 1976 to cater for tourists who want to 'live like a prince'. Even if you cannot afford to stay, ask for a tour of the Royal Suite – it is out of this world! **Mangkunegaran Palace Hotel** (tel: 5683) at Jln Man-gkunegarn is, by contrast, disappointing. This noble house has a small pool, gardens and air-conditioned rooms from US$16 single, US$19 double, but is in serious need of renovation. **Hotel Cakra** (tel: 5846) at Jln Riyadi 21 is a smart colonial-style place with all mod cons and well-priced rooms from 27,900rps single, 32,900rps double. It doesn't have a pool, but is very centrally located.

Ramayana Guest House (tel: 2184), a little way out of town at Jln Dr Wahidin 15, is ideal for couples who find Solo's cheaper *losmen* grim ('I would not touch them with a bargepole' was one com-ment) and who need somewhere quiet and clean to relax. Room prices start at

13,500rps (22,000rps with air-conditioning) and include a good breakfast and afternoon snack. The nearby **Hotel Dana** (tel: 3890) is a reasonable fallback, with similarly priced rooms and a certain old-world charm. **Losmen Putri Ayu** (tel: 6154) at Jln Slamet Riyadi 293 is fair value at 10,200rps fan, 20,400rps air-conditioned.

Budget accommodation can be a problem. Many backpackers hit Solo late at night – if from Malang, very late. The priority is to find a cheap room, any room, to collapse in for the night; something better can be tracked down in the morning. The first place to head for is **Westerners** (tel: 3106) at Kemlayan Kidul 11, a small alley running between Jln Gatot Subroto and Jln Yos Sudarso. Pak Mawardi and his family are wonderfully friendly people who have developed the art of hosting travellers to perfection. They offer small, clean rooms at 3500rps single, 4500rps double, two larger rooms at 7000rps, free tea and coffee, good information, bicycle rental, laundry service, Western breakfast and lots of outside eating areas. If full and this is common, try **Hotel Kota** at Jln Slamet Riyadi 113 (rooms from 6000rps, central location) or **Losmen Fortuna** at Jln Ronggowarsito 24 (rooms at 5000rps, near Westerners). If all else fails, you will have to spend a night at **Hotel Central** on Jln Achmad Dahlan. This place has poky, but clean, cells at 3500rps and gets very mixed reports. 'It is an art deco masterpiece – like a rough version of the Savoy in Brighton!', said one couple. 'We didn't have time to admire the architecture,' complained another, 'We were more concerned with the noisy staff, the centipedes in the toilets, and the vomit from past guests on the mirror in our room . . .'.

FOOD

Every area of Java has its speciality *nasi* dish. Solo's is *nasi liwet*, or coconut rice with chicken and vegetables. Solonese street food is excellent. Look out for *nasi pecel* (rice with green leaves, beansprouts and hot peanut sauce) and *kembal* (rice-cakes and noodles in sweet milk). *Nasi rames* is dry (rice with some noodles and a bit of everything) and *nasi soto* is much the same sort of thing, but with some sauce poured over it to make it into a soup. At the night market, which runs all the way down from Jln Teuku Umar to the main *kraton*, the *warungs* and stalls lay out loads of tempting little snacks, usually costing only 100 or 200rps per dish. You can eat your fill, trying a bit of this and a bit of that, for under 2000rps a head. The night market is particularly famous for its chicken rice and *susu* drinks. Walk down Jln Slamet

Riyadi and you will find 30 or 40 little stalls selling *srabis* – light crispy pancakes with rice pudding, absolutely delicious. There are good Western eats (chips, toast, pancakes, breakfasts) at **Warung Makan Serba Ada**, opposite Hotel Central and cheap beer/Indonesian snacks at nearby **Warung Gaya Baru**. Two good bakeries cum Western restaurants are **New Holland Pub & Restaurant** on Slamet Riyadi and **La Tansa Bakery** down Imam Bonjol. **American Donut** on Jln Slamet Riyadi has popcorn, hot dogs and burgers. Right next door is **Makan Moesik**, a cosy air-conditioned video bar showing Western films (entrance 3000rps, free before 10 p.m.). **Mataram** restaurant, opposite the tourist office, offers good Chinese food and the big **Hotel Cakra** offers special Javanese set lunches and dinners at 4500rps per head.

MOUNT BROMO

From April to October, when skies are clear and sunrises good, Bromo is probably the highlight of any Indonesian tour. The rest of the year, when rains are frequent and spectacular sunrises few, it is often a waste of time. You can most conveniently visit Bromo as a stopover between Solo/Yogya and Bali, but do bypass it for Malang if the weather looks sour!

This active 2302-m-high volcano stands within a vast 12 km wide crater, which is the moonscape 'sea of sand' you walk across to the rim. Just to its right is the almost perfect cone of Mt Batok, while on the opposite (south) side is Java's highest peak, Mt Semeru, at 3676 m. Since 1950, when Bromo had its last major eruption, there have been several minor eruptions. One took place on 5 June 1981, when hundreds of backpackers were up on the crater waiting for the sunrise. They all fled in panic – none of them thought to take a photograph. On another occasion, in 1987, the volcano blew out a lot of ash and gas, changing the colour of the crater basin from orange-brown to grey-black.

There is a certain thrill of excitement to climbing Bromo. It is home to the fire god Betoro Bromo and you just do not know when he's next going to lose his temper! His sporadic moans and groans bring instant offerings from the Tengerrese people who inhabit the surrounding area. They are a gentle, friendly people with almost Tibetan features, who are believed to be descended from refugees from the ancient Hindu-Javanese kingdom of Majapahit. Once a year, on the fourteenth day of the last month of the Tengerrese year (usually February), they all troop up to the lip of the crater at midnight for the annual appeasement

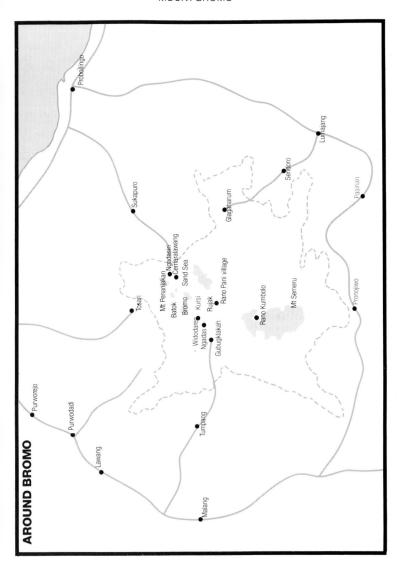

AROUND BROMO

Probolinggo

Lumajang

Sukapuro

Senturo

Pasirian

Glagaharum

Mt Penanjakan Ngadasiri
Cemaralawang
Sand Sea
Rano Pani village

Tosari

Batok
Bromo Kursi
Rujak
Widodaren
Ngadas
Gubugklakah

Rano Kumbolo

Mt Semeru

Pronojiwo

Purworejo

Purwodadi

Tumpang

Lawang

Malang

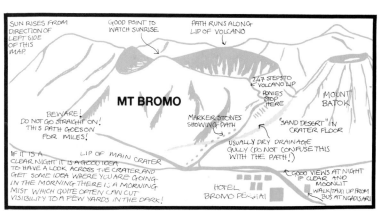

SUN RISES FROM DIRECTION OF LEFT SIDE OF THIS MAP.

GOOD POINT TO WATCH SUNRISE

PATH RUNS ALONG LIP OF VOLCANO

MT BROMO

247 STEPS TO VOLCANO LIP
PONIES STOP HERE

MOUNT BATOK

BEWARE!
DO NOT GO STRAIGHT ON! THIS PATH GOES ON FOR MILES!

MARKER STONES SHOWING PATH

"SAND DESERT" IN CRATER FLOOR

USUALLY DRY DRAINAGE GULLY (DO NOT CONFUSE THIS WITH THE PATH!)

IF IT IS A CLEAR NIGHT IT IS A GOOD IDEA TO HAVE A LOOK ACROSS THE CRATER AND GET SOME IDEA WHERE YOU ARE GOING IN THE MORNING. THERE IS A MORNING MIST WHICH QUITE OFTEN CAN CUT VISIBILITY TO A FEW YARDS IN THE DARK!

LIP OF MAIN CRATER

HOTEL BROMO PERMAI

GOOD VIEWS AT NIGHT IF CLEAR AND MOONLIT
WALK/TAXI UP FROM BUS AT NGADISARI

ceremony of Kasada. It is a magical experience – the best time of all to visit Bromo.

ARRIVAL/DEPARTURE

Bromo is most commonly approached via the town of Probollingo on the main Yogya-Surabaya road. Probollingo is ll hours by train from Yogya (dep. 7.30 a.m. daily, 3500rps third class), six hours by bus from Banyuwangi (2700rps) and two hours by bus from Malang (1400rps). From the minibus station in Probollingo (2000rps by *becak* from the new bus terminal) you can take a colt (1000rps, two hours) up to Ngadasiri village, a few kilometres below Bromo. If you arrive after 5 p.m., when the colt service stops, charter a minibus to Ngadasiri (12,500rps for up to 12 people, one hour) from Wira Bromo Travel Service, 50 m from the bus-station. Or stay overnight in Probollingo at the **Ratna Hotel**, a short 500rps *becak* ride from the bus or train station. This place looks luxurious, but has nice economy rooms from 3500rps double including breakfast. Good cheap local food is served at **Warung Nekmat**, only a few doors down from Wira Bromo Travel, although Probollingo's best cuisine is found at **Panorama** restaurant, some 3-km out of town on the way to Bromo (150rps by *bemo*).

On arrival in Ngadasiri, report to the office at the bus-station to pay your entrance fee (1000rps) to the Bromo national park. Then brace yourself for the steep 3-km hike up the hill (40 minutes) to Cemoro Lawang at the rim of the crater. If you don't want to walk you can go up by taxi for 1000rps per person. Ngadasiri has a few cheap *losmen* (**Yoschi's Guest House**, 2 km before Ngadasiri, is particularly nice) but most travellers continue straight on to **Hotel Bromo Permai** at Cemoro Lawang. It is then far less of a walk to the volcano in the morning. The Bromo Permai has cheap dormitory rooms from 3500rps, better rooms from 10,000 to 33,750rps and a nice-looking bar-restaurant. Don't eat here though – the food is terrible. Take an ice-cold beer, by all means, to recover from the walk up, but stroll back 100 m to the **Cafe Lava** for your evening meal. Don't feel obliged to stay at the Permai either – all the way up the hill from Ngadasiri to Cemoro Lawang, villagers are out offering cheap *losmen* accommodation at around 2/3000rps per person, inclusive of breakfast. The Permai is, however, the only place with electricity, although the generator shuts down at 10 p.m. sharp.

When you are ready to leave Bromo, go down to the small tourist information office at Ngadasiri. It sells seats on daily express buses to Denpasar (10,500 to 12,500rps), Yogya (9000 to 14,000rps) and Jakarta (25,000rps). Alternatively, take a public minibus (regular departures from 7 a.m. to 9.30 a.m.) down to Probollingo, and then an express bus (9 a.m., 10 a.m., ll a.m., 5750rps) to Denpasar or a regular bus to Yogya/Solo/Malang. Trains from Probollingo to Banyuwangi, for Bali, offer good scenery and are not as crowded in third class as Javanese trains usually are.

SIGHTS

Depending on the time of year, your hotel/*losmen* will wake you between 3 a.m. and 3.30 a.m. for breakfast. The idea then is to make a leisurely one and a half hour trek to the inner rim of the volcano, arriving just in time for the sunrise. It is not a very popular idea, but most people manage it. Whatever you do, do not miss breakfast – hiking up a volcano with nothing but a malaria tablet in your stomach is *not* a pleasant experience, take it from me! On the walk up to the crater, take it easy. Quite apart from the altitude, you do not want to reach the top with too much of a sweat on. It is very cold up there at night – around 36-41°F (2-5°C) June to September and 50-59°F (10-15°C) November to May. Take along some warm clothing and/or a sleeping bag and equip yourself with good walking shoes, an umbrella/waterproof (in case of rain) and a torch.

From the Bromo Permai hotel, it is an easy 3-km stroll out to the crater. Walk up the hill, down the other side and look out for the small path (right) leading down to the crater basin. Then follow the series of white markers across the sand to Bromo. If lost, just follow the line of ponies being led by the locals (they charge 6000rps for the return trip if you are too lazy to walk!). The final leg, which even the ponies cannot help you with, is a stiff climb up 247 steps to the crater rim. Most people turn left at the top and take only a few steps before stopping to watch the sunrise. Adventurous types turn right at the top of the steps, walk l.5 km round the rim, take in the sunrise without the crowds, go down to Ranopani (a scenic three-hour stroll), hop on a jeep to Ngadas, do the pleasant 13-km walk to Gubugklakah, and make Malang via Tumpang (two colt trips) by nightfall.

Don't feel obliged to see Bromo at night. The crater itself is just as impressive during the day as it is by sunrise, when you march with hundreds of others and wait for the sun amid much chatter. However, if you do go up for dawn, don't, like the local tourists, vanish as soon as the sunrise happens. Hang around for a while and get some decent photos!

Early morning mist around Mount Bromo

Mount Bromo crater

MALANG

Situated in the mountains 90 km south of Surabaya, Malang is one of Java's most attractive towns and a nice spot to rest up for a few days as it is cool, untouristy and fairly relaxed. Travellers stop here for thouree reasons: to break the long journey between Bali and Yogya, to make the approach to Mt Bromo (Malang is a far more livable base than Probollingo) and to jump off to the little-visited plantations and nature parks of east Java.

Malang is the kind of place one instinctively likes. Developed in the late eighteenth century as a coffee-growing centre, it still has a perceptible colonial air. In the town centre, leafy parks and gardens vie for attention with tall-steepled churches and old Dutch hotels and mansions. Up in the hills, the recreational resorts of Batu and Selecta provide excellent scenery and walks. Dotted around town and on the outskirts too, grotesque military monuments (the legacy of Sukarno) contrast vividly with rustic Hindu temples dating back to the tenth century. Malang's elevation of 450 m means that it enjoys an eternal springtime – temperatures rarely rise over 75°F (24°C).

ARRIVAL/DEPARTURE
Air
Merpati offers daily flights to and from Jakarta, Bali and Lombok. Their office is at Jln Jagung Suprapto 50 (tel: 27962).

Road
There are two direct buses a day from Bali: the non air conditioned Bali Indah (8250rps) and the Simpatik air conditioned (10,750rps). The cheapest bus seats to Bali from Malang are sold by Bali Indah (8000rps) at Pattimura bus-stand. For Solo, there is a choice of a train (dep. 1.30 p.m., arr. 9.30 p.m., 8000rps second class, 5800rps third class), a direct night air conditioned bus (dep 7 p.m., arr 4 a.m., 9000rps) and a few day buses via Kediri. Malang to Kediri is three hours (1300rps) and you must leave early as the last bus from Kediri to Solo is 1 p.m.. All buses to Solo (and Batu/Selecta) leave from Malang's Dinoyo terminal. To get to Bromo, take a bus to Probollingo (two hours, 1400rps), then a *bemo* up to Ngadasiri (two hours). Or take a colt to Tumpang (45 minutes) and then walk 22 km up to the crater rim. This is the 'real' travellers' route, very scenic but hard work! To or from Banyuwangi costs around 4000rps by bus, and the journey takes about nine hours.

TOURIST SERVICES
For tourist information and maps, see Sudar Sono ('Ignored Boy') at Helios Hotel. What he doesn't know about Malang is not worth knowing. The other budget lodge, Bamboe Denn, also has good information. The official tourist office on Jln Tugu does not.

The GPO (open from 8 a.m. to 2 p.m.) is on the south side of the *alun-alun* square, the Immigration Office is at Jln Raung 2 and Bank Bumi Daya (open from 8 a.m. to 1 p.m., closed Sunday) is opposite Hotel Pelangi.

SIGHTS
Sightseeing is cheap and easy by colts (little blue minibuses with destinations posted) and *becaks*. Malang has some very fine Hindu ruins and it is worth taking a day out to see them. From Pattimura bus-stand, take a colt 12 km north to **Candi Singosari** (250rps, 20 minutes). This small Shiva shrine is a fine example of thirteenth-century Singosari architecture and houses the ashes of Kertanegara, the dynasty's last king. It is notable both for its unique base, which doubles as the inner sanctum (*cella*) and for the distinctive pop-eyed faces poised over each of its four arches. Only the top level of the temple has ornamentation – the rest was left uncompleted. The two huge Dwarapala guardians in the court-yard are believed once to have stood at the main gateway to the Singosari capital. Most of the shrine's other treasures have been shipped to the Leiden museum in Holland.

From Singosari, it is 20 minutes by colt to Blimbing (250rps), then half an hour to Tumpang (300rps). Ask to be put off at **Candi Jago**, which is another thirteenth-century temple, said to be the burial place of Singosari's fourth king, Vishnuvardhana. This shrine is small and compact, with lively friezes running around the base and upper levels too. Ask the gatekeeper for xeroxed information on the reliefs, which depict both Hindu and Buddhist legends. A fierce image of eight-armed Shiva is propped up in the grounds and although the roof of the shrine has caved in you can climb the steps for views of the surrounding countryside.

From Jago, take another colt (15 minutes, 250rps) on to **Candi Kidal.** If you have time or inclination for only one temple, make it this. Kidal is a relatively large sanctuary, beautifully situated in a shady jungle clearing, with first-rate carvings. Completed in 1260 in honour of Anusapati, the second Singosari king and well renovated in 1988/9, it stands today as perhaps the most stunning example of east Javan architecture – a real gem!

Very few tourists make it to the **Army Museum** on Jln Ijen, – either because it closes early (12 noon daily) or because they prefer the cool hill resort of **Selecta**, 20 km north on the slopes of Mt Arjuna.

MALANG

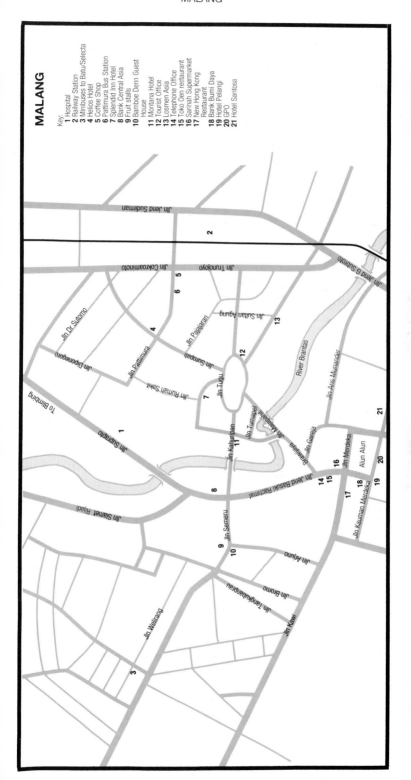

MALANG

Key:
1 Hospital
2 Railway Station
3 Minibuses to Batu/Selecta
4 Helios Hotel
5 Coffee Shop
6 Pattimura Bus Station
7 Splendid Inn Hotel
8 Bank Central Asia
9 Fruit stalls
10 Bamboe Denn Guest House
11 Montana Hotel
12 Tourist Office
13 Losmen Asia
14 Telephone Office
15 Toko Oen restaurant
16 Sarinah Supermarket
17 New Hong Kong Restaurant
18 Bank Bumi Daya
19 Hotel Pelangi
20 GPO
21 Hotel Santosa

Selecta is famous for its striking mountain scenery, terraced flower gardens and apple orchards. At Selecta Pemadian there is a fine open-air swimming pool and pretty picnic gardens of poinsettia, bougainvillaea, tiger-lilies and roses. Admission is a stiff 1000rps, but the two poolside restaurants (one Chinese, one Indonesian) are cheap and good. **Pemadian Hotel** (tel: Batu 23) has a beautiful setting and rooms/bungalows at 17,000/30,000rps, inclusive of breakfast. **Hotel Santosa II**, Jln Selecta-Tulungrejo (tel: Batu 66) is cheaper at 7000rps per person, including food. To get to Selecta, take a three-wheeler to Dinoyo bus station (150rps), then a minibus to Batu (300rps), finally another minibus (350rps) up to Selecta. The whole trip takes around an hour and it is worth stopping off at Batu for the views and for the fun market next to the minibus terminal.

ACCOMMODATION
Places to stay are few and far between. **Hotel Pelangi** (tel: 27456) at Jln Merdeka Selatan 3 is a large colonial hotel with a central location, stylish rooms from 25,000rps fan to 40,000rps air-conditioned, and full facilities. **Hotel Splendid Inn** (tel: 23860) at Jln Mojopahit 4 has lots of old Dutch character (sunken baths, antique furnishings, homey atmosphere etc.) and rooms from 24,500rps single, 31,000rps double. The new-look **Hotel Montana** at Jln Kahuripan 8 is exceedingly popular. The cheapest room is 30,000rps, but you will have to be here first thing in the morning to get one! The same goes for the mid-range **Malinda Hotel** (tel: 23402) at Jln K H Zainul Arifin 39, which charges 10,000 to 15,000rps for clean doubles. **Helios Hotel**, only two minutes' walk from the bus-station at Jln Pattimura 37, is the budget travellers' centre in Malang, with cheap rooms (7000rps single, 8000rps double), informative staff, free breakfast, nice gardens and a Dutch-speaking owner who spends his whole day running around in gay pyjamas – and why not? If full, try **Bamboe Denn** hostel (tel: 24859) at Jln Semeru 35 – 1500rps for a dormitory bed ('Cheapest beds in the world!' enthused one real traveller) and part of the deal is that you have to talk to the students studying English there.

FOOD
Toko Oen, opposite Sarinah supermarket on the square, is the top eating spot in town. It is an all-in-one patisserie, ice-cream palace, coffee-shop and high-class restaurant. The epic menu has Western, Chinese and Indonesian food (try the *wienerschnitzel* with paprika sauce – a snip at 5000rps) and the atmosphere and decor exist out of time. 'The whole place reminded me of a beach pavilion restaurant,' observed a friend, 'the taped organ muzak, the lighting, the wicker lounge chairs, the deco pillars ... If there was a boardwalk here and an ocean, it would be perfect!' Toko Oen is open daily from 9 a.m. to 9 p.m. only, so do not turn up late for dinner.

At Malang Plaza in the town centre, there are **Kentucky Fried Chicken**, **Dunkin' Donut** and hot (often cold) dogs. The **Pasar Senggol** night market on Jln Majapahit by the river has a wide variety of cheap and delicious snacks, including the local speciality of *terang bulan*, a kind of (very) sweet pancake. Go Chinese at **New Hong Kong** restaurant on Jln A R Hakim, near the *alun-alun* and try **Minang Jaya's** 20-course west Sumatran spread at Jln Besuki Rachmat 111 – it's your big chance to experiment with Padang cooking!

KALIBARU
Kalibaru is a good little base from which to discover east Java. You can see a typical Dutch coffee plantation here, then make side-trips to the turtle beach of Sukamade, to the game park of Baluran and to Ijien Plateau for the mountain sunrise. Kalibaru's slight elevation, 500 m above sea-level on the southern slope of Mt Raung (3,330 m) makes it ideal for coffee-growing. From here down to nearby Glenmore are the old Dutch settlements where Java's largest plantations came into being. At first they planted only coffee and rubber, but just recently they switched to cocoa, which is better for export. Most of Kalibaru's cocoa goes to Holland, although a fair amount of it ends up at Nestlé's chocolate factory in Bandung. Coffee is still produced, although mainly by local people who have agreed to transmigrate to Sumatra. The Government gives them a coffee tree apiece and two hectares of land. In Java, as a whole, there is far more cocoa being grown today than coffee.

As yet, Kalibaru is only popular with Dutch travellers, who usually drop in by private bus from nearby Malang, on their way to Bali. They arrive just after the rains (between April and July) when the plantations are at their most green and luxuriant. Kalibaru's limited accommodation is full then and you would be wise to book ahead to avoid problems in finding accommodation.

From Kalibaru, there is not much point in hanging round any longer in east Java. There are some gloriously rugged volcanoes in this part of the world, but nowhere special to settle. Your next obvious port of call would be Malang (for Bromo) or Bali.

ARRIVAL/DEPARTURE

The only real drawback to Kalibaru is getting there. It takes around eight hours from Bali by the following route: bus/ferry from Denpasar/Gilimanuk to Ketapang on the eastern tip of Java; *bemo* from Ketapang down to Blambangan bus-station in Banyuwangi (40 minutes, 500rps); another *bemo* on to Genteng (one and a half hours, 500rps); finally a Jember bus marked 'Yuangga' to Kalibaru (one hour, 200rps). From Malang, get a bus going to Jember, then change for Kalibaru. It is a seven-hour trip costing less than 2000rps total.

ACCOMMODATION

Off the bus in Kalibaru, walk (or hire a horse-drawn cart for 500rps) to the *back* of the railway station, where you will find two adjoining guest houses. **Margo Utomo Homestay** (tel: Kalibaru 23) is a virtual museum of accumulated Dutch art and is, in fact, built in the style of a plantation home. The manager, Mr Soekotjo, is a charming and erudite host. He is more used to Dutch travellers, but speaks English just as well. His rooms are well-furnished, clean and quiet and cost US$15.5 single, US$19 double. Meals are good value at 6000rps apiece. **Susan Homestay**, right next door, is similarly priced but is not half so good.

SIGHTS

After breakfast, Mr Soekotjo will take you out on a short plantation tour for a nominal fee of 2000rps. His guest house is on a small 7-hectare farm which grows cocoa and coffee, plus back-up crops of pepper, cinnamon, nutmeg, cloves, coconuts, banana and avocado. This is an excellent opportunity to learn all about the multifarious produce of Java. In the afternoon, visit the large government plantation 1 km out of Kalibaru or take a bus (or car from Margo Utomo) to **Glenmore**, 17 km further down the road. An English plantation owner called Mr Glenmore founded this station over 50 years ago to transport his coffee to Surabaya. Access to the plantation is restricted, but the owner of **Losmen Glenmore** (cheap rooms at 5000rps) can probably set up a tour for you. This whole area has wonderful scenery so bring lots of film for your camera!

From Kalibaru, you can travel 80 km south west to **Sukamade**, also known as Turtle Bay. This famous 3-km-long beach is one of the few places left on Java where you can still watch giant sea turtles (leatherbacks, hawksbills and green turtles) laying their eggs in the sand. Your best chance of seeing them is from 10 p.m. to 3 a.m. on moonlit nights between October and March. You may wait only an hour to see the turtles coming up the beach, or you may be there all night.

Watch out for the old turtles, who craftily dig lots of 'bogus' holes in the sand before laying their eggs in the real one. The young turtles just go 100 m up the beach and lay in the first hole dug. They are the easiest to spot. You can get to Sukamade by *bemo* from Glenmore, or by hired car from Margo Utomo in Kalibaru. Don't attempt this trip from January to April, however, as there are seven rivers to cross (and no bridges) and during the rains the road becomes impassable. At Sukamade, you can camp out on the beach (special platforms have been constructed for visitors) or take 10,000rps rooms at **Wisma Sukamade** *losmen*.

Mr Soekotjo also arranges car tours out to the **Ijien Plateau**, a 2,243-m-high volcanic lake (no swimming) sandwiched between Mts Ijien and Merapi. It is a very barren and deserted place – few tourists have made it up there yet – but the scenery is awesome. You leave Kalibaru around midnight to reach the plateau for sunrise. The 7-km ascent from the base to the top is pretty steep, but if you think that is hard work, just watch the local guides climbing in and out of the crater carrying 30-kg bags of sulphur! The other popular approach to Ijien is from Banyuwangi – first a mini-bus to Jambu (17 km), then another to Licin (10 km). Try to hitch a lift on a truck on to Sodong from Licin, otherwise brace yourself for a long 17-km ascent with a guide and pony.

When you are ready to leave Kalibaru, take a bus to Genteng, then a *bemo* to Banyuwangi. If you need to stay the night here, try **Hotel Baru**, Jln Pattimura 82-84 (large airy rooms from 4000 to 8000rps) or **Losmen Anda** at Jln Basuki Rachmat 36 (5000rps single, 7000rps double). Or take a *bemo* 6 km up the road to Ketapang for deluxe rooms (17,500rps fan, 22,500 air-conditioned) at **Hotel Banyuwangi Beach** near the ferry.

From Ketapang, it is only 30 km north (one hour by *bemo*, 600rps) to Wonorejo, which is the entrance to **Baluran National Park**. This is the best – and the most accessible – of Java's game reserves, well worth a diversion to see. The parklands surround the vast cone and open-sided crater of Mt Baluran (1247 m), which occupies the whole north-east corner of Java. The unusually extensive savannah grasslands dry out completely between May and October, making it easy to see, in such open land, the rusa deer, bantang bulls and feral buffaloes which graze there. It has been called Java's one bit of Africa – the game-watching conditions are unique. It is also one of the few game parks in the world where you can divide your time between wildlife-spotting and lying on a beach!

You need a permit to visit Baluran. This is issued at the PPA office in Banyuwangi (Jln A Yani 108, tel: 41119), where you can also book accommodation and get sketch-maps of the park. From the guard-post just inside the reserve at Wonorejo (which also issues permits) it is a pretty boring 12-km walk down a forest trail to **Bekol**, the park headquarters. There is a small resthouse at Bekol (2500rps per person, no electricity) and a small viewing platform overlooking a large waterhole. From here, in the dry months, you can see animals coming out of the jungle to drink, usually in the early morning or the late afternoon. Bekol's resident guide, Julian, speaks good English and offers jungle treks at dawn for 2500rps. There is a similar deal at **Bama Beach**, 3 km away from Bekol on the shore, where Cianto, the friendly lodge caretaker charges 2500rps per dormitory bed, 1000rps per meal and 2000rps per person for early morning treks. Herds of wild buffaloes and deer are commonly seen, as are peacocks, jungle fowl, black monkeys, macaques, civet cats and even leopards and monitor lizards. You will need a guide to avoid large spiders hanging out of the bush and sudden plummets down concealed water-holes. It is worth bringing your mask and snorkel to Bama as the water is calm and clear and there is some nice coral to be seen only 200 m out. The beach itself is a narrow strip of white sand (busy at weekends, otherwise deserted) leading off to a series of little coves accessible only at low tide.

Sumatra

Sumatra is a good deal less developed than Java and a lot greener. There is far less laid on for tourists so you have to do a lot more for yourself, which is not necessarily a bad thing. Travelling through Sumatra takes a bit more stamina and considerably more patience than travelling through Java. Accommodation is rather more spartan, even if cheaper, and transport is unpredictable to say the least. The hassle-factor is larger (lots of students wanting to learn English) and it is rare to find privacy anywhere. This said, Sumatra is a land of smiling faces, rustic charm and peaceful simplicity – a really good place for adventure-seekers!

THE LAND

Coming in from Java or Malaysia, the first thing you will notice is the wonderful sense of space; there are no crowds in Sumatra, and no traffic congestion either. Although four times larger than Java (some 2,000 km long and up to 400 km wide) this island has four times less people: only 26 million, or 15 per cent of Indonesia's total. In relief, Sumatra comprises a high mountain chain running over 160 km along the western coast and containing numerous volcanic peaks. Mountain lakes, like Toba and Maninjau occupy the intervening valleys between the mountains, while towards the south the rivers flow inland causing swampy land. Profitable plantations of oil, palm and rubber take up most of the suitable lowlands, but some 60–70 per cent of the total land area of Sumatra is still dense forest and tropical jungle. In these rain forests lives the richest and largest fauna in Indonesia – not only wild elephant and tiger, but orang-utan, big black *siamang* monkeys with their booming calls, tapirs, Malayan bear, jungle cats, clouded leopards and the very shy (and very hairy) two-horned rhinoceros, which is rarely seen. Despite the creation of reserves to protect the wildlife (notably at Gunung Leuser National Park in north Sumatra), the wholesale destruction of primary jungle by greedy profiteers has placed both the forest and the island's large mammals in the conservation frontline.

The popular part of Sumatra is in the north – the hill station of Bukittingi, the beautiful Lake Toba with its Samosir island, the volcanoes of Brastagi and the orang-utan sanctuary near Bukit Lawang. The south doesn't have much to offer. It is primitive, it is not high enough to be out of the heat and, most depressing of all, the rain forests are being wiped out. Most travellers start their Sumatra tour at Padang (going north) or at Medan (going south). They generally come into Padang from Jakarta, either by boat or by air. A brave few take the bus. The most common approach to Medan is by boat from Penang, although more people are now flying in from KL or Singapore. A £40 air-ticket is money well-spent to avoid all those long tiring bus journeys within Sumatra.

CLIMATE

Being right on the equator, Sumatra is subject to variable weather. It rains everywhere from September to December and then come the 'local' showers of January-February, when it can be dry in Padang and teeming down in Bukittingi, or vice versa! It dries out during March and between May and July it is positively dry. In climate, Sumatra is very similar to Java, i.e. very hot and very humid. Temperatures range from 72–88°F (22–31°C) in the lowlands, and from 61–79°F (16–26°C) at Lake Toba. March to May are the hottest months, January to February the coolest, but the difference is never more than 2°C. The peak season for tourists is June to August – big crowds from Australia (surfers bound for Nias) and Europe (summer holidays).

HISTORY

Until Dutch and British planters took it over in the nineteenth century, Sumatra was a land of dense rain forest where wild animals roamed free. A thousand years ago, it was the most important island in the Indonesian archipelago, as well as the cultural centre of South-East Asia. Srivajaya, in the Palembang river valley, was colonised by Hindus around the second century and rapidly extended its influence. By the twelfth century, this powerful Buddhist empire controlled not only Sumatra, but the western end of Java and the east coast of Malaysia. During the thirteenth century, shortly after the arrival of Islam on Sumatra's northern shores, Srivajaya became seriously weakened and in 1377 it was conquered by Java, settling the age-old naval rivalry between these two places. The Javanese then sent a great army to conquer west Sumatra, which was ruled by the independent Malay kingdom of Minangkabau. According to legend, the chiefs of both sides agreed to settle the issue with a fight between two bulls. The Malays thought of a ruse and, allowing a calf to starve for ten days, they bound sharp knives to its horns and set it free to run full-tilt against the belly of the Javanese buffalo. The starving calf, mis-

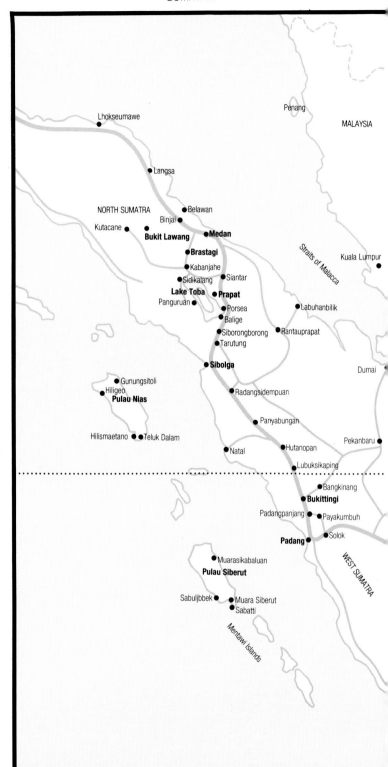

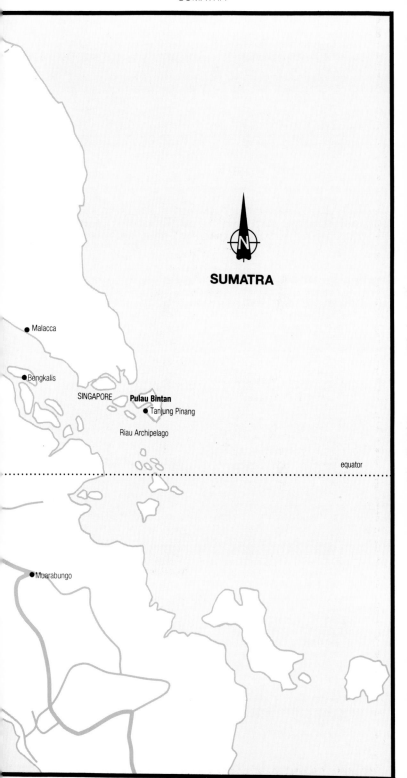

taking the opposing bull for its mother, stabbed it to death trying to find milk. To commemorate their victory, the Malay conquerors named their land and people '*Minang Kabau*' or conquering buffalo.

By the late fourteenth century, Minangkabau had gained much of the influence which Srivajaya had lost and was in control of the whole of Sumatra. In 1680 however, when King Alip died without leaving any direct heirs, the kingdom was divided into three parts and soon fell into complete decadence. The European history of Sumatra can be summed up as the struggle between the British and the Dutch for possession of the island, of the victory of the Dutch (by treaty in 1824) and of the long-drawn-out struggle which this nation had to obtain control over the natives. The last king of Minangkabau died in 1849 – his portrait hangs in the King's House near Bukittingi.

PEOPLE AND RELIGION

The Sumatrans are a jungle people. They are shorter, darker and more wiry than the Javanese and they speak far less English. Of the numerous ethnic groups on the island, the best known are the matriarchal Minangkabau of west Sumara, the Christian Batak of north Sumatra and the aboriginal inhabitants of the islands of Nias and Mentawai. The religion of Sumatra is predominantly Islam, though Protestant missionaries have made some headway amongst the Batak and in Nias, as can be seen in Lake Toba with its churches and schools. The odd thing about the **Minangkabau** is that although it is an Islamic society, it is also a matriarchal society, which on the surface of things, is a real conflict! Community and family life centre around Muslim mosques and traditional *adat* houses (with their distinctive saddle-backed roofs, decorated with buffalo horns), but even today the descent of property is through the female line and when a man marries a Minang woman he moves to her house. She has control over the family land and assets and runs the family business – although (curiously) the man still has a lot of say in the household of his sister! It is quite an involved system, but it works very well.

As for the **Bataks**, they were among the most warlike tribes of Sumatra and cannibalism became their main form of defence – a permanent deterrent to any stranger who intruded on their territory. This antagonism towards aliens can be understood when one learns that the Bataks were pushed from their homelands in Thailand and Burma by migrating Mongolian and Siamese tribes. When they arrived in Sumatra, they headed straight for the highlands around Lake Toba, believing that the natural barrier of the mountains would best protect their kingdom. Like the Minangkabau, their architecture is typified by high-gabled saddle-shaped roofs adorned with geometric designs and buffalo horns. Although the Toba Bataks were converted to Christianity in the 1860s, most are still animists, and ancestor worship still forms an important part of their culture. *Bahasa* Indonesian is the official language of Sumatra, but the Bataks have their own dialect. The local greeting is *horas* and the natives will appreciate you using it.

DOMESTIC TRANSPORT

Getting around Sumatra requires time and patience – it must have the most 'flexible' transport system in Asia. Bus and boat schedules are totally meaningless – everything goes when it goes! Having taken a plane or boat from Jakarta to Padang, or from Singapore to Pekan Baru, or from Penang/KL to Medan, you will now have to come to terms with the buses. Sumatran buses are famous. They often have two drivers, two break-down men and a whole heap of spare tyres aboard. Most of them have seats in rows of three. Only one company, ALS, has seats in twos, which gives you a bit of room. But they are all jammed full with chickens, people with huge boxes and chain-smoking locals. The worst bus trip you are likely to experience is the 12-16 hour marathon between Toba and Bukittingi. Taking on anything longer, you can expect all sorts of delays:

> We took a 60-hour bus journey up from Yogyakarta to Bukittingi. It wasn't a very healthy bus and every time we stopped they tried to repair it. It was so funny, because they were all squatting round this battery with a great big hole in it. They tinkered with it for a bit, then they had lunch, then a three-hour sleep. And then they came out and the battery was going. I do not know how they did it. Later on, the driver appeared with the dashboard. It was broken in half – just two bits of wood. He took that down with him and half an hour later it was fixed. I do not know how he did that either.

Note: the Trans-Sumatran Highway was finished in 1988, but then it was flooded, so it is being repaired again. If all goes well, it will soon be 'only' 22 hours by bus from Palembang up to Bukittingi.

ENTERTAINMENT/SHOPPING

Local music and dance, together with traditional arts like silver, hand-weaving, embroidery and woodcarving, are most accessible in tourist centres like Toba,

Bukittingi and (to some extent) Padang. In most other places, you must look really hard to find the culture, strong though it is. Sumatra is about ten years behind Java in terms of entertaining tourists and is light years behind Bali when it comes to selling its beautiful handicrafts. Because tourism is so low-key, however, you can often pick up some great bargains! Particularly good buys are the *ikat* and *songket* weaving of Bukittingi and the batak blankets of Brastagi and Toba.

ACCOMMODATION

Out of Medan (which has the quality hotels), accommodation in Sumatra is remarkably cheap – about half the price of Java. I went through the country on 10,000rps a day and that took in accommodation (upmarket *wisma* guest houses or cheap batak-style *losmen* with sweeping roofs), food, a couple of beers, sightseeing and extensive travel by bus.

FOOD

The main dish is rice, to which all the other ingredients add flavour and variety. Typically, Sumatrans flavour their food with a careful blend of dried and fresh spices – garlic, candlenut, ginger, turmeric and shallots. Rice is usually served with red-chilli *sambal*, a hot side dish and pickles. Many dishes are cooked in *santan*, the liquid from grated coconut, flavoured with chillis and topped with peanut sauce. West Sumatra claims to be the birthplace of the beef curry *rendang*. It is very dry, has hardly any sauce and as a travelling food it can last for months! Another Minang speciality is *gulai ikan*, a delicious fish curry cooked in coconut milk, served in a marinade of garlic and red chillies. Padang is famous for its hot, spicy food, Samosir island for its multi-dish 'smorgasbord' and Bukittingi for its mouthwatering stuffed pancakes called *murtabak*. In Sumatra, it is essential to be adventurous with food. In most places, you just don't have any kind of a choice!

LANGUAGE

Bahasa Indonesian is understood everywhere on Sumatra nowadays, regardless of the myriad local dialects spoken, since it is the common language of the schools. Even more so than in Java (cf. page 133 for vocabulary), a little *bahasa* goes a long way. If the local lads bother you to teach them English, insist that they return the favour!

MISCELLANEOUS

Full information on visas, currency, time, electricity, and local transport are given in the introductory section to Java as a whole.

PADANG

Padang is the gateway to west Sumatra and its capital city. It is well known as a centre of learning and a great many Sumatrans come to study at the big university here. There is not much to see or do – travellers generally visit the museum, laze on a beach and then fly out. However, the city has a certain small-town charm (you would never guess this is the third largest city in Sumatra!) and is surprisingly neat and clean. Being so close to the equator, Padang gets a lot of rain and can be terribly hot, just like its food. Backpackers waiting for a boat out to Jakarta can cool off at the nearby beach of Air Manis. Others, with more time to spare, can take a ten-day adventure trip to Siberut, a lost island which is the home of primitive tribes.

ARRIVAL/DEPARTURE

Air

As a major gateway to Sumatra, Padang receives a lot of traffic through Tabing Airport, 6 km from the town centre. You can fly to or from Jakarta for 135,000rps (inclusive of airport tax) on Garuda, or for 115,000rps on Merpati or Mandala. Garuda connects Padang with Medan, Pekanbaru and Singapore and Merpati has one flight a week which goes to Siberut Island.

From Tabing airport into town costs 4000rps by taxi (only half as much if you start walking!), or 100rps by local *bis kota* from the main road.

Sea

A luxurious way to travel Jakarta-Padang-Sibolga is on the Pelni ship *Kerinci*. It leaves Teluk Bayur, Padang's main port, at 11 p.m. every second Sunday for Jakarta, returning to Padang every other Friday. Fares are between 24,000 and 63,000rps and the journey takes 27 to 33 hours. The *Kerinci* goes north every other Saturday night, and back to Padang on a Sunday. The trip takes 11 hours and costs 10,800 in economy class, including adequate food, plenty of deck space, privacy and fresh air. The bus to Sibolga, on the other hand, costs only 6000rps and includes even more hours of travel, but does not include food and those other advantages.

Road

Nobody enjoys the long, boring and hot bus journey up to Padang from Palembang at the southern tip of Sumatra. A typical comment is 'Don't do it! Fly, catch a boat, anything, but don't do it!' If you must go to Jakarta by road, book with ANS at Jln Pemuda 15, across the road from Padang bus-station. Their bus costs 27,000rps, takes 'only' 36 hours,

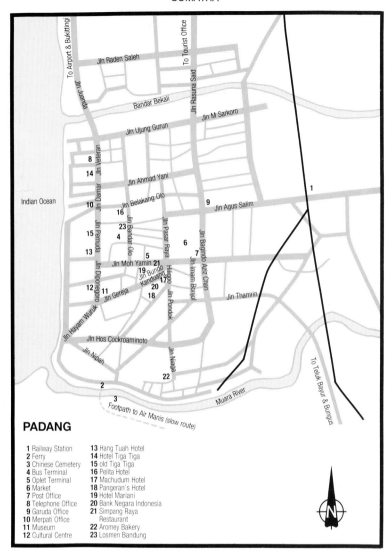

PADANG

1 Railway Station
2 Ferry
3 Chinese Cemetery
4 Bus Terminal
5 Oplet Terminal
6 Market
7 Post Office
8 Telephone Office
9 Garuda Office
10 Merpati Office
11 Museum
12 Cultural Centre
13 Hang Tuah Hotel
14 Hotel Tiga Tiga
15 old Tiga Tiga
16 Pelita Hotel
17 Machudum Hotel
18 Pangeran's Hotel
19 Hotel Mariani
20 Bank Negara Indonesia
21 Simpang Raya
   Restaurant
22 Aromey Bakery
23 Losmen Bandung

and doesn't break down as often as others. There are cheaper buses (18,000rps) but they are not air-conditioned.

Buses leave every few minutes for Bukittingi (1100rps) from Padang bus-terminal. If you arrive in Padang by air, you can pick one up from the main road outside the airport. The NPM express bus is best. It gets to Bukittingi (92 km) in just two hours. Enjoy the fantastic scenery along this route.

TOURIST SERVICES
Padang's best tourist office is the Kanwil Postel (tel: 28231) way out at Jln Khatib Sulaiman. You can get there by *dokar* (1000rps) or by *oplet* 269 from the *oplet* station. This office is open from 8 a.m. to 2 p.m. Monday to Thursday, 8 a.m. to 11.30 a.m. Friday, 8 a.m. to 1 p.m. Saturday. Ask the friendly staff for a west Sumatra 'tourist map' – it is free and very useful. Further information can be obtained from Tunas travel agent (tel: 21313) at Jln Pondok 86b.

The post office at Jln Bagindo Aziz Chan 7 is an excellent introduction to Sumatran 'rubber time'. It is open from 8 a.m. to 4 p.m. Monday to Friday – 'sometimes till 9 p.m.' says the tourist office – 8 a.m. to 12 noon Saturday and 'sometimes for a couple of hours' on Sundays! The Immigration office (tel: 21294) on Jln Khatib Sulaiman, near the tourist office, is very co-operative. One couple got a five-day extension on their Indonesian visa here after being told it was 'totally impossible' in Medan. How much you pay for an extension is 'up to

Outskirts of Bukittingi

The pineapple market in Padang

you', they reported, but a donation of 5000rps should do it! You will find the telephone office at Jln Veteran 47, and C V Eka Jasa Utama moneychanger (better rates than the banks) on Jln Niaga. Garuda (tel: 23224) is located at Jln Jend Sudirman 2, Merpati (tel: 21303) is opposite the bus-station at Jln Pemuda 45a, Mandala (tel: 21979) is at Jln Pemuda 29a and Pelni Lines (tel: 22109) is at Jln Tg Priok, Teluk Bayur harbour.

TRANSPORT AROUND TOWN

Use *oplet* minibuses for local transportation. They go anywhere in town for 100 to 150rs – far better than horse-drawn *dokars*, which don't move for less than 500rps. Padang's central bus terminal is on Jln Pemuda and the *oplet* station (and taxi-stand) are close by on Jln M Yamin.

SIGHTS

Padang's one sight of consequence is the **Adityawarman Museum** at the junction of Jln Diponegoro and Jln Gereja. Built in the shape of a traditional Minangkabau *adat* house, with high-peaked roofs, carved and painted walls and two rice barns out front, it is very impressive to look at. The displays inside, mainly antiques, textiles and heritage items from all over west Sumatra, are good but poorly presented. Entrance to the museum is 250rps, and opening hours are 8 a.m. to 6 p.m., Friday until ll a.m., closed Monday. Across the road is **Taman Budaya** Cultural Centre, where you can watch practice sessions of traditional Minang dance and music every Sunday, from morning to afternoon. The Minangkabau folk orchestra is similar to *gamelan*, with xylophones (*talempong*), bamboo flutes (*salung*), strings (*rebab*) and cowhide drums (*gandang*). The Cultural Centre is open 9 a.m. to 2 p.m. daily and there is nearly always something going on – art exhibitions, *panca silat* performances, stage plays, poetry readings, etc. Check the board for upcoming events.

If you do not mind rustic facilities, **Air Manis** beach is a good place to stay while in Padang. To get there, take a minibus (150rps) from the *oplet* terminal to Teluk Bayur harbour. Opposite the harbour, a flight of steps leads up and over the hill (2 km, 30 minutes) to the beach. Stay at **Papa Chili Chili's Homestay**, so named because the food there is always hot and spicy! His place is a charming little shack right on the beach, with simple rooms from 2000 to 5000rps and good cheap homestyle cooking. The great man is often not there, but his son Ali and daughter Yusna are entertaining hosts. Ali speaks good English and sets up treks to the local waterfall (a superb walk, even though you feel like a mountain goat at the end) and two-day fishing trips which are apparently not to be missed.

The beach itself is geared to total relaxation, as one guest related: 'Every day at 3 p.m. four brown cows walk down the beach in search of garbage and food. Around 4.30 p.m., the childen/vendors come by with banana, coconut and rice treats to carry you over to dinner. As the technicolour sunset light-show begins, one dragonfly will buzz you continually if you sit on the beach. Soon after 6 p.m., a bat will fly random patterns between the boats and the palm-stump to the left. This will happen every day, but soon the days will cease to exist – just on and on and on, like the waves and the clouds, a continuum of change and "same-same".'

The two pretty little islands lying offshore from Papa Chili's are 'Small Banana Island', which you can wade over to at low tide and 'Big Banana Island', for which you must pay Ali 5000rps to paddle over to. The larger island has the coral and the beautiful beaches, but neither island has bananas. The goats ate them all, and now there are only coconuts and no goats. A short ten-minute walk along the beach from Papa Chili's brings you to the rotting hulk of a ship and a prostrate stone figure, his head bowed in grief on the deck. This petrified person is Malin Kundang, a local lad who, according to legend, sailed to Java to seek his fortune. He returned in a beautiful boat, with a beautiful wife, and then offended the gods by publicly disowning his poor old mother of whom he was ashamed. To punish his crime, they waited until Malin Kundang set sail for Java again and then whipped up such a storm that his boat was driven ashore and wrecked on the rocks. As soon as the vessel hit the beach, so the story goes, it was turned – along with Malin Kundang and his beautiful wife – into stone.

Avoid Air Manis at weekends when all the domestic tourists roll in. Try **Bungus Bay**, 22 km south of Padang, instead. This is another palm-fringed beach with good swimming and memorable sunsets. Ali's waterfall is nearby, a crippling one-hour climb up the side of a mountain and you can swim there too. Canoes and *prahus* can be hired out to the various small islands in the bay and there are a couple of fishing villages north along the beach. Stay at **Carolina** guest house (rooms from 10,000 to 30,000rps) or **Pasir Putir** *losmen* (around 7000rps a night). Bungus is a scenic one-hour ride from Padang by *oplet* (500rps).

Siberut is the largest of four islands, the Mentawais, which lie about 100 km off Sumatra's west coast. Some 65 per cent of this island's interior is still covered by dense tropical rain forest and the aboriginal tribespeople, long isolated from the outside world, still believe in magic and live by hunting. Guided tours to Siberut have grown like mad. They have been running two ten-day tours a week out of Bukittingi (US$100 per person, inclusive of food, accommodation, guide and transport) for the last year or so and already it has made a difference. In the three touristy villages they take you to, all the locals now wear T-shirts and queue up demanding cigarettes. You don't actually see primary jungle unless you hire a local guide and go up into the hills. There are two guides in Muara Siberut, the main town, who have been showing scientists around for many years. They don't have official licences and they are a lot cheaper than the guides from Bukittingi, but they know a lot more. For around 60,000rps a person, they will take groups of five or more out on long two-week treks right into the island interior, camping out in the bush to see animals close up and visiting primitive tribes who have never seen a white person before. You can go with fewer people, but it costs more. Don't believe anyone who tells you that you can't do it on your own. You don't need a permit to visit any more, and Muara Siberut now has decent facilities – three restaurants, two *losmen* and about a dozen stores. Three or four ferries a week go there from Muara harbour in Padang, the 10/11 hour trip costing 10,000rps to sleep on deck, US$100 for a six-berth cabin. Every Monday, Merpati flies in and out of Siberut from Padang for around 17,000rps.

ACCOMMODATION

Of Padang's more expensive hotels, the **Mariani International** (tel: 25466) at Jln Bundo Kandung is easily the travellers' choice. It has good security, nice tropical gardens, a helpful true-travel office and air-conditioned rooms from 25,000 to 30,000rps. **Pangeran's Hotel** (tel: 26233) at Jln Dobi 3-5 is a comfortable modern-style hotel in quiet surroundings, with a central location and air-conditioned rooms from 31,625rps single, 37,950rps double. The new **Pangeran Beach Hotel** at Jln Juanda 79 has a pool.

In the mid-range, choose between **Padang Hotel** (tel: 22563) at Jln Azizcham 28 and **Hotel Hang Tuah** (tel: 26556) at Jln Pemuda 1. Both these places are clean and well managed, with rooms around 10,000rps fan, 20,000rps air-conditioned. Two good cheapies are **Losmen Bandung**, Jln Bandar Olo 37 (7000 to 10,000rps) and **Pelita Hotel**, Jln Jawadalam IV-23 (2500rps single, 4000rps double). The old backpackers' favourite, the **Tiga-Tiga** at Jln Pemuda 31 (100 m from the bus station), has rooms at 3500rps single, 7500rps double and a 1500rps dormitory. Don't confuse it with the new Tiga Tiga at Jln Veteran 33 which charges twice as much for

rooms twice as good (hot water, fan, breakfast, etc.).

FOOD

If you have been anywhere else in Indonesia, you will know that Padang is famous for its (incandescent) cuisine. Padang food is left to ferment in spices for three days before they even serve it to you – which is why it is so hot! There are Padang restaurants all the way from Java to Bali, but to sample *nasi padang* at source go to **Simpang Raya** at Jln Mohd Yamin 125, opposite the *oplet* stand, or **Roda Baru** upstairs at Jln Pasar Raya 6, in the market buildings. Don't risk it anywhere else – bad Padang food is absolutely *grim*! The swanky **Taman Sari** at Jln A Yani 23 tones down its Padang fare for Westerners, but is best known as a place to enjoy Sundanese and seafood in air-conditioned comfort. Two good Chinese restaurants in Jln Pondok are **Chan's** at No. 94 with live music at night and **King's** at No. 86 with top-quality food and service and prices to match. **Pangeran's Hotel** has the only steak-house in town and **Aromey Bakery** is famous for its cakes. **Mah Kota Restoran** on Jln Pondok, near the Grand Hotel, serves many kinds of traditional Minang dishes and **Restoran Kubang** at Jln Mohd Yamin 138, near the bus station, does cheap and tasty *martabak* pancakes.

BUKITTINGI

The heartland of the Minangkabau people and culture, Bukittingi is Sumatra's answer to Bali's Ubud – the hill-station with Western food, Western sounds and interesting little cafes which close at midnight. Located 930 m above sea level, this is a very cool, pleasant and livable place with a charm all its own. The clock tower in the square, built by the Dutch in 1827, has given Bukittingi its pseudonym of 'Big Ben Town', but the name literally means 'high place'. Surrounded by three volcanoes, Tandikat, Singallang and Merapi, it is also known as Tri Arga or 'town of three mountains'. Of all Sumatran towns, Bukittingi is the one most geared to travellers' needs. Through the various guest houses you can book sightseeing tours, culture shows, treks to Siberut Island and all your onward travel. Accommodation and food are ultra-cheap and very good. Shopping and crafts are better than anywhere else in west Sumatra. The people are welcoming, the climate comfortable and the sights worth at least a week. All in all, Bukittingi is a travellers' mecca!

ARRIVAL/DEPARTURE

On arrival in Bukittingi, take an *oplet* (100rps) from Aur Kuning bus station, 2 km south east of town to Jln Ayani for

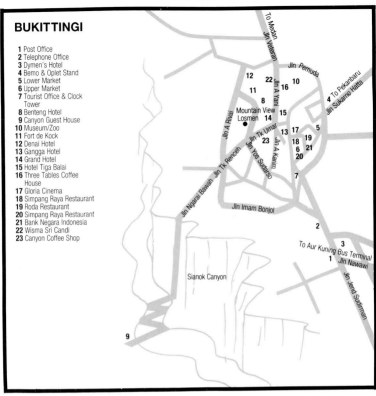

BUKITTINGI

1 Post Office
2 Telephone Office
3 Dymen's Hotel
4 Bemo & Oplet Stand
5 Lower Market
6 Upper Market
7 Tourist Office & Clock Tower
8 Benteng Hotel
9 Canyon Guest House
10 Museum/Zoo
11 Fort de Kock
12 Denai Hotel
13 Gangga Hotel
14 Grand Hotel
15 Hotel Tiga Balai
16 Three Tables Coffee House
17 Gloria Cinema
18 Simpang Raya Restaurant
19 Roda Restaurant
20 Simpang Raya Restaurant
21 Bank Negara Indonesia
22 Wisma Sri Candi
23 Canyon Coffee Shop

the hotels. Coming in by bus, the short and scenic one and a half hour ride from Padang (1100rps) is a total contrast to the endless 16-18 hour trip from Praphat/ Lake Toba. If you buy tickets direct from the Aur Kuning station, ALS and ANS sell seats on the non-air-conditioned bus to Praphat for 7500rps and the air-conditioned bus for 12,000rps. The 4 p.m. departures are the best: they drop you at Andilo Travel in Praphat (for boats to Toba) between 4 and 6 a.m. next morning. Buying from the guest houses in Jln A Yani, expect to pay 1000rps extra in commission. Ganga Hotel sells seats on a 'special tourist bus' to Praphat, leaving at 8 p.m. twice a week. It costs 15,000rps per person, takes only 12/13 hours and includes stops at hot springs and the equator. The Ganga has a good ticketing service for Jakarta (23,000rps, or 30,000rps air-conditioned, 36 to 48 hours), Bandung (26,000rps, or 39,500rps air-conditioned), Yogya (32,500rps) and – the marathon journey to end them all – for Bali (43,500rps, or 63,000rps air-conditioned) which takes around four days! The Three Tables Coffee House offers buses to Sibolga (6000rps, 12 hours) and Medan (10,000rps, or 15,000rps air-conditioned), also share-taxis to Padang (40,000rps, seats eight) or to Praphat (US$100, seats eight). It

also sells a good-value flight ticket from Padang to Jakarta (Mandala) for 93,000rps – much cheaper than Garuda or Merpati. This price includes bus-travel to Padang and transport from Jakarta airport to the city.

If you are on your way to Singapore and do not want to go from Medan or Padang, you can save time and money by taking a bus from Bukittingi (3500rps, six hours) to Pekan Baru, then a riverboat (15,000rps, 50 hours) to Tanjung Pinang. If two days' standing on deck (without a cover) is not your idea of fun, fly Pekan Baru to Tanjung Pinang (40,000rps) or to Batam (53,800rps). When in Pekan Baru waiting for a boat or plane, stay at **Tommy Place**, Pekan Baru Riau 41D – 7000rps by taxi from the airport (or 200rps by *oplet* from the main road); 125rps by *oplet* from the bus-station, ask to be put off at Jln Nangka.

TOURIST SERVICES

The tourist office (tel: 22403) beside the clock tower is a waste of time. You will get much better information from Iko Sakato travel service (tel: 22822) at Jln A Yani 13, or from local guides like Ad at the Three Tables Coffee House.

The post office is at Jln Sudirman 75, open from 8 a.m. to 4 p.m. weekdays, until 12 noon Saturday. Next door is the telephone office, with a 24-hour overseas

A horse-drawn taxi rank in Bukittingi

calls service (26,000rps for three minutes to the UK, 22,750 to US/Australia). You can change money at Bank Negara Indonesia (open 8 a.m. to 2 p.m., closed Sunday) in the Pasar Atas market building, but rates are not good. Books can be bought, sold and exchanged at the bookshop next to the Coffee Shop in Jln A Yani.

TRANSPORT ROUND TOWN

Bukittingi is a small, compact town, ideal for walking, although the steep levels, connected by steps, take a bit of getting used to. *Oplets* charge a flat fare of 100rps and horse-drawn carts (*bendi*) ask considerably more. The Three Tables Coffee House has cars for hire – 60,000rps per day with a driver, 80,000rps with a guide – and Ganga Hotel rents out motorbikes at 17,500rps per day.

SIGHTS

Every Saturday and Wednesday, Bukittingi's central market is a fiesta of colourful stalls and busily bargaining local people – don't miss it. Above the market, in the centre of town, is the **zoo**, which is a disaster. 'Very sad and depressing', mourned one visitor, 'The animals look ill and act psychotic – it is like a concentration camp. The one thing I wanted to see – the Sumatran tiger, has been dead for the last three years. All they've got now is a stuffed one!' The zoo is open from 8 a.m. to 5 p.m. daily and admission is 400rps. A further 200rps admits you to the **museum** inside the zoo complex, which *is* worth going to. Built as a traditional family house in 1844, opened as a museum by the Dutch in 1934, this has an eye-catching exterior (Minangkabau architecture at its best) and, inside, well-presented historical and cultural displays. Ask the curator to show you his foreign banknote collection. Outside, stroll around and enjoy the views – the zoo is situated on a hilltop at the highest point in town. Of the three volcanoes visible from here, the only one you can climb is **Mt Singgalang**. Take a bus to Batu Sangkar village (one hour), stay overnight at one of the *losmen*, and rise early for the pre-dawn ascent and sunrise views. The 100-m deep **Sianok Canyon** is a 4-km walk from the town centre. To get there, head down Jln A Yani into Jln Tk Umar and keep straight on. To catch the sunlight over the canyon, you need to visit between 9 a.m. and 3 p.m. when the sun is high. There are lots of birds and animals (especially black gibbons) around here, so keep your eyes peeled. The new **Canyon Guest House**, at the bottom of the 4-km-long chasm, is a good cheap place to stay. Just before the canyon, a path leads left off the main road to the silversmith village of **Kota Gadang**, a long 12-km hike away.

Lake Maninjau, 30 km south west of Bukittingi, is a beautiful crater lake – perfect for relaxation – with exceptional scenery and some nice walks for the energetic. The best time to visit is late afternoon, for stunning sunsets. The lake is good for swimming, and you can hire canoes and bicycles to go across or around it. Minibuses run direct to Maninjau from Aur Kuning bus station, but the last 12 km are a hairy one and a half hour descent round 47 hairpin bends, so do not travel on a full stomach! Three good places to stay (all with rooms around 3000 to 7000rps) are **Beach House** right on the lake, **Amani**, an old Dutch guest house full of antiques and **Coffee House**, a bit rickety, but run by nice people.

To discover the several out-of-town attractions, hire a guide or take an organised tour. Bukittingi currently has over 30 guides, only a handful of whom have red cards and are qualified. The rest have white cards and are termed 'escorters'. Ask around at the Ganga, the Coffee Shop and the Coffee House for the best four guides – Ad, Ed, Lala and Bujang. Their charges (25,000rps per day) are best shared by a group. Many places along Jln A Yani, notably Parindo Travel at Hotel Grand, sell one-day sightseeing tours by minibus for 12,000rps per person. The beautiful countryside alone is worth the cost of this trip, which also provides a number of really worth-while photo stops and fascinating insights into the culture and traditions of the Minangkabau people, courtesy of good English-speaking guides. Tackling this as an independent (even hiring a group minibus) you will take a lot longer to find points of interest and will not have any explanation of them. Bring a towel and swimming costume, also plenty of camera film!

Most tours start at **Tabek Patah**, a popular viewpoint, and move on to **Sungai Tarab**, an authentic old coffee mill still driven by water-wheel. The small town of **Batu Sankar** has a lovely old Meeting House, beautifully decorated with floral motifs, and **Lima Kaum** is the site of some sanskrit stones found in the fourteenth century. The **King's Palace**, just up the road from Lima Kaum, is a photographer's dream – a majestic structure recently restored (1970) in all its original splendour with a soaring ten-point roof and a huge rice-barn out front. A short stop at **Balimbing**, to see a 300-year-old traditional house is followed by swimming at **Lake Singkarak** and shopping for crafts at **Pandai Sikat**. This weaving and wood-carving village, 10 km from Bukittingi, has some beautiful things for sale – you pay 40,000rps (£15) for silk embroidery tapestries which take a month or more to make on primitive wooden looms – but before you splash out, just ask yourself what you are going to do with them back home. These pieces are not as functional as, say, batik sarongs!

Tours are best value on a Tuesday, when you get free transport and free admission (normally 500rps) to the big bullfight at **Koto Baru**. This event, which starts around 5 p.m., is not a bloodsport. Two bulls lock horns in a muddy field until one runs away to fight another day. When the loser makes his break, the field is suddenly full of of zigzagging locals going 'Ay-yay-yay! Ay-yay- yay!' and having the time of their lives. Bullfights sometimes happen on a Saturday too, although the venue is not always Koto Baru but sometimes a different neighbouring village. If not on a tour, and you want to take the chance, hop off the bus from Padang before going into Bukittingi.

ENTERTAINMENT

Traditional Minangkabau dancing takes place at the zoo between 1 and 3 p.m. every Wednesday, Saturday and Sunday. For evening entertainment, there are traditional art performances – music, dance, self-defence and folk theatre – at Jln Cindua Mato 10 (in front of the Gloria cinema at the market) from 8 to 10 p.m. every Wednesday and Saturday. Tickets (5000rps) are sold at Ganga guest house or at the door. On the way home, take a stroll down to the Lower Market – folk musicians play for pin money here between 9 and 11 p.m. The only other nightlife is (irregular) parties at the Three Tables Coffee House.

SHOPPING

There is a great selection of batik materials on the top floor of the **Confeksi** covered market opposite the Gloria cinema. All the locals shop here and prices are very reasonable. Take local buses out to **Kota Gadang** for gold and silver jewellery, and to **Pandai Sikat** (cf. Sights) for woodcarvings, silk embroidery and loom weaving. The Wednesday/Saturday market in the town centre runs from 7 a.m. to 5 p.m. and has everything from crafts and antiques to silks and spices.

ACCOMMODATION

Until the swish new **Garuda Hotel** (with pool) is completed (7 km out of town on Jln Veteran), Bukittingi's top place to stay is **Hotel Denai** (tel: 21460) at Jln Rivai 26, below Fort de Kok. It is a bright, cheerful place with rooms from US$27 single, US$30 double and luxury cottages at US$55. The nearby **Benteng Hotel** (tel: 21115) at Jln Benteng 1 is the highest-situated hotel in town, with scenic views, a good restaurant, well-furnished rooms from ll,500 to 34,500rps and bags of old-fashioned charm. Also on the way up to the fort, **Mountain View Hotel** (tel: 21621) at Jln Yos Sudarso 3 is actually a mid-range *losemn*. Pay 9000rps for a nice double room with tiled bathroom, and get one with a view of the valley. Right next door, **Wisma Bukittingi** (tel: 22900) has a quiet situation, friendly people, rooms from 5000 to 10,000rps, and a great motto: 'Fresh weather – you feel at home'. The new **Wisma Sri Kandi** (tel: 22984) at Jln A Yani 117 is very central, and very well priced at 7,500rps single, 10,000rps double. Every room has a sink, a writing desk and a party-size double bed – real luxury!

The cheaper *losmen* are concentrated along Jln A Yani in the centre of town. They all charge around the same – 2/3000rps single, 3/4000rps double, 4/5000rps triple – and many of them handle bus ticket bookings for Sumatra, Java and even Bali. The **Ganga Hotel** (tel: 22967) at No. 70 is possibly the best deal – 3000rps for regular rooms, carpeted and clean; 7500rps for superior rooms with shower and Western toilets. Avoid noisy rooms near the mosque and arrive early to get one with a window! The Ganga has good information, a laundry service and free tea and coffee. Further down Jln A Yani, **Tiga Balai** has singles for 2000rps, doubles for 3000rps, a TV lounge, good noticeboard and friendly people. **Singallang Inn** has one-price rooms at 3000rps and (working) showers. The communal eating area is great for meeting people. **Murni's**, opposite, is very popular, despite offhand staff. **Grand Losmen** isn't grand at all, but you could do worse. There are lots of other places so ask around.

FOOD

The street carts of Bukittingi (wandering *warungs*) do fantastic *martabak sayur* or vegetable spring rolls, although only at night. They are 600rps a time and a really tasty treat. The *martabak manis* are just as good – really thick pancakes stuffed with chocolate, nuts and crunchy sugar. They cost 400rps and I could eat them all day! Other popular street snacks are *sate ayam*, grilled corn on the cob with roasted peanuts, and *sayak*, a sweet and sour fruit and vegetable meal. Go to the big Pasar Atas market to find the full selection of local fare and try Padang-style food at the *warungs* on the junction of Jln A Yani and Jln Tengku. Try Chinese food at **Selecta** restaurant near the clock tower, go Indonesian at the **Simpang Raya** opposite the clock tower and tuck into cakes, pastries and fresh breads at the little bakery opposite the Grand Losmen. Most Westerners eat out at Jln A Yani's three 'coffee houses'. The **Singallang Coffee Shop**, opposite Ganga Hotel, does offbeat dishes like *soto Madura* along with Western-style omelette and chips. The smug **Coffee Shop** is a real one-upmanship place – full of real travellers going on about who's done the most daring trip recently. Unless you have just crawled off a 60-hour horror bus from Yogya, you are ashamed even to sit down! Better by far is the **Three Tables Coffee House** which actually had nine tables when I was there. This is a friendly hangout with delicious snacks, good music and chatty, informative staff. Like the Coffee Shop, it specialises in traditional travellers' fare – chips, banana pancakes, fruit salads and toasted sandwiches.

NIAS

For those who want to go to an island and get away from the tourist scene and not spend a lot of money, Nias still offers many opportunities. It is a popular surfing spot (especially during the November to December peak season) and a good escape for people who have been travelling for a year and who just want to collapse on a beach with a good book. An eight-hour ferry ride from Sibolga, off the west coast of north Sumatra, Nias is the home of rice growers, stone-age tribes and swarms of anthropologists. Of interest for its ancient villages, primitive customs and fine beaches, this once-remote island used to be the centre of a megalithic culture which began around 3000 BC and lasted well into the twentieth century. The hilltop villages have stone-paved streets, lined with unique stilted houses, and if you stay here long enough you may see the so-called leaping warriors of Nias, who jump over huge stone obelisks in the tradition of their pagan ancestors.

Watch your health on Nias. Recently, there have been continuous reports of malaria in the jungle interior and a massive cholera outbreak on the north of the island. So far, Teluk Dalam and the south seem to be okay, but take *both* types of malaria tablets and protect yourself against mosquitoes after dark.

ARRIVAL/DEPARTURE

You have got to be dedicated to visit Nias – I travelled for a whole week just to spend three days there! If you cannot afford 75,000rps for the SMAC flight to the island from Medan, pay 6500rps for the 10-12 hour bus ride from Bukittingi to the port-town of Sibolga. Off the bus, local touts will quickly sell you a boat ticket to Nias (much more convenient than going all the way to the harbour) and you can check out likely departure times at the various *losmen*. If you get stuck in Sibolga (as many people do) do not suffer in cheap, grim quarters, splash out 9000rps for a decent double room at **Hotel Pasar Baru** in New Market, near the bus-terminal. From Sibolga, there is one passenger boat a day, except Sunday, to the northern port of Nias, Gunung Sitoli, (6200rps, eight to ten hours), but it often breaks down. The big *Helena* cargo boat to Teluk Dayam, the island's southern port, leaves every three days or so (6000rps deck, 12,000rps cabin, 12-14 hours). However, it is not on any schedule, so it is really pot luck if you catch it. 'Like most travellers', commented one couple, 'we headed for the beaches, the culture and the jungle treks of south Nias. We arrived on a Wednesday and were told three days running that the *Helena* was leaving "tomorrow". Eventually, it was Saturday and the boat to the south didn't go and the boat to the north had engine failure. So there wasn't going to be a boat until Monday, because nothing leaves on Sunday. Two more days in Sibolga – we were going crazy! To our surprise, a boat left on Sunday after all – it went to the north, and we took a perilous bus journey (6500rps, four to ten hours) down to Lagundi beach from Gunung Sitoli. Leaving Nias was a problem also. We waited in the south three days and finally took a bus back up to the north – it was the only way to get out!'

SIGHTS/ACCOMMODATION

So, is it really worth the hassle of going there? Well, Nias is nice once you get to the south. The two most interesting villages are only 12 km apart and you can walk or cycle to most of the local sights. Teluk Dayam, the harbour town, has a few waterfront *losmen* (try **Effendi's**; rooms from 5000 to 8000rps) and a couple of Padang-style restaurants. Lagundi is a long horseshoe-shaped beach with good coral and surf at the top and good swimming in the centre. *Losmen* here are very cheap (1000-2000rps per room) but very simple. Bring a torch, a few candles and some food supplies. If you are here for the coral and the surfing, stay at **Sea Breeze** or **Happy** up on the north beach – they have the best food. Down at the sand beach, try **Magdelena** or **Yianti**. Both places arrange good side-trips to **Bawamataluo**, a traditional village with war-dancing, a chieftain's 'palace' and some sacrificial stone tables, to **Hilisimaetano**, where stone jumping over 2-m-high piles of stones is performed most Saturdays by trainee warriors and to **Botohili**, a delightful village of old-fashioned stone houses and unique customs. A lot of visitors to Nias, however, get stuck on the beach and see nothing of the local culture, so go on, make the effort!

SAMOSIR (LAKE TOBA)

The centre of Batak culture is the island of Samosir on Lake Toba, the largest lake in South-East Asia. At 900 m above sea-level, it provides a cool weekend retreat for wealthy Sumatrans from oil-rich Medan and a relaxing haven for travellers on a budget. There is not much to do on Samosir except read, write and play cards, but there are some good hill walks for trekkers and the lake is good for swimming. The island has several villages of historical interest, with royal tombs, cannibal courts and megalithic monuments. The Batak Toba are a gentle, friendly people who have recently converted to Christianity. For just £1 a night you can stay in one of their high-peaked *adat* houses on the water's edge and share their calm and unhurried way of life.

ARRIVAL/DEPARTURE

Boats go to Samosir from the town of Prapat on the northern shore of Lake Toba, 174 km from Medan. You can approach Prapat by bus from Bukittingi (12-16 hours), Sibolga (four hours) or Medan (six hours). On arrival, take a *bemo* (100rps) from the bus-station down to Andilo Travel (tel: 41548) at Jln Sisingamangaraja 41, above the pier. Here you can enjoy a meal and forward-book your onward travel – buses to Brastagi (five to six hours, 2000rps), Medan (2000rps), Sibolga (3000rps), Bukittingi (8000rps) and Padang (9000rps) – before boarding a boat over to Samosir. Boats do not work to any fixed schedule, but there is usually one every two hours between 9.30 a.m. and 6 p.m. out to Samosir and between 7 a.m. and 3 p.m. back to Prapat. The crossing takes one hour, the one-way fare is 500rps, and boats drop off and pick up from all the major *losmen* at Tuk-Tuk and Ambarita.

There are also irregular ferries to Tomok from Ajibata, 2 km from Prapat by minibus. Prapat's main pier has a smaller Andilo desk (useless) and a chaotic market – avoid it. Also avoid travel agent touts at the bus-station. They will tell you the last boat to Samosir has 'gone' and then will try to sell you both their boat and their accommodation.

Use Prapat to change money (at the post office above Andilo, if the banks are closed) since you cannot do it on Samosir. Near the post office is a telephone office open for 24 hours for overseas calls. Andilo has a few cheap rooms for 3000rps and **Wisma Danau Toba** (tel: 41216) at Jln P Samos 15 is the big resort hotel with rooms from 18,000rps. A good restaurant in Prapat is the **Asia**, 30 m below the post office.

Note: the express bus to Bukittingi via the equator (12/13 hours, 15,000rps) leaves every Monday and Friday at 6 a.m. – tickets from P T Dolok Silau, Jln Sisingamangaraha 113, Prapat, or from Gokhon library, Tuk Tuk.

TUK-TUK

Of the three tourist centres on Samosir Island (the other two are Ambarita, 3 km north and Tomok, 5 km south) Tuk Tuk peninsula has by far the best choice of accommodation. Most of the *losmen* here, as elsewhere on the island, are typical Batak buildings with sweeping saddle-back roofs, many of them in superb lakeside locations. **Tony's** has batak houses at 2-3000rps and sells nice weaving. This is a good place to check out how much they should cost before visiting the markets in Tomok and Ambarita. Other recommended cheapies are **Abadi** (next to Tony's) **Antonius** (towards Tuk Tuk Timbal) and **Judita** (near Toledo Inn). **Carolina Cottage** (tel: 41520), on the southern tip of the peninsula is always full. It offers good food, a lively atmosphere, clean rooms at 6-12,000rps and excellent views of the whole lake. **Toledo Inn** on Tuk Tuk is the island's most upmarket accommodation, with hot water, a nice beach and luxurious rooms from US$15 to 20.

The speciality food on Samosir (offered by every second *losmen*) – is 'smorgasbord'. This potpourri of assorted dishes is around 2000rps per person with fish and 5000rps with fresh suckling pig, but you only get these prices if there is a group of you. Every *losmen* has a restaurant, but Tuk Tuk has a few independent eating places like **Pepy's** and **Lekjon's**, which turn out first-rate European fare. You must watch what you eat on Samosir – a lot of *losmen* wash utensils in the lake or make tea from its water, so stomach complaints are common.

For information, go to **Gokhon Handicrafts Library** near Tony's *losmen*. Friendly Bernicke speaks good English, knows a lot about the island and distributes a good map. He sells books (English, German, Scandinavian and Dutch), copies tapes, rents bicycles, sells batak blankets and offers massage. His giant chess game (100rps a go) is a popular feature and he sells tickets for the Saturday night batak music/dance show at nearby **Laster Joni**. Tuk Tuk's other main nightspot is **Bernard's** with the occasional disco.

TUK TUK TIMBAL

This is the little 'thimble' or peninsula just off the Tuk Tuk mushroom going towards Ambarita. The single losmen, **Tuk Tuk Timbal** is run by a friendly Dutch-Indonesian couple and the food is

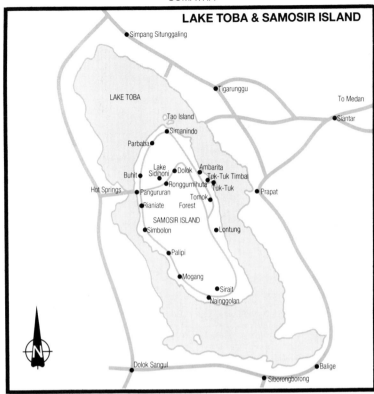

LAKE TOBA & SAMOSIR ISLAND

excellent. Just down the road is **Mr Mas**, a cosy place with Dutch cooking and home-made German cakes. It has the best swimming around, being situated away from the bay and having clear, clean water.

AMBARITA

Ambarita, an hour's walk from Tuk Tuk, has some stone chairs. There are three megalithic complexes here, documenting the practice of ritual cannibalism for which Samosir is notorious. The first features 300-year-old stone chairs where neighbouring chiefs would discuss the fate of a captured enemy. From there, they moved on to a second megalithic cluster to pronounce sentence. South of Ambarita is the third complex with a 'breakfast table' where the hapless prisoner was beaten to death, decapitated, chopped up on a stone, cooked with buffalo meat and washed down with blood. This is what local guides will tell you anyway – the Bataks commonly exaggerated their cannibalism to deter strangers from their shores.

Ambarita also has a small market (go shopping for striped Batak blankets, wood carvings, Chinese porcelain and old Dutch coins), a post office (open 8 a.m. to 2 p.m., closed Sunday) and a scruffy tourist information centre behind the stone chairs. Only in Ambarita can

you find a sandy beach. Stay at **New Rista** (5000rps per room) or at **Rohandy's** (1500/2000rps) right on the lake. **Gordon's**, a couple of kilometres beyond Ambarita on the way to Simanindo, has very nice bungalows down by the water's edge from 3000 to 5000rps. It is remote, but the food is good. Minibuses go there from Tomok and Ambarita.

TOMOK

The Bataks' lust for blood is further demonstrated by the tomb of King Sidabuta in Tomok, west of Tuk Tuk. The bloodstained coffin stands opposite ritual statues of a buffalo sacrifice, together with executioners. Don't let local lads charge you anything to see the graves – donations are entirely voluntary. They will describe the tombs, and the trees planted beside them, as 2,000 years old, but they probably date only to the sixteenth century. Tomok also has a busy market, a small museum and several fine traditional houses. But the beach is not clean, so few Westerners stay here. **Roy's** *losmen*, set back from the beach, has cheap rooms at 2/3000rps. **Toba Beach Hotel** (tel: 515562) charges 30-35,000rps and has a private beach.

AROUND THE ISLAND

Minibuses shuttle back and forth between Ambarita and Tomok every half-

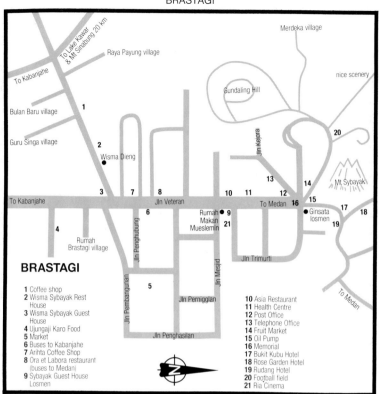

BRASTAGI

1 Coffee shop
2 Wisma Sybayak Rest House
3 Wisma Sybayak Guest House
4 Ujungaji Karo Food
5 Market
6 Buses to Kabanjahe
7 Arihta Coffee Shop
8 Ora et Labora restaurant (buses to Medan)
9 Sybayak Guest House Losmen

10 Asia Restaurant
11 Health Centre
12 Post Office
13 Telephone Office
14 Fruit Market
15 Oil Pump
16 Memorial
17 Bukit Kubu Hotel
18 Rose Garden Hotel
19 Rudang Hotel
20 Football field
21 Ria Cinema

hour or so until dark. They sometimes go to the village of **Simanindo**, 16 km from Ambarita on the northern tip of the island. The main attraction at Simanindo is the huge house of a Batak king, which has been restored as a museum. Here you can study the Batak tomb sites – the oldest sarcophagus dates to the seventeenth century and is ornately carved with figures and ornaments. The more recent are plain and decorated only with a simple cross.

When the new ring road around the island is completed (due 1990) you will be able to make the circuit by pushbike or motorbike – hire these from Carolina's or Gokhon library in Tuk Tuk. But Samosir is a place for walking – a myriad trails lead through the hills to hidden valleys, paddy fields and gushing waterfalls. John at Andilo Travel (Prapat) has full information on walking and motorbike trails and hands out a photocopied map. He will show you where to find the many interesting animals up in the mountains – white buffalo, wild pig, monkeys, birds and snakes. The best mountain walk starts from Ambarita. A hundred metres before the Protestant Church, follow the road up through the coffee plantations to the Christian tomb. From here, you can commence the climb (approximately four hours) up to the village of **Dolok**. Stay overnight at **Mr Jenny's**, a great little *losmen* with rooms for 1000rps, then walk 12 km on to **Lake Sidihoni**. Return along the same road.

BRASTAGI

Brastagi is a lovely, dusty old town surrounded by jungle and volcanoes, a worth-while stop between Medan (65 km north) and Lake Toba. The volcanic soil is so rich here that Brastagians say it takes six months for a fence to become a hedge. Because of its high elevation, 1,400 m above sea level, Brastagi has a cool healthy climate all year round. Founded by Dutch plantation owners in the 1920s, the town is today a market centre for the warm, sociable Karo people, whose distinctive horned-roof houses adorn several neighbouring villages. The name Brastagi has two possible derivations. In the first, *bras* means rice, *ta* is hour and *agi* is younger brother/sister. Thus the popular market call of 'Come, brother/sister, it is time to buy some rice!' The market is only recent, however, so this explanation is unlikely. The more probable derivation is from the Sanskrit word *braspati* meaning 'spirits of the soil' – there are numerous sacred places around Brastagi which, the Karo believe, house spirits which protect the trees, the rivers and the villages.

ARRIVAL/DEPARTURE

You can do the two-hour trip to Medan by bus (every 15 minutes from Sentosa coffee-shop at the bus-station, 750rps) or by share-taxi (every 30 minutes from Ora et Labora coffee-shop opposite the bus-station, 2500rps). Getting to Prapat, for Lake Toba, is less easy. There is no 2000rps 'combined' bus ticket this way round! You have to take three separate buses: from Brastagi to Kabanjahe (30 minutes, 150rps) to Siantar (three to four hours, 1000rps) and to Prapat (one hour, 300rps). On the way to Siantar, there are two worth-while stop-offs: **Si Piso-Piso Waterfall**, the highest waterfall in Sumatra and the **King's Palace**, a fine 200-year-old example of Karo architecture. A special taxi to Prapat (50,000rps, seats five) stops at both places and is sold by touts outside Wisma Sybayak.

To get to Bukit Lawang (cf. Medan section) from Brastagi, take a local bus to Sei Wampa (750rps), then another to Binjei (200rps), then a third to Bukit Lawang (900rps). There is one direct bus daily (1900rps, five to six hours) from outside Ora et Labora restaurant, Jln Veteran. Mr Pelawi at Wisma Sybayak offers popular three-day jungle treks to Bukit Lawang at 50,000rps per person, inclusive of food, guide, porters and all transport.

TOURIST SERVICES

Wisma Sybayak and Hotel Ginsata, at either end of the main street, Jln Veteran, are the best sources of information. The post office, near the monument at the bottom of Jln Veteran, is open from 8 a.m. to 2.30 p.m. Monday to Thursday, Friday until ll a.m., Saturday until l.30 p.m. Just below it, the telephone office is open 24 hours for overseas calls. Time your calls precisely here, to avoid arguments over the bill later! You can also phone from Wisma Sybayak – it is more expensive, but you get English-speaking assistance. Change money here too as there are no banks in town. Go swimming at the Rudang (1000rps/day) and Rose Garden (3000rps/day) hotel pools. Most travellers use the Rudang.

SIGHTS

If you think Brastagi is just a one-street town, check out the guest comments books at Wisma Sybayak – there are enough ideas here to keep you busy for a fortnight! Mr Pelawi provides guides for the two local volcanoes – 15,000rps (one to three people) to **Mt Sibayak**, 25,000rps to **Mt Sinabung**. Of the two, Sibayak (2,094 m) is the easier to climb and you can soak in hot springs on the way back. A guide is advisable, since it is *very* easy to get lost in the jungle. If you do it yourself, get a photocopied map (none too reliable) from Wisma Sybayak, hop on a minibus to Daulu Junction (300rps, 20 minutes), walk 4 km (or another minibus, 200rps) to Semangat Gunung village at the foot of the mountain, and climb up the hills (three and a half hours) and down the steps – not the other way round. Wear proper footgear for the wet slippery trails, take some snacks (anything for energy), do not get separated from your travel companion and mark your trail in case you are forced to come down the same way you went up.

After your climb, relax in **Lau Debuk-Debuk** hot springs, a short stroll from Daulu Junction. The turquoise-coloured water here is very good (suggested one traveller) if you are suffering from any infections. 'Stay in the water for about an hour, and clean the wound with cotton soaked in the water. The spring is rich in sulphur and very healing.' Back on the main road, you can walk (or hitch a lift) 2 km on (towards Medan) to **Sikulikap Waterfall**. This is a lovely spot also, with some good jungle walks.

If you want to climb Mt Sinabung (2,450 m) without a guide, start out as early as possible. It is a six-hour walk up and four hours down (on your knees!). Take a minibus from Brastagi to Kabanjahe (200rps), then another on to Singarangalang (500rps). Start from Mardingding – past a small lake, after 20 minutes' walk, you come to a junction where the path splits into two. Take the right fork (by the farmhouse) and then another 20 minutes on, when the path divides again. The jungle starts immediately after this. Take the left turning and follow the path all the way up. There is at least a three-hour walk through dense jungle and one and a half hours through stones and bushes. From the top, take the same way down again. The last hour of the ascent is especially steep so bring a torch, just in case, and food and water too. Mr Pelawi can suggest places to stay, but it is still a good idea to take a tent or sleeping bag. The views from the top of this volcano, while not as impressive as Sibayak, will reward your efforts, but not on a cloudy day.

Pelawi's latest 'discovery' is the orang-utan research station at **Ketembe**, north of Kutacane in Aceh province. Situated right in the middle of Gunung Leuser (the largest national park in South-East Asia) it has well-preserved jungle, wild orang-utans, hornbills, rhino and even tiger. Wisma Sybayak offers treks there, or you can do it yourself – take a bus from Brastagi to Kebonjahe (ll km, 30 minutes, 150rps), change to Kutacane on a Garuda/Selian bus (five to six hours, 2200rps) and get a third bus to Ketembe (one hour, 500rps). In Ketembe, stay in the guest house next to the Alas River and walk alone or hire guides (10,000rps

Children nit-picking, Lake Toba

Batak-style guest houses in Samosir

per day) for two- to four-day jungle treks. Pa Ali, the coffee-shop owner in Ketembe, does good food and arranges cheap guides. You can sleep on mattresses in his *warung* for 1000rps.

SHOPPING
Shop for Batak ornaments and antiques at **Namaken Souvenir Shop** or **Crispo Antiques** in Jln Veteran. The central market, best on Tuesday, Friday and Sunday, has a good selection of sarongs (lovely designs) and Balinese-style *ikat* too. In the market, **Nandi Pen's** stall (Keleng Br Purba) sells Batak weavings and Karo traditional cloth at reasonable prices.

ACCOMMODATION
Brastagi's top hotels are north of town: **Rose Garden Hotel** (tel: 20099) at Jln Peceren 1, **Rudang Hotel** (tel: 43) and **Bukit Kubu** at Jln Sempurna. All three have comfortable rooms from 20,000 and 40,000rps and good bar-restaurants. Stay at the first two for air-conditioning, pool and 3-star facilities: at the Bukit Kubu for golf, horse-riding and old-style colonial charm. There is not much in the mid-range, just a few hilltop bungalows like **Karo Hill** (9000rps double) on Jln Jaranguda, 2 km out of town. For cheap 3000-4000rps rooms at **Wisma Sybayak**, Jln Udara 1 (tel: 20953), arrive before noon as this place is permanently full. The food and gardens are a big draw and so is Mr Pelawi the manager. He is a retired English schoolteacher who has compiled an astonishing amount of information (and maps) for tourists. He even confirms air tickets. If you cannot get a room, take a mattress-bed on his floor for 1000rps or stay at **Sibayak Rest House**, opposite, until one comes vacant. Nearby **Wisma Dieng**,Jln Udara 27, has double rooms only at 5000rps. **Ginsata Hotel**, Jln Veteran 79, charges 3000/4000rps for singles/doubles. The manager, Mr Paligan ('Mr Bullshit') is a good guide.

FOOD
Check out the special Karo Batak food in the market. There are many stalls here and the dish to ask for is *babi panggang*, roast pork, rice and blood sauce. **Ujung Ali** *warung*, about 2.5 km out of town on the way to Kebonjahe, is an excellent place to sample Karonese cooking. **Rumah Makanan Muslim** restaurant, next to the cinema in Jln Veteran, does cheap and excellent Muslim curries, but leave some room for the *sate* sold outside. **Siang Malam**, on the corner of Jln Trimurti, is tops for Chinese and European food and is far friendlier than the overrated **Europa** and **Asia** restaurants. Most travellers eat at **Wisma Sybayak** (seafood, Chinese and European) and drink coffee at **Erwin Purba**, next to the market – real coffee beans only!. For something completely different, try Brastagi's own special drink, *bandrek*, made from freshly ground ginger and served piping hot. Like many people, I could never decide if it was absolutely delicious or absolutely undrinkable.

MEDAN
The capital of north Sumatra, Medan is important purely as an entry or exit-point for Penang or peninsular Malaysia. Once the seat of the Dutch plantation owners before the war, it is no longer the 'Paris of Sumatra'. The city centre is today a hell's kitchen of exhaust fumes, buzzing two-stroke engines and noise. It is like a mini-Bangkok, but with few redeeming features. Founded as a seventeenth-century sultanate, the name Medan means 'battlefield' and it often feels like it. Women travellers get particularly hassled and several of them have ended up making complaints at their embassy. If you survive the first day (which is all most people allow before moving on to Brastagi/Toba) you may believe the second interpretation of Medan's name, which is *madan* or 'recovered from illness'. Once the home of a traditional Karo healer called Patimpus (his statue is in the street of the same name) and still a centre of doctors and hospitals, the town has many hidden attractions to revive the shell-shocked traveller – parks, temples, mosques, palaces, old colonial buildings, even a crocodile farm and a Chinese food market. It is also the best approach to the orang-utan research centre at Bukit Lawang, which is something special.

ARRIVAL/DEPARTURE
Air
The major western gateway to Indonesia, Medan is a good place to arrange international flights. Penang-Medan flights are operated by MAS, cost around US$50 and take just 20 minutes to cross the narrow Melaka Strait. Medan-Jakarta is serviced by Garuda (163,400rps for midday flight, 139,400rps for evening flight), Mandala (118,500 for morning flight, 108,000rps for afternoon flight) and Merpati (108,600rps). Medan-Singapore is covered by Garuda and Singapore Airlines (US$258) and Medan-KL by Garuda and MAS (US$120).

Medan's steamy, chaotic Polonia airport has lockers in its domestic lounge, where you can leave bags for 500rps per piece per day. The domestic terminal has much better facilities (snack bar, restaurant and book stall) than the international terminal. From airport to town centre (2 km) costs 5000rps by taxi or (if you walk 300 m to the outside gate) 1000rps by trishaw.

Sea

The *Gadis Langkasuka* sails for Penang at 6 p.m. every Tuesday and Thursday (sometimes Saturday too) from Medan's Belawan harbour. The comfortable ll/12 hour trip costs 41,850rps deck, 48,350rps cabin and tickets are sold by Eka Sukma Wisata Tour, Jln Brigend Katamso 62A. You must be on this boat by 4 p.m. at the latest – that is when the customs men go home. Pelni ships go from Belawan to Jakarta every Monday at noon (48 hours, 36,200rps deck, 49,000rps fourth class), to Padang every Tuesday at noon (12 hours, 26,000rps) and to Tanjung Pinang for Singapore (30,000rps). Buy tickets from the Pelni office (tel: 25100) at Jln Sugiano 5, or, perhaps more convenient, from Jacky at the Indian Food Centre or Arthur at Tapian Nabaru *losmen*. To get to Belawan harbour, 26 km north of Medan centre, pay 2000rps for the tourist bus or catch a 'Damri Patas' public bus from the junction of Jln Getah and Jln Puteri Hijau (200rps). Have 150rps handy for the port entrance charge.

Road

There are very regular buses to Prapat (2000rps, four hours) from Sisingaman-garaja station and to Brastagi (750rps, two hours) from the terminal on Jln Iskander Muda. The Indian Food Centre offers taxis to Prapat (7500rps) and to Brastagi (1500rps). The 'Pem Semesta' bus for Bukit Lawang picks up from the corner of Jln Iskandermuda and Jln Binjei. On arrival in Binjei (30 minutes, 200rps), tell the driver to drop you at Lapangan and hop on a second bus to Bukit Lawang. Bus tickets to Bukittingi, Sibolga and Jakarta are available from the ALS office (tel: 22014) at Jln Ama-liun 2a, or from the Indian Food Centre.

TOURIST SERVICES

Far better than the mediocre tourist office (Jln A Yani 107) is the Indian Food Centre at Jln Kediri 96. This place is a classic example of an enterprising indi-vidual (in this case, manager Jacky) taking on the role of tourist officer and doing it ten times better than paid officials. A whole wall of his restaurant is given over to useful information, not only on Medan but on the whole of Sumatra.

The post office, an historic old Dutch building, is centrally located on Merdeka square. To make overseas calls, go to Indosat in Jln Perintis Kemerdekaan. They give a special 25 per cent discount between 12 midnight and 6 a.m. and accept collect calls and credit-card calls for a number of countries. It is important to change money in Medan before ven-turing inland, where banks are few and far between. Bank Negara Indonesia, Jln Pemuda 12 and Bank Bumi Daya, oppo-site Danau Toba Hotel, offer the best rates. Merpati, Garuda and Mandala are all close together on Jln Brigend Katam-so. MAS (tel:: 51933) has a small, efficient office at Hotel Danau Toba, Jln Imam Bonjol 17 and is open from 8.30 a.m. to 4.30 p.m. weekdays, until 3 p.m. on Saturday. You will find Singapore Airlines in the Polonia Hotel, Jln Jen Sudirman and SMAC (for flights to Nias) at Jln Imam Bonjol 59. Mitra Book Store, two minutes' walk from the Indian Food Centre, has second-hand books for sale and exchange. Medan has consulates for UK, USA, West Germany and va-rious other countries – check the tele-phone directory.

SIGHTS

You can see Medan's few sights in a morning, by motorised *becak* (around 1500rps for a 15-minute ride), by yellow minibus (standard fare 150rps) or on foot. The **Maimoon Palace**, at Jln Katam-so 66, is good for a wander, even if you cannot go inside the building (now gov-ernment offices). Built by the Sultan of Deli in 1888 in a mixture of architectural styles (Oriental, Middle Eastern and Western) this fantastic structure is best visited in the early morning, although you can drop in at any time (even midnight!). From here, it is a short stroll over to the **Great Mosque** on Jln Sising-amangaraja, a beautiful Moroccan-style edifice built by the Sultan of Deli in 1906. The **Mayor's Office** on Jln Balai Kota,is a supreme example of Dutch colonial architecture. It dates to 1908, and is open to the public from 9 a.m. to 2.30 p.m. Monday to Thursday, Friday till ll a.m., Saturday till 1 p.m. The **Bukit Barisan** war museum at Jln H Zainul Arifin 8, is open the same hours and has military displays from the Second World War, the War of Independence and the 1958 Sumatran rebellion. On Jln Teuku Umar, the new (and very pretty) Indian temple is modelled on the Sri Mariam-man temple in Penang. Just up the road from Tapian Nabaru *losmen*, an interest-ing Chinese temple burns huge 'crema-tion houses' of paper and wood at midnight – contact Jacky at the Indian Food Centre to arrange a visit. He can also arrange *becaks* (500rps per person return) to the **Crocodile Farm** 7 km out of town at Asam Kumbang village, near Sunggal. Some 1,500 crocodiles live here and feeding time is 4.30 p.m. Finally, if you need a rest from Medan's crazy traffic, there is a large, relaxing park at Jln Sudirman, in front of the Elizabeth Hospital.

Bukit Lawang, 87 km from Medan, has an orang-utan rehabilitation centre, one of only two places in the world where they still exist in the wild. Orang-utans are presently facing extinction – there are

MEDAN

Key:

1 Airport
2 Railway station
3 Bank Bumi Daya
4 Post office
5 Belawan bus station
6 Central minibus station (Sambu)
7 Wampu bus station (for Brastagi & Bukit Lawang)
8 Bus to Bukit Lawang
9 Indian Food Restaurant
10 Tapian Nabaru Hotel
11 Wisma Sybayak Transit Accommodation
12 Hotel Sumatra
13 Prapat bus station (for Toba)
14 Eka Sukma Wisata (Penang ferry agent)
15 Tip Top restaurant
16 Tourist office
17 Hotel Danau Toba
18 Pelni office
19 Siguragura Hotel
20 Maimoon Palace
21 Hotel Garuda
22 Deli Plaza shopping centre
23 Hotel Polonia
24 Chinese food street
25 Garuda office
26 Merpati office
27 Medan zoo

To Prapat

To Delitua

Jln Singamangaraja

Jln Rahmadsyan

Jln Puri

Jln Amaliun

15

Jln Surabaya

Jln Selat Panjang

Jln Semarang

Jln Martinus Lubis

Jln Veteran

Jln Letjen Haryono MT

Jln Pandan

Jln Sambu

Jln Bawean

Jln Rupat

Jln Perintis Kemerdekaan

Jln Ceribon

12

13

21

24

Jln Bandung

Jln Bogor

Jln Pandu

26

Jln Brigjen Katamso

14

20

2

5

6

Jln R Bola

Jln Kesenian

Jln Pemuda

16

Jln Balai Kota

19

25

Jln Palang Merah

18

Jln Sugiono

Jln Warni

27

To Belawan

Jln Putri Hijau

22

Jln Tembakau Deli

4

Jln R Saleh

3

17

Jln Teugku Daud

Jln Tuan Sri Lanang

9

Jln R A Kartini

23

Jln Letjen Suprapto

Jln Imam Bonjol

1

Jln Diponegoro

Jln H Z Arfin

Jln Hang Tuah

Jln Jend Sudirman

Jln H Ir Juanda

Jln Mongonsidi

Deli River

Jln Guru Patimpus

Jln Jend Gatot Suroto

10

Babura River

Jln Gajah Mada

Jln Hasannudin

Jln Hayam Wuruk

Jln Syailendra

Jln Iskandar Muda

8

11

To Brastagi

Jln Sei Wampu

7

To Binjai

only about 1,000 left in the Sumatran jungles. These lovable long-armed apes are bred in zoos all round the world and are sent here to be trained to live in the wild. It often takes seven to ten years to achieve this. The actual centre is at Bohorok, a steep half-hour walk from Bukit Lawang to the river, then across by canoe. The cost of the boat is included with the 3000rps permit for three days' stay issued by the PPA office (open 24 hours) in Bukit Lawang village. Orang-utan feeding times (usually 7.30 a.m. and 3.30 p.m.) are posted here also. 'Go on the morning feeding trip', suggests one traveller, 'because the orangs sometimes do not turn up in the afternoons and it is a hot steep climb through the jungle for nothing!' Times *not* to go to Bukit Lawang are busy weekends, when loads of Medan day-trippers turn up and the rainy months of September to November, when the boat often cannot cross the river to the rehabilitation centre because of high water.

In the village, rooms at **Wisma Bukit Lawang** (4/5000rps) are much better than at **Wisma Leuser Sibayak** (3500rps single, 5000rps double), but the Sibayak has far better information and food. Everybody recommends the Sunday night buffets: 'A bit expensive at 3000rps, you may think, until you get halfway down the 20ft table and realise that your plate is piled high and you haven't got a bit of everything! Three trips might do it, so if you intend going, skip all other meals that day!' Both lodges hire out guides for jungle treks at around 10,000rps per person per day. The area round Bukit Lawang is one of the largest remaining tracts of primary jungle in Sumatra, so you can expect value for money. Another good idea is to rent a tyre and drift down the river to Bohorok – three hours of unexpected obstacles. You emerge from the river at the first large bridge you come to and drip onto the bus back. The bruised bits only really ache the next day.

ENTERTAINMENT
If you fancy a swim, use the pools at the Danau Toba (1500rps/day) or Tiara (5000rps/day) hotels. The Danau Toba is open to the public, so avoid busy afternoons when all the locals dive in. There is a good disco at the Danau Toba and lots of billiard tables too. For a cheap, soothing massage (8500rps/hour) go to the 24-hour parlour at Hotel Dirga Surya.

SHOPPING
Bargain hard for antiques, bamboo weaving, Dutch pottery and woodcarvings at the arts and crafts shops along Jln Jen A Yani. For batik sarongs, shirts and paintings, try **Batik Semar** at Jln H Z

Arifin 105 – it is a two-minute walk from the Indian Food Centre and stocks mainly Solo produce. **Deli Plaza** in Jln Balai Kota is a good place for general shopping. It sells cheap English tapes and all kinds of imported goods and clothes from all over the world. Rather less appealing are the heaps of second-hand clothes found along Jln Mongonsidi – they are apparently donations from European people for the refugees in Indonesia!

ACCOMMODATION
There is a lot of competition between Medan's top hotels, so big discounts are possible. The last time I was there, the large and well-established **Danau Toba International** (tel: 327000), Jln Imam Bonjol 17, was offering a 'permanent' 50 per cent discount, bringing the cost of an air-conditioned double room down to less than £20 a night! Great value this, especially with a pool, bowling alley, two bars, three restaurants and all other 4-star facilities included. The brand-new **Tiara Medan** (tel: 516000) in Jln Cut Mutiah is, however, Medan's leading hotel, an ultra-modern place with pool, bar-lounge, grill room, health centre and air-conditioned rooms from US$41 single, US$45 double (plus 10 per cent taxes). For half these prices you can enjoy a quiet comfortable stay at the **Polonia Hotel** (tel: 325300), Jln Jen Sudirman 14, with a pool, fitness centre, first-class Chinese restaurant and air-conditioned rooms with in-house video.

There is not much in the mid-range. **Hotel Sumatra** (tel: 24973) at Jln Sising-amangaraja 27 has clean fan rooms with bathroom for 15,000rps (ask for one at the back, off the noisy main street) and a few air-conditioned rooms around 20,000rps. The air-conditioned coffee shop is a bonus and guests get free transport to the airport. **Hotel Dirga Surya** (tel: 323433), Jln Imam. Bonjol 6, in front of the American Consulate, is an older place but quieter, asking 25,000rps for fan rooms, 35,000rps for air-conditioned. **Hotel Wai Yat** (tel: 321683), Jln Asia 44, has a reputable restaurant and rooms from 20,000rps.

At the bottom end, try **Tapian Nabaru Hotel** (tel: 512155) at Jln Hang Tuah 6. It is a clean, quiet little place (totally removed from the city noise) with a breezy 2000rps dormitory and double rooms with fan for 4000rps. Manager Arthur speaks Dutch and English, and is both helpful and informative. Good breakfasts, real (free) coffee, small garden and only a short walk to the brilliant Indian Food Centre – who could ask for more? If full, try **Hotel Irama** down a small alley at Jln Palang Merah 1125, by the junction of Jln Listrik and close to Hotel Danau Toba. Clean and friendly, it has dormitory beds for 2000rps and small, stuffy rooms (no fan) at 3000/4000rps. **Sigura Gura** at Jln Lt Jen Suprapto 2K, near the Garuda office, is for emergencies only – grim little cells (with fan) at 5000rps. The **Hotel Garuda** at Jln Sisingamangaraja 18 has a range of rooms from 7000 to 17500rps and is worth the extra expense.

FOOD

Medan has a lively little Chinatown which really comes into its own at night, when the twin food streets open up off Jln Bogor. The first street, Jln Selat Panjang, is where to try *dim sum*, steamed *momos*, hot *sate* Padang and excellent seafood. Don't miss the *mie pansit* at **Mie Pansit Tiong Sim** stall. The other street, Jln Semarang, has more atmosphere and an even better choice of dishes. Try the *foo yung hai* at **Lili's** *warung*, it is special! The stalls open up at 7 p.m. and close around 1 a.m. (on Saturday night, around 4 a.m.).

Of the many Chinese restaurants in town, **Restoran Mikado** (tel: 26863) at Jln Pelangkaraya 1 is tops for seafood. Come in a group and order a selection of dishes – a real blowout will not cost you more than 10,000rps a head. For Western food, go to **Tip Top Restaurant** at Jln Jen A Yani. It is an all-in-one eating house – a combined cafe, restaurant, lunch room, patisserie, ice-cream palace and bakery – with nostalgic live music from 7 to 11 p.m. A few doors down, **Lyn's Cafe** does superb steaks and spaghetti bolognaise. At the huge **Deli Plaza** shopping centre, on the corner of Jln Balaikota and Jln Getah, you will find a **Kentucky Fried Chicken** and a whole host of Chinese, European, Indonesian and Padang fast-food specialists. At Jln Kediri 96, the **Indian Food Centre** offers authentic Bombay-style *birianis*, *thalis*, yogurt cocktails and *dosas* at very reasonable prices. Manager Jacky provides games (backgammon, draughts, scrabble), ice-cold beers, a reliable travel/tour service and up-to-date information on just about everything.

Bali

With its vibrant culture, scenic beauty and white sandy beaches, Bali has become, in the mind's eye of millions of people, the epitome of the exotic far-away island paradise. Yet if its name has long been evocative of magical romance, it has only recently become Indonesia's most popular tourist attraction. Tourists have been coming here for over 50 years, but it was only when the Reagans dropped in on their way to a Tokyo summit in 1986 that President Suharto and his government positively earmarked Bali as the tourist highspot in their 13,677-island archipelago. It was about this time, too, that the cheap-deal flights offered by Garuda decisively transformed Kuta and the surfing spots around the southern peninsula into an Australians' Torremolinos.

If this is the end of your South-East Asia tour, you will want at least a week in Bali – to shop for crafts, to laze on beautiful beaches, to explore the island by jeep, to sample the delicious food (a real change after all that Indonesian *nasi goreng!*) and to tune in to the local music and dance – before heading on home. If Bali is your first stop, give yourself an extra few days to acclimatise to Asian temperatures and humidity, and save yourself some culture shock by getting out of noisy Kuta or Denpasar as soon as possible!

THE LAND

Lying off the eastern end of Java, Bali is a small, rugged and mountainous island covering an area of 5,558 sq km. Depending on traffic conditions, you could drive the 130 km east to west across it (along the north coast) in just four and a half hours and the 85 km from north to south (i.e. Kuta to Singaraja) in two and a half to three hours. The island is split in two by a high mountain range which includes Mt Agung (3,200 m) and three other large volcanic peaks. A beautifully terraced expanse of fertile land descends south of the mountains all the way down to the Indian ocean. Denpasar, the capital and the tourist belts of Sanur and Kuta are located on the eastern and western coasts of the southern part of the island. The peninsula of Nusa Dua on the southern tip is fast developing as a resort.

Despite the inroads of tourism, the old Bali of traditional ways and unchanged customs goes on behind the scenes, even at busy commercialised Kuta beach. And it doesn't take more than a half-hour drive out of any of the main tourist areas to find the 'real' Bali – with its sculpted rice-terraces, colourful temple festivals and smiley people – perfectly intact. It is amazing how strong the religious tradition of the Balinese people still is. It is wrong to assume that because Kuta has become ruined by tourism, they have lost all their culture. They are always going out to some festival, wedding or funeral and half the reason (if not the whole reason) they tolerate the tourism excesses of Kuta is to *pay* for all those celebrations!

If you take out Denpasar, Kuta, Sanur and Nusa Dua, all located in one very small south sector of the island, and travel just 16 km outside of them, you have completely left tourism behind. The second Bali is the lush, tropical hinterland of beautiful countryside and tiny unspoilt villages where people are genuine and friendly, don't speak any English and are just happy to see you. Rent a bicycle, ride 5 km out of Kuta and suddenly you are in the ricefields. Everyone is laughing and smiling and shouting 'Hello mister, how are you?'. It is the real Bali and it is obvious that most tourists do not bother to go there. What they miss are all those ceremonies, temple festivals and cremations one comes across unexpectedly while cycling or driving around in the countryside. You just have to be there when it happens and if you get stuck in Kuta you will never know about it.

Something else you will notice away from the tourist spots is a lot of people. Bali has a population of 2.6 million and is densely populated. Few people own much land and those who do do not own much (a father's death means the subdivision of his land among his sons, resulting in plots too small to be profitable) but none of it goes unused. The hinterland of Bali (what the locals in Kuta call 'the Wild West') is actually rice terraces all the way up the lower slopes (until they are no longer feasible) and immaculately laid-out plantations of rubber, bananas, coconuts and cloves. There is nothing 'wild' about Bali any more, it is almost completely cultivated!

HISTORY

In terms of their history, the Balinese are the last surviving remnant of the old Hindu empire that once held sway in Java. Gajah Mada, chief minister of Java's Majapahit kingdom, subjugated Bali in the mid-fourteenth century and ruled from his capital at Gelgel near Klungkung. The introduction of east Javanese influences led to an astonishing burst of artistic, musical and architectural energy which has continued on (albeit in

BALI

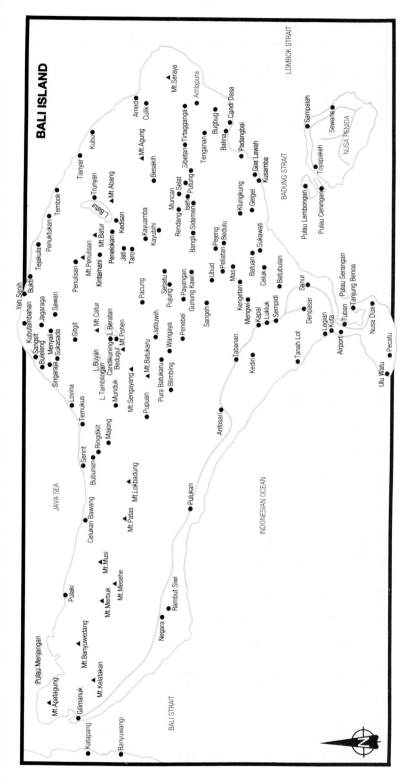

a commercialised form) right up to the present day. The main thrust came early on, when the Majapahits were forced out of Java by the spread of Islam and migrated to Bali with all their top scholars and artists in 1478. This was the springboard for the development of a unique Bali-Hindu culture, a fascinating synthesis of the Bronze Age animism of the Balinese natives and the polytheistic Hinduism of the new Majapahit rulers. A very proud people, the Balinese today consider themselves far superior to their Javanese neighbours, partly because they have an ancient heritage, (the connection [dim though it is] with the old royal family of Yogya) but also because of their alleged descent from the warrior caste of Rajasthan in India. When the Dutch invaded in 1908, Balinese royalty dressed up in ceremonial robes and, preferring mass suicide (*puputan*) to surrender, charged the Dutch machine-guns armed only with *kris* daggers. The few survivors lost their kingdoms to the new Dutch colonial government, but retained their palaces and became respected as patrons of the arts.

MUSIC AND DANCE
The powerful religious sense of the Balinese finds its main expression in the arts and every person seems to be an artist in some form, whether it is painting, weaving, carving, basketry or just making decorations for the family temple. Music and dance are taught from a very young age and almost every village has a group of musicians who perform on special religious occasions. The instruments are collectively referred to as the *gong*, after the largest and most obvious member. In the larger towns, many neighbourhood associations (*banjars*) have *gongs* and groups of dancers who perform at major festivals. Most villages have two orchestras: *leggong* (or *gong kebyar*) for welcome dances and special events and an *anklung* which plays mainly at birth and wedding ceremonies. A third *gamelan* set called a *gender* is also sometimes present, for cremations. Balinese *gamelan* is a good deal livelier and noisier than its (rather soporific) Javanese counterpart. *Gamelan* bands play with great gusto and participants rarely (unlike at Yogya) disappear or stop for a chat in the middle of a performance.

Dances are very spectacular (as are costumes) and artistes use their hands, head and eyes to great effect. There are over 200 dances in the Balinese repertoire and all are unique to the island. The famous trance dances of Ubud (Bali's cultural heartland) derive, for instance, from a time when serious outbreaks of malaria afflicted the villagers, inspiring them to communicate with the gods in a state of trance. This evolved through the centuries into a whole range of religious dance forms. The majority of these are highly stylised and take their themes from the old Hindu epics of the Ramayana and the Mahabaharata, or from local folklore. No visit to Bali would be complete without seeing a performance of the *Kecak* or monkey-dance at Ubud. Here you have 100 men seated in a dark, torch-lit circle, chanting, clapping, hissing and shouting in perfect polyrhythmic harmony. It is quite a spectacle! Less invigorating, but just as watchable, is the dazzling *legong* dance (performed by young girls of astonishing grace and muscular dexterity), the *Baris* warrior dance (for the men, this one, with lots of those-who-are-about-to-die heroics) and the pantomime-like *Barong* or *Kris* dance (performed by giant puppets on stilts). All these entertainments, plus the Balinese version of the Ramayana classical dance drama, are best seen in their complete form and at Ubud. Don't waste your money on inferior cut-down versions at Kuta.

RELIGION
ost of Bali's prolific artistic activity is directed towards decorating temples, celebrating weddings and funerals, or making offerings to the gods. Gods, good and bad, must be appeased daily with offerings of food or flowers in home temples, village temples or regional temples of the Mother Temple of Besakih, as well as by the roadside, in doorways, or among the Foster's cans on a bar table (do not worry, by the way, if you step on these 'offerings' as you walk along the road as the gods have already eaten the essence!). The Balinese may have adopted the veneer of Hinduism (indeed, 95 per cent of the population are theoretically Hindu) but they remain at heart superstitious, spirit-fearing animists. You will not, for instance, find many of them going for a swim with the tourists because there are too many mind-boggling monsters and demons in the sea!

Religion governs every aspect of Balinese life, from birth to death. The centre of community life is the temple and each village must have at least three. Since each one of Bali's 20,000 temples is subject to a three-day festival and since there are only 210 days in the Balinese year in which to celebrate them, there is always a festival going on somewhere on the island. Cremations, for which families scrimp and save for years and then dig their long-dead relatives up again, are especially fun occasions since they represent the liberation of the soul. Significantly, most of the money the Balinese make out of tourism goes not on achieving a higher standard of living, but on affording bigger and better funerals!

Tips

Although the Balinese have become used to tourists and can generally speak more English than people in other parts of Indonesia, they have a very polite social etiquette and always appreciate efforts to conform to their local traditions. While anything (including topless bathing) may go in Kuta, it is most certainly not tolerated elsewhere. To avoid offence and to make life easy for the travellers who come after you, be mindful of the local customs:

- Wear a sash tied around your waist at temples and ceremonies. You can pick one up cheaply in the local market.
- Wear sensible dress (no bikinis and beachwear) in public places and on local transport.
- When taking photographs, respect Balinese religion and privacy.
  Don't climb onto the temple walls or shrine, do not put yourself on a higher level than the village elders and do not snap people bathing in public places or rivers.
- Women are not allowed to enter temples when menstruating and it is rude to walk in front of people when they are praying.

SHOPPING

Shopping in Bali is nothing like as cheap as it once was. The influx of tourism has sent prices soaring and shopkeepers do not haul you off the street to buy any more, they sit and wait for you to come in. Over the short space of 18 months (from late 1987 to early 1989), the average Balinese wage virtually doubled and this was mainly because tourists did not know the real value of goods and paid far more than they needed to. If you want fair prices, be prepared to bargain as though your life depended on it and try to shop alone to avoid paying commissions to 'guides' or touts. The cheapest shopping is in the off-season months of February and March, when all the Aussies have gone home and shopkeepers drop their prices radically.

Bali is famous for its ethnic 'handmade' crafts and if you know what you are looking for there are some truly excellent pieces to be found at bargain prices. Don't buy anything on the first day however, take the time to wander round, to compare prices, and to see the difference between quality art and tourist tat. There is a great deal of massproduced junk about, churned out by cottage industries (or 'factories') for the benefit of the undiscerning big spender. In general, it is best to shop for crafts in the villages that actually produce them. For paintings and carvings, go to Ubud and to the villages of Mas and Peliatan just below Ubud. For stone sculptures, make your way to Batubulan. Bratan

and Celuk have a name for weaving, gold and silverwork, while the art market at Sukawati sells woodcarvings and *ikat* textiles at really low prices. It is incredible what deals you can get in the villages, without even having to bargain!

Kuta and Sanur are boutique-land and shopping for leathers, handbags, accessories and fashion clothes is much better here than in Bangkok. There is a far better range of produce and a lot of it is original stuff, not copies. Shop prices are theoretically fixed, but you can often bargain 10 to 20 per cent off goods with labelled prices and up to 30 per cent on items without a tag. Fashion shirts go from between 15000 and 20000rps and top-quality leather jackets, made to your own design, can be had for as little as £80. Experienced travellers shop around, then buy in bulk (a number of different items) from one shop. This is a particularly good idea if you are flying home from Bali and need lots of presents for friends. The more you buy, the better price you get. Take the basic Bali singlet, for instance. You can get them for as little as 1000rps apiece (normal price 3000rps) if you buy a couple of dozen! The bottom price on a T-shirt is 3000rps, on a normal button-up shirt with collar around 5000rps (from a market stall) and on a ladies' dress from 4 to 6000rps, depending on length and fabric. Flat-heel fashion shoes in leather come in all colours of the rainbow and start at around 30,000rps, but you can bargain down to 20,000rps, with a second pair for only 18,000rps. If you want them made up, they will let you choose the style and the leather type. Readymade shoes go from around 16000rps in the shops along Kuta's Legian St, but they will not often have your size.

In Bali, as in Bangkok, there are a lot of fake designer watches peddled on the streets. Most of them come out of Hong Kong (Bangkok has its own Lacoste and Rolex factories, but the CIA is cracking down on all home-produced copy goods in Thailand) and most of them are okay. A friend of mine, an experienced buyer who knew what he was looking for, bought 30 watches in Kuta. Three months later, 20 of them were still working. Copy watches (sold mainly in Kuta) start at around 45000rps. Early in the morning, you cannot bargain the touts down below 25000rps, but go at around 9 or 10 p.m. at night (which is when they usually pack up) and you can often haggle down to 10 or 15000rps. This ploy goes for all goods sold on the streets – the evening is the best time to buy.

Buying jewellery (especially silver) is a risky business. A lot of so-called 'cheap' silver is, in fact, silver-plated copper, which tarnishes after a week. There is no easy way of telling good from bad silver (even the plated stuff is hallmarked!). The only tip I can offer is that silver-plate is much brighter and whiter than the genuine article. If you are staying in Kuta, Sanur or Ubud, ask your hotel/ *losmen* to get someone reliable off the street. Otherwise, stop off at Celuk on the way up to Ubud. There is a wide range of silver jewellery here, most of it is genuine and (if you avoid the more touristy shops) it is very cheap.

CLIMATE
Bali is only 8 degrees south of the equator, which means that it is hot and humid all year round, particularly in the centre of the island. There are only two seasons: hot and dry from April to September and hot and wet from October to March. The wettest months are December and January, but even then the rains are interspersed with periods of glorious sunshine. Temperatures range from 75–82°F (24–28°C), and the hottest months are May and early October.

There are two peak seasons for tourists: mid-December to mid-January (Christmas, New Year and Australian summer holidays) and July-August (European summer holidays, Australian winter break). At these times, accommodation is in short supply, rooms are not discounted, shopping is most expensive and rates for car hire go through the roof. Whenever you go, there will always be tourists at Kuta and Sanur.

ARRIVAL/DEPARTURE
There are several travel agents in Kuta, offering cheap air/rail/bus travel into Java, as well as budget flights to Europe, Australia and Asia. Most agencies are reliable (try Perama on Legian St, tel 51551) but do not pay any money until you have seen your ticket!

Air
Bali's Ngurah Rai airport (tel: 5101l) has adjacent terminals for domestic and international flights. Airport services include tourist information, money-changing, left luggage and an expensive bar. On arrival, book a taxi from the counter at the exit. Fares are fixed and you can go to Kuta (3 km, 3200rps non-air-conditioned/4500rps air-conditioned) to Denpasar (13 km, 6800/9000rps), to Sanur (10 km, 8700/12000) or to Nusa Dua (12 km). Alternatively, you can walk out of the airport onto the main road and hail a passing *bemo* (minibus) into Kuta for just 350rps. If you do not want to stay in Kuta itself, you can get a second *bemo* (from *bemo* corner) on to the other resorts. Many travellers take a taxi from the airport to Denpasar's Kereneng station, then a minibus up to Ubud.

Perama offers international flights to Singapore (US$125), Bangkok (US$245) and Kuala Lumpur (US$149), also domestic flights to Bandung (10l,090rps), Jakarta (100,760rps), Lombok (33,500rps) and Yogya (55,880rps). If leaving Bali by air, have your airport tax (9900rps international, 2650rps domestic) ready. This is *not* included with the cost of your ticket.

Note: many people like to fly from Bali straight to Yogya. You miss Bromo, but in the rainy season (when views are poor) this is probably just as well. The other popular flight is the short 20-minute trip to Lombok, sold by Merpati. Those wishing to island-hop through the islands of Nusa Tenggara and thence on to Australia can take advantage of Merpati's regular flight from Kupang (Timor) to Darwin (Australia).

Road
Coming in from Java, it is a short 20/30-minute ferry crossing (fare 400rps, departures every hour or so) from Ketapang over to Gilimanuk on Bali's western tip. Remember to correct your watches – Bali is one hour ahead of Java. From Gilimanuk, there are regular buses (three hours, 1500rps) down to Ubung bus-station, 2 km north of Denpasar. From Ubung, it is a short *bemo* ride into Denpasar, from where you can travel into any of the southern resorts.

Perama sell straight-through tickets from Denpasar to Bandung (train ll,200rps, bus 25,500rps), to Jakarta (train 13,100rps, bus 29,500rps), to Probollingo (train 5,100rps, bus 8000rps) and to Yogya (train 8,300rps, bus 13,000rps). If departure times do not suit you, shop around at other travel agents. Alternatively, arrange your own transport – local buses run every half-hour or so from Denpasar (Ubung station) to Gilimanuk, for Java. Cross over by ferry to Ketapang (move watches *back* one hour!) and hop on a bus (hourly service) to Malang, Jember or Probollingo.

TOURIST SERVICES
The main 'Badung' tourist office (tel: 23602) is in Jln Surapati, Denpasar. There is a smaller (more convenient) tourist information centre in Kuta's Art Market, at the end of Jln Bakungsari. It is open from 9 a.m. to 2 p.m. Monday to Saturday and has information desks for Bali, west Java and east and central Java. Handouts include island map, calendar of events, festival list, and *Bali Tourist Guide*. Services include car rental, hotel reservation, sightseeing tours, tourist health insurance, parcel-packing and a small post office, open from 8 a.m. to 4 p.m. Monday to Saturday.

The main GPO is inconveniently situated on Sanur Road, midway between Denpasar and Sanur. It is open from 8 a.m. to 4 p.m. weekdays, 8 a.m. to 1 p.m. on Saturday. There is a 50rps charge for each letter collected at the poste restante. If staying in Kuta, have your mail sent to the post office at the tourist office, or to the postal agent in Legian St, next to Peanuts disco.

International phone calls are best made from the airport. Connections are far quicker and better here than at Denpasar (24 hour service at the telephone office on Jln Veteran, near tourist office) or at Kuta (small telecommunications office near Peanuts disco on Legian St, open 8 a.m. to 6 p.m. Monday to Saturday, three minutes to the UK costs 26000rps). When planning calls home, bear in mind that Bali is seven hours ahead of London GMT.

Kuta has several money-changers on Legian St (usually open from 9 a.m. to 6 p.m., shop around for the best rate) or you can go to Panin Bank next to Peanuts disco (open from 8 a.m. to 2 p.m. Monday to Thursday, until 11 a.m. Friday, until 1 p.m. Saturday). Bank Central Asia at 39 Cockroaminto St, Denpasar, is where to go if you have spent all your money in Kuta and need a fresh injection of cash on a visa or master card.

The main Garuda (open from 7.30 a.m. to 4.30 p.m. weekdays, 9 a.m. to 1 p.m. Saturday) and Merpati (open 7.30 a.m. to 3 p.m. weekdays, 9 a.m. to 1 p.m. weekends) airline offices are in Denpasar. Most people use the Garuda/Merpati desks at the airport, or the (pleasantly air-conditioned) Garuda desk at the Kuta Beach Hotel.

Important note: if you are flying out of Bali, you must *reconfirm your air tickets* (do it yourself, do not trust a travel agent) at least 72 hours before departure. If you do not, you could lose your seat!

GETTING AROUND THE ISLAND

Bemos (open-air jeeps with bench seating down the side) or minibuses are a cheap, convenient way of getting round Bali. You can get from Tirtagganga to Singaraja (halfway around the island) for just 900rps (about 30p!) by public *bemo*. Some useful fares include Kuta-Denpasar 400rps, Kuta-airport 350rps, Kuta-Legian 300rps and Denpasar-Sanur 350rps. Denpasar has four bus/bemo terminals: the Tegal depot is for Kuta, Legian, Sanur, Nusa Dua and airport; Kereneng services Ubud and eastern Bali; Ubung depots for the north and west of the island; and Suci is for Benoa (Turtle Island). If you are in a hurry (public *bemos* often stop to pick up/drop off passengers) or do not fancy being one of 20 people crammed into a 12-seater minibus, you can charter your own *bemo*. Chartered *bemos* are a particularly good idea for routes like Kuta-Sanur (6000rps one-way) which are not covered by public *bemos* and for others like Kuta-Ubud (15000rps one-way) which would otherwise involve time-consuming transfers (i.e. Kuta to Tegal station in Denpasar, 300rps; Tegal to Kereneng, 300rps; Kereneng to Ubud, 1000rps). If you get a few people together, chartering a *bemo* can work out as cheap as travelling by local transport. You can even charter a *bemo* by the day for around 25,000rps, which works out cheaper than hiring a jeep and you do not have to worry about insurance or the cost of gas.

Notes: watch out for pickpockets on crowded *bemos*, especially on popular routes like Kuta-Denpasar and Denpasar-Ubud. Never get into an empty *bemo* with two or three men inside – there have been cases of robbery. Never board any *bemo* before agreeing the price with the driver first (if not sure, ask your hotel or a fellow passenger).

Hired vehicles are a great way of touring the island at leisure, stopping where and when you want to snap photos, to admire the countryside, or to take in a passing festival. This said, there are a few drawbacks. Many roads are in poor condition and other vehicles have an unnerving habit of pulling out of side-roads without indicating. If these were not enough, Bali's legions of stray dogs are fond of sunning themselves in the middle of busy main highways. It is a bit of an assault course really (look out for the traffic sign: '50kms an hour only – Better late than end in the hospital') but fun. Whatever vehicle you hire, the first thing to check is your horn – in built-up areas, you will be hitting this every few seconds! Other things to check are brakes, lights, tyres, indicators and steering. Make sure you get insurance (limited though this may be) in with the price of rental. Fuel is very cheap (only 400rps [15p] for a litre) and it is wise to fill up (since tanks invariably start out empty) as soon as you set off. You will be asked to produce your International Driving Licence (endorsed for motorbike, if you are hiring one) and you may have to leave your passport as security. Applying for a Balinese licence is a costly and time-consuming business and not recommended! Motorbike hire is cheap (between 6000 and 10,000rps a day, depending on size and age of the machine) but accidents are very common. It is far safer (and not much more expensive) to get two or three people together and hire a jeep. As with motor-

A Balinese temple

bikes, the rates vary according to season and to how long you hire for. There are numerous rent-a-car places in Kuta, Sanur, Ubud, etc. and shopping around will get you a Japanese jeep for 25,000rps per day, if you hire it for three days or more. Few companies are keen to rent out cars, jeeps or motorbikes for just a day.

Pushbikes are by far the cheapest (1500rps/day) and the most relaxing way of getting around outside of the cities. Peddling into small country villages often evokes a better reaction from (often shy) local people than if you roar in by noisy jeep or motorbike. Hilly mountain roads make some routes hard going, but you can always load your bike onto a passing *bemo*!

KUTA

Kuta gets a lot of bad press, not all of it deserved. The metamorphosis from sleepy fishing village to Benidorm-style resort is complete, but the magnificent sunsets and the long golden-sand surfing beaches remain. Kuta has hot water, foam beds, international food, iced beer, cocktails, cheap tapes, T-shirts and lots of good nightlife. Few travellers have any complaints about that, especially if they have just rolled in from spartan Java or Sumatra. Kuta's main problems are pollution, noisy traffic, lack of planning and too many people trying to make a living out of tourists. It is on Kuta beach itself that you can gauge the full horrors of tourism – the rudenesses of drunken surfers has rubbed off on the locals and it is impossible to sit on the sand for more than five minutes without being hassled to buy something or insulted when you won't. If you let the locust swarm of traders, massage ladies and hawkers wash over you without protest, you can have your hair plaited and beaded, your fingers and toes manicured, your whole body massaged with sun-oil, you can buy your gaily-coloured sarong, beach-shorts, swimsuit and souvenirs, you can drink your cold beer, have a newspaper delivered, buy a big bag to get all your gear back to the hotel – you can do all this for less than £10 and from the comfort of your newly purchased 180 × 60 cm beach-mat!

Kuta has its points, but do not stay too long. When you have had enough of beach hassle, stodgy Western food, frenetic bars, noisy discos, hard-sell hawkers and eye-catching shops, it is time to move out!

ACCOMMODATION

Despite the recent tourist boom, room prices in Bali remain fairly low. There is a lot of cut-price competition between the (innumerable) hotels and *losmen* and while full occupancy is starting to force the rates up slowly, on an international standard Bali remains dirt-cheap. In Kuta, good rooms with private shower, toilet, fan, verandah, etc. go for around £4 single, £6 double and breakfast is thrown in for free. If you want air-conditioning (a blessing in the hot season!) you are looking to pay around £12 single, £15 double, per night. There is a smattering of luxury hotels, with all mod cons, charging between £30 and £60 per double room and all these places are pleasantly low-level. Since 1966, none of Bali's hotels have been allowed to build above the level of the coconut trees! On arrival in Kuta, be prepared to look around. If you arrive late, take the first clean place offered and hunt out something better in the morning. When looking, be warned that garden hotels and guest houses are susceptible to mosquitoes (not a problem if you have a net) and that some 90 per cent of rooms in Bali, not just in Kuta, have single beds (couples need to do some extra legwork). In practice, finding a good place to stay is rarely a problem. There are hundreds of establishments to choose from and although the places mentioned below are good, you may well turn up something better by speaking to other travellers. Kuta's cheaper (and quieter) *losmen* often lie off the main route. **Ronta II**, off Popies Lane 2, has large self-contained bungalows with their own garden, shower and fan at 8000rps single, 14000rps double. Next-door **Lillie's** is similarly priced and almost as good. In Popies Lane 2 itself, **Suji's** (tel: 52483) has very quiet bungalows with huge rooms at 10000rps single, 15000rps double. Slightly upmarket, **Aquarius Beach Inn** (tel: 51762) on Legian St is a popular family hotel with good-value rooms (hot water, bath, spacious interior) at around 20,000rps fan and 35,000rps air-conditioned. Rooms are bungalow-style, ranged around nice gardens and the small pool is a treat. **Panorama**, behind Agung bungalows (near Peanuts, towards Popies Lane 2) has double bungalows with self-service kitchen and lounge at only 17,500rps. It is half the price of the more fêted Agung and the pool is better. **Walon**, just below Fat Yogi's in Popies Lane, is real value for money – large self-contained bungalows (with party-size double beds!) for only 20,000rps. **Pendawa**, near the beach, is very central. This place is wonderfully quiet (an important consideration in Kuta) and the rooms are well priced at 25,000rps for two. If you have more money to spend, try **Adi Dharma Cottages** (tel: 51527) in Legian St (lovely pool and gardens, pleasant sit-out restaurant, friendly staff and cosy air-conditioned rooms with

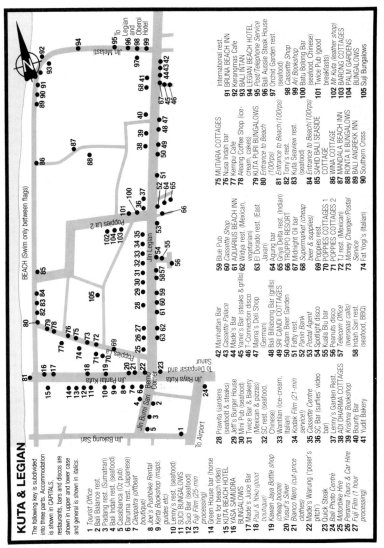

KUTA & LEGIAN

The following key is subdivided into three parts. Accommodation is shown in CAPITALS, restaurants, bars and discos are shown in upper and lower case and general is shown in *italics*.

1 *Tourist Office*
2 Bali Balance rest.
3 Padang rest. (Sumatran)
4 Bali Indah rest. (seafood)
5 Casablanca (Oz. pub)
6 Daruma rest. (Japanese)
7 *Cleopatra (offbeat boutique)*
8 *Joe's Pushbike Rental*
9 *Kerta Bookshop (maps, guides etc)*
10 Lenny's rest. (seafood)
11 SUCI BUNGALOWS
12 SUCI BUNGALOWS
13 *Fuji Film (25-min processing)*
14 *Green House bar (horse hire for beach rides)*
15 KUTA BEACH HOTEL
16 YASA SAMUDRA BUNGALOWS
17 Made's Juice Bar
18 *Paul & Yoko (good boutique)*
19 *Kawan Jaya Bottle shop (cheap booze)*
20 *Yusuf's t.rest.*
21 *Bianco Nero (cut-price clothes)*
22 *Made's Warung ('poser's pitch')*
23 Quick Steak
24 *Bali Photo Centre*
25 *Motorbike Hire*
26 *Perama Tours & Car Hire*
27 *Fuji Film (1 hour processing)*
28 Prawata Gardens (seafood & steaks)
29 Jeff's Burger House
30 Mini Pub (seafood)
31 Twice Bar & Bakery (Mexican & pizzas)
32 SC rest. (seafood, Chinese)
33 Wantilan (ice-cream, Italian)
34 *Kodak Film (21-min service)*
35 *Cassette Centre*
36 SC Bar (surfies' video bar)
37 Lenny's Garden Rest.
38 ADI DHARMA COTTAGES
39 *Krishna Bookshop*
40 Bounty Bar
41 Yudit Bakery
42 Manhattan Bar
43 Cassette Palace
44 Made's Bar
45 Yanie's Bar (steaks & grills)
46 T-Connection disco
47 Mama's Deli Shop (German)
48 Bali Billabong Bar (grills)
49 SRI CANDI COTTAGES
50 Adam Beer Garden
51 Fatty rest.
52 Panin Bank
53 *Postal Agent*
54 Spotlight disco
55 Kuala Blu bar
56 *Telecom Office (overseas calls)*
57 T.J. rest. (Mexican)
58 Indah San rest. (seafood, BBQ)
59 Blue Pub
60 *Cassette Shop*
61 AQUARIUS BEACH INN
62 Widya rest. (Mexican, vegetarian)
63 El Dorado rest. (East Javan)
64 Agung bar
65 Ginya Delta rest. (Indian)
66 TROPPO RESORT
67 Midnight Oil bar
68 Supermarket (cheap beer & supplies)
69 Poppies rest.
70 POPPIES COTTAGES 1
71 POPPIES COTTAGES 2
72 T.I rest. (Mexican)
73 *Money Changer/Postal Service*
74 Fat Yogi's (Italian)
75 MUTIARA COTTAGES
76 Nusa Indah bar
77 *Aleang Coffee Shop (ice-cream, cakes)*
78 KUTA PURI BUNGALOWS
79 KUTA PURI BUNGALOWS
80 *Entrance to Beach (100rps)*
81 *Entrance to Beach (100rps)*
82 Tony's rest.
83 Kuta Seaview rest.
84 *Entrance to Beach (100rps)*
85 SAHID BALI SEASIDE COTTAGE
86 WINA COTTAGE
87 MANDALA BEACH INN
88 RONTA II BUNGALOWS
89 BALI ANGREKK INN
90 Southern Cross
91 International rest.
92 BRUNA BEACH INN
93 Kerangmas Cafe
94 LEGIAN BEACH HOTEL
95 *Post/Telephone Service*
96 Bali Aussie Steak House
97 Orchid Garden rest. (seafood)
98 *Ari Bookshop*
99 *Cassette Shop*
100 Batu Bolong Bar
101 Twice Pub (good breakfasts!)
102 *Mr Kuta (leather shop)*
103 BARONG COTTAGES
104 PALM GARDENS BUNGALOWS
105 Suji Bungalows

---

phone, fridge, tiled bathroom, huge double beds, etc)., from US$25 single, US$30 double. In the same range, there is **Yasa Samudra** (end of Jln Pantai Kuta, near beach) with bar-restaurant, pool, laundry service, safe deposit and smart rooms at US$15/18 fan, US$22/25 air-conditioned. **Barong Cottages** in Poppies Lane 2 attracts the young crowd (nice pool with sunbeds, friendly staff, good atmosphere, fan doubles at US$14, air-conditioned rooms at US$16 single/ US$18 double). **Poppies I Cottages** on Poppies Lane I has swish self-contained bungalows (US$37 + 15 per cent tax), immaculately kept gardens and a pool.

If you want a lively mid-range resort, try **Troppo Zone** (tel: 51591) at Puri Rama Jln Legian. Food is magnificent (the head chef learnt his skills at the Sydney Boulevard!) and rooms go for US$45 a double. 'It is the number one 18 to 35 resort in Bali!', enthused a guest, 'The perfect scene for any young person who wants to drink and eat himself into oblivion!' There are several places like this, the most popular being **Bali Intan Cottages** off Jln Legian. Here you have a beach-front pool with swim-up bar, a good restaurant, luxurious cottages at US$56/60 (cheaper rooms at US$50/55) and lots of live-wire atmosphere. Still central and rather more sedate, the big **Kuta Beach Hotel** has po-faced staff but great facilities. Superior bungalows cost US$50 single, US$60 double and entertainments include 'the intimate informality of magic organ, will enchant your dinner every Tuesday, Thursday and Saturday'.

Not far from noisy Kuta are **Pertamina Cottages**, beautifully situated on a quiet stretch of beach close to the airport. Rooms cost US$56 single, US$60 double and suites start at US$550. For something really special, travel up to Legian Beach (an extension to Kuta Beach) and check out the high-class **Bali Oberoi**. 'This is how we know you want Bali to be' claims the literature. Actually, it is an exclusive club-type hotel as far removed from real Bali as you could imagine, but the superb private beach, the tastefully designed bungalows (US$105 single, US$l15 double) and the 5-star facilities (palm-shaded pool, shopping arcade, beauty salon, tennis courts, 18-hole golf course, etc., help you forget that. And every room has a luxurious sunken bath! If you cycle up above the Oberoi on Legian, there are some very quiet and secluded self-contained bungalows for rent, at about US$100 a day, with staff attending to your every whim. Remember, there is no need to settle for second-best in Kuta – it has accommodation to suit every taste and pocket!

FOOD

There is no problem in finding somewhere to eat at Kuta. You are spoiled for choice! Restaurants and bars come and go, but here are a few suggestions: **Made's Warung** is where all the foreign trendies (many of them resident) go for coffee (great capucchino) and lunch. Full of poseurs, clothes designers and Australian rock stars, it is definitely *the* place to be seen in Kuta. As one *aficionado* commented: 'When you come here, you bring yourself and your style'. Service is slow, but you can enjoy excellent jazz sounds and spot famous people while you wait for your food, which, when it arrives is great. Somewhere else to enjoy Indonesian fare is **Penang** restaurant, just past the Sari Club on Jln Legian. It is authentically Balinese (little plates of everything, all you can eat for 4000rps) and local people like it. Don't confuse this place with the similarly-named **Padang** in Jln Bakung Sari (near tourist office) which is famous for its Sumatran-style dishes. Try the marinaded beef with rice – only 1000rps and really tasty!

For a Western-style feast, I would suggest **Yanie's** off Legian St (best hamburgers in Bali by far) or **TJ's** in Poppies Lane (great Mexican food) or nearby **Poppies** (just to say you have been there). Seafood is good at **Indah Sari** on Jln Legian (near Peanuts), where you can have all the lobster, king prawns and fish *satay* you like for less than £5. If you have a taste for Indian food, a trip to **Griya Delta** (behind Panin bank on Jln Legian) is a must. Best tikkas and tandoories I have tasted in South-East Asia and not too expensive. On Jln

Legian itself, there is **Fatty's** (Japanese and Western), **Twice Bar & Bakery** (steaks, wines and cakes) and **Blue Pub** (cheapest beer in town). For really cheap food, dive into a local *warung*, go to the night market (open 6 to 11 p.m., wide choice of Chinese and seafood dishes) or just pick and choose from the various street carts – *satays* are great over here and it is incredible what they can do with goat! A banana-leaf dish of *tahu* (Indonesian-style tofu, served with bean-sprouts, peanut sauce and chillies) rarely costs more than 200rps and is delicious. However, do watch out for the dreaded Bali Belly. This is caused by drinking unbottled water, drinking too much alcohol (lowers the resistance to disease) or just by picking up something bad in the local food. As anywhere else in Asia, it is important, when eating from the street, to ensure that food is freshly cooked and not just reheated.

ENTERTAINMENT

When not lazing on the beaches, hanging out in restaurants, or chatting to the Balinese (an entertainment in itself – they have an amazing sense of humour), you can drink beer and watch endless videos in numerous bars (many stay open till 2 a.m.), or bop away until dawn at an earsplitting disco. There is a whole Australian sub-culture happening on Kuta and at night it turns into a raucous tinsel-town of bright lights and pulsating music. The big scene is Legian St. From beer-bars like **S C Club** (great wall videos) and **Kuala Blu**, you can cross the road to **Peanuts** disco, which only gets going around midnight (i.e. after all the happy hours at the various bars have finished). **Peanuts** is the definitive Kuta night-spot. The sign outside – 'T-shirts, singlets, shorts and thongs are bloody welcome!' – tells you that. Inside, it is maelstrom of heavy rock music and swaying crowds of surfies. Peanuts is open from 8.30 p.m. till the 'early hours' and the 4000rps admission fee includes two free beers.

Every Kuta sub-group has its own favourite disco. If Peanuts is for Aussies and animals, then **Club 66** (on the road out to Legian, halfway between Kuta and Oberoi Hotel) and **Chez Gado-Gado** (up on Legian beach) is where the Europeans and resident trendies go after a beer or two at **Goa** bar (2/3 km out of Kuta). For something a little better, I would suggest **Number One** disco out at Sanur, near the Bali Hyatt. The drinks are expensive and you have to dress fairly smartly, but the atmosphere is really good. Another popular nightspot is **Benny's** on Kuta beach, which attracts some of the best musicians in South-East Asia.

For more sedate evening entertainment, you could take in a traditional dance show (*leggong, barong, baris,*

The sea temple, Tanah Lot

Rice fields, Bali

kechak, Ramayana etc.) at one of the hotels (tickets sold by many agents in Kuta or Sanur) although you would do much better to wait until Ubud or Peliatan.

SANUR

If the noise and hype of Kuta doesn't appeal, then the long and narrow beach of Sanur (only a short *bemo* or taxi-ride away) certainly will. Hotels are more expensive here and so is the food, but the sea is much calmer and ideal for windsurfing. There is far less hassle from massage ladies and beach vendors, and the offshore coral reef makes for good snorkelling (watch out for sea urchins). There are plenty of places to hire out snorkelling equipment, windsurfers and parasails and most hotels can arrange boat-trips out to nearby Turtle Island, which is famous for its turtles, sea-temple and beautiful coral. At low tide you do not need a boat – you can just wade over.

Most of Bali's first-class hotels are at Sanur and a lot of them have swimming pools and front the beach. Top of the heap is the **Bali Hyatt** (tel: 8271) with landscaped gardens and luxury bungalows from US$70. The newer **Sanur Beach Hotel** (tel: 8801l) is ideal for couples and families, with useful facilities and very livable rooms from US$75 single, US$85 double. Most nights (arrive by 7 p.m., for 7.30 p.m.), there is a value-for-money US$20 buffet dinner featuring Balinese dances. In the mid-range, there is **Segara Village Hotel** with a nice pool, pleasant restaurant and quiet bungalows from US$25. Right next door, **Tourist Beach Inn** has economical rooms at 10,000 to 15,000rps, although **Sanur Indah**, near the post office, is probably the best budget bet with twin rooms at 10,000rps to 12,000rps. There are lots of other cheap *losmen*, so ask around.

Sanur village has several good places to eat. There is a popular little *warung* (no name) near to Sanur Indah guest house on Jln Sindhu, serving cheap and tasty Balinese snacks. Nearby **Carlo's Bar** does great seafood and so does **Kulkul Restaurant** on Jln Tanjung Sari. **Umasari**, next to No. 1 disco in Bali Hyatt St, has a vast menu and popular fish dishes/cocktails. The dance programmes on Monday/Thursday nights are good. Finally, there is **Swastika II** restaurant on Jln Tanjung Sari. This place offers a bit of everything (including Italian food) in a breezy garden setting.

NUSA DUA/TANJONG BENOA

Recently, concerned that tourist development might spoil Balinese culture if it were allowed to spread all over the island, the Government decided to concentrate it all in one place, and selected Nusa Dua. This is the new jet-set 5-star tourist spot on the southern peninsula and no small hotels are allowed. Nusa Dua is totally geared to international-class package tourists and business travellers. The beach here is a beautiful white stretch of sand and the sea is ideal for swimming and windsurfing. The offshore coral reef is the best place on Bali to try diving and several agencies (try P T Baruna Water Sports at Nusa Dua Beach Hotel) offer good-value three-day diving courses at around 100,000rps. Nusa Dua has the advantage of being very close to Kuta and Denpasar, without the noise and hassle of either place and it is only ten minutes' drive from the airport. The two recommended hotels are **Hotel Bali Sol** (tel: 71510/l) with rooms from US$76 single, US$142 double and **Nusa Dua Beach Hotel** (tel: 71210) where a night of 5-star luxury costs less than £40!

Nusa Dua is only a 20-minute drive from Kuta. For comparison, try Tanjung Benoa, another ten minutes on. This is a pleasantly self-contained spot, where you can do most things without having to move very far from the beach. Start perhaps with a meal at **Jeladi Snack Bar** (nice Italian food), move on down to the beach for a massage, go for a swim (snorkelling is nothing special here, but the water is very clear and you get to see a sample of the local fish), then wander for two minutes down the beach to **Benoa Marine Recreation** and try out the watersports (parasailing, jet-skiing, water-skiing, water-scooters, etc.) or get a group together and charter a boat to go fishing/diving. Benoa is good both as an away-day excursion from Kuta, or as an overnight stopover. There are now three decent places to stay: **Hasan Homestay** (twin rooms at 15,000rps), **Chez Agung** (nicer doubles with bathrooms at 25,000rps) and **Puri Joma** (classy twins from US$25).

ULU WATU

Bali is famous for its many good surfing spots. Ulu Watu, 19 km south west of Kuta (40 minutes' drive), is an excellent example – it has a long, long reef break and the surf rolls in from miles out! Also at Ulu Watu is a spectacular sea temple, offering striking views of Bali's volcanic profile. It is dramatically poised on the lip of a cliff which plunges 90 m straight down to the Indian Ocean. About 500 m before the temple (where the path ends), a forest trail leads down (about 20 minutes' stroll) to the surfing beach. On the beach are some half-dozen bars cum restaurants, all with good views (especially at sunset). There are no bungalows, but you can buy or hire surfboards here. Out of the water, ask the local lads to direct you to the nearby limestone caves which are beautiful. Back on your

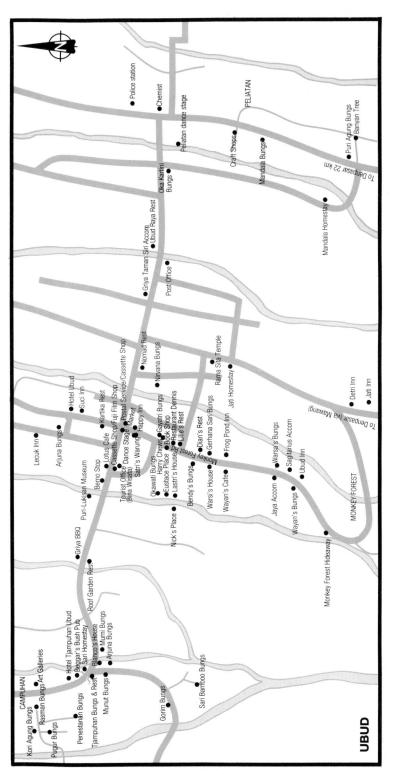

N

Police station
Chemist
PELIATAN
Peliatan dance stage
Puri Agung Bungs
Banyan Tree
Craft Shops
Mandala Bungs
To Denpasar 22 km
Oka Kartini Bungs
Mandala Homestay
Ubud Raya Rest
Griya Taman Siri Accom
Post Office
Nomad Rest
Nirvana Bungs
Rama Sita Temple
Jati Inn
Detri Inn
Postal Service/Cassette Shop
Fuji Film Shop
Hotel Ubud
Kartika Rest
Suci Inn
Jati Homestay
To Denpasar (via Mawang)
Lecuk Inn
Arjuna Bungs
Lotus Cafe
Cassette Shop
Dance Stage
Market
Gayatri Bungs
Restaurant Dennis
Lillie's Rest
Frog Pond Inn
Warsa's Bungs
Bemo Stop
Book Shop
Gerhana Sari Bungs
Sagitarius Accom
Puri-Lukisan Museum
Tourist Office (Bina Wisata)
Satri's Warung
Happy Inn
Harry Chews
Dian's Rest
Ubud Inn
Okawati Bungs
Eustace Place
Lastri's House
Monkey Forest Rd
Jaya Accom
Griya BBQ
Bendy's Bungs
Warsi's House
Wayan's Cafe
Wayan's Bungs
Nick's Place
MONKEY FOREST
Roof Garden Rest
Monkey Forest Hideaway
CAMPUHAN
Hotel Tjampuhan Ubud
Beggar's Bush Pub
Sari Homestay
Blanco's House
Arjuna Bungs
Kori Agung Bungs
Rasman Bungs Art Galleries
Murni Bungs
Pugur Bungs
Penestanan Bungs
Tjampuhan Bungs & Rest
Munut Bungs
Gorim Bungs
Sari Bamboo Bungs

UBUD

motorbike (the paths are too narrow for jeeps), look out for a sign (about 1 km out of Ulu Watu, heading back to Kuta) for another surfing beach called **Nyang-Nyang**. Only enthusiasts make the long, perilous one-hour descent down to this one, but it is definitely worth a stop for the views.

DENPASAR

Denpasar may be Bali's capital, but it is a dirty, smelly city and few travellers go there. Actually, there is no need to. Everything you need (banks, airline offices, travel agents, postal services, tourist information, etc.) can be found in Kuta, Sanur or even Ubud. In addition to Denpasar's regular tourist services (listed on pages 209-10), there is an immigration office (tel: 27828) round the corner from the GPO and a Pelni Lines office (tel: 4387) on Jln Pelabhun Benoa. A few consulates (Australia, Japan, Germany, USA, Holland, New Zealand, etc.) are located in Denpasar, although if you are British, French or Canadian and you lose your passport, you will have to go to Jakarta! Due to the lack of tourist interest, most of Denpasar's better hotels and guest houses have closed up, but **Adi Yasa** at Jln Nakula II is still a good bet, with friendly staff and clean rooms from 7000rps to 10,000rps. Denpasar has a busy covered market (best around dawn), a couple of cheap-eats night markets (in Kumbasari and in the Kereneng bus terminal) and a semi-interesting museum on Jln Wisnu (open mornings only, admission 200rps). Unless you want to go shopping (try the government-run **Sangraha Kriya Asta Handicrafts Centre** at Tophati) that is just about it.

AROUND THE ISLAND

To see what Bali is like away from Kuta, hire a jeep and tour the island. Either share the cost of a self-drive jeep or (since not everyone fancies driving on Bali) hire a car with driver at only 15,000rps per day extra. Before setting off, buy a good road map (from any bookshop) and check with the tourist office to see if any local temple festivals or ceremonies will coincide with your route.

The following route starts from Kuta, covers most traditional points of interest and includes suggestions on where to spend the night. How long you are on the road is up to you. Many travellers do a lightning three to four day tour (overnighting in Ubud, Candi Dasa, Lovina, etc.) while others opt to see everything in a fortnight, but even if you are in a hurry, you must allow for spontaneous detours to follow a colourful procession, or to drop in on a temple event. Most of Bali's best 'sights' are off the beaten track and

if you zip around the island with a 'been-there-done-that' attitude you will miss them all.

The obvious place to head for out of Kuta is **Ubud**, located in the hills north of Denpasar. To get there, take the Sanur Rd out to Sanur (12 km, 20 minutes), then drive due north to Ubud (41 km, 1 hour). Stop off along the way to visit the various crafts villages (**Celuk** for silverwork, **Mas** for woodcarvings, etc.) but do not buy anything from the live show-rooms. You will get much better prices at the smaller roadside workshops.

Ubud, the cultural centre of Bali, makes an excellent base. It is convenient, pretty central and there is lots to see and do. Along with the nearby village of **Peliatan**, it is also one of the best places to see traditional dance. *Leggong, baris, kebyar* and *kechak* dances are all regularly performed and the small Bina Wisata tourist office on Jln Raya (open from 8.30 a.m. to 7.30 p.m. Monday to Saturday) gives full details and sells tickets. Ubud was, until quite recently, a calm and peaceful haven away from the noise and clamour of Kuta. This is no longer true. The main tourist route is now a mini-Kuta of craft shops, travel agents, motorbikes, *bemo*-men and dance-show touts, but people still hang out in Ubud for weeks on end and it is easy to see why. Quite apart from the arts and crafts, the music and dance, the cheap food and accommodation, the colourful shops and markets, the cool climate and the overall spiritual atmosphere, you only have to walk a short way in any direction to find some of the best scenery in the island interior. Ubud is essentially a place for long relaxing walks and although there are bicycles, motorbikes and jeeps for rent, most people buy a *Bali Pathfinder* from the tourist office and set off on foot.

Real Ubud, where the better accommodation is, starts at the bottom (not the top!) of Monkey Forest Rd and across the suspension bridge at nearby Campuhan. Here you can still find the restful atmosphere and the beautiful countryside that attracted travellers in the first place. Several *losmen* (mainly bungalows) have an attractive situation overlooking, or even in, the rice fields. Down Monkey Forest Rd, you will find **Happy Inn** (lovely family, 8000rps with fan/toilet); **Eustace Place** (good views, 15,000rps); **Gerhana Sari** (nice gardens, 8000rps to 15000rps); **Warsa**'s (good food, rooms from 10,000rps); **Sagitarius Inn** (family-style bungalows from 15,000rps); **Ubud Inn** (cool pool, rooms with hot water at US$20); and, in the rice fields opposite, **Wayan Rudita**'s bungalows (8000rps single, 10,000rps double). Down at Campuhan bridge, there is **Pondok Tjampuhan** (brand-new place,

Hindu temple, Bali

great restaurant, scenic situation, ultra-comfy rooms at US$20) and **Homestay Sari** (backpackers' choice, clean rooms on terraced hillside at 6000rps single, 10,000 for two). Beyond the bridge, up the hill, choose between **Hotel Tjampuhan** (pleasant upmarket cottages, picturesque setting, US$24 single, US$32 double), **Pugur** (clean and quiet, run by friendly local artist, 10,000rps single, 12,000rps double), **Kori Agung** ('Stay with us for Memorable One', US$25 for two) and **Rasman** (helpful manager, large two-person bungalows at 15,000rps).

Ubud is quite as good as Kuta for eating and food is cheaper. Down Monkey Forest Rd, you will find **Lilie**'s (popular travellers' fare), **Canderi**'s *warung* (friendly breakfast spot) and **Dian**'s (great *lumpia* spring rolls). Along the main road, is **Ary**'s **Warung** (try the *gado-gado*), **Lotus Cafe** (good coffee, cheesecake and vegetarian snacks) and **Nomad Restaurant** (the place to go for late-night feasts). Two of Ubud's best eateries are located on either side of Campuhan bridge – **Murni**'s **Warung** (nice situation over the river, but a bit pricey) and **Pondok Tjampuhan** (romantic atmosphere, soothing *gamelan* sounds, superb Italian food and cocktails). Get up early one morning for the fish *satay* at the morning market.

Most of Ubud's tourist services (post office, airline reservation offices, travel agents, bookshops, *gamelan* cassette shops, etc.) are strung along the top of Monkey Forest Rd (see map). When shopping, check prices and quality before buying. Look along Jln Raya for patchwork bedspreads (double-sided, double-size, under £10) batik shirts/dresses (around £2/3), fashion clothes, silver, tapestries, etc. High-class carvings in wood and bamboo can be found at **Bloom's** and *ikat* weavings at **Jain's Place**, both at the bottom of Monkey Forest Rd. The best art shops are up the hill at Campuhan and every man and his brother wants to sell you paintings. All in all, you cannot go far wrong, just as long as you remember to bargain hard!

Leaving Ubud, it takes 20 minutes by jeep down to the weaving centre of **Gianyar**. Drop in on the Pertenunan Setai Cap Cili workshop (on your left as you enter town) to see the many looms used for *ikat* weaving. The threads are tie-dyed beforehand to produce a blurred edge pattern. A short drive further south takes you past Kusamba to **Goa Lawah**, the bat cave, which houses thousands of the creatures in a flap or hanging out. From here, it is only 15 minutes (turn right off the main road, drive 2 km down to the docks, turn left just before a row of demolished houses) to **Padangbai**. This is a narrow white-sand beach in a calm and secluded bay, ideal for snorkelling. Padangbai is the ferry-point for Lombok and three boats go there (in theory at least) every day. Stay at **Rai Beach Inn** (huge two-storey bungalows at 15,000rps) or **Padangbai Beach Inn** (small self-contained cottages at 6000rps). Try the seafood at **Celagi** restaurant and hire a boat to go snorkelling (ask for Wayan – he knows all the best diving spots). Back on the main road, drive on 7/8 km and look out for a 'Balina Dive' sign on the right. This marks the way down to **Balina Beach**, another quiet spot with good snorkelling and diving. **Balina Beach Bungalows** have rooms from US$10 to 30, including breakfast. The other operation, **Puri Buitan Cottages**, has a pool, bar, restaurant and one-price rooms at US$20. It also offers open-water diving courses up to **Padi** licence (four to five days, five dives) at US$200.

From Balina, it is only 4 km along the coast to the new backpackers' beach resort of **Candi Dasa**. This is another place like Kuta of ten years ago – here, you can wander down the beach and locals stuff items of clothing or carvings in your pockets for next to nothing, just to get a bit of money. Candi Dasa is a small golden beach (very beautiful) and it has a national park. There is a whole series of little white-sand coves leading off it and none (as yet) have a single hawker or massage lady on them! The beach at Candi Dasa is lined with *prahus* (Indonesian outriggers) which you can hire for 6000rps an hour (one to four persons) to go diving at the two little offshore islands. It is a nice trip, but not essential – the coral is just as good 300 metres out from the shore. Swimming is good, but you can only use the beach at low tide. At high tide, it simply vanishes! If staying over, shop around. Candi Dasa has a wide range of accommodation, but there is a huge price difference between them. You can pay anything between 6000rps and 36,000rps for what is effectively the same room. I found **Wiratha** to be the best cheap deal (charming self-contained bungalows from 8000 to 10,000rps), although **Rama Pensione** near the lagoon (spacious doubles for 7000rps), and **Sari Jaya**, with its prime beach location (12,000rps for two), are also recommended. Most places offer discounts if you stay a week or longer. In the village, eat at **TJ's** (steaks, toasted sandwiches, a bit of everything really, in an elegant Japanese garden setting) or **Murni's** (famous for its 'stuffed everything'!). Most restaurants have good seafood – Western dishes like smorgasbord are less successful – and a lot of them offer evening buffet deals where you can watch an (amateurish) music or dance performance.

A short way back along the main road from Candi Dasa (a pleasant 3-km morning walk) is the ancient Bali Aga village of **Tenganan**. Situated in the hills, surrounded by lush forests, it is populated by an Aga tribe who resisted the impact of Hinduism and who still retain many of their ancient ways. Tenganan is famous for double *ikat* cloth (warp and weft pre-dyed separately and to a pre-set pattern, producing an interesting and intricate cross-weave) but the village has become over-commercialised of late – locals now sell palm-leaf *lontars* (religious manuscripts) with 'I love Bali' messages written on them! Avoid the nearby walled-city temple, with its rip-off 'donation' book and its kitsch painted roosters. If you must buy something, bargain for bamboo instruments. Tenganan is a bizarre place (quite different from the rest of Bali) but rather fun. Try to see a tooth-filing ceremony – very unusual!

Tirtagganga, 18 km inland from Candi Dasa, is worth an overnight stop. There is an old water-palace here (built 1947, but it looks ancient!) with two freshwater pools to swim in. The surrounding scenery – a wide amphitheatre of glistening rice-fields – is fantastic and so are the sunrises. For the views, stay up on the hill at **Kusumajaya Inn**, run by a friendly, loquacious Balinese policeman. His rooms are 6000 to 12,000rps, inclusive of a good breakfast. Down by the water-palace there is **Dhangin Taman Inn** with double rooms from 4000 to 8000rps. If you want to try one of the many beautiful walks round here, the owner will draw you a map.

From Tirtagganga, you can travel up to Singaraja (for the northern beaches) in one of two ways. The quick option, only three hours by jeep, is the road running up between the mountains (Agung and Seraya) to the hot, dry and deserted north-eastern coast. Look out for the salt factory – huge upturned pillars of salt standing on a black-sand beach – near **Tembok**. If time permits, stop off at **Yeh Sanih** for a relaxing soak in the freshwater springs. The slower route from Tirtagganga takes you an hour north to **Besakih**, the 1,000-year-old mother temple of Bali. From here you can climb **Mt Agung** (3,142 m), the island's highest peak. The many *losmen* in Besakih village (try **Arca Valley Inn**) will tell you that you need a guide, but you do not – all you need from them is a night lamp. For the sunrise, start up the mountain at 2 a.m. It is a hard five-hour climb (especially the last part) but worth it. From the village, head straight up the hill, past the big temple on the left, until you reach a small temple on the right. There is a fork to the right just beyond this, but do not take it. Keep straight on

and continue through the forest to the top. Agung volcano last erupted in 1963, covering one-quarter of the island in lava! Back on the road and continuing north east, you will soon come to **Mt Batur**, which also had a 1963 eruption. Batur and its huge volcanic lake are best viewed from **Penelokan**, perched high on the crater rim, but arrive early as the mist comes in after 2 p.m.. Many people walk (45 minutes) or *bemo* (600rps) down from Penelokan to **Kedisan** to cross the lake by boat and climb the mountain. Buy your boat ticket from Kedisan police station (to avoid hassle) and at Toya Bungkah, on the other side of the lake, take any trail leading up to the peak. It is a three-hour ascent and you do not need a guide. Toya Bungkah has several cheap places to stay. Try **Mountain View Losmen** at the Air Panas (hot springs) or the nearby **Losmen Gununa**. The local dance school lays on evening entertainments.

However you approach the north-coast centre of **Singaraja**, arrive well before dark. That way, you will not have to stay overnight. The town has a few adequate *losmen* (**Hotels Gelasari** and **Sentral** on Jln A Yani), a couple of Chinese restaurants (**Gandhi** and **Segar**, also on Jln A Yani) and a worth-while morning market, but is otherwise grim. Most travellers head straight out to **Lovina Beach**, a few kilometres further on, which offers black volcanic sand, calm sea, good snorkelling and lots of peace and quiet. Coming in from Singaraja, look out for the various *losmen* signs on the right. They begin some 6 km out, at Anturan (stay at **Baruna Cottages** or **Jati Reef**) and run 5 km on through Kalibukbuk village (try **Nirwana** or **Banyualit Beach Inn**) to Lovina. Rooms are generally cheap, between 5000rps and 25,000rps per double and (as everywhere else on Bali) a good breakfast is included. If you do not want to eat at your *losmen*, there is **Superman**'s *warung* (tasty local snacks) or **Khie Khie** Chinese restaurant (good seafood) both at Kalibukbuk. Many places hire out boats to the offshore coral reef (3000rps per person) for snorkelling. The famous hot springs 8 km beyond Lovina (look out for the Air Panas sign) are your big chance to soak away all your travel cares in beautiful surroundings. If travelling there by *bemo* (20 minutes), get off at the bottom of the hill and hop on the back of a motorbike (or walk) the final leg.

Only 20 minutes' drive east of Singaraja, the charming little village of **Menyali** offers visitors a real slice of traditional Balinese life. Here you can see a 'library' of ancient *lontars* (palm-leaf writings), tune into some of the best *gamelan* music in the north and, if the mood takes you, even set up a Balinese-style wedding! I did it. Well, where else in the world can you get married for £70, supported by two *gamelan* orchestras, a full dance troupe and a curious cast of hundreds?

Menyali is a typical Hindu village of around 2,000 people. It divides into two *banjars* or communities and has three main temples (for Brahma, Vishnu and Shiva) and 12 family temples. Most people work on the land. Menyali has just one *losmen* at present. This is **Rumbia Homestay**, run by the village headman, Suamba. He lets out bright, simple rooms at 10,000rps per person, inclusive of all meals and as much tea/coffee as you can drink. For the same amount again, he gives expert tuition in *gamelan* and dance.

Important note: visits to Menyali are by prior arrangement only. This village has no wish to be flooded with tourists. To book, write to I Gede Budasi, Jln Surapati 198, Kubujati, Singaraja.

There is a big waterfall at **Gitgit**, which you have to pass if you are heading back south to Denpasar. It is a bit of walk off the main road (2 km), but if you are an adventurous swimmer these falls are really good fun – the best jacuzzi of your life! Most people, however, head straight down from Singaraja to **Bedugul** (30 km, 45 minutes). There is a large and beautiful lake here, with a recreation park (entrance 200rps) and a picturesque pagoda-style lake temple. Bedugul has a colourful flower and vegetable market – very photogenic – which runs from 7 a.m. till late every day. The area offers good walks and you can hire boats to go out on the lake. About 3 km south, there is a temple to the water goddess with an orchid market on Sundays. In Candikuning, about 0.5 km before the botanical gardens, **Ashram** *losmen* has nice rooms at 15,000rps, a good bar-restaurant and a master chef who gives cooking courses to tourists! A decent second-string is **Hotel Bedugul** with rooms from 15,000 to 25,000rps.

From Bedugul, it is an hour's drive south to the royal temple at **Menwgi**. Of the many thousands of temples on the island, this is the second largest and probably the most beautiful. Surrounded by a moat, it houses fine *merus* (like pagodas) and pavilions. About 1 km below Mengwi you can turn off right to visit the important sea temple of **Tanah Lot** (prettily poised atop a rocky islet, best seen at sunset) or just go back to Kuta.

LOMBOK

Following on from the success of Bali, which has become rather crowded of late, the Indonesian Government is trying to extend the tourist trail to other islands and in particular to Lombok. In the case of Lombok, it is proving to be very successful due to similarities in art and culture and its close proximity to Bali. Although only the western coast has so far been geared up for tourism, the recent purchase of much of the northern and eastern coast (by rich Australians) suggests that Lombok is a destination of the future – look to this island developing rapidly in years to come.

THE LAND

Geographically, Lombok is a small island with an area of 4,700 sq km. It divides into the mountain ranges of the north, dominated by high Mt Rinjani, and the dry flatlands of the south. The eastern side is drier (and less populated) than the west, but the whole island is subject to droughts. In 1971, for instance, there was a severe famine in the south, caused by poor rains. To counteract this, the Government introduced dry (*gora*) rice which is able to produce a crop without any water. The experiment was so successful that Lombok gained a new nickname, *Bumi Gora* or 'Land of Dry Rice'. Today indeed, rice is one of the island's main exports, along with coffee, cattle and tobacco. Fish and *kang-kung* (water-spinach) are sent to Bali and pumice stone (to furnish walls for high-rise hotels) goes to Hong Kong. However, Lombok society is geared totally to rice. If the harvest is good, the people can afford to get married. If it is bad, they tend to get divorced. Marriage and divorce are very common on Lombok, especially since men (under Muslim law) are allowed up to four wives! The south may be dry, but (as in Bali) it is the cultural heartland of the island with a strong tradition of music, dance, weaving and pottery, etc. Unlike Bali, however, it has very few places to stay. Certain parts of the south are becoming more popular now (e.g. Kuta beach), but the main tourist infrastructure is still concentrated to the west – at Sengiggi Beach, at the offshore Gili islands and at the three connecting provincial towns of Mataram/Ampenan/Cakranegara.

PEOPLE AND HISTORY

With a population of 2.3 million, Lombok is quite densely peopled. As in Bali, such overcrowding has prompted the Government to introduce family-planning and transmigration programmes. Thousands of people are now being resettled on the adjoining island of Sumbawa, which shares a common government with Lombok. Rather ironically, Lombok itself received a wave of migratory Balinese, who have successfully entrenched themselves to the west of the island, holding fast to their Hindu beliefs, building temples and establishing

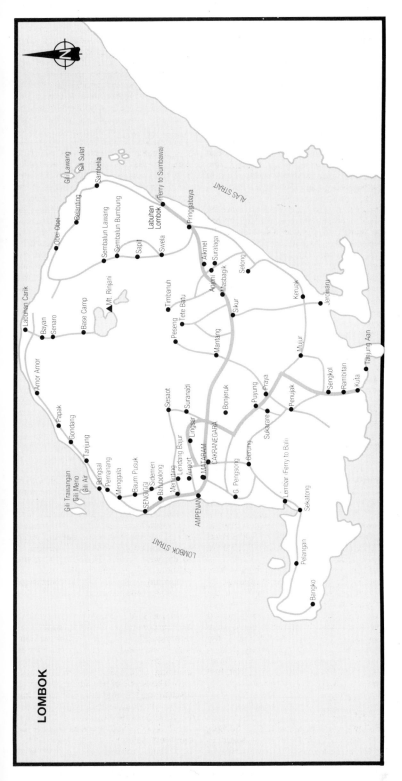

strong *banjar* communities. At present, while 80 per cent of the population are still Muslim Sasaks and 10 per cent Christians and Buddhists, the most enterprising 10 per cent are the Hindu Balinese who have brought their knowledge of tourism to the island and who are now capitalising on it.

The native people of Lombok are the Sasaks. They originally colonised the island from east Java around the seventh and eighth centuries AD and their name is thought to derive from the bamboo rafts they used to cross the straits. The other interpretation of the word *sasak* – 'one who leaves his country to find another' – is, however, the more likely. To begin with, the Sasaks were animist and worshipped the gods of the earth, wind and sky, but then they received the Hindu-Javanese influences of the Majapahit Empire (who invaded from east Java in the fourteenth century) and later the Islamic zeal of Sunan Prapan (who arrived from north Java in the early sixteenth century). In the seventeenth century the western part of Lombok was invaded from Bali by the the Raja of Karangasem, while the east was overcome by groups of Muslim traders. The Balinese seized control of the whole island in 1849, but were heavily defeated in 1894 when the Sasaks enlisted the help of the Dutch. Lombok promptly reverted to being predominantly Muslim – under Dutch colonial rule – with only the western part remaining Hindu. Even today, there is constraint between the Sasaks and the Balinese. The old joke that you cannot see Lombok in Bali, but you can see Bali in Lombok (i.e. because this island still has many powerful reminders – palaces, temples, etc. – of the pre-Dutch Balinese kingdom) has worn rather thin amongst the Sasaks and you will make no friends by repeating it in their company! The 'lingua franca' of the island is still Sasak (albeit blended with Balinese) and the most popular greeting you will hear is *gak ba jok emba*? or 'where you go?'

RELIGION

The religion is a little more complicated. A few Sasaks are still animist (mainly in the centre, towards the mountains) but the great majority are Muslim. These divide into the orthodox 'Five Prayer Islam' (**Waktu Lima**) and the revolutionary 'Three Prayer Islam' (**Waktu Telu**). The latter group, who account for some 30 per cent of Sasaks, pray three (not five) times a day and abstain from pork and alcohol. The Waktu Telu have leanings towards Hinduism – they worship lingam-type monoliths, offer incense and flowers and, at one particular temple (Lingsar), they even pray together with Hindus at the full moon!

Note: with Muslim influence so strong, you should dress sensibly on Lombok – no sleeveless T-shirts and shorts; ladies, and men must wear sarongs or long trousers to enter temples.

ENTERTAINMENT

The Sasaks have just as strong a tradition of music and dance as the Balinese, but you have got to look around to find it. There are weekly cultural performances at Narmada (inside the summer palace) every Sunday, admission 500rps and Sengiggi Beach Hotel holds a worthwhile 'Lombok music night' from 7.30 to 9.30 p.m. every Sunday (US$15, with buffet dinner), but apart from that there is nothing much laid on for tourists. The Sengiggi event is worth catching since it uses the very best local dancers and *gamelan* players. If you miss it, a good tour agent (like Satriavi) can arrange a private showing at around 100,000rps – quite cheap if there are 20 of you! Sasak *wayang* plays – based not on the Ramayana or Mahabaharata legends (as elsewhere in Indonesia), but on the tale of Amir Hamzah, Mohammed's uncle – are performed all over the island, but you just have to be there when they happen. If you are keen on martial arts, traditional *peresean* fighting – using rattan canes and cowhide shields – is demonstrated at Aphm-Taman Ria Cilinaya in Cakranegara from 4 to 6 p.m. daily. In olden times, this form of combat was used to select the king's troops.

SHOPPING

The other thing that everybody goes to Lombok for nowadays (apart from to get away from Bali) is to do business. This is because ethnic handicrafts (fabrics, artefacts), weaving and baskets – cost so much less here than on Bali. The little men who come to the hotels to show you various antiques, carvings and materials are usually much cheaper than the shops – about half the price if you bargain hard! The small carved boxes with animal motifs (frogs, buffalo horns, etc.) are attractive novelty buys, and if you want something bigger, ask to be shown a few carved house doors. They're beautifully decorated and the frames and hinges are usually thrown in for free. Your hotel can usually suggest somewhere to arrange shipping.

What Lombok is really famous for is its fabrics, notably the so-called *kain songket* (interwoven with silk, gold or silver thread) and the normal *kain biasa* (plain or striped cloth, with geometric patterns or floral decorations). The traditional set for a lady is a *kain songket* and shoulder shawl, while the men wear a *batik kain* sarong with attached sash. Most fabrics are woven in the *ikat* method, i.e. from pre-dyed yarn, often done by elaborate processes like tie-dye, etc. One colour is used for the backing cloth, while a second is introduced later (as a cross-weave) to furnish the design. *Ikat* is woven in rayon (cheap and nasty), pure cotton (10 to 15,000rps per metre) and silk (30 to 35,000rps per metre). Good-quality *ikat* is soft and colour-fast, and if it is batik, the pattern should be equally clear on both sides. Sukarare is the main centre for weaving (it certainly has the best selection of designs) but you will often find cheaper prices in Mataram town – try Pertenunan Rinjani factory at 44-46 Jln Pejanggik, or Selamat Riyadi on Jln Ukirkawi.

ORIENTATION
On arrival on Lombok, you will be struck by the total contrast of this island to Bali. Out of the small airport, you go straight into the countryside, driving down long avenues of towering palm-trees, flanked by banana plantations, rice-paddies and quiet secluded beaches. It is a real breath of fresh air! Coming from Bali, you will also notice a big difference in the plant and animal life. The pre-Darwin naturalist Sir Alfred Wallace made a study of evolution in this area and came to the conclusion that the flora and fauna of Asia ended at Bali. There was no tropical vegetation, no elephants, rhinoceros or tigers to be found east of it. Suddenly, on Lombok, was found the dry, cacti-growing terrain and the marsupial life-forms of Australasia. So he placed what is now known as the 'Wallace Line' between Bali and Lombok. Not that you will notice much difference in climate between the two islands – Lombok's temperatures range from 40°F (21°C) (night only) to 86°F (30°C) in the October to March rainy season and from 75-88°F (24-31°C) in the April to September dry season. The peak tourist season is August to October, when lots of Europeans roll in on their summer holidays. The most beautiful month is August, when there is no rain and the scenery is at its best.

Regarding where to stay, you have got quite a choice. Over the past five years, development has switched from the inland towns of Mataram and Ampenan (noisy and dull) to quiet and peaceful Sengiggi Beach, which is now quite a resort location. A lot of backpackers assume that Sengiggi is expensive (not necessarily so) and head up to the three small Gili islands off the west coast. These are okay, but you do tend to get stuck on them (boats back and forth are erratic) and at night the mosquitoes come and eat you. As one victim reported, 'Paradise by day can turn into a bloodsucker's ball at night!'. Several people are now basing themselves at Ampenan in order to arrange a trek up to Mt Rinjani (spectacular and well worth doing) while just as many are heading on down to Kuta, the new tourist attraction on the south coast. This Kuta is nothing like its namesake on Bali – quite the reverse in fact. Apart from Sengiggi, I would rate it as the best place to stay on Lombok at present, particularly if you are on a shoestring budget.

ARRIVAL/DEPARTURE
Air
Merpati flies several times daily between Denpasar (Bali) and Mataram (Lombok). The short 20-minute hop costs 33,500rps one-way and 67,000rps return. On arrival at Lombok's Selaparang airport, wind on your watch (Lombok is one hour ahead of Bali) and book your taxi (prices posted) to Sengiggi, to Ampenan-Mataram-Cakranegara, or to Kuta Beach. A few of the larger hotels have reservation desks in the arrival lounge and offer free taxi transfers.

Sea
There are at least two boats daily between Padangbai (east Bali) and Lembar (west Lombok). Timings are irregular, but ferries usually depart around 9 a.m. and 2 p.m. The crossing takes four to five hours and the one-way economy fare is 3850rps. Tickets are available on board. At Lembar, you can catch mini-buses up to Ampenan-Mataram-Cakranegara (2000rps) or to Sengiggi (3500rps).

Ferries also run two to three times daily from Labuhan Lombok (east Lombok) over to the neighbouring island of Sumbawa. The economy fare is 2250rps and the crossing takes around three hours.

TOURIST SERVICES
Most of these are located in the three-in-one capital of Ampenan-Mataram-Cakranegara, some 10 km south (30 minutes by road) from Sengiggi Beach.

The main tourist office (tel: 21866, 21730) is in Ampenan at Jln Langko 70. It is a friendly, informative outfit, open from 7 a.m. to 2 p.m. Monday to Thursday, until 11 a.m. Friday, until 1 p.m. Saturday. There is a small post office across the road (open from 8 a.m. to 2 p.m., Friday until 11 a.m.) but the main GPO (and poste restante) is south of Mataram town on Jln Ismail Marzuki.

In Ampenan, there is Garuda (tel: 23762) near the tourist office, Pelni Lines (tel: 21604) at Jln Kapitan 1, Bank Negara Indonesia (best place to change money) on Jln Langko, Kantor Imigrasi (immigration office) on Jln Udayana, leading out to the airport and several tour-travel agencies strung along Jln Langko. In Mataram, you will find Merpati (tel: 22226) in the Selaparang Hotel and a telephone office (for overseas calls) a few doors along.

TRANSPORT AROUND THE ISLAND

Recent improvements have led to bigger, better roads all over the island and from the main *bemo* terminals at Ampenan and at Sweta, 1 km out of Cakranegara, you can get a *bemo*/minibus to almost anywhere. This is handy, since most inland sights (traditional villages, historical sites, etc.) are within 20 km of Ampenan-Cakra. However, not everybody enjoys travelling by public *bemo* – their routes are strictly regulated (e.g. from Sengiggi to Ampenan is only 250rps, but then you have got to get another *bemo* for 150rps on to Mataram/Cakra) and they are continually stopping to pick up/drop off passengers, which can be very frustrating. Horse-drawn carts or *dokars* are also slow, but they are a cheap and authentic way of seeing round the towns and countryside. Hiring one for a day's sightseeing (5/6000rps) saves all that tiresome *bemo*-hopping from one village to the next and you have got the driver all to yourself!

SENGIGGI

Until Kuta and other budding resorts get their act together, Sengiggi Beach has to be the best base for travellers on the island. This is a glorious 4-km-long stretch of white sand with (as yet) never more than a handful of people on it at any one time. The water is calm and clear, ideal for swimming and the beach drops away suddenly into an undersea coral wonderland. Quality wood-carvings are sold along the beach at low prices and so are fishing/snorkelling trips around the bay in *sampan* outriggers (around 5000rps per hour). Views across the Lombok Strait to Bali and Mt Agung are fantastic, especially at sunset. It is an idyllic spot and you can lie on the sand all day long without a single gems-salesman or massage-lady bothering you!

Sengiggi now has a wide range of accommodation, with more appearing all the time. At the top end of the beach, with the best location and views, you will find **Sengiggi Beach Hotel** (tel: 23883). This is Lombok's most pleasant hotel, with a 4-star rating and facilities to match. At US$40 single, US$50 double, the standard rooms (ask for a downstairs one, with access to the beach) are within the pockets of most mid-range travellers and represent superb value for money. It is worth paying a little extra (US$60 single, US$70 double, plus the usual 21 per cent taxes) for one of the thatched-roof bungalows. These are equipped with every modern comfort, face onto a better beach and some have fine sunset views. Each room has its own balcony, shaded by cool palm trees. Facilities include tennis, snorkelling, scuba diving, sailing and windsurfing and there is a lovely pool with sunbeds. Even if you cannot afford to stay here, it is worth calling in for the Sunday night dinner-dance show (US$15 + taxes). This features traditional Lombok dances plus a superb buffet of authentic Lombok dishes – try *ruap-ruap* (vegetable salad with grated coconut), *ayam panggang* (honey-roast chicken), *paseuh* (fish satay), *dabu-dabu* (tuna fish), *kang-kung* (Lombok's famous water-spinach) and *taliwang* (*the* Lombok sauce, made from chillis, coconut oil, garlic, sliced shallots, shrimp paste – a really hot one!).

Mascot Hotel, 200 metres below Sengiggi Beach Hotel, is brand-new mid-range accommodation with a good stretch of sand, nice gardens, small restaurant and well-furnished duplex bungalows from US$25 single, US$27 double, inclusive of taxes and breakfast. It is trying hard and the staff are extremely friendly. A short walk below this, the **Granada Hotel** has one-price rooms at 30,000rps net. They have air-conditioning, colour TV and a pleasant garden setting, but are small and claustrophobic and not especially recommended. Further down the road (set back off the beach) you will come to the cheaper *losmen*. Best bet is **Pondok Sengiggi**, run by an Australian lady married to a Sasak man. It is an interesting little place, much-loved by backpackers, with clean rooms at 4000rps single, 5000rps double and big double bungalows (completely self-contained) at 10,000rps. Soon, there will be a few new-style bungalows (with attached shower) at 15,000rps. Arrive 11 a.m. (check-out time) to snap up any rooms going. The busy little restaurant has a pleasant garden setting and a vast menu – try Lombok specials like *pelecing kang-kung* (spinach in hot chilli sauce, very tasty, very hot!) or *kang-kung goreng* (stir-fried spinach). As elsewhere, the big dish on offer is fresh lobster at 25,000rps per kg. **Melati Dua**, just below the Pondok, has nice gardens, a modest restaurant and self-contained bungalows from 25,000rps with toilet/shower.

If you do not want to eat at a hotel/*losmen*, check out **Denn's Restaurant** near the Mascot Hotel. This is a popular late-night hangout with cheap and authentic snacks, ice-cold beer and groovy Western sounds. Denn himself is a likeable young man who enjoys talking to Westerners. Another inexpensive place to eat, if it is still there, is the small *warung* next to Pondok Sengiggi. Then there is **Sunshine** restaurant between Granada and Sengiggi Beach Hotel, with good (if expensive) seafood and a breezy location overlooking the sea.

The Barong dance, Bali

GILI ISLANDS

The three tiny islands of Gili Air, Gili Meno and Gili Trawangan lie off the north-western coast of Lombok and represent, in the eyes of one jaded traveller, 'the ultimate escape from the insanity that is Bali'. They have no roads, no cars, no motorbikes and no electricity. What they do have is clear waters, fantastic coral, lovely white-sand beaches and lots of peace and quiet. The living is cheap – a standard two-person beach hut with outside toilet/*mandi* (and three meals a day) is only 8000 to 12,000rps – but the food is dull and it is a good idea to bring your own.

To visit the Gili islands, either hire a car for a one-day fishing/snorkelling trip (25,000rps from, say, Mascot Hotel in Sengiggi) or, if you want to stay over – make your own way up to Bangsal dock for a boat over to the islands. To reach Bangsal, go to Rembiga (125rps *bemo* ride from Ampenan, or walk 1 km left out of the airport), take a 500rps *bemo* (one and a half hours) to Pemenang and then hop on a *dokar* (150rps) for the harbour. It is worth arriving at Bangsal before noon. There are several boats daily out to Gili Air (20 minutes, 500rps) and three or four to Gili Meno (40 minutes, 800rps), but there is often only one boat a day (one hour, 2000rps) to the furthest island of Gili Trewangan. A strong swimmer, with fins, could make it over from Air to Meno, but travellers who miss the Trewangan public boat usually club together and charter their own boat – around 12,000rps one-way to Meno, 20,000rps to Trewangan.

Gili Air is the most popular island, probably because it is the nearest to the mainland. Small and lush (you can walk across it in one hour), it reminds many travellers of a typical Greek island. The water is clear and calm, there is a good beach and the coral begins very close to the shore. Most of the accommodation is down at the southern end of the island, around the harbour. **Makmur** is typical of what is found here – plain bungalows on stilts, with shutter-windows, a little sit-out porch and (at Makmur only) steel four-poster beds with bright-red mosquito nets! **Hans** and **Tiga** also get positive mentions.

Gili Meno is the most beautiful of the three islands and has spectacular blue-mushroom coral. It is also supposed to have malaria, but the one traveller I met who caught it wasn't taking sensible precautions. Meno's accommodation is all on the east beach and while most of them are simple bungalows (try **Mallia's Child** or **Matahari**) a few high-class places (like **Inda Cemara**) are coming up now, with air-conditioning and luxury facilities. If package tourism ever happens here, it will happen first on Meno.

Gili Trewangan is a nice place to relax, with a good beach and fine snorkelling. A little larger than Air, it also has some pleasant walks. The only two gripes are the strong currents (do not get too close to the coral) and the bad food (a lot of people seem to get sick here, probably from eating off plates cleaned in local water). Trewangan has about 12 *losmen* now, all located on the east coast. Stay at **Fantasi** (run by lovely Lily) or at **Pak Majid**. Both these places are clean, with good food.

TOURING THE ISLAND

To see the island properly and at leisure, you will need at least four days, twice that if you want to climb Mt Rinjani (cf. Ampenan, below). Most people, however come to Lombok to sit on a beach, and rarely spend more than a day sightseeing. They either take a US$25 day-tour (air-conditioned bus, English-speaking guide) with a reliable travel agent like Satriavi (53 Jln Langko, Mataram, tel: 21788; branch office at Sengiggi Beach Hotel) or they arrange their own transport. A good way of touring the island – if you do not mind the poorly surfaced roads – is by motorbike. Bikes can be rented out from local people in Cakranegara for around 10,000rps per day. Chartered *bemos* or cars (around 40,000rps per day with driver) are easily hired thourough the *losmen* in Ampenan-Mataram-Cakra, but check them over thoroughly before setting off!

The following route takes a full day, covers the main tourist spots and can be started from either Sengiggi or from Ampenan. Don't feel obliged to see everything, but do make time for unexpected stops and detours – as in Bali, the best 'sights' are out there on the country roads and in the villages.

Ampenan is a good central starting point. See the old harbour (once used for tourist boats, now used by local fishermen who sit hunched on the skeleton moorings like birds of prey) and then visit **Museum Negari Nusa Tenggara Barat** on Jln Banjar Tiler, south of Jln Langko. Admission is 200rps and it is open from 8 a.m. to 1.30 p.m. Tuesday to Thursday, Friday until 10.30 a.m., Saturday until 12.30 p.m. Ampenan has a few decent *losmen* (**Horas**, **Latimojong** and **Wisma Triguna**) in Jln Koperasi, a comfy air-conditioned hotel (**Wisma Melati**) in Jln Langko, two popular restaurants (**Pabean** and **Cirebon**) in Jln Pabean and several *warungs* (some of the best *mie goreng* I have tasted in Indonesia!) running down Jln Pejanggik.

Note: if you have time to spare, Ampenan is an excellent place to arrange treks up to **Mt Rinjani** in the north. This

3,726-m dormant volcano is Indonesia's third highest peak and the experience of climbing it is something quite special! Centuries ago, the mountain blew its top, leaving a 6-km rim and a 300-m drop to the large crater lake below. Rinjani last moved in 1942, pushing up an ash cone on the lake's edge called Gunung Baru or 'new mountain'. Views from the top are astounding – especially at sunrise – but getting up there is hard work! Sturdy boots are in order and you will need a good sleeping bag and warm clothing for cold nights. Contact Eddy Batubara at Wisma Triguna, Jln Koperasi. He offers two, three and four-day volcano tours (porterage, sleeping bag and food included) and is a chatty, ever-smiling travelling companion.

From the museum in Ampenan, drive through to neighbouring **Mataram**. This is a pleasant little town, its broad avenues lined with nut-trees planted by the Dutch. Mataram is the capital of Lombok, but the only thing likely to hold your interest is the Pertokoan Aphm Cilinaya entertainment complex. This has the one-and-only nightspot on the island – the **Chili Disco** – also a supermarket, a billiard hall and a small cassette centre selling local 'pop' tapes. Mataram's luxury hotels range from the quaint **Suranadi Hotel** ('Located in a very cold place, but in the daytime we get enough sunshine that way you can lay down in the sunny day to dry your body relaxation') to the stylish **Hotel Granada**, Jln Hatta (tel: 23138) with air-conditioned colonial-style rooms at 24,000rps and nice gardens. Cheap accommodation is not that good in Mataram and most budget travellers stay in Ampenan. Three pleasant restaurants are **Plamboyan** (Western, Japanese, Indonesian), **Sekawan** (seafood) and **Garden House** (Western, Chinese, Indonesian), all located in Jln Pejanggik.

Down the road at **Cakranegara**, the old royal court of **Puri Mayura** is a pretty thatched-roof pavilion, situated in the middle of a small artificial lake, which was once used as a court of justice and as a meeting hall for Lombok's Balinese kings. The Hindu king who built it (in 1744) showed respect for his Muslim wife by dotting Islamic statues round the pavilion, which is otherwise in the Hindu architectural style. Over the road is **Pura Meru**, the largest and most important Hindu-Balinese temple on Lombok. It was built in 1720 to unify the various Hindu factions existing on the island at that time and comprises three *merus* or temples: one for Brahma (seven tiers), one for Vishnu (nine tiers) and one for Shiva (ll tiers). Kept under strict lock and key, it is sufficient to view it from the pavilion. Another good reason for visiting Cakranegara is its **Sweta Market**,

huge, colourful and very good for photography. It is best and busiest around 9 a.m. and you can ask any *bemo* driver for directions as they all know it. While in town, why not pick up some traditional Lombok music-tapes? You will find the best selection at **Toko Dua**, Jln Selaparang 60. In the same road, if you want to stay over, there are two good mid-range hotels, **Hotel Mataram** and **Selaparang Hotel**, both with rooms at 15,000-30,000rps. Backpackers favour the **Losmen Astiti** in Panca Usaha (cheap rates, free breakfast, bike and car rental). For food, sample the *ayam goreng* (special fried rice) at the great little **Warung Taliwang** in Jln AA Gde Ngurah.

From Cakra, it is a scenic 20-km drive south (40 minutes) to the rural weaving village of **Sukarare**. Here traditional fabrics are woven on old wooden hand-looms in unique, often complex, patterns and designs. The main two cloths produced are *ikat* (where the pattern is made before weaving) and *songket* (where the pattern is in the weaver's head, demanding great skill and concentration to produce). Sukarare is a Muslim village and most weavings made here go into co-operative shops for sale. You can get cheaper prices by buying direct from women on the street, but to see the full range of produce visit Taufik Weaving Co., one of the larger co-operatives. Bargain hard here for handwoven tablecloths (20,000rps), belts (3500rps), sarongs (20,000 to 50,000rps), *songket* (20,000rps) and complete *bagulambung* ladies' sets (sarong, belt, shawl and jacket) at around 30,000rps. Weaving may be pricey at Sukarare – particularly the *songket* pieces woven with gold and silver thread – but quality is excellent. When bargaining, count on paying 30 per cent less than the first asking price (this village has really caught on to tourism) and go into shops on your own to avoid paying commissions to guides/*bemo* drivers. If you want to see the weavers at work, visit before noon.

A further 15-km drive south (30 minutes) brings you to **Penujak**. This is one of Lombok's many pottery villages, where clay pots for everyday use (simple in design and primitive in style) are produced. Arrive around 1-2 p.m. to see the workers and shop for vases, bowls, crockery and teapots (with attractive snake-motif spouts) in the small showroom. Everything is very cheap – no item over £1!

Continuing south, you will come first to **Sengkol** (notable only for its Thursday market) and then – half an hour out of Penujak – to **Rambitan**. Stop here to see a typical Sasak village, delightfully quaint, with rustic rice-barns, large water-containers (for ablutions before prayers) and corn hanging out to dry from rickety thatched huts. It is a fascinating insight into what is (sadly) a dying culture. The villagers, dressed in traditional black costumes, are getting rather too used to tourists – the women now charge for photos and the kids hassle you to buy dubious bits of rock. Rambitan has an old thatched-roof mosque (Masjid Kuno) on top of the hill and a small art shop (selling inferior weaving) at the bottom.

From Rambitan, it is 9 km (25 minutes' drive) on to **Kuta Beach**. This is a magnificent 100-km stretch of deserted golden sand, with a whole string of beautiful bays leading off it. Swimming and snorkelling are excellent and (because the waves break right out on the edge of the bay) the water is always mirror-calm. More and more travellers are *bemo*-hopping down here from Mataram (Sweta to Praya to Sengkol to Kuta), to stay for weeks. However, it is still possible to walk for miles along the beach without seeing another European face. The only time that the sleepy fishing village comes alive is when hordes of people from all over the island turn up for the annual *nyale* festival of February-March.

You would never guess it, but Kuta was once a very important kingdom. It had a beautiful princess called Mandalika who threw herself into the sea rather than choose among her many ardent suitors. This way, she believed, she would become something to be enjoyed by all men. What she became, in fact, was a small *nyale* fish (baby eel) which nowadays washes up in great numbers on Kuta beach around the time of the festival. Another name for Lombok is *putri nyale* or land of the beautiful fish-princess, and the islanders believe that if they attend the festival and eat the fish they will find great good fortune. At present, Kuta only has basic cottage-style accommodation (the best is **Andas**, with good food and its own generator; if it is full, try **Yellow Flower Cottages**). At present, there is talk of a 5-star Sheraton Hotel at Kuta, while in the adjoining bay of **Tanjung Aan** (4 km east) a luxury resort with air-conditioning, sunken baths, running water in every room, etc., is poised for completion.

Heading back north, you will want to visit **Narmada**, 10 km east of Cakranegara. Here, in the centre of a vast recreation park (open from 8 a.m. to 6 p.m. Monday to Saturday) is one of the great achievements of Balinese architecture – the summer water-palace of the King of Karangsem. This is built on a low terraced hill, descending sharply into a river valley, in miniature replica of Mt Rinjani and its crater lake. It was constructed in 1727 (some say 1805) to allow the king to continue to make offerings when he was too old to climb the real mountain! Just inside the park entrance, on the left, is the 'green house' with the king's rooms, while the wooden pavilion above the (new) swimming pool is where the aged ruler used to gaze down on local bathing beauties and choose his bedmate for the night. The Narmada complex is superbly landscaped, with tiered gardens, water pools and Western-style fountains built into traditional Balinese compounds of interlocking courtyards and pavilions. Avoid busy weekends, however, when it is packed!

A short drive north (3 km) brings you to **Lingsar**, the oldest and most sacred Hindu temple in Lombok. Originally built in 1714 by the first Balinese migrants to arrive on the island, it was rebuilt in 1878 as a symbol of unity between the Hindu-Balinese and the Waktu Telu-Sasaks. Here, on different levels of the temple (Muslims downstairs, Hindus upstairs) the two faiths offer common prayers for plentiful rains, good crops, etc. If you want to feed the sacred eels in the Waktu Telu temple, there are hard-boiled eggs (their favourite snack) for sale at the *warungs* outside.

A good place to finish off, especially around sunset, is **Batu Bolong** cliff temple. This is located off the main road, midway between Ampenan and Senggigi. From the top of the temple, which is situated on a low rocky promontory, the king used to cast virgins into the sea as offerings. The temple itself is nothing special, just a crumbling old seventeenth-century ruin, but if you look around the rock-pools below it, you will spot many amphibians (reminders of human evolution from the sea) coming in to land!

Index